# The Spanish-Cuban-American War and the Birth of American Imperialism

VOLUME II: 1898–1902

IUPUI
UNIVERSITY LIBRARIES
COLUMBUS CENTER
COLUMBUS, IN 47201

Philip S. Foner

# The Spanish-Cuban-American War and the Birth of American Imperialism 1895-1902

VOLUME II: 1898–1902

Monthly Review Press
New York and London

Copyright © 1972 by PHILIP S. FONER
All Rights Reserved

Library of Congress Catalog Card Number: 79-187595

First Printing

*Monthly Review Press*
116 West 14th Street, New York, N. Y. 10011
33/37 Moreland Street, London, E.C. 1

MANUFACTURED IN THE UNITED STATES OF AMERICA

# Contents

|       |                                                              |     |
|-------|--------------------------------------------------------------|-----|
| XV.   | Cuban-American Relations During the War                      | 339 |
| XVI.  | The Devastated Island                                         | 379 |
| XVII. | Prologue to Military Occupation                              | 388 |
| XVIII.| The Treaty of Paris                                          | 406 |
| XIX.  | Military Occupation: The Brooke Administration               | 422 |
| XX.   | Military Occupation: The Wood Administration                 | 452 |
| XXI.  | U.S. Economic Penetration of Cuba During the Occupation      | 466 |
| XXII. | The Cuban Labor Movement During the Occupation               | 484 |
| XXIII.| Failure of the New Annexationist Drive                       | 514 |
| XXIV. | The Cuban Constitutional Convention                          | 534 |
| XXV.  | Origin of the Platt Amendment                                | 559 |
| XXVI. | Congress Adopts but Public Opinion Rejects the Amendment     | 578 |
| XXVII.| Cuba Resists                                                 | 593 |
| XXVIII.| Cuba Yields to Force                                        | 613 |
| XXIX. | The Battle Over Reciprocity                                  | 633 |
| XXX.  | The Republic of Cuba                                         | 655 |
|       | *Reference Notes*                                            | 673 |
|       | *Index*                                                      | 705 |

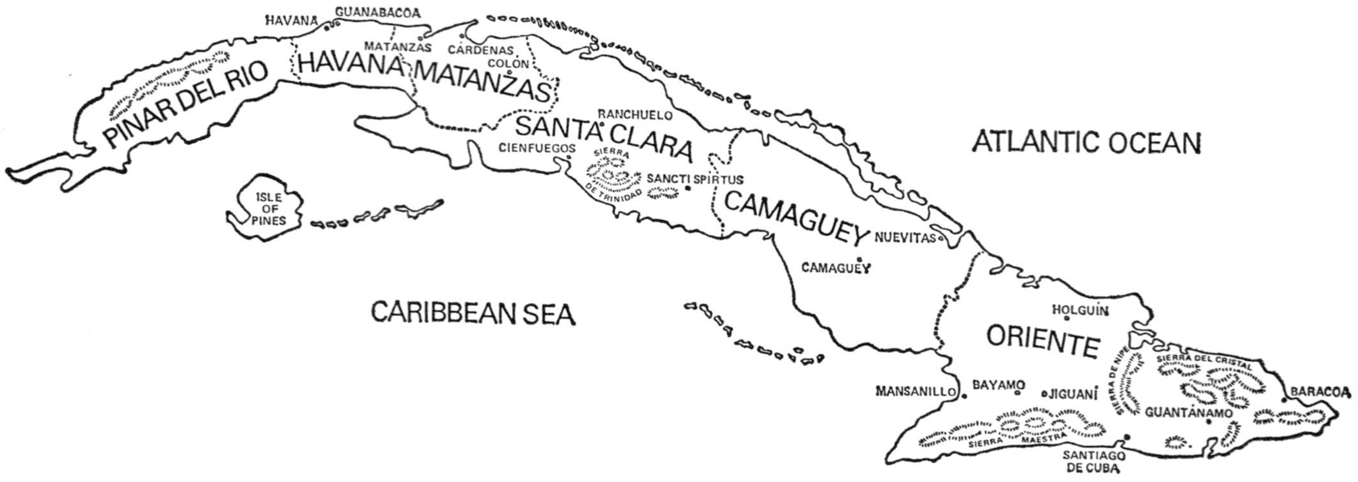
HAVANA
GUANABACOA
PINAR DEL RIO
HAVANA
MATANZAS
MATANZAS
CÁRDENAS
COLÓN
SANTA CLARA
RANCHUELO
CIENFUEGOS
SIERRA DE TRINIDAD
SANCTI SPIRTUS
CAMAGUEY
NUEVITAS
CAMAGUEY
ISLE OF PINES
ATLANTIC OCEAN
CARIBBEAN SEA
ORIENTE
HOLGUÍN
BAYAMO
JIGUANÍ
MANSANILLO
SIERRA MAESTRA
SIERRA DE NIPE
SIERRA DEL CRISTAL
GUANTÁNAMO
BARACOA
SANTIAGO DE CUBA

## CHAPTER XV
# Cuban-American Relations During the War

WHEN THEODORE ROOSEVELT, Lieutenant-Colonel of the United States Voluntary Cavalry—the Rough Riders—wrote a book describing the Spanish-American War, the American humorist Finley Peter Dunne said of it (through his mouthpiece, Mr. Dooley): "If I was him, I'd call th' book 'Alone in Cuba.' "[1] After one has read the vast majority of books by American historians dealing with this war, one is left with the impression that the United States alone was responsible for the victory over Spain, that the Cubans were either not present during the fighting or served no useful function in the war, and made little contribution to the final outcome.* Is it surprising then that in 1951, John F. Kendrick, an American historian and a veteran of the Spanish-American War, complained: "Not one American in 10,000 realizes how important the Cuban army was in our Spanish war.... Our histories simply state that we did it all.... Isn't honor overdue where honor was earned?"[2]

Although Cuban revolutionists had wanted only political recognition and material aid from the United States, they faced the reality of armed intervention with the determination to assist the American expeditionary forces, and in conjunction with them, to achieve a quick victory over Spain. The real question was whether the United States intended to ignore the Cuban army in the war, as its refusal to recognize the insurgent government would seem to indicate.[3] The answer to this question was not slow in coming. The War Department had

---
* The latest but by no means the only example is H. Wayne Morgan's *America's Road to Empire: The War with Spain and Overseas Expansion*, published in 1965. In the entire discussion of the Spanish-American War, there is not a single mention of a Cuban participant.

already decided to utilize the Cuban forces. On April 9, 1898, Secretary of War Alger and General Nelson A. Miles, commanding general of the United States Army, sent Lieutenant Andrew S. Rowan with the famous "Message to García." It was a verbal message since the United States was not yet at war.

It is precisely because of this "Message," which has been called the "most famous utterance emanating from the Spanish-American War," [4] that many Americans know the name of even a single Cuban general—Calixto García.* Unfortunately, the legend which has grown up around Lieutenant Rowan's dangerous mission has created the impression that a heroic American, without knowledge of Spanish and unfamiliar with the territory occupied by the Cuban troops, practically single-handedly overcame insuperable obstacles to complete his task. That there were Cubans whose assistance made the success of the mission possible is either ignored or barely mentioned in most accounts of the mission, including Lieutenant Rowan's own memoirs.†

Rowan planned to reach Cuba from Jamaica, but when he arrived in the British colony, he found that he could not continue. He was finally put in contact with the Delegate of the Revolutionary Junta in Jamaica, who introduced him to Comandante Gervasio Savio of the Liberating Army. Savio, who regularly transported mail and passengers between Jamaica and Cuba, was willing to take Rowan to Cuba provided the Delegate of the Cuban Revolutionary Government in New York instructed him to do so. Secretary of War Alger then asked Estrada Palma to request Savio to transport Rowan to Cuba. The request was granted, but the Cubans in New York insisted that Rowan pay for his passage, and the War Department paid the Cuban government the required amount. This payment was kept to be used as a proof of the existence of a Cuban government.

Savio carried Rowan to Cuba in his small boat, arriving at Ensenada de Mora where, as usual, a detachment of Cuban soldiers was waiting for him. Rowan had been able to converse with Savio in English since

---

\* Elbert Hubbard's short story, "A Message to Garcia," published as a book in 1898, had sold about four million copies by 1955. (Alice P. Hackett, 60 *Years of Best Sellers, 1895-1955*, New York, 1956, pp. 12-24.)

† This myth was reinforced in the motion picture produced in 1936 with Wallace Beery in one of the starring roles. Reissued on television, it has served to continue the myth in recent years.

the Cuban had learned the language in Jamaica. But now he was turned over to Cuban soldiers who spoke only Spanish. Asked what his objective was in Cuba, Rowan said only in broken Spanish: "Mi desea ver General García" (I wish to see General García) and "Mi tener mensaje para General García" (I have a message for General García). Escorted by the *mambises* who guided him through sign language, Rowan (or "Mister" as he was called by the Cubans) moved toward the encampment of General Salvador Hernández Ríos, chief of the division of Manzanillo, located at El Chino, at the other side of the towering Sierra Maestra. Through narrow paths in the jungle, wading across rivers, the detachment went up the mountain until they found a path at the top along which they could travel safely. After crossing the Sierra Maestra, the detachment met a patrol of Cuban cavalry, led by Lt. Eugenio Leopoldo Fernández Barrot, aide of General Hernández Ríos. Fernández Barrot spoke English, and after he had learned of Rowan's objective, took over the task of escorting him to García's headquarters. As the patrol advanced, the news came that García had captured Bayamo. It was in this city, on May 1, 1898, that Rowan delivered his "Message to García," after first having identified himself with a letter of introduction from the Revolutionary Junta in Jamaica.[5]

Rowan's message was designed to arrange for military cooperation between the United States and the Cuban armies, and García was to make known his requirements so that assistance could be dispatched. García sent Rowan back to the United States on May 2 with a Cuban military mission consisting of General Enrique Collazo, Colonel Carlos Hernández, and Lt. Col. Dr. Gonzalo García Vieta. The Cubans carried military data, maps, memoranda, and a message to the Secretary of War. Dated Bayamo, May 1, 1898, and written by García in English, the message read: "To the Sec. of Ward [sic] U.S.A.—Dear Sir: I confer into Gen. E. Collazo my entire confidence full powers to slate [sic] in view to you giving particulars of importance verbally, of great value for further intelligence between that Department and this Army."[6]

Arriving in the United States after an uneventful journey, Rowan reported to his superiors in Washington and related a tale of his trip in which the Cuban hardly appeared, thereby launching the legend of the "Message to García." Collazo and his companions had interviews with Secretary Alger and General Miles in Washington during which they informed the Americans of García's military plan, requested approval of it, and the military supplies to carry it into effect.[7] At this time, García reported that his forces, consisting of 3,000 men, were well armed with Remingtons and Mausers captured from the Spaniards, but were very short on ammunition, having only "enough ammunition for five or six shots."[8]

In a letter to Gómez, informing him of Rowan's visit and the events that followed, García outlined his plan in detail. He had asked the United States

> to disembark for me arms and munitions for 15,000 men at a point agreed upon on the north coast so that I can attack, supported by the North American fleet, the port of Gibara and the city of Holguín. It is true that Lt. General Salcedo has fortified Holguín with 10,000 men and that the whole line is occupied. But the surrender of this enemy fort would signify the definitive and absolute triumph of our arms in Oriente. General Ríos is now marching on Manzanillo to complete the siege of the city; General Rabí is doing the same in Palma Soriano and Santiago de Cuba, and while General Menocal and Capote are doing the same at Gibara and the ports of the north coast, where we are awaiting the American reinforcements, I will direct myself against Holguín.
>
> As soon as this plan achieves its results, I was thinking that, at the head of 8,000 or 10,000, I would go to Occidente and place myself at your disposal. . . .[9]

It is clear from García's letter that the campaign against Spain would begin in the East and then move on to the West, where the decisive and final battles would be waged. This was in keeping with the initial plan of General Miles. While the Cubans, reinforced with arms and ammunition and well supplied with food, would launch an offensive in the East, supported by the U.S. fleet, the U.S. Army would attack Puerto Rico before undertaking the decisive campaign in Cuba. When the occupation of Puerto Rico was completed, the United States would land in the eastern region where the Cubans had already engaged and weakened the Spaniards. Then would begin the occupation of Cuba from East to West.

With the understanding that the Americans would wage their principal campaign in the western portion of the island around Havana, and assured by General Miles that supplies would be rapidly dispatched to him from the United States, Gómez sent a message to several chiefs of the Department of Oriente expressing his opinion that it was "glorious and just that the three military corps of the military department of Oriente should each contribute the largest possible number of veteran volunteers which, forming a complete division, would march, representing Oriente, to seize the beautiful laurel of conclusive victory. And I cherish the hope that the whole army of Oriente, which was the first to march to the end of the island and plant the flag of the Republic there, should now also be the first to be filled with the magnificent and sincere spirit of this second military enterprise. . . ." Thus it was that Gómez detached a sizeable portion of the Liberating Army from the East and sent it on the long trek westward.[10]

But without informing Gómez, the Americans had changed their military plans. When Rear Admiral Pascual Cervera's Spanish flotilla, after a report that it was sailing for the United States, slipped into Santiago Harbor on May 19, 1898, the main American effort was changed from the West to the vicinity of Santiago.* The Puerto Rican expedition was abandoned for the time being, and everything was concentrated on obtaining victory in Oriente as a means of ending the war quickly.[11]

Gómez was thus isolated in the central province of Las Villas with forces which had been detached from Oriente, and was unable to be present during the action in the East.† Unaware of the confusion over early plans caused by the change in American strategy, newspapers in the United States used this state of affairs to raise the charge that the Cubans were half-hearted in the war effort. But N. G. Gonzales, editor of *The State,* published in Columbia, South Carolina, who was with

---

* For three weeks, people in the United States, especially those in the cities along the Atlantic Coast, lived in continual alarm of an attack by Spanish warships. Actually, "The Phantom Squadron," as Cervera's fleet came to be called, was in no position to inflict any real damage and no one knew it better than Cervera himself. (Millis, *op. cit.,* pp. 168-69.) Cervera's fleet crossed the Atlantic without approaching the United States and without engaging the U.S. fleet, crossed the Caribbean, and finally sailed into the haven of the Bay of Santiago de Cuba. The common remark in the press before Cervera's fleet was located at Santiago was that it was similar to Josh Billing's flea: "When you try to put your hand on him you touch the place where he recently was."

† General Mario G. Menocal, who was in charge of the detached Cuban force, claimed that Calixto García knew of the change in plans before Gómez made the disposition from the East to the West, but failed to notify the Commander-in-Chief in time. (Eduardo Rosell Malpica, *Diario de Campaña,* Habana, 1916, p. 343.) There is no other evidence to substantiate this charge.

Gómez in Cuba, put the record straight: "We are in a position to know that if the original plan of campaign had been carried out, Gómez would have marched from central to western Cuba, attacking the Spanish posts en route, capturing them if possible and effecting a junction with the United States forces near Habana for an assault on that city. But Cervera's entrance into Santiago changed the direction of the war and Santiago became the objective of the only movement by land."[12]

Although the U.S. War Department all but forgot about Gómez and his men once the plan of campaign was changed, the Cuban *Junta* organized an expedition to re-enforce the *mambises* in central Cuba. Most of the volunteers were Cuban cigarmakers from Key West and Tampa, but a few were Americans, including N. G. Gonzales, editor of *The State*\* and Grover Flint, author of *Marching with Gomez.* When the expedition was ready to sail, after months of training in Tampa under General Emilio Núñez, Colonel Acosta and General Julio Sanguíly, a detachment of some fifty Negro troops from the Tenth Cavalry was added.[13] That the expedition left at all was due mainly to the persistent efforts of General Núñez. For weeks, Núñez visited the army headquarters in Washington and Tampa, pleading for ships to carry the expedition, and food, arms and ammunition desperately needed by Gómez. Finally he succeeded in obtaining two vessels, the *Florida* and the *Fanita,* and late in June, the ships left Key West with several hundred Cubans, a score of American volunteers, the Negro cavalrymen, hammocks, hats, saddles, shirts, suits, blankets, corn meal, beans, coffee, pork, canned beef, bacon, hard bread, two dynamite cannons, 4,000 Springfield rifles, 500,000 Springfield cartridges, 454,000 Spanish Remington cartridges, 200,000 Mauser cartridges, 200 Colt's revolvers and 31,000 cartridges for them.[14] A few days later, Gonzales wrote in his diary, which he entitled, *In Darkest Cuba*:

> Headquarters Cuban Army, camp near Palo Alto, Camaguey. Wednesday, July 6, 5:10 a.m.—Within forty yards of me, sitting in his hammock, writing, is an old man called Maximo Gomez. Camped around in the thickets and palm groves are 2,000 Cuban soldiers. Our expedition has succeeded. We have found and re-

---

\*In announcing Gonzales's departure for Tampa to join General Núñez's staff, James Henry Rice, Jr., his successor as editor of *The State,* noted: "He has long been imbued with a desire to free Cuba from Spanish bonds and now goes to prove his faith by his works." (*The State,* May 13, 1898.)

lieved Gomez. And no one who is not here to see and hear for himself can realize how potential are those words, "found and relieved." [15]

In a touching passage, Gonzales described the condition of the men who were fighting with Gómez:

> I have written of General Gomez's *escolta* or escort, numbering about 150, and referred to the first half dozen who rode by as being uniformed. But the others! The tears came into my eyes and I felt a strange thrill down my spine when there passed these, the picked body-guard of the Commander-in-Chief of the Cuban Army, who ought to be the best equipped in the service. Here is a great *guajiro* . . . with a beard like a thicket, barefooted and riding a straw saddle. Next, a little boy of 12 or 13, naked to the waist, but with a big rifle on his pommel and a proud look in his eyes. Then, a huge Negro, stark naked except for a breech-clout of rags. Great God! What a force with which to have baffled Spain so long! No one man in a hundred with a whole suit of clothes—all torn and worn, with stomachs swollen from long subsistence on green fruit; yet men and boys who could ride forty miles after three days without solid food, and go on picket duty immediately after with the utmost alacrity and cheerfulness.
>
> And when the outlying brigades and regiments began to come in! Colonels, lieutenant-colonels and majors with the remnants of uniforms torn and patched; young men with fine, open faces, men of education and society, doctors, lawyers, engineers, former residents of cities, who with a smile spoke of their privations—how they had lived on green mangoes—which are worse than green peaches and taste like turpentine—palm nuts, horses, mules, donkeys, snakes! No complaints. They joked about it, felt in their pockets for a little *picadura,* rolled it into cigarettes with the inner leaf of the palm for supper, shrugged their shoulders, and smiled. Many of their horses had gone down the throats of these starving men before the green fruit came, and they had left from one to seven cartridges in their belts.
>
> But there came the worst spectacle of all, the remnant of a Negro regiment of infantry commanded by Jose Maceo, eighteen months dead. These men were without hats or shoes, and many of them had only a rag about their loins. They had made a forced march of 60 miles in obedience to the summons, over fearful roads, but with wonderful hardihood took up their camp duties immediately, without rest or food. Naked, but with rifles and cartridge boxes. I noted one whose rifle had worn a great sore on his shoulder, and his cartridge box another on his hip. Another, a mulatto, who

had returned from New York to fight at the beginning of the war, had been two years without hats or shoes. He had come all the way from Habana province, 400 miles, to go on with the fighting.

Remember that there were all men to whom Spain had offered terms—amnesty, food, positions in her army—if they would content themselves with autonomy, and give up their struggle for independence. We at home speak with pride of Marion and his men;* let us not withhold the need of justice to the Cubans of all classes who have undergone, in the same cause of liberty, sufferings tenfold as great, and continued in two wars, for thirteen years.

Oh, it was a pleasant thing to see them get a square meal out of Uncle Sam's tins of corn and beef, and it was as pleasant to see them this morning putting over their burned backs the brown canvas blouses. . . .[16]

This expedition was the last of the volunteer regiments to reach Gómez during the war. Tomás Estrada Palma announced in mid-June, 1898 that the Cuban *Junta* had no funds to fit out additional regiments, even though 400 Cuban cigar workers were ready to leave from Tampa, where they were training.[17] *The State* appealed to the War Department in self-interest to underwrite a new expedition: "The value of Cuban allies is known to be great and at each step in the occupation of Cuba it will become more apparent. Inured to the climate, familiar with the topography of the island, burning up with zeal to right Cuba's wrongs and able to supplement the inexperience of American troops with wise suggestions at critical times, they will be a tower of strength to the army."[18] But Washington had all but lost interest in the campaign waged by Gómez against the Spanish in central Cuba, and the plea went unheeded.† All attention was directed toward eastern Cuba where García was in charge of the Liberating Army.

On May 26, in response to García's request, the first cargo of supplies arrived at the port of Banes on the *Florida*: 7,600 Springfield rifles, half a million bullets, 150,000 rations and other military equipment as

---

\* Francis ("Swamp Fox") Marion was the guerrilla leader of the American revolutionary army during the War for Independence.

† William Randolph Hearst got the brilliant idea of delivering a sword worth $2,000 to General Gómez. But the sword did not reach Gómez until the war was over, and the Cuban General refused to accept it. "Those imbeciles in New York, with two thousands dollars to waste," he exploded. "It would have bought shoes for my barefooted men, shorts for their naked backs, cartridges for their useless rifles. Take it away. . . ." (Willis J. Abbot, *Watching the World Go By*, Boston, 1933, pp. 207-08.)

well as mules and horses. On June 6, Colonel Carlos Hernández, one of the men sent to the United States with Rowan, arrived at Banes on board the *Gloucester*, bringing with him a message from General Miles. The commanding general of the United States Army informed García of the American plan to disembark several thousand men on Cuban soil and then to attack the city of Santiago de Cuba by land and sea. That same day, García sent a message to Miles pledging his full cooperation: "Since for me your wishes are a command which I obey with great pleasure, I am taking the necessary measures to bring together as soon as possible, an appreciable number of forces at the place you indicate. . . . All my subalterns have orders not only to protect the disembarkation of the American forces and to give them whatever services they need, but also to put themselves unconditionally under your orders." García pointed out the presence of six Spanish warships in the bay of Santiago, described the defenses of the city, noting that there were 12,000 Spanish soldiers between Santiago de Cuba and Guantánamo, and 3,000 others under arms. Since it was clear that the Spaniards expected to obtain reinforcements from Holguín, García reported that he had called in forces from Camagüey to maintain continual pressure on that fort, thereby preventing the strengthening of the Santiago garrison.[19]

As soon as he had sent his message to Miles, García set about fulfilling the Cuban part of the plan outlined by the American general. Realizing that not a few Cubans feared that American soldiers were coming only in order to take over Spain's role in governing the island, García issued a proclamation to all chieftains in the Eastern Department emphasizing that the "American soldiers are landing in Cuban territory to help us free Cuba," and that it would be shameful if Cubans did not cooperate "in the defense of their Fatherland on the battlefield. . . . Those who are trying to save their lives by hiding themselves justly deserve the scorn of their fellow-citizens." [20]

Following the strategy worked out by García, the Liberating Army began to prevent the strengthening of Santiago's defenses. The fourth Cuban division, under the command of General Luis de Feria, was put in position to cut off General Luque's army in Holguín, while a Camagüeyan division, commanded by General López Recio, was placed in Victoria de las Tunas to cut off Spanish reinforcements from Camagüey. While the Spanish forces in Holguín were being isolated, caught between the Sierra Maestra and the units placed by García, a similar process was taking place in the areas surrounding Santiago. The first Cuban division commanded by General Pedro A. Pérez was placed facing the 6,000 Spanish soldiers, under General Pareja in Guantánamo. A small division, unfortunately vastly outnumbered by the enemy, was placed near Manzanillo to try to prevent the soldiers under Brigadier Luis Escario from moving to Santiago or, at least, to harass them en route. García realized that this was a weakness in the defense of Santiago, but he hoped to reinforce this small division, which was commanded by General Salvador Hernández Ríos.[21]

Having moved the various divisions to where they could most effectively impede Spanish reinforcement of the Santiago garrison, García abandoned his encampment at Mejía, facing Holguín, and began a forced march, which in five days—June 14 to 19—was to take him and his force of four thousand men across the highest mountains of Cuba to the outskirts of Santiago de Cuba. In the early hours of June 19, the white-haired, seventy-year-old General reached El Aserradero, completing the difficult journey through the passes of the Sierra Maestra.[22]

Even before García arrived at El Aserradero, Cubans and Americans had been cooperating closely. Admiral William T. Sampson, who was in command of the American fleet off Santiago, anxious to check the defenses of Santiago, had sent Lieutenant Victor Blue to the headquarters of General Jesús Rabí. The Cuban general escorted the American naval officer around the area of Santiago, pointing out the batteries which should be the target of a naval bombardment. The bombardment began on June 16, and Sampson reported to the Secretary of the Navy that "the batteries were silenced completely." In the same report, Sampson pointed out: "Cubans great assistance at Guantanamo. . . ."* This was a reference to the capture of Guantánamo Bay by American marines and Cuban soldiers.[23] Accounts of the battle placed special stress on the role of the Cubans. Thus one report observed:

> The insurgents now with the marines number only 80, but they show splendid bearing, are clever scouts and invaluable in skirmish

---

* Sampson also noted the importance of the Cuban force blocking a Spanish advance from Guantánamo to Santiago: "The Spanish forces at Guantánamo are vainly attempting to reach Santiago, as the Cubans hold the intervening territory." (*The State*, June 21, 1898.)

work and seem to have an utter contempt for the Spanish marksmanship.

These little black men, when ordered forward into the struggle, go unconcernedly toward the Spanish lines, absolutely without fear of the foe. In fact the Cubans have joined the marines in scouting for a mile all around the American camp and it is believed that their cooperation accounts for the failure of the enemy to make an attack last night. The insurgents know the ground so well that it is impossible for the Spanish bushwackers to get close enough to do any damage.[24]

With the capture of Guantánamo Bay, Sampson's fleet blockading the harbor of Santiago had a place to refuel since it could now take on coal in safety.

On June 16, General Pérez of the Cuban Army paid an official visit to the American fleet, and for the first time during the war, a Cuban flag was seen at the masthead of an American warship and was saluted. As General Pérez boarded the Marblehead, a salute of honor was fired and he was received by a guard of honor.[25] This was the prelude to the widely-publicized visit to the fleet by General García. On July 20, García conferred with Sampson, at the Admiral's invitation, on the cruiser *New York* to discuss the plan of campaign and the places at which the American expedition would disembark. French E. Chadwick, who had met García at General Rabí's camp, escorted him aboard the *New York* and was present at the interview, wrote later that "García made a highly favorable impression. . . . He inspired much confidence in Sampson who was ordinarily not in a hurry to trust others in this way."* In his work, *A History of the Spanish-American War*, R. H. Titherington emphasizes that García won Sampson's approval by being a man "of the most frank and attractive manner and of a very military appearance." [26]

Sampson and García did not see eye-to-eye on the place where the Americans should disembark. García felt the disembarkation should occur to the west of Santiago de Cuba, and he had concentrated his troops at El Aserradero in order to protect this operation. When Sampson remained unconvinced, it was decided to postpone the decision until the arrival of General William R. Shafter, head of the American expe-

---

\* Suffering from seasickness, García told Chadwick: "As bad as are the roads in Cuba, your roads, Capt. Chadwick, are worse." (Associated Press dispatch, *The State*, June 21, 1898.)

ditionary army.[27] When he left the *New York*, García sent the following message to the United States: "I am greatly obliged for the efforts of the American people in securing the independence of Cuba, and I shall do all I can to defeat the Spaniards quickly."[28]

Before the American troops were disembarked, Shafter went ashore and conferred with Sampson and García in the latter's camp at El Aserradero. ("The Cuban commander's tent," wrote a correspondent present at the conference, "is a rude hut, covered with leaves, and containing only a meagre camp outfit."[29]) At the conference in the Cuban military headquarters, Sampson and Shafter finally agreed upon the plan proposed by García for the disembarkation of the American expeditionary force.\* This plan called for the disembarkation of the troops at Daiquirí and Siboney, places which García knew well since the area contained property belonging to his family. The operation would be protected from the sea by the American fleet and from the land by the Cubans, who were to defend the area where the landing was to be made and the approaches to Santiago, in order to prevent Spanish reinforcements to the city.[30] There was one phase of García's plan, however, which Shafter rejected. Aware that the Cuban forces facing Escario's troops at Manzanillo were too few in number to prevent the Spanish soldiers from effectively reinforcing the Santiago garrison, García proposed that General Rabí be sent with a contingent of Cuban soldiers to the banks of the Contramaestre River where they could block an advance toward Santiago. But Shafter insisted that every unit of the Liberating Army in the area of Santiago be employed to protect the disembarkation of the American army.[31] This decision, as we shall see, was to have unfortunate consequences.

García was pleased that Shafter had lost no time in consulting him. But he must have wondered how the huge General—Shafter weighed over 300 pounds—would be able to function in the terrible heat of Cuba's eastern province, precisely at the time of the year when the weather was most oppressive. During the conference, Shafter, clad in a thick woolen uniform more suited for winter frontier duty in the United States (where he had spent most of his time in the Army, fighting the Indians who were protesting being driven off their land) than

---

\* Margaret Leech mistakenly describes this as Shafter's plan. (*In the Days of McKinley*, New York, 1959, p. 243.) Actually, the American general relied almost entirely on García for advice as to the best place to land.

for the tropics, had been on the verge of collapse. Captain Aníbal Escalante Beatón, a member of García's staff, voiced the opinion of all Cubans who had watched Shafter at the conference:

> In our judgment, it was a grave error of the North American General Staff to send on a war undertaking of this type, a soldier like Shafter, who, because of his physical makeup, would be . . . unable to act with the precision which the situation required, especially in a territory like ours in which the climate caused him such great suffering. General Shafter was not the man for the post. . . .[32]

As everyone familiar with the situation knew, the selection of Shafter reflected the United States' total unpreparedness for an overseas expedition in the tropics. "Our nation," wrote an American Red Cross worker with the U.S. Army, "could hardly have been less prepared for war if Spain had the ordering of our national affairs. The nation was unprepared in every branch of the service."[33]* On April 1, 1898, the military establishment consisted of 26,040 enlisted men and 2,143 officers, who were to form the nucleus of a new army of 275,000, and train the recruits for the invasion of Cuba. Following the declaration of war, when the volunteers and state militia began to assemble in southern camps at New Orleans, Tampa, Mobile, and Chicamaugua, where they might be acclimatized to tropical Cuba, it was realized that the problem of equipping and training them was worse than had been anticipated. Not a single regiment of the militia was fully equipped, and many men were in the camps with nothing that a soldier needed save enthusiasm. Only one government arsenal, which could equip 400 men a day, was in a position to manufacture materials of war. The government, therefore, had to depend upon private manufacturers who were more interested in amassing profits from inferior supplies than in serving their country. The food which constituted the basis of the soldiers' rations was supplied by men who saw an opportunity to cash in on the nation's need. Early enough, soldiers were supplied with "em-

---

* The most comprehensive study of the status of the U.S. Army on the eve of the war and the chaos that emerged after war was declared is Graham A. Cosmas, "An Army for Empire: The United States Army in the Spanish-American War," unpublished Ph.D. thesis, University of Wisconsin, 1969. However, the study is of little value for an understanding of the role played by the Cubans before and after April, 1898, and has nothing at all on Cuban-American relations during the war.

balmed beef" which made them violently ill and caused more than a few deaths.[34]

Shafter was given command of the expeditionary force to Santiago de Cuba, and, on April 29, 1898, established his headquarters at Tampa, Florida. The city was totally unprepared to handle the thousands of men who kept arriving. A single railroad line reached Tampa, connecting it with the rest of the country, and on this line, both troops and cargo trains had to pass. The result was that the Tampa spur was continuously congested, and regiments competed with each other in snatching trains to carry them to camp. When troops did arrive, they found that their military equipment was on cargo trains which could not get through. Troops were ready for training in Tampa, but the trains with artillery, guns, munitions, uniforms, medicines and provisions, horses and mules were stranded 100 to 150 miles from their destination. Apart from everything else, Tampa as a port was not suitable for embarkation of the army of 20,000 men whom Shafter commanded. Among other deficiencies, it simply did not have adequate wharfs to accommodate simultaneously several transport ships and warships.[35]

Already in Tampa the troops were suffering intensely from the heat, for they had been provided with woolen uniforms. Attached to General Shafter's headquarters were officers of the Cuban Liberating Army who had been sent by Gómez and García to help the Americans prepare for an invasion of the tropics. But in the continuous confusion and chaos, their advice was never sought, and when given, was generally ignored.[36]

On May 30, knowing now that Cervera's fleet was in Santiago, Secretary of War Alger ordered Shafter to begin preparations to sail for Cuba. It was hopeless to expect Shafter to comply with this order; the problem of organizing the expedition was simply beyond his experience and capacity. On June 1, General Miles arrived in Tampa to see what he could do to bring order out of the chaos and persuade Shafter to begin moving out. Shafter refused to set a date for the departure, but finally promised he would be ready on June 4th. But on that date, he telegraphed Washington that it was impossible for him to fulfill his promise. General Miles, in a dispatch on the same day to the Secretary of War, gave the reason for the postponement:

> Several of the volunteer regiments came here without uniforms; several came without arms, and some without blankets, tents or

camp equipage. The 32d Michigan, which is among the best, came without arms. General Guy V. Henry reports that five regiments under his command are not fit to go into the field. There are over 300 cars loaded with war material along the roads about Tampa. ... Every effort is being made to bring order out of confusion. ... To illustrate the embarrassment caused by present conditions, fifteen cars loaded with uniforms were sidetracked twenty-five miles away from Tampa, and remained there for weeks while the troops were suffering for clothing. Five thousand rifles, which were discovered yesterday, were needed by several regiments. Also the different parts of the siege train and ammunition for same, which will be required immediately on landing, are scattered through hundreds of cars on the side-tracks of the railroad. Notwithstanding these difficulties, the expedition will soon be ready to sail.[37]

The explanation proved unsatisfactory to Washington. Sampson was growing increasingly impatient for cooperation from the army, repeatedly cabling that without an attack by land, the continued blockade of the harbor was quite senseless. Moreover, the "fair weather" might end any day and the hurricane season would be on. The expedition would then really be in trouble.[38]

Orders for the departure flew to Tampa from Washington, and Shafter decided to leave even if it meant that cannons taken to Santiago would never shoot a shell since the munitions would have been left behind on some railroad spur. But now a new difficulty arose. Shafter explained it in a letter to Henry C. Corbin, Adjutant General of the Army, on June 7:

> I know to you in Washington it seems we are awfully slow in getting off. ... The great difficulty ... is that the place was overestimated and its capacities are exceeded. The whole army has to go down over one little track, and it takes time. It is not as though we could walk up to a city wharf and march on board. Every thing has to be loaded on freight cars, as wagons can't get within half a mile of the wharf. If I could load it in wagons and drive to the ships, I could load it very much quicker. I am glad that, except in loss of time, however, it is not going to do any harm, as Mr. Cervera seems to be safely bottled up.[39]

On June 8, the embarkation began in the midst of great disorder. Regiments stole railroad cars from each other in order to be the first to reach the piers, and in several cases, this was accomplished at gunpoint. The contingent of Rough Riders, led by Colonel Theodore Roosevelt, had been assigned the *Yucatan* along with a regiment of veteran infantry and one of volunteers from New York. After a fist fight, the Rough Riders seized control of the *Yucatan*, and then announced that only four companies of regulars could come aboard. The New York volunteers then sent a contingent on a launch which seized a transport assigned to another regiment. To add to the confusion, it was learned that the army transports could not carry all of the men and their equipment. Part of the supplies were therefore left behind.[40]

The Fifth Army Corps, under the command of General Shafter, sailed with a fleet of thirty-two transports, carrying some 819 officers and 15,058 enlisted men, in addition to mules, horses, teamsters, packers, clerks, several Cuban generals, foreign military attachés, and correspondents. The convoy had hardly started when a report of a phantom Spanish fleet was heard. Fear arose that it was dangerous to proceed, but since no one dared to recall the transports, they loitered until it was learned a week later that the ghost fleet was only three American merchantmen. On June 14, the expedition got under steam again.[41]

On June 20, in the early hours of the morning, Shafter's expedition reached the Bay of Santiago where the bulk of the U.S. fleet stood guard. It had made its way to the coast of Cuba without interruption and without having to fire a single shot.[42] What remained now was to solve the problem of disembarking so many thousands of men, mules, horses, wagons, ambulances, food and war suplies. Once Shafter and Sampson had accepted García's plan at the El Aserradero conference on June 20, the Liberating Army proceeded to carry out the role assigned to it. General Cebreco's division placed itself in the mountains to cut off possible reinforcements from the Northwest, while two Cuban units in numbers of approximately five hundred men each were transported to the east of Santiago by American ships, and, together with the Cubans already there, took Daiquirí and defended the beachhead. During the landing process, several additional Cuban units were shipped to the area. Meanwhile, the U.S. fleet bombarded the coast in a maneuver to give the Spaniards the impression that the disembarkation would take place at Cabañas, a maneuver strengthened by the fake attack by the Cuban troops led by General Rabí. But it was at Daiquirí and Siboney, as had been planned, that the Cubans concentrated their main force, occupying the village and the area immediately around it, including the bay of Siboney, and forming a protective ring between the Spaniards and the expeditionary army.[43] "The Cuban insurgents," wrote a correspondent with the expedition, "bore their share in the enterprise honorably and well. Five thousand of them, in mountain fastness and dark thickets of ravines, lay all last night on their guns, watching every road and mountain path leading from Santiago de Cuba to Guantanamo. A thousand of them were within sight of Daiquiri, making the approach of the Spaniards under cover of darkness an impossibility."[44]

The United States forces went ashore in a heavy surf on beaches covered by fifteen hundred Cuban troops while other Cuban units attacked Spanish troops in the interior, preventing them from advancing to the area where the landing took place. Thus protected, the expedition disembarked without having to fight a single Spaniard.[45] As General Arsenio Linares, in charge of defending Santiago de Cuba, wrote, "Without the help of the Cubans, the Yankees never could have disembarked. The assistance of the *insurrectos* was extremely powerful. A proof of this is that the North Americans disembarked only where the insurrection was strongest."[46]

Writing from Siboney on June 27, García informed Estrada Palma that the Cuban promise to protect the American landings had been fulfilled. He expressed the hope that this was only the opening phase of Cuban-American cooperation until final victory. "My only preoccupation," García emphasized, "is to draw together our good relations with the allied army, and I have no doubt that before the campaign ends, all the people of the United States will be convinced that we do not lack the conditions to govern ourselves."[47]

García's high hopes quickly faded as friction developed between the Cubans and the Americans, and his dream of what the end of the campaign would bring turned into a nightmare.

One point at issue was the role to be played by the Cubans in the joint operations. After the landing troops and equipment had been consolidated, Cuban troops performed the invaluable service of erecting various fortifications, emplacements, and trenches around the approaches to Santiago.[48] While they continued to do this throughout the siege of the city, García was furious when he learned that Shafter had insisted on assigning the Cubans to these duties solely. The Cubans were to be used to carry supplies and dig trenches for the Americans. García immediately protested that his men were not "pack-mules," and that, weak and emaciated from having been deprived of sufficient food for a long period, they could not be expected to build roads, dig trenches, and carry supplies for long stretches on end. He insisted that they be assigned to worthier tasks.[49]

Even before the Americans landed in Cuba, the people of the United States had been led to believe that in the war against Spain, little assistance would come from the Cuban Army. On May 22, 1898, the Washington correspondent of the New York *Tribune* wrote that "it is now definitely known that little or no assistance from the vaunted 'armies of liberation' need be expected." [50] The failure of most newspapers to mention the role of the Cubans in assisting Lieutenant Rowan deliver his "Message to García" was part of this effort to belittle Cuban contributions. While this anti-Cuban attitude ceased during the battle of Guantánamo and the landing at Daiquirí, it was only a temporary halt. The objection García raised to having the Cubans assigned to carrying supplies, building roads and digging trenches, gave the American correspondents the opportunity to launch a campaign of slander against the Cuban Army. Americans who received their impressions of the Cubans from dispatches of correspondents at the front were led to believe that the men of the Liberating Army would not work, would not fight, and were interested only in stealing food from the Americans. The Associated Press correspondent in Cuba was particularly vicious in his slanders, and since his dispatches were carried in hundreds of newspapers, they helped to create an extremely hostile opinion towards the Cubans. A typical A.P. dispatch read:

> The Cubans with the advance forces, in spite of the good behavior of their comrades at Guantanamo, seem to be worthless. All day they sit in the shade of their palm-thatched camps and at night they smoke cigarettes and gorge on Uncle Sam's rations, while in sight of them Uncle Sam's boys, with empty stomachs and not a bit of tobacco for their pipes, build roads all day under the blazing sun and sleep on their rifles under the starlight sky at night.[51]

Unfortunately, the American military commanders who knew better, and later admitted that such reports were a tissue of lies,* did nothing

---

* Although he did nothing to contradict the correspondents' dispatches while he was in Cuba, on his return to the United States in August, General

to contradict the correspondent. But when the Associated Press correspondent wrote from Cuba that the Cubans were killing Spanish prisoners, the War Department in Washington asked General Shafter for a report. Shafter wired: "Dispatch as to killing prisoners by Cubans absolutely false. No prisoners have been turned over to them, and they have shown no disposition to treat badly any Spaniards who have fallen into their hands."[52] In an editorial entitled, "The Lie Nailed," *The State* observed on July 9, 1898: "That much is settled officially, but it is quite impossible for Gen. Shafter to hunt down each one of the numerous misstatements of facts in regard to the Cubans; and in justice to them and to us, this misrepresentation ought to cease forthwith. The most certain way to stop it is to recall that correspondent." But the A.P. correspondent remained in Cuba, and his dispatches denigrating the Cuban contribution to the war continued, as did those of other correspondents of leading American papers. It is hardly surprising that the Cubans should have resented being pictured as leeches who sunned themselves while the Americans did the fighting for them.

Another cause of friction was the tendency of American officers to use the Cubans as scapegoats for their own errors. This emerged at the very beginning of the campaign in the action at Las Guásimas. After the landing at Daiquirí, Shafter ordered Brigadier General H. W. Lawton, head of one of the two infantry divisions of the Fifth Army

---

Wheeler publicly rebuked the reporters for lying about the role of the Cubans in the war. He conceded that there was friction between the Americans and the Cubans, but declared that this was not the fault of the insurgents. Partly it was due to language differences; the Cubans could not clearly understand orders when translated poorly, and they often seemed "harsh and abrupt." The Cubans had never refused to dig trenches and build roads, especially when they understood the importance of this work, but owing to their physical condition they could not persist too long. "They had been living mostly on fruits and vegetables, and did not possess the strength for the hardships which well fed soldiers have to go through." The charges of pilfering were greatly exaggerated. About 20,000 people had come out of Santiago without anything to eat. When the American soldiers were pushing ahead in an engagement, they had to discard their rolls containing provisions. While some of this was stolen by Cuban soldiers, the majority were taken by destitute people who came out of Santiago. (*The State*, Aug. 18, 1898.)

Charles Johnson Post, an American soldier in the war, later wrote bitterly of "the war correspondents who "sneered at the Cubans and ridiculed their rifles, and their fighting. The correspondents knew nothing of it." (*The Little War of Private Post*, Boston, 1960, pp. 126-28.)

Corps, to take a defensive position on the Santiago road beyond Siboney. In the vanguard of Lawton's column were Cuban troops under the command of General Castillo Duany and Colonel González Clavell, while in the rear was the American cavalry, dismounted because of lack of horses, commanded by Major General Joseph Wheeler, a veteran of the Confederate Army. During the entire day of June 23, the Cubans kept up a fire against the 1,500 Spaniards who had fortified themselves in Las Guásimas, but in keeping with Shafter's instructions, had not advanced against the entrenched position. Lawton's infantry division also remained where it was stationed. But when night fell, Wheeler determined "to get first blood" by moving ahead of the rest of the army. He pushed one of his brigades, under General S. B. M. Young, in front of Lawton's men. Young's brigade included the Rough Riders, who were also eager to draw first blood.

At dawn on June on June 24, the regulars, with Wheeler and Young at the head, and the volunteers, the Rough Riders, led by Lieutenant Colonel Theodore Roosevelt and Colonel Leonard Wood, launched their "little independent war" against the Spaniards. Wheeler's men were able to escape Lawton's attention, but Young's division came in contact with the Cubans who had been occupying the road which led to Las Guásimas and engaging in fire with the Spaniards. Colonel González Clavell urged Young not to proceed with the rash action, but made no impression on the headstrong General. González Clavell furnished the Americans with information on the position of the Spaniards and a few guards for the march, but he refused to join the absurd venture. Later, Young publicly criticized the Cubans for having "abandoned" him in the undertaking, and the newspapers in the United States charged the Cubans with cowardice for not having joined the attack.

While the Spaniards were driven back at Las Guásimas, the Americans suffered heavier casualties than did the enemy. Actually, as was later substantiated by the Dodge Commission investigating the conduct of the war, the Spaniards had already decided to abandon Las Guásimas because of the losses they had sustained from the fire of the Cubans throughout the previous day. In any event, the reckless skirmish at Las Guásimas, the first engagement of the American army in the war, had no military significance. But it began the spreading of a false picture of the role of the Cubans in the campaign. Soon the Cubans were blamed for the heavy losses sustained by the Americans at Las Guásimas.[53]

The American version of the Cubans' role during the attacks on El Caney and San Juan further intensified friction between the allies. On June 30, the order came for the advance on Santiago. The morning of July 1, the outer defenses east of Santiago were attacked. Brigadier General Adna R. Chaffee, who began the major engagement, afterwards known as the Battle of San Juan Hill, used a contingent of 1200 Cubans in opening the road in the direction of El Caney, a fortified village which the Spaniards occupied. Chaffee acknowledged that "they [the Cubans] were very useful to me." [54] Meanwhile, another contingent of Cuban soldiers was in position to prevent the arrival of Spanish reinforcements from the North.

Shafter's plan called for a quick seizure of El Caney, to which were assigned Lawton's division and an independent brigade of regulars, some 7,000 men in all, and a contingent of 1200 of the Cuban division of González Clavell. As soon as these forces attacked, the remaining 8,000 men were to move down the road to San Juan Hill, guided by an observation balloon as they passed through the woods. It was estimated—and with this Lawton agreed—that it would take two hours to capture El Caney with its garrison of 1200 men. But, despite the bravery exhibited by many of them, chaos and confusion prevailed among the American troops. By splitting his forces at the very outset of this major engagement and underestimating the strength of the Spaniards despite Cuban reports to the contrary, Shafter had doomed all chances of a quick victory. The observation balloon sent up above the advance guard gave away to the Spaniards where the American forces were stationed, and they responded effectively. The smoke from the black powder in the rifles of the Americans also made them an excellent target, while the artillery, also equipped with black powder, was more of a disadvantage than an aid.

The triumph at El Caney took eleven hours, not two, and it took 81 dead and 370 wounded from the Americans. The Cubans, who were fighting with the Americans, also suffered serious losses. For the final assault on El Caney, General Lawton asked for reinforcements from General García, and a platoon of Cuban infantry joined the Americans in entering the village and driving the Spaniards out of the fortified houses.

Nevertheless, as part of an attempt to explain the failure of the Americans to achieve the quick victory anticipated and the heavy losses incurred, the American command circulated a report that the Cubans had again let down their allies. They had fulfilled their assignment of guiding the Americans to their objective, went the report, but had then considered their mission accomplished; while Lawton's men were engaged throughout the day in heavy fighting to take the village, the Cubans had sat on a hill well to the rear, keeping up an ineffective long-range fire, and at no time during the battle had they come down to join the attack.

The truth of the matter was that the Cubans fought in the ranks throughout the day with Chaffee's and Ludlow's men, and suffered losses along with the Americans. And the troops which finally broke into El Caney included a Cuban contingent. But the canard against the Cubans continued despite all evidence to the contrary. Indeed, when a few years later, the United States commemorated the bloody action at El Caney by erecting a memorial on the site of the battle, there was no mention on the tablet of the Cubans who had participated in the operation and had cooperated to help achieve the victory.[55]

The same American reluctance to share credit for victory with the Cubans was exhibited after the battle of San Juan, yet the Cuban troops under González Clavell were in the thick of the battle throughout, and in the final assault on the hill, they scaled the heights together with the American troops. In his account of the battle, French Ensor Chadwick emphasized the contributions of an anonymous Cuban soldier "who showed perfect valor and was very useful in destroying the barbed wire with his heavy machete."[56] But such courage counted for nothing with many Americans. After the Battle of San Juan Hill, Stephen Crane, the New York *World* correspondent with the American army, reported that "both officers and privates have the most lively contempt for the Cubans. They despise them."[57] Not to be outdone, the Associated Press correspondent wrote that "the name of Cuban is usually wreathed with camp profanity, and very rarely is a kind word spoken of them. In fact, in some quarters there is a disposition to prophecy an early collision between our men and the Cubans."[58]

With so many Southerners as officers and privates in the American army, the fact that the Cuban army was composed largely of Negroes was enough to earn this contempt, regardless of the contribution it made to the campaign. The contemptuous term "nigger" became the one most commonly used by American officers and soldiers—and newspaper correspondents—to describe the Cuban fighters.* "Bandits" and "dagoes" ran it a close second.

Even though the Battle of San Juan Hill had almost ended in disaster, the costly victory had opened the road to Santiago. It only remained for Shafter to move in on the tightly blockaded city, which was in desperate straits for food, and with his artillery and the guns of the American fleet, force the Spaniards to surrender. But Shafter, who had talked freely before El Caney and San Juan of the need for a speedy victory, now informed Washington of his intention of retreating. He was almost totally incapacitated by discomfiture and illness. Due to the heat and his enormous bulk, and given to gout, he suffered physically to the extent that he rarely left his headquarters.** This probably affected his presence of mind. In any case, his decisions were hesitant, and he was repeatedly racked by fears and extreme pessimism in regard to the success of the campaign in progress.[59]

Not even the destruction of Cervera's fleet as it ventured out of Santiago Harbor could induce Shafter to attack.† It did, however, provide correspondents with a new opportunity to spread lies about the Cubans. Thus they wrote that the Cuban soldiers tried to slaughter

---

\* Cuban Negroes were not the only ones subject to such scurrilous attacks; even Negroes fighting in the American Army were looked down upon by Southern white officers and privates. (George Kennan, *Campaigning in Cuba,* New York, 1899, pp. 100, 128, 143-44.) However, one Southern officer in a dispatch to the New York *Evening Post* wrote of the fighting around Santiago: "If it had not been for the Negro cavalry, the 'Rough Riders' would have been exterminated. I am not a Negro lover. My father fought with Mosby's Rangers, and I was born in the South, but the Negroes saved that fight, and the day will come when General Shafter will give them credit for their bravery." (Reprinted in *Literary Digest,* Aug. 27, 1898, p. 248.)

\*\* When the Dodge Commission held its investigation at Washington into the conduct of the war, Shafter testified: "I was nearly prostrated . . . when I would sit up it would make me dizzy. . . . I had a beastly attack of gout so that I could not wear a boot for a week, and had to wear a gunny sack on my foot, and I could not climb my horse, and would have to build a platform to climb up on." (*Senate Document* 201, 56th Congress, vol. VII, p. 3197.)

† On the morning of July 3, Cervera attempted to make his escape. As the column of ships emerged from the bay, the Americans opened fire, and one by one the Spanish ships were destroyed. By 11:35, within less than two hours all save one had been lost, and 10,000 Spanish sailors who might have been used in the defense of Santiago could not now be employed.

the crews of Cervera's ships as they crept up on the shore after the naval battle, thereby "arousing the indignation of the American sailors who witnessed the act." [60] Admiral Cervera, in his official report to the Spanish government, made no such charge. After describing his plight and that of his men cast ashore naked, he wrote: "The insurgents had captured about 200 men, and with them five or six were wounded. The insurgents tendered their services, which I thankfully declined. 'We have surrendered to the Americans,' I told them. 'If you have surgeons with you, kindly permit them to attend to the wounded, several of whom are in a very bad condition.' This was done." [61] Unfortunately, Cervera's tribute to the Cubans received little attention in the American press, while the fabricated slanders of the correspondents was front-page news.

Pressured by Washington to move, Shafter hit upon an excuse to justify his inaction. On July 4, the day following the American naval victory at Santiago Bay, he wired Washington:

> There appears to be no reasonable doubt that Gen. Pando succeeded in entering Santiago last night with his force said to be about 5,000 men. This puts a different aspect upon affairs and while we can probably maintain ourselves it will be at the cost of considerable fighting and loss. Gen. Lawton reports that Gen. Garcia who was to block the entrance of Pando informed him at 10 o'clock last night that Pando had passed in on the Cobra [sic] road. Lawton says he cannot compel Gen. Garcia to obey my instructions and if we intend to reduce Santiago we will have to depend alone on our own troops and that we will require twice the number we have. . . . [62]

Thus it was the Cubans, and General García in particular, who had made an attack impossible. Actually, Shafter's statement was untrue. General Pando was not in Santiago; he was completely cut off by the Cubans.[63] The only reinforcements to arrive in Santiago were those under General Escario and they were not 5,000.

Naturally, Shafter did not mention that the situation he complained of was caused by his own strategic error. García, it will be recalled, had realized very early that one of the major provisions of the plan of attack on Santiago required that all Spanish reinforcements be prevented from reaching the city. He had therefore placed contingents of the Liberating Army in sufficient strength to prevent such reinforcements. Where this was accomplished, the Spaniards were effectively halted. A Spanish force of about 10,000 men under General Luque endeavored to reach Santiago from Holguín some seventy miles away, but was prevented from doing so by repeated attacks of Cubans concentrated in that district. Smaller Spanish units under General Pareja at Guantánamo were also blocked by General Pedro A. Pérez. However, the Spanish forces at Manzanillo under General Escario (whom Shafter called Pando) were confronted by a small contingent of Cubans under General Francisco Estrada. García knew that the vastly outnumbered Cubans were not in a position to prevent Escario's troops from reaching Santiago, and prior to the disembarking of the Americans, he had urged Shafter to allow him to send troops under General Rabí to the area of Manzanillo to close the pass to the Spaniards. Shafter rejected this request, insisting that all Cuban units protect the landing. After the disembarkation, García again urged Shafter to allow him to send Rabí with two thousand men to attack the Spanish column of four thousand under Escario before it reached Santiago. (García's plan called for Rabí's force to rendezvous with other Cubans at Aguacate in order to execute an ambush.) But Shafter again turned down the appeal, arguing that he did not wish to weaken his forces further and that Escario's troops would be dealt with just as well in Santiago.

It came as no surprise, therefore, that Escario's troops were able to cover the one hundred miles from Manzanillo to Santiago without being turned back or destroyed by the outnumbered Cubans. But the Spanish troops did not advance unimpeded. The 3,700 men and 148 mule train of supplies were supposed to cover the distance in six days in a forced march. Until their ammunition ran short, Colonel Estrada's 600 men did not let the Spaniards rest, attacking and harassing them in a series of skirmishes, ambushes, snipings, sorties and feints. The forced march of six days stretched to eleven days. The Spaniards suffered 27 killed, 71 wounded, and sustained other damage—all inflicted by a poorly-equipped band of *mambises* one-sixth the size of the enemy. So worn out were Escario's troops when they reached Santiago that they were unable to play an effective role in the defense of the city. Moreover, in the five days the column had been delayed, El Caney and San Juan had been taken and the Spanish fleet had been destroyed. As the Spanish military historian José Müller y Tejeiro noted, the 600 Cubans had delayed Escario's column long enough to nullify most of its value to the defense of Santiago. In "An Unwritten Chapter of the Santiago Siege," the Springfield *Republican* of January 15, 1899 noted: "General Shafter was severe on the Cubans because Escario's column succeeded in entering the beleaguered city. Yet it was due solely to the persistent, harassing attacks by those Cubans along the whole route of Escario's long march that the Spanish reinforcement of some 3500 men did not enter Santiago several days before Shafter's forces had come up to the attack upon the town. General Escario did not enter the Spanish lines until the war was over, and it is the Cuban insurgent, ragged and hungry, to whom we must credit that important service to the American army."

After the surrender of the Spaniards at Santiago, García received support for his advance to Shafter. Colonel Escario freely admitted that had General Rabí reinforced Estrada, his worn-out troops would have been routed! [64]

Nothing of the above, of course, appeared in any of Shafter's dispatches. Having found a scapegoat for his own inadequacies, he kept referring to the reinforcements from Manzanillo—whose number he exaggerated—to justify his inaction at Santiago. Over and over he emphasized that "the Cuban forces are not to be depended upon for severe fighting," and that "we will have to depend alone upon our own troops." [65] Yet it was General Nelson A. Miles himself, in his report to the Secretary of War, November 5, 1898, who accused Shafter of having shifted to the Cubans the blame for his own error in preventing García from effectively blocking Escario's column. In view of the attacks upon the Cubans in the Santiago campaign by American correspondents,* General Miles' words on that point are worth quoting:

---

\* Stephen Crane charged throughout the Santiago campaign that the Cuban soldiers "would not fight, but stayed in the rear to eat up rations and steal the belongings of American soldiers." (New York *World*, July 14, 21, 28, 1898.) In an article entitled "The Santiago Campaign," the Associated Press correspondent wrote, "The Cubans have proved a sorry disappointment throughout the campaign even to their warmest friends. They have been everywhere, except where the battle raged, but their chief and favorite state has been near the commissary. . . . . The more our commanding officers see of the Cubans, the less they appear to think of them, either as soldiers or as men. . . . Poll the United States troops in the province of Santiago de Cuba today and 99 out of every 100 will say in almost so many words: 'We have bought a gold brick in "Cuba Libre."'" (*The State*, July 28, 1898.)

It will be observed that Gen. Garcia regarded my requests as his orders, and promptly took steps to execute the plan of operations. He sent 3,000 men to check any movement of the 12,000 Spaniards stationed at Holguin. A portion of this latter force started to the relief of the garrison at Santiago, but was successfully checked and turned back by the Cuban forces under Gen. Feria. General Garcia also sent 2,000 men, under Perez, to oppose the 6,000 Spaniards at Guantanamo, and they were successful in their object. He also sent 1,000 men, under General Rios, against 6,000 men at Manzanillo. Of this garrison, 3,500 started to reinforce the garrison at Santiago, and were engaged in no less than 30 combats with the Cubans on their way before reaching Santiago, *and would have been stopped had Gen. Garcia's request of June 27 been granted*. . . .[66]

No one can read this paragraph and deny that the Cuban troops, ragged and starved though they were, furnished valuable aid to the Americans in taking Santiago. They successfully blocked movements of Spaniards from Holguín and Guantánamo, and those from Manzanillo would have been headed off, "had Gen. Garcia's request of June 27 been granted."

Yet Shafter thought only of snatching full credit for himself. He extended his own lines in front of García's troops and virtually ignored the Cuban General during the final stages of the siege of Santiago. While waiting for reinforcements, Shafter had sent three demands for the surrender of the city, and General José Toral, who was in command after the wounding of General Linares in the battle of San Juan, was given time to cable Madrid for instructions. On July 8, Toral proposed that he evacuate Santiago and take up his stand at Holguín, where the battle could be fought in the open country without danger to civilians. General García immediately advised Shafter not to agree, pointing out that Toral was only maneuvering to prolong the war. But Shafter no longer listened to García, and urged Washington to accept Toral's proposal. On July 9, he received a blunt telegram endorsing García's advice: ". . . Your message recommending that Spanish troops be permitted to evacuate and proceed, without molestation, to Holguín is a great surprise and is not approved. The responsibility of destruction and distress to the inhabitants rests entirely with the Spanish commander." Shafter was informed that President McKinley insisted he was to "accept nothing but an unconditional surrender, and [you] should take extra precautions to prevent the enemy's escape."[67]

When General Miles arrived with an expedition, Shafter finally had to act. The bombardment of Santiago began on July 10. The fourth demand to surrender was sent on the morning of the 11th, and Toral, impressed with the increased forces before him, asked for time to confer with his superiors. On that day, July 11th, a two-day truce was arranged, but before its expiration, a meeting of the opposing commanders on July 13 resulted in an extension until 5 o'clock July 14, and in arrangements for a further conference.[68] In the second conference, Toral offered to capitulate on the basis of repatriation of his soldiers and retention of their side arms. Shafter was ready to accept these terms, but Secretary of War Alger rebuked him: "It is not possible that you are entertaining the proposition of permitting the Spanish to carry away their arms. Such a suggestion should be rejected instantly. You have been instructed the terms of surrender acceptable to the President, and they must be concluded on those lines."[69]

On July 16, Toral surrendered unconditionally, and on that day, in the shadow of the ceiba tree—*el árbol de la paz* (the tree of peace) —situated between San Juan and Canosa, the armistice was signed. The Spanish officers were permitted to retain their side arms and the privates their personal property. All Spanish soldiers in eastern Cuba were to march to Santiago and deposit their arms.[70] The formal surrender of Santiago took place on July 17 with the signing of the terms by representatives of the United States and Spain. On that day, General Shafter with his staff and escort entered the city. At 9 a.m., General Toral formally surrendered the plaza and all stores, and at noon, the American flag was raised over the Governor's palace and the band played the Stars and Stripes.[71]

In advance of the surrender of Santiago, and in anticipation of it, President McKinley on July 13 had ordered that, pending further orders, existing Spanish laws should be maintained in the occupied territory. All Spanish officials who were willing to serve were retained where consistent with military rule. Existing laws would operate and Spanish judges would continue to administer the law of the land. Under the supervision of the American military governor, the Spanish constabulary would be preserved. General Chambers McKibben was appointed temporary Military Governor of Santiago, but he was succeeded on July 20 by General Leonard Wood.[72]

A week after the fall of Santiago, an American officer in the Eighth Regiment of Ohio Volunteer Infantry wrote to President McKinley from his camp near the surrendered city:

> When the true story of the Santiago campaign is written, if it ever is told, the people of the United States will be astounded and amazed. Barring the matchless courage of the private soldiers, the personal efficiency and devotion of the subordinate officers and the patriotism, it will make the most shameful page in American history.[73] *

The most shameful part of this page occurred on the day of the surrender of Santiago by the Spaniards. As the senior Cuban Commander present, García had quite rightly expected to participate in the surrender negotiations and to share in the control of the city after its surrender. After all, the Cubans had been fighting in eastern Cuba since 1895 and had inflicted tremendous damage on the Spaniards before the Americans entered the war. Since then, the Cubans had been active militarily either independently or in joint military combat with the Americans. Moreover, it had not been bad Spanish strategy but Cuban preventive measures which had kept the Spaniards from breaking the encirclement of Santiago. Not only are Cuban and Spanish sources unanimous on this point,[74] but Shafter himself acknowledged this. On July 15, two days before the surrender, he wired Washington: "I do not believe that Toral is trying to gain time in hopes of getting reinforcements. *Cubans have forces in vicinity of all Spanish troops....*"[75] One can easily imagine what would have been the result if the thousands of veteran Spanish soldiers in Holguín, Guantánamo and other parts of Oriente had arrived in Santiago to continue the battle against the weary, disease-racked armies of Shafter commanded by a man too discouraged and too physically incapacitated to lead them effectively. By blocking and then immobilizing the Spanish reinforce-

---

* Almost a year later, Victor F. Lawson, publisher of the Chicago *Record*, wrote: "At Santiago Gen. Miles was compelled to do nothing and allow Avoirdupois Shafter to make a reputation—and what a reputation he made!" (Lawson to William Curtis, June 16, 1899, Victor F. Lawson Papers, Newberry Library, Chicago.)

ments, the Cubans, as Shafter acknowledged in his dispatch to Washington, made Toral's unconditional surrender inevitable.

Yet in callous disregard of the Cubans' contribution to the victory, Shafter did not permit them to take part in the conferences leading to the city's surrender, nor in the official ceremonies ratifying the terms of capitulation. No Cuban was permitted to sign the surrender. After this, Shafter rubbed salt into the Cubans' wounds by forbidding all armed *insurrectos* to enter Santiago, and as a final insult, he informed García that the Spanish civil authorities would remain in charge of all municipal offices until it was convenient to change them for others— the very thing against which the Cubans had so long fought.*

The Americans' excuse for the failure to invite the Cubans to take part in the occupation of Santiago was that they were afraid that the revolutionists would indulge in acts of vindictiveness against the Spaniards and in an orgy of looting.[76]† In fact, the Associated Press correspondent wrote from Santiago, following an interview with Shafter, that the reason "the Cubans were greatly disappointed at the step taken by the American commander was that they had confidently counted upon having Santiago turned over to them to loot and plunder, as they had in succession sacked Daiquiri, Siboney and El Caney." [77] Since none of these places had been sacked, it was clear that a huge propaganda campaign was afoot to slander the Cubans and thereby justify their exclusion from the surrender. What makes this all the more reprehensible is that Shafter had received assurances from García and other Cuban generals as early as July 4 that the "insurgents will not interfere with any of them [the Spaniards]" after they had surrendered and were disarmed.[78]

---

\* Later García pointed out that Shafter "had given me a distinct promise that the Americans and Cuban troops should enter the town together; that promise he has denied, but nevertheless, it was so." (*The State*, Sept. 28, 1898.)

† The same reason, it is worth noting, was given for the exclusion of the Filipino independence fighters from Manila during the take-over of the city from the Spanish, even though Manila fell as a result of a joint American-Filipino attack, 12,000 Filipino troops helping to capture the city. Likewise, the Puerto Rican independence fighters were kept out of San Juan during the surrender because, as one contemporary writer put it, "it was feared that the Puerto Ricans who had assisted in the investment of the city would produce a scene of rapine and slaughter." (H. K. Shackleford (General George A. Nelson, pseudonym), "Yankee Doodle in Puerto Rico or Routing the Spanish at San Juan," *Complete Stories of the Present War*, July 20, 1898.)

To the Cubans it was obvious that the United States wished to utilize their army for a military victory, and obviously also, without giving them any credit for it. In his General Orders No. 26, July 19, 1898, to the U.S. troops, on the successful outcome of the campaign against Santiago, Shafter did not make a single reference to the Cuban Army. The victory was entirely "the work" of the U.S. soldiers.[79]

To his credit, General García refused to swallow the American insult to the Cuban Revolution and to himself as its chief spokesman in Oriente. On July 17, he sent Máximo Gómez his letter of resignation as Lieutenant General. After describing the role the Cubans had played, which had "contributed so much to the success of the operation" at Santiago and Shafter's insulting conduct, "in everything relating to the capitulation," he noted that the only course left to him was to resign "in an irrevocable sense since I am not ready to keep on obeying the orders and cooperating with the plans of the American Army, and I don't want it said that I am obeying the orders of my government. . . . I have no other way of protesting against the attitude of the American government. . . ." In the course of his letter, García informed Gómez: "I do not obey North American orders."[80]

That same day, July 17, García sent his famous letter of protest to Shafter. Famous, that is, in Cuban history, but generally ignored by American historians, none of whom have ever reprinted it. The letter, bearing the address, "*Campos de Cuba Libre,*" went:

> Sir: On May 12 the government of the Republic of Cuba ordered me, as commander of the Cuban army in the east to cooperate with the American army following the plans and obeying the orders of its commander. I have done my best, sir, to fulfill the wishes of my government, and I have been until now one of your most faithful subordinates, honoring myself in carrying out your orders as far as my powers have allowed me to do it.
>
> The city of Santiago surrendered to the American army, and news of that impotrant event was given to me by persons entirely foreign to your staff. I have not been honored with a single word from yourself informing me about the negotiations for peace or the terms of the capitulation by the Spaniards. The important ceremony of the surrender of the Spanish army and the taking possession of the city by yourself took place later on, and I only knew of both events by public reports.

I was neither honored, sir, with a kind word from you inviting me or any officer of my staff to represent the Cuban army on that memorable occasion.

Finally, I know that you have left in power in Santiago the same Spanish authorities that for three years I have fought as enemies of the independence of Cuba. I beg to say that these authorities have never been elected at Santiago by the residents of the city; but were appointed by royal decrees of the Queen of Spain.

I would agree, sir, that the army under your command should have taken possession of the city, the garrison and the forts.

I would give my warm cooperation to any measure you may have deemed best under American military law to hold the city for your army and to preserve public order until the time comes to fulfill the solemn pledge of the people of the United States to establish in Cuba a free and independent government. But when the question arises of appointing authorities in Santiago de Cuba under the special circumstances of our thirty years strife against Spanish rule, I cannot see but with the deepest regret that such authorities are not elected by the Cuban people, but are the same ones selected by the Queen of Spain, and hence are ministers appointed to defend Spanish sovereignty against the Cubans.

A rumor, too absurd to be believed, General, describes the reason of your measures and of the orders forbidding my army to enter Santiago for fear of massacres and revenge against the Spaniards. Allow me, sir, to protest against even the shadow of such an idea. We are not savages ignoring the rules of civilized warfare. We are a poor, ragged army as ragged and poor as was the army of your forefathers in their noble war for independence, but like the heroes of Saratoga and Yorktown, we respect our cause too deeply to disgrace it with barbarism and cowardice.

In view of all these reasons, I sincerely regret being unable to fulfill any longer the orders of my government, and, therefore, I have tendered today to the commander-in-chief of the Cuban army, Maj. Gen. Máximo Gómez, my resignation as commander of this section of our army.

Awaiting his resolution, I have retired with all my forces to Jiguaní.

I am respectfully yours,

CALIXTO GARCIA, *Major General*.[81]

García's letter was not made public in the United States until a week after the surrender of Santiago. However, it was known that

García and his men were enraged by their exclusion from the surrender negotiations and being prohibited from entering the surrendered city. On July 20, newspapers carried an Associated Press report from Santiago describing this development, which pointed out "the increasing strained relations between the Americans and Gen. García's Cuban soldiers. Indeed, the situation has now reached a point where there is practically no communication between the armies, and their relations border on those of hostility rather than the relations which one would suppose should exist between allies."[82] (This must have sounded strange coming from a reporter who had done his best to create such hostile relations.) Such reports alarmed the Cuban *Junta* in the United States, and the leaders quickly sought to allay any impression that Cubans were ungrateful to the United States, or resented American conduct of the war, or doubted that she would live up to her promises to help achieve Cuban independence. Domingo Méndez Capote, the vice-president of the Republic of Cuba, was in New York at this time, and on July 22, after consulting with Estrada Palma, Benjamín Guerra and Horatio S. Rubens, he issued a statement disassociating the government he represented from García's reported differences with Shafter. (Since García had not bothered to send his resignation to the provisional government from which he had received his post, but had only communicated with Gómez, it is understandable that Capote was not inclined to be sympathetic with the General.*) "If there is any such misunderstanding between García and Shafter," Méndez Capote declared, "I regret it very much. . . . We have the utmost faith in the pledge made in our behalf that we may enjoy our liberty as an independent republic. Under the circumstances, we will certainly fulfill the pledges we have made as to complete cooperation, and will do all in our power to assume our part in the conflict."[83]

The very same day that the press carried Méndez Capote's assurance to the United States, García's letter to Shafter was published in

---

* García later declared that he had sent his resignation to Gómez instead of to the provisional government because "there is no government." (*The State,* Sept. 28, 1898.) This was not a new point-of-view. In June, 1898, he had written to Estrada Palma that "the Cubans must accept the fact that there is in reality no government in Cuba since the Council of Government actually is incapable of fulfilling the most elementary duties." (Calixto García to Tomás Estrada Palma, June 27, 1898, original in Archivo Nacional, Havana, and reprinted in *Boletín del Archivo Nacional,* 1936, pp. 108-12.)

the newspapers. There was now no question as to whether or not there had been a misunderstanding. "Scorching But Very Dignified," was the heading over the letter in a number of papers. Editorial reaction was generally favorable to García.* "Without doubt he deserves better treatment than to be ignored in the hour of victory," declared the Chicago *Journal*.[84] The Louisville *Dispatch* was even more forthright:

> García's letter places Gen. Shafter in a very bad light if it is true. It is a dignified and able protest against the discourtesy shown him and his army after the victory was won, even to the extent of neglecting to inform him as to what was going on. It is a protest against the policy of recognizing the appointees of the Queen of Spain to conduct affairs in the city of Santiago, and the most eloquent and touching part of it is the answer to the charge that he and his army are barbarous. On that point Gen. García fires a shaft at Shafter which must have penetrated even his 315 pounds of flesh to the heart."[85]

García's letter had brought no response from Shafter, but the storm aroused by its publication in the United States forced the U.S. general to explain his action. In doing so, in a report to Washington, he distorted the cause of the break with the Cuban military leader. "The trouble with Gen. García was that he expected to be placed in command at this place, in other words, that we would turn the city [of Santiago de Cuba] over to him." García had made it quite clear in his letter that the Cubans agreed that the Americans should take possession of Santiago, and that the Cuban Army's role should be subject to Shafter's approval. He objected strenuously to continuation of Spanish rule over the city as an insult to all that the Cubans had fought for. The Cuban Army sought only to play a part, under the command of the Americans, "until the time comes to fulfill the solemn pledge of the United States to establish in Cuba a free and independent government." Shafter was obviously annoyed at being reminded of the purposes set forth by Congress in the Joint Resolution when the United States declared war against Spain, for he reported to Alger that he had told García "that the question of Cuban independence could not be considered by me."[86]

The Cuban *Junta* refused to comment on Shafter's explanation.

---

* García later reported that he had "received from the United States thousands of letters of congratulations." (*The State*, Sept. 28, 1898.)

However, Estrada Palma urged all Americans not to confuse García with the Cuban people, for the General spoke only for himself. "There is no danger that the Cubans will permit a slight misunderstanding of one of their countrymen, even of a general, with an American to affect the successful issue of the campaign." [87] Estrada Palma was correct in pointing out that the dispute would not affect the Cuban contribution to final victory. Indeed, García himself, after he withdrew his forces to the interior, drove the Spaniards out of Gibara and was besieging Holguín when news of peace came.[88] But Estrada Palma was incorrect when he declared that García spoke only for himself. In the last week of July, 1898, a large body of citizens of Santiago de Cuba signed a petition addressed to President McKinley, in which they supported García for having protested Shafter's refusal to consult the Cubans on the terms of the surrender and to allow the Cuban troops to enter the city. Moreover, they strongly endorsed García's resentment over the fact that Spanish officials were retained in office. The petition thanked "the people of the United States for delivering us from the insufferable yoke of Spanish rule," but expressed dismay at the fact that Spanish officials still governed the liberated city:

> We hope that the present state of affairs at Santiago, where Spaniards are still the administrators of our interests, property and fate, will be brief; that the city may soon be turned over to the Cubans, and that our flag may enter, the flag of Cuba waving triumphant beside the American flag, as Cuban soldiers fought side by side with the Americans against the common enemy.[89]

This moving petition was ignored in Washington. After all, President McKinley himself had stipulated before the surrender of Santiago that Spanish laws would be continued and Spanish officials allowed to administer them!

Washington also ignored an appeal from Dr. Julio Henna, president of the Puerto Rican section of the Cuban Revolutionary Party, calling upon the United States to arm and equip a company of Puerto Rican exiles in New York to accompany the American Army in its invasion of Puerto Rico. "They would go as interpreters, scouts, guides and soldiers," Dr. Henna suggested.[90] But Washington wanted no interference from Puerto Ricans with its plan to annex the island.* Moreover, the Administration felt that Admiral Dewey had been too cooperative with the Filipino independence army,† and it did not want any trouble to develop on the Puerto Rican scene.

Throughout the first days of August, the end of hostilities was expected momentarily. It came on August 12. Secretary William R. Day for the United States, and Jules Cambon, the French ambassador to the United States, acting for Spain, signed a protocol which would form the basis of a definite peace treaty. The provisions for the general armistice were:

1. Spain would relinquish all claims of sovereignty over and title to Cuba.

2. Puerto Rico and other Spanish islands in the West Indies, and an island in the Ladrones to be selected by the American government, would be ceded to the United States.

3. Cuba, Puerto Rico and other Spanish islands in the West Indies should be evacuated immediately and commissioners, within thirty days after the signing of the protocol, should meet at Havana and San Juan to arrange and execute the details of the evacuation.

4. The United States would occupy and hold the city, bay and harbor of Manila, pending the conclusion of a treaty of peace which would settle the status of the Philippine Islands.

---

\* On July 20, Henry Clews, a Wall Street banker, and writer of a nationally-syndicated Weekly Financial Review, said that Wall Street's view on the question of Puerto Rico was that "the island of Porto Rico must become absolutely and unqualifiedly the property of this government." (*The State,* July 20, 1898.) The following day, a dispatch from Washington read: "The authoritative declaration was made today that the island of Porto Rico is to be held as a permanent possession of this country as the price of the war." (*Ibid..,* July 21, 1898.)

† Immediately after the battle in Manila Bay, Dewey had suggested that the Filipino chief, Emilio Aguinaldo, might be able to render valuable services in the war against Spanish forces on the island. Aguinaldo and his men assumed a strong offensive after the fall of Manila, placing large parts of the island under the effective rule of the Filipinos. Navy Secretary Long, alarmed by this developmet, cautioned Dewey to be careful in his relations with the Filipinos lest they get the idea that the United States favored independence for the island after Spanish rule was overthrown. "It is desirable, as far as possible, and consistent with your success and safety, not to have political alliance with the insurgents or any faction in the island that would incur liability *to maintain their cause in the* future." (Navy Department *Annual Report,* 1898, Appendix, p. 101. Emphasis mine. P.S.F.)

5. The United States and Spain would each appoint commissioners to negotiate a treaty of peace, the commissioners to meet at Paris not later than the first of October.

6. On the signing of the protocol, hostilities would be suspended and notice to that effect would be given as soon as possible by each government to the commanders of its military and naval forces.[91]

President McKinley announced a suspension of hostilities on the same day, August 12, and orders were issued to the American naval commanders in Cuba, Puerto Rico and the Philippines raising the blockades.[92] The Administration now faced the problem of informing the Cuban revolutionary leaders of the protocol ending the fighting, without, at the same time, establishing official relations with them since that might appear to be recognizing the existence of a Cuban government. McKinley therefore sent Charles E. Magoon to New York to attempt to persuade the leaders of the Cuban *Junta* to notify the leaders of the Revolution of the cease-fire in a purely personal message. Magoon met with Estrada Palma and Horatio S. Rubens, and conveyed McKinley's wishes. But Rubens insisted that notification of the protocol must be transmitted to Cuba by Estrada Palma in his official capacity as the Cuban Republic's Minister to the United States. "Why," Rubens asked, "do you appeal to Estrada Palma unless you recognize in him the Cuban representative, and the only means of communication to bring about the required action?" When Rubens and Estrada Palma refused to budge from this position, Magoon consulted the White House, and after several telephone conversations with McKinley, agreed to the Cubans' terms. A cable was sent by Estrada Palma to General Bartolomé Masó, "President of the Cuban Republic in Santiago de Cuba," and it was signed "Minister and Delegate Plenipotenciary to the United States." It read:

> I have this thirteenth day of August, 1898, accepted in the name of the Cuban provisional government, the armistice proclaimed by the United States. You should give immediate orders to the army throughout Cuba surrendering all hostilities. Preliminary terms of peace, signed by representatives of Spain and the United States, provide that Spain will relinquish all claim over and title to Cuba.[93]

The joyous news reached the Cubans in arms during the next few days. On August 17, Máximo Gómez received the news in Camagüey.

In an informal address, he congratulated the Cuban people on the end of the war. "He would rather," an on-the-spot reporter wrote, "that Cuba should have completed herself the achievement of her independence, but that had not been done, and he was grateful to the Americans for coming to the rescue, and he recognized the peace they had made as binding upon the Cubans." [94]

Two days later, a moving ceremony took place at Punta Alegre in central Cuba. The little schooner which had brought some supplies to Gómez's forces was about to return to the United States with several Americans who had been through the campaign. At 6:30 A.M., the vessel was about to depart when Gómez came aboard with General Carrillo, Captain Santos, and several other Cuban officers. Taking a package from an attendant, Gómez unrolled and exhibited a silken Cuban flag, stained and faded. Addressing Captain Santos, he observed that this was the flag of Peralejo, where Antonio Maceo had defeated Martínez Campos, and that Santos, because of his services to the Cuban cause as the pilot of many relief expeditions, had merited the honor of holding it. Gómez then took another package from the orderly and opened it, exhibiting a smaller Cuban flag. *"La bandera de la invasión,"* he explained. This was the flag he and Maceo had used in the famous march through Cuba in 1895-96 from one end of the island to the other. It was passed from hand to hand, caressed and returned to the orderly.

Then Captain Santos, his face beaming, seized the signal halyards, and began to fasten the flag of Peralejo to the cord preparatory to raising it to the masthead. But Gómez stopped him, and ordered Santos to bring an American flag. One was quickly found in a locker of the cabin, and under Gómez direction, the Stars and Stripes was attached to the halyards, and the two flags were raised together, the American above the Cuban. At the same time, the cornets on the wharf sounded the *Himno de Bayamo,* the Hymn of Bayamo, the Cuban "Marseillaise."

> "The 'old Man' took off his black slouch hat," wrote an American at the scene, "and watched the flags go up the line and ripple out in the morning breeze. He continued for fully a minute to gaze up at them with a solemn, rapt expression on his grim features. Standing a few feet away by the main mast, I could see every working of his lean, brown face and could well divine the thoughts

that passed through his mind. After many years of hardship and struggle and sacrifice, after ten years of one war and three of another unparalleled in privation, after failure and exile and the bitterness of hope deferred, he looked at last upon the flag of Free Cuba, floating over the blue waters."

Withdrawing his gaze from the flags, Gómez lifted his black hat at arm's length above him, and cried out: "*Viva Cuba!*" The officers and men on the schooner and those on the wharf, their hats off, echoed, "*Viva!*" "*Viva la Libertad!*" cried Gómez. "*Viva!*" responded the crowd. "*Vivan los Americanos!*" cried Gómez. "*Viva!*" the crowd echoed.[95]

The Spanish-American War, *la Guerra Hispano-Cubano-Americana*, as the Cubans more correctly call it, "the little splendid war," as John Hay called it in a letter to Theodore Roosevelt, had lasted three months and twenty-two days, 113 days in all. To many Americans and to nearly all American newspapers, the speedy victory over Spain was due entirely to the might and power of the United States. "We have gone to the rescue of the Cubans and won their war for them," was the common refrain.[96] But here and there a few voices were heard pointing out that the victory was due not alone to the blows delivered against Spain by the forces of the United States. As one contemporary noted: "The saving factor, despite our nation's total unpreparedness for the war, was Spain's impoverished condition due to the damages inflicted by the Cubans over the years."[97] This was a correct evaluation. As we have clearly seen, the Cubans, by their persistent and self-sacrificing struggle of over three years, to say nothing of the more than two decades of struggle that preceded the second War for Independence, had reduced Spain to a condition of extreme financial exhaustion, and had rendered her people war-weary to a point bordering on hopelessness. Before the United States entered the war, Spain had lost 100,000 men and drained the dregs of her resources. Her army in Cuba was spent up in the cities and towns, sickened and incapable of effective fighting. The countryside, controlled by the Liberating Army, afforded no substance for Spain's troops, and the occupation of the interior by the Cuban forces made retreat impossible from cities attacked by the United States as well as reinforcement to the beleaguered cities. Moreover, the fact that the Spanish armies in fortified towns were dependent for provisions upon imports from Spain, made the American blockade terribly effective.

In short, Spain surrendered not only because one stronghold in Cuba—Santiago de Cuba—was taken, but because her other troops in the island were weakened and decimated by years of Cuban efforts, and because the Cuban forces prevented the Spanish units from uniting and continuing resistance. This, together with the American naval and land forces, brought final victory.

## CHAPTER XVI

# The Devastated Island

"FREE CUBA—free and unutterably desolate." Thus an American correspondent wrote as the war came to an end.[1] After more than three years of "total war," Cuba lay in ruins. The armies of Spain and Cuba had swept back and forth over the land, carrying ruin with the torch at every trip. What was missed by one army was destroyed by the other. The incendiary fires had consumed houses and everything else around them. In livestock Cuba had been self-sustaining at the beginning of the war. The upland in the central portions of the island provided ample sustenance and conditions for the thriving of cattle. But all this changed when General Weyler ordered his army to kill all horses and cattle in the country that could not be utilized by the Spanish, in order to prevent accession to them by the *insurrectos*. Now the pastures were empty; nearly all the livestock was gone. Of the three million head of cattle in 1895, only ten percent remained. The chief industry of the province of Puerto Príncipe had been cattle raising, but only about 25,000 cattle were now left out of the hundreds of thousands previously on the ranches. Over nine-tenths of the cattle of Matanzas and Santa Clara Provinces had disappeared; less than 100,000 remained of well over a million animals.

The sugar industry was in a deplorable state. Cane fields and mills had been destroyed; crop cultivation had been neglected, and the mills which had survived could not grind because they lacked cane. Planters had little or no capital to resume operations. The 350 sugar mills had been reduced to a mere 40, and these had no cane, fuel, equipment or capital. In the cities and towns, the factories connected with the sugar industry were hardly operating. The same chaos existed in the tobacco and coffee industries; indeed, all industry appeared at an end.

The roads were completely out of repair and impassable in many

379

parts of the island. "All we have for roads," wrote an American from Oriente, "are ditches, some 16 and 20 feet deep, which have been washed out among the undergrowth by the heavy rains." The few railroads were out of repair. Bridges and telegraph lines all over the island were down and practically useless. Eastern Cuba, where so much of the fighting had taken place, had become "almost a wilderness." [2] Nor was central Cuba much different. "In marches of 200 miles," wrote an American just returned from Camagüey, "I neither saw a house, nor a cow, calf, sheep or goat, and only two chickens. Sugar, coffee, tobacco and rum are staple products of Cuba. In all that time and all that journeying we encountered of these nothing but tobacco, and not half a sufficiency of that. The country there is wilderness." [3]

There was no food except in the towns, and these, outside of Santiago Province, were still held by the Spanish garrisons—for under the armistice, the Spaniards were to occupy the towns until replaced.* Since the Cuban soldiers were not permitted to occupy the towns, they remained in the surrounding countryside, without food and slowly starving. "The Cuban Army is dying with hunger," wrote Lieutenant Colonel Carbonne to Gonzalo de Quesada. "General Menocal took me to see his weak, tottering, and squalid soldiers—made so on account of the want of food and actual necessities of life." [4] Since the United States did not press for immediate evacuation of the entire island by the Spanish soldiers, as called for in the protocol ending hostilities,† the

---

* As we have seen, Brigadier-General Leonard D. Wood was placed in charge of Santiago de Cuba after the surrender of the city. He later became head of the military department of Santiago, created on August 10, 1898, and consisting of the Province of Santiago as it was evacuated by the Spanish. The Province of Puerto Príncipe was attached for a time, but was administered by Major General Lawton. Lawton was a soldier rather than an administrator, and since his services was needed elsewhere, he was supplanted on October 12, 1898 by General Wood. Thus there were two provinces under American administration before the control of the whole island was transferred by Spain. (Willis Fletcher Johnson, *The History of Cuba*, New York, 1920, vol. IV, p. 140; "Report of the War Department," *House Document* 2, 56th Cong., 1st Sess., vol. IV, p. 140.)

† *The State* charged the Administration with deliberately plotting the delay of the evacuation of Cuba by the Spanish soldiers so as to provoke the Cuban Army into acts of looting. "If the Cuban soldiers enter the towns to loot a town of its food supply, there will be an illustration of the necessity for a big force of American troops to keep down this 'banditti' and for a long delay in permitting the formation of a government by the people of Cuba." (Nov. 5,

condition of the Cuban Army grew worse with each passing day. "The troops are upon the utmost verge of starvation," wrote General Pedro Betancourt in October, 1898. "Their sufferings are terrible, and something must be done, and that quickly, if they are not to perish. These people are today the true reconcentrados of Cuba." [5]

The plight of the people was equally tragic. Of the 50,000 inhabitants of Santiago at the time of the surrender, 15,000 were sick. (In addition there were in and about the city about 4,000 sick Spanish and 5,000 sick American soldiers.) The inhabitants were just returning from a horrible pilgrimage to Caney, where they had gone to get out of the besieged city. There some 15,000 people of all ages had been herded under frightful conditions, and many died on the way back while the others were too weak and exhausted to bury them. The streets of the city were filled with heaps of decomposing filth and the rotting carcasses of horses and dogs. Frightful odors came from abandoned houses, speaking strongly of the dead within. Smallpox and yellow fever were raging, and clouds of smoke hung over the city, from funeral pyres where many bodies for which burial was impossible were being burned. On one day there were 216 deaths in the city, and the average was about 200 per day. Half the people were threatened with starvation.[6]

Havana was crowded with several thousand *reconcentrados;* sometimes they were found dead in the streets and in their filthy quarters, where disease and starvation were rampant. Thousands lacked food, clothing and medicine. Puerto Príncipe, a city of 30,000, was in miserable sanitary condition as were all the other Cuban cities and towns.[7] Desolation, starvation and chaos prevailed everywhere. Some merchants and a few large planters seemed prosperous, but the people had no means with which to buy supplies, and merchants were holding the available supplies at prices prohibitive to the starving people. A large proportion of the rural and village population was sick from malaria. Guerrillas who had served with Spain were still in the mountains, and people were afraid to return to their farms.[8]

The war had not only practically destroyed the economic base of

---

1898.) Actually, the discipline of the starving Cuban soldiers during the months following the protocol of peace and their refusal to loot the towns so as to avoid creating the impression that they were bandits, is a remarkable tribute to their patriotism.

life on the island; it had wiped out a significant part of the population. Those who had survived the concentration camps were further weakened by the blockade of the Cuban ports by the United States fleet during the war. For her bread, Cuba had for many years prior to the war been dependent upon the United States, though Spanish restrictions on trade were such that she often imported American flour by way of Spain. With the blockade, the cities were cut off from these supplies. Not even a ship of the Cuban Relief Committee was allowed through the blockade to relieve the starving population. "We are at this port with a ship laden with supplies," Clara Barton wrote from Key West on May 20, 1898, "waiting until the time shall come when we may be able to reach Cuba and there relieve any and all persons who are suffering." [9] The ship, the *State of Texas,* remained in Key West, loaded with 1,400 tons of food, medicine and clothing for the relief of destitute Cubans while Miss Barton tried vainly to obtain permission from Admiral Sampson to enter Havana. (The U.S. Navy insisted that no supplies could be landed in Cuba until American troops could guard them to prevent provisions from being diverted to the use of Spanish soldiers.) "Thus," J. Gardner, Miss Barton's assistant, wrote angrily, "the navy of a nation that was making war in the name of 'humanity' was used as a barrier to prevent food from reaching the starving people for whose sake the war was waged." [10]

The *State of Texas* was joined by other ships loaded with supplies for the Cubans, and all were finally allowed to land in Santiago after the surrender of the city. On July 19, a reporter wrote from Santiago that "Miss Barton yesterday began distributing supplies and relieving thousands of cases of distress from hunger and sickness." [11] By the end of August, Clara Barton could write that "Santiago is relieved; it has more supplies than it wants, both of ours and the Government. It is now an independent place, that has fought its way to freedom, desires to resume its normal conditions and its business and does not consider itself longer an object of charity; does not want to be pauperized and does not hesitate to say so. We have left in the warehouses more than they will ever know what to do with." [12]

Under General Leonard Wood, Military Governor of Santiago, starvation and disease were fairly checked in the city. One of the first things Wood did was to establish a Sanitary Department. Men were recruited to clean up the city. Prices were cut, especially on meat and sorely needed food for the weakened and anaemic people, and the army issued large amounts of rations. (Rations were issued to 18,000 people daily on an average.) The average daily death rate was reduced from 200 to 10.[13] This was a notable achievement, but it had been carried through with a high hand. Wood demanded complete obedience to whatever he decreed, and Santiagans who opposed his measures "were publicly horswhipped in the streets of Santiago."[14] "In dealing with Latin races," Wood once wrote, "it is not advisable to yield under pressure, unless one is prepared to give up everything and submit to be ruled."[15] As early as the late summer of 1898, Wood, in the words of the Cuban historian, M. Márquez Sterling, showed that "he preferred conquering to governing."[16]*

Outside of Santiago de Cuba, however, conditions were still desperate. The Cuban Central Relief Committee and the Red Cross met with considerable opposition from U.S. Army commanders when they tried to relieve suffering outside of Santiago. The Relief Committee complained that "some Ten Thousand dollars worth of our supplies were forcibly seized by order of Col. [Duncan] Hood of the U.S. Army and our distribution to the thousands of suffering at Gibara, Holguín and other places was abruptly brought to an end." Actually, much of the supplies intended for the "suffering Cubans" in these and other towns ended up with the U.S. armed forces. "The army grasps at everything," Clara Barton complained. W. E. Cramer, one of her assistants, wrote from Gibara that so much of the Cuban relief supplies had been seized for "military necessity" that "further work with the remainder would amount to practically nothing. . . . No better example of the utter incompetence of the army official could be found that is shown in this act of 'necessity' for the confiscation of food intended for *reconcentrados* and given by the American people to feed starving Cubans."[17]

As a result of a strong complaint against this "outrage," some of the confiscated supplies were returned.[18] But a continual struggle took place between the U.S. government and the relief organizations. The former insisted that it could handle the problems in Cuba by itself

---

* Wood also showed a tendency to glamorize his work, hiring an agent, A. E. Mestro, to publicize his activities in Cuba. Mestro met with newspaper editors in the United States and boasted of the sternness with which Wood operated in Santiago. (A. E. Mestro to Wood, Oct. 16, 1898, Leonard Wood Papers, Library of Congress.)

and the Cuban Relief Committee and the Red Cross pointed out that the government talked big and did little, and placed obstacles in the way of these organizations when they tried to relieve suffering. On October 25, 1898, Miss Barton noted sadly that "the scores of nameless obstructions have rendered efforts at relief well-nigh useless." In a direct appeal to President McKinley, she wrote: "There still exists much suffering in Cuba, especially in those districts where but little, if anything has been distributed since the raising of the blockade and the opening of the ports." [19]

Clara Barton was not exaggerating. In many parts of the island starving people searched for any kind of food. Rats, mice and even diseased animals were devoured, and roots and grasses were used to assuage hunger. "Even the birds which habitually fed themselves from left-overs," writes Rafael Martínez Ortiz, "perished from hunger. And this is an island of the tropics where the exuberance of nature appears to offer subsistence in abundance." [20] A special problem was the children of dead *reconcentrado* parents. "They were like herds of hungry neglected animals," wrote one observer, "literally perishing of filth and hunger." [21]

It is in the correspondence of the Central Relief Committee and the Red Cross agents in Cuba, collected in the Clara Barton Papers, that one gets a vivid picture of what Miss Barton called "the indescribable, prolonged and unmitigated distress of the people." [22] These reports were written at a time when American military commanders, especially General Leonard Wood, were boasting that the provinces under their command were fully on the road to recovery.

From Trinidad came the report late in September, 1898, that "the people have been without supplies of any kind with the exception of corn and a few vegetables for months, and have been obliged to eat even the dogs and carcasses of dead animals where obtainable." [24] W. S. Warner, Cuban Relief Committee and Red Cross agent, wrote from Gibara in mid-October: "I send you with this in a separate package a suit of clothing in rags that I have had thoroughly disinfected and washed as a sample of the condition of the people here. I would suggest that it be hung in the window of some of the great Broadway retail clothiers with a placard stating its purpose: an object lesson to [the] American people on the condition of the Cuban farmer. The women have no clothing." A week later, he sent the following observation about Gibara: "I have seen wretched towns in Honduras, Guatemala, and the Central American Republics, but never any so wretched as this."[25] "*Tons* of quinine are needed," he appealed. "There is literally not an ounce. . . . Every thing is needed that these people eat, use or wear, for they have absolutely nothing and absolutely no money to buy with."[26]

In mid-October the following report came from Guanabacoa:

> In regard to the condition of the people here, you may believe me and rest assured that the stage of misery and starvation and sickness is *more than ever*, and on the *increase*. . We not only have the reconcentrados whose ranks death has thinned out by the thousands, but we have the once respectable and self-supporting classes, who are suffering everything and dying for want of food. They could not go along the street and feed from garbage barrels to eke out a miserable life for a short time; nor could they beg in the streets passing the day sitting on the sidewalks or in door ways, but could only live in despair until death came.[27]

Early in November, the agent in Guanabacoa sent a tragic dispatch:

> A very large amount of supplies is required. . . . Here in this town they are dying at the rate of thirty to fifty a day now. In the house next door to me sixteen have died. . . . Today the mother of a family of fourteen is dead; father, mother and seven children, none of them small; boys of twenty years, girls of fifteen, starved to death; remaining alive yet. . . . The younger girl of about seven is now in my house, her oldest sister of sixteen is bloated to her arms, the oldest boy a spectre. Of this we have it all around us. They are thrown into the garbage cart and sent away to be buried in a trench with hundreds of others, and not covered until the trench is filled, and then only a few inches of dirt is thrown on the top layer—no coffins of course allowed. . . . At this moment I hear the garbage cart passing to the next door, to remove the dead mother I have already written about. Poor woman and poor people. . . .[28]

From Matanzas there was a shocking report:

> No one who has not been here and seen their wretchedness can appreciate at all the dreadful condition of a large part of the entire suburban population. Starvation, disease, and death everywhere, without the means of warding them off. . . . It is hard to see the grown people here, but a sight of the little ones would soften the

hearts of the most indifferent. The legs and arms of many of them are not larger than your thumb, and when their bodies are exposed you can see every bone. Colorless, hollow-eyed, and sunken-cheeked, they are indeed wrecks of the pitiless barbarity of Gen. Weyler and the inhumanity of the Spanish Government.[29]

And so it went throughout most of Cuba. ("You know better than anyone what destitution exists everywhere on this island," a Red Cross agent wrote to Clara Barton on October 20, 1898.[30]) Reports poured into the Cuban Relief Committee and the Red Cross describing deaths from starvation and disease, especially smallpox. Writing from Holguín in late October, Warner reported: "Smallpox is in all parts of the city, and there are no records to show the number of cases, as there is not even *one* doctor in the town for the [Spanish] army or citizens. The army is losing about thirty per day by smallpox, and it is probable that there is about the same number of deaths among the more wretched Cuban citizens, especially women and children." [31] The reports told of people anxious and willing to work but with "nothing to work with and no seed with which to sow the ground." [32] Accompanying these reports were appeals that "something be done," that food, medicines and clothing be shipped quickly to Cuba.* Agents complained that the U.S. Government was not doing enough and was confining itself to daily food rations to the starving population of only a few cities while the promise of farm tools, seeds and domestic animals too often remained just that—a promise. Agents complained, too, that too much of American assistance went not to the peasants but to promote big enterprises in sugar and tobacco.[33]

Besides stressing the terrible plight of the Cuban people, the reports emphasized that the Cubans were eager and anxious to rebuild their wrecked country. Self-help and mutual aid were almost universal. Tools were passed around from farmer to farmer, and plows were pulled by men, even by women.[34] "One family, consisting of a father, mother

---

* As early as August, 1898, Clara Barton wrote: "If six months ago it was necessary for us to reach Cuba for relief, it is doubly necessary now.... For those who are left alive the need is terrible." The Central Cuban Relief Committee made the same point in an appeal to the American people, reminding them that "even with the establishment of peace on the island, the unfortunate 'concentrados' have nothing to which they can return, excepted desolated fields and ruined homes. Food and clothing will be needed to help them along until they can take care of themselves." (Clara Barton to S. E. Barton, Aug. 8, 1898, and Circular, signed by Stephen E. Barton, chairman, Central Cuban Relief Committee, both in Clara Barton Papers, Boxes 39, 43, Library of Congress.)

and children, having obtained a plow," wrote a reporter from Matanzas, "the boys yoked themselves to it while the father held it for breaking up the soil." [35]

In their reports all agents stressed the desire of the Cubans for education. Especially touching was a report dealing with the nineteen asylums established by the Red Cross, under Clara Barton's supervision, for the care of orphans. "We found them anxious to learn," wrote one of Miss Barton's assistants. "At one of the inspection visits, Miss Trotzig asked a little boy of five what she should bring him on her next visit. (One of his playmates had a toy watch.) She said to him, 'Would you like a watch?' He thought for a moment, and then he said, 'If it is just the same to you, I would rather have a book.' " [36]

In the asylums about 1,000 Cuban children were cared for and taught to read and write. Some were children of soldiers in the Liberating Army whose mothers had died in the concentration camps. "How many fathers who did not expect to see their sons alive, found them in the asylums of the Red Cross, alive and healthy, knowing how to read and write, do sums and raise corn," wrote a contemporary Cuban.[37] In addition to the orphan asylums, the Red Cross set up hospitals and infirmaries in Cuba. Writing of an inspection tour she made of the hospitals, infirmaries and asylums, this same Cuban observed: "Miss Barton's popularity in Cuba is amazing. Everywhere she received a most enthusiastic ovation. She was received at all the railway stoppings by committees of authorities, associations, clubs, ladies; and the populace, in confused masses, offered her honors, titles, flowers, and applause." [38] Another Cuban writes: "Not a few of the Cuban children born from 1898 to 1900 were called Clara or Claro, a spontaneous token of gratitude to Clara Barton who had saved so many lives." [39]

Slowly Cuba began the painful recovery from ruin. The United States government, the Cuban Central Relief Committee and the Red Cross made important contributions to this recovery. But as one student has noted: "The Cubans themselves probably did more to rescue Cuba from want and desolation than the Americans." [40] In December, 1898, Robert P. Porter, McKinley's special commissioner to Cuba, wrote: "It is easy to discern the omens which point to the coming prosperity of the whole island under intelligent and honest government." [41]

But whose government would it be: Cuba's or America's? Would it be an American possession, a truly independent republic, or a pseudo-independent republic? The answer would soon come.

## CHAPTER XVII
# Prologue to Military Occupation

THE JOINT RESOLUTION OF CONGRESS, embodying the Teller Amendment, adopted April 20, 1898, stated that "the United States hereby disclaims any disposition or intention to exercise sovereignty, jurisdiction, or control over said island [of Cuba] except for the pacification thereof, and asserts its determination, when that is accomplished, to leave the government and control of the island to its people." On the first anniversary of the passage of the Teller Amendment, the *Journal of the Knights of Labor* commented bitterly: "By the adoption of the Teller resolution by Congress we pledged ourselves to withdraw from Cuba. Did we do it? On the contrary we sent regiments of American soldiers there to compel, by force of arms, the Cuban citizens to submit to our demands."[1]

The process of transition from the Teller Amendment to military occupation began soon after the United States declared war. Although the Cuban revolutionists had hailed the Joint Resolution, they were anxious to obtain clear and precise information as to the intentions of the United States toward Cuba, and how the "self-denying" clause of the Resolution would be carried out. They were becoming increasingly concerned, moreover, by the campaign of slander in the American Army, suspecting that there was a sinister purpose behind the lies.*

---

* A number of newspapers in the United States reached the same conclusion. The Boston *Transcript* observed: "For political ends it may be deemed expedient by those who are anxious we should have Cuba for ourselves, to sow distrust of insurgent capability, either for war or peaceful government, in the minds of the army and the public." If the campaign picturing the Cubans as worthless allies continued, warned the Minneapolis *Times,* "the American flag will never come down in Cuba even though we are most solemnly pledged to assert no permanent jurisdiction in that island." However, the Cleveland *Leader* urged its continuation since it "may furnish an easy solution of the Cuban

N. P. González, editor of *The State* who was close to the Cuban revolutionists, voiced their concern when he wrote early in the war: "There seems to be in process of development a systematic scheme to misrepresent the Cubans in arms, with a view to the preparation of public sentiment for an evasion of the terms of the Congressional resolution recognizing the independence of Cuba. It looks to me as if the foundation were being laid—in lies—for the indefinite control by the United States on the theory that the Cubans favoring independence are in a small and weak minority and have failed to contribute to the redemption of the island. There may be big money for the trusts and syndicates in the government of the island by the Republican party until 1901, and some fat jobs for Republican politicians." [2] Henry Clews, writing of Wall Street's attitude toward what policy should be adopted toward Cuba once the war was won, gave real substance to González's analysis: "The United States must absolutely occupy Cuba, and hold it under military rule until the people are prepared for a self-government that will be satisfactory to this country." [3]

In May, 1898, the Cuban Council of Government urged Estrada Palma to obtain information on this subject, particularly what parts of Cuba were to be occupied by the American Army, for how long, and under what conditions. He was instructed to learn "who will have authority to keep order and tranquility" during the American intervention, to work for official recognition of the Cuban insurgents by the United States, and make the Americans understand that "there will be here no other order of things than that founded on our Constitution." To bolster this action, Domingo Méndez Capote, the vice-president of the revolutionary government, was sent to Washington, after the surrender of Santiago de Cuba, with ample and complete powers to work with Estrada Palma in whatever manner considered necessary.[4]

Méndez Capote's mission was a failure. The American authorities, he reported, would not tolerate any interference with their plans for Cuba. He found in Washington that "great fears and marked prejudices exist concerning the real purpose of the Cuban revolutionary element

---

problem. While our Government disavowed a purpose of conquest, it may be absolutely necessary for us to keep Cuba and make it a part of the United States." (*Public Opinion*, July 28, 1898, p. 104; *The Literary Digest*, July 30, 1898, p. 124.)

and of its actions now that it found itself free of Spanish domination and felt itself the owner of the destinies of the country."[5]

What this meant soon became evident. Although Calixto García had been cruelly disappointed by the failure of the American authorities to acknowledge the value of Cuban contributions to the victory over Spain, he had not lost hope that they were ready to grant the Cubans the right of self-government. In a circular issued on July 17, before he left the area of Santiago de Cuba, García urged all Cubans and especially the members of the Liberating Army, to make sure that "the best order should reign everywhere, that respect for people and property—all rights of man—should become a fact, and that each one of us should be its most faithful guardian and defender." This was urgent, García emphasized, for "only in this way shall we prove to the world that we have full right in desiring to be free and independent," and only in this way would it be possible to convince the American nation that the Cubans should be permitted to proceed to create a Republic "with the right to occupy a place among the nations of the earth." "It will exalt us in the eyes of the American people," he stressed.

To carry forward this program, García outlined in detail the steps to be taken in the cities and towns occupied by the Liberating Army and those which would be evacuated by the Spaniards. He called upon the chiefs of the divisions "to conduct elections for a Mayor and Councilmen who should be elected by universal suffrage in which every Cuban over the age of twenty-one should participate." Until the central government of the Cuban Republic was organized, the Mayor and Councilmen in the cities and towns, "elected by popular vote," and assisted by the Liberating Army in keeping order, would conduct governmental functions.[6]

García's plan clashed immediately with the decision of the American authorities to maintain absolute control of Cuba. As far as the government and its military representatives in Cuba were concerned, any talk of occupation of towns and cities by the Cuban Army and of Cuban self-government was out of the question. The Administration desired above all conditions which would ensure opportunities for investment of American capital. "Properly directed," exulted Major General Fitzhugh Lee in August, "Cuba will have a great commercial future. Its unbounded and great resources will be very rapidly developed by American push, vigor and capital."[7] But "properly directed" meant, of course, directed by men who would have the proper respect for the interest of Americans, and the Cuban revolutionaries clearly did not fit the bill. With its provision for universal suffrage, García's plan threatened to give the common people of Cuba—the peasants and workers, many of whom were Negroes—too large a voice in the affairs of the island, and it is hardly to be expected that men who believed that Negroes in the United States were not ready for self-government should welcome the prospect of Cuban Negroes participating actively in the government that would replace Spanish domination. Charles G. Baylor, a Rhode Island Negro leader, made this clear. "Nearly all the leaders and fighters in the Cuban army of liberation," he wrote in the Richmond Planet of July 30, 1898, "are men who, if in South Carolina, Mississippi or Louisiana would be made to ride in the 'Jim Crow Cars,' and would be refused the right to occupy a private residence on Beacon Street, in Boston. You see the proposed Afro-Cuban Republic was too close to our own Cuba and Armenia to suit either the northern or southern plutocrats. . . . The *Planet*, a Negro weekly published in Richmond, not only endorsed Baylor's interpretation, but in an editorial advised Gómez and García to stand up squarely against the Americans, even if it meant taking up arms once again, or else they would never live to see a truly independent Republic of Cuba. "Their fate will be that of Gen. Emilio Aguinaldo in the Philippine Islands. The United States will never recognize him or his government, and he, too, will be forced to fight not only the Spaniards but the Americans as well."[8]

It is not surprising, therefore, that García's plan was quickly vetoed. Indeed, General H. W. Lawton, the newly appointed military commander of Santiago Province, wired the War Department on August 16 asking for "definite instructions as to policy to be observed toward the Cuban Army. . . . These people still maintain their organizations, are scattered through the country in vicinity of city, are threatening in their attitude, and keep the inhabitants stirred up and panicky by threats and acts of violence."[9] Lawton offered no evidence to justify his charge that the Cuban Army was engaging in "threats and acts of violence," and as for being "threatening in their attitude," he meant, of course, the desire of the Cubans who had fought for so many years for independence and self-rule to have a voice in the destiny of their country. As one U.S. newspaper correspondent wrote indignantly: "This inflammatory class demands and urges the recognition of Cuba for Cubans."[10] Naturally, this reasonable and logical demand came into conflict with the concept of "Cuba for Americans." Shafter put it clearly in a dispatch to Washington on August 16: "A dual government can't exist here; we have to have full sway of the Cubans."[11] The Administration agreed. The United States, and it alone, would exercise authority over Cuba, and the Cubans must understand this fact at once. "Interference from any quarter will not be permitted," McKinley notified Lawton.[12] When Enrique Trujillo, editor of *El Provenir,* organ of the Cuban Revolution published in New York, arrived in Santiago de Cuba in the summer of 1898 and applied to General Wood, who had replaced Lawton as military commander, for a license to establish a Cuban paper, the request was rejected. "The character of the proposed publication was not considered desirable by the general," wrote a reporter from Santiago. The paper, it was felt, would advocate the right of the Cubans to govern themselves.[13]

These developments were by no means accidental. Despite the Joint Resolution of Congress, a campaign had begun in the United States not long after the war started, to pave the way for American annexation of Cuba. To be sure, in the U.S. Army's leaflet, "Spanish Words for Soldiers," to be used by the men who would land in Cuba, the first two sentences read: "We are your friends" and "We do not want Cuba."[14] (The soldiers were urged to "Keep this for Reference.") However, many newspapers regarded it as mere propaganda. On June 22, 1898, before the Americans had landed at Daiquirí, the Chicago *Tribune* was arguing for Cuba, Puerto Rico' and the Philippines: "All of these islands will belong to us by sovereign right of honorable conquest. . . . They will be American soil from the moment the Stars and Stripes float over them. . . . Annexation of all three is the natural outcome." Even earlier than this, on May 23, 1898, the Chicago *Interocean* had announced: "We must at least control the destiny of Cuba for many years, and eventually annex it." Of course, the Teller Amendment stood in the way, but this was simply a declaration of Congress and if conditions warranted its repeal, it could be withdrawn by Congress.* Early in July, a leading newspaper editor pointed out that the

---

* "What, So Soon!" *The People* commented in noting the attempt to revoke the Teller Amendment. It predicted that the "Amendment will be stretched enough to admit our capitalists completing the work upon which they lashed the nation." (June 19, 1898.)

war itself might yet provide the ground for dumping the Teller Amendment:

> There was not then [at the beginning of the war] the remotest thought among us of taking Cuba for ourselves. . . . But the sweep of war is like that of the whirlwind—no man can tell where it may reach.
> We have interfered to give Cuba a better government and we therefore stand morally responsible to the civilized world for the character of its government. The present insurgents may be able to establish one that we can afford to be responsible for; but if not, our responsibility continues.[15]*

This seemed to imply that at least the Cubans would soon have the opportunity to prove that they were capable of establishing "a better government." But most American papers were not willing to suspend judgment. Before the war ended, the press began to picture the Cubans as "a base rabble unfit for freedom and self-government," and to praise the Spaniards for having realized this all along.[16]† On July 24, 1898, *The People,* organ of the Socialist Labor Party, called attention to this development, and warned that it was "part of American imperialism's scheme to annex Cuba":

> The papers begin to beam with an abuse of the insurgents whom only the other day they were praising to the skies. These insurgents then were "noble patriots sacrificing their lives for freedom's cause." They were "valiant champions of liberty." Now they are "valiant eaters of American provisions"; then they were daring patriots, braving death for their island's liberation from Spanish cruelty," now they are "daring skulkers behind the American

---

* Joseph H. Choate, a leading Wall Street lawyer, made the same point in an address to the American Bar Association. "The Government," he declared, "must not be held too rigidly to purposes and expectations declared before the commencement of the war and in utter ignorance of its possible results. . . . In war events change the situation very rapidly." (New York *Tribune,* Aug. 19, 1898.)

† By the time of the surrender of Santiago de Cuba, the Cubans and Spaniards had virtually swapped places. The Cubans were now regarded as the enemy and the Spaniards as America's ally against a revolutionary mob unfit for freedom. "In Santiago after the surrender," Walter Millis notes, "the American and Spanish troops fraternized in a spirit of mutual admiration for each other and mutual contempt for the Cubans." (*op. cit.,* p. 363. *See also* Associated Press dispatch from Santiago de Cuba, in *The State,* July 21, 1898.)

lines, patriotically protecting themselves from Spanish Mauser bullets." The truth is the Cubans have not changed; it is the American imperialists who have come out into the open.

*The State* put it more succinctly: "Robbery of reputation is now the preliminary requisite to robbery of territory."[17]

Pro-imperialist newspapers warned that the idea that the Cubans were ready for self-government was an illusion. The pledge of "Cuba for the Cubans" was no longer binding, declared the New York *Tribune,* for it presumed that the Cubans were ready for self-government, a presumption which was "false and unsubstantial." Anarchy would be the result of entrusting government to rabble made up of so many "ignorant niggers, half-breeds and dagoes," and, declared the New York *World,* "we are not spending our blood and treasure in putting down one anarchy in Cuba for the sake of setting up another."[18] Scores of papers featured the conclusion of the Associated Press correspondent that "the Cuban leaders are vain and jealous, and if they were given self-government the odds that those who failed to get places of prominence and profit would in the course of a month start a revolution against those who had fated better than they."[19] The Detroit *Tribune* suggested that the United States, "for a long time at least," would have to occupy Cuba and administer its government. If the Cubans did not like it, it might be necessary to bring about "the military subjugation of the people we went to war to save." The Hartford *Post,* published by McKinley's private secretary, John Addison Porter, praised the President's foresight in refusing to recognize the Cuban Republic. "Had it not been for our chief magistrate, these good-for-nothing allies of ours would have been established as an independent nation." The Cleveland *Leader* was happy because "the Cubans have displayed their worthlessness thus early in the struggle. Their conduct may furnish an easy solution to the Cuban problem. While our Government disavowed a purpose of conquest, it may be absolutely necessary for us to keep Cuba and make it part of the United States."[20]

It was all brutally summed up by the military spokesmen for American imperialism. General S. B. M. Young, one of Shafter's divisional commanders, declared that "the insurgents are a lot of degenerates, absolutely devoid of honor or gratitude. They are no more capable of self-government than the savages of Africa."* And when Shafter himself was asked by reporters following his return from Cuba, "How about self-government for the Cubans," he replied tersely: "Self-government! Why these people are no more fit for self-government than gun-powder is for hell."† He added, with evident relish, that "we have taken Spain's war upon ourselves." [21] In short, the United States' purpose in Cuba after the war was the same as that of Spain's before it—to crush the Cubans' desire for independence!

That England should be followed in her colonial policy was a constant cry in the annexationist press. The lesson for the United States was clear: Cuba with its "crude and ignorant population, largely composed of Negroes," should be administered in a firm, deliberate fashion after the manner of the British crown colony. The United States should accept the British lesson that the "relationship of the white men to the tropical people must be that of dominance." [22] Joseph Chamberlain, England's Secretary for the colonies and a leading architect of British imperialism, approved of linking Cuba with England's imperialist approach to conquered people. On arriving in New York in September, 1898, he told reporters: "The United States now finds itself in much the same position as ourselves in Egypt. We are bound to put down rebellion, and we shall stay there until we do." He predicted that the United States would stay in Cuba at least as long as England would remain in Egypt.[23]

Evidently the McKinley Administration viewed this analysis with favor. On September 30, with obvious satisfaction, William R. Day forwarded the President a clipping from the London *Times* which compared the situation in Cuba with that in Egypt; it contained the typical slander that "to give up the island to the power of such persons (as the Cuban insurgents) would be worse than to perpetuate Spanish ascendency," and went on to conclude: "It is obvious enough that the administration of Cuba will have to be controlled by, in some shape or form, the United States. . . . In Cuba, the United States will have

---

* The pro-imperialist British *Saturday Review* seconded this viewpoint, but used an American illustration: "The Cubans or the Filipinos are quite as unfit for selfgovernment as a plantation of Louisiana Negroes, and the country that has conquered them must govern them." (vol LXXXVI, Oct. 8, 1898, p. 458.)

† *The State* commented caustically: "If the Cubans are no more fit for self-government than Shafter is for the command of an army we would be very sorry for them." (Dec. 19, 1898.)

to grapple with the work of governing a population unfit to rule itself."[24] It is not difficult to understand Day's satisfaction. American imperialism had found the strategy by which to rob the Cuban people of the independence to which they were clearly entitled. By repeating over and over again that the Cubans were unfit for self-government, the path was cleared for indefinite American occupation of the island. One newspaper predicted as early as September, 1898 that the occupation would last "until the Cubans shall weary of it and seek relief in accepting annexation or in such territorial form of government as the President may offer."[25]

While all this was occurring, the Cubans were not mere passive spectators. Cuban patriotic clubs were formed in many cities, the members of which wore insignias in their buttonholes on which was inscribed the Cuban flag and the slogan: "Let the United States abide by the Congressional resolution."[26] All over the island, the Cuban flag, with the lone star, made its appearance. "Now the symbol of successful revolt, if not of attained sovereignty, it floats over every town in Cuba," wrote a reporter following a tour of the island in the fall of 1898.[27]

Meetings were held in Cuba demanding a clear-cut declaration from the United States that Cubans would be allowed to govern themselves. "We believe, and would urge," a meeting in Santiago de Cuba declared, "that our own people are capable of fulfilling the international obligation to establish a government for the island. All patriotic Cubans desire a government of their own as compensation for the sufferings and heroism of our army, and the definite establishment of the Cuban republic, with Cuban authorities, in accordance with the resolutions of the United States Congress."[28] But there were even bolder declarations. *La Independencia* of Santiago reminded the United States that "we are a people who have proved by the way we liberated our country from Spanish tyranny that we can resist aggression and oppression whenever it comes and in whatever form."[29] Two American officers, following a visit to every Cuban Army camp in the island, reported that "from these men who have struggled and suffered for three long years for their ideal of freedom, resistance is to be feared to any solution of the problem not having for its basis independence." They predicted that the Cuban soldiers might very well "take to the field and wage a guerrilla warfare against the Americans if any form of government short of absolute independence for the Cubans is established in the island."³⁰

Such reports brought an outcry from the American press accusing the Cubans of ingratitude for even thinking of turning against those "who have spent millions of dollars to free them, whose blood, shed in their behalf, is hardly dry upon their hills, and whose food they are now eating." But *The State* put the case for Cuba clearly:

> The very aspirations for independence which the press of the United States held to be so praiseworthy when expressed against Spanish rule are claimed now as unpardonable impudence when expressed against American rule. They must take what we choose to give them, and be what we choose to have them, and that last is a cringing set of slaves. Befool yourselves as you may, that is at the bottom of the anti-Cuban feeling now being worked up.³*

It was in this disturbing atmosphere that a Cuban delegation arrived in the United States to determine the American government's ultimate purposes in the island.

On October 1, 1898, the Council of Government had convoked an assembly of delegates to study and work out solutions for problems facing the country. Previous to this, the Council released an "Exposition to the President of the United States," explaining the nature of the projected gathering. The Council noted that since it had been constituted for war, its authority "terminated when peace arrived," hence the need for a new body which would seek to speak for Cuba "in political matters. Our actions are directed toward all peoples without distinctions, differences, or exclusions." The "Exposition" added that when the preliminary assembly had paved the way, a General Consti-

---

* Praising N. G. González and his paper, *The State*, for its treatment of the Cuban question, General Emilio Núñez wrote: "If we are fortunate enough to have many champions as yourself in the American press no doubt that we will see the flag of the Lone Star float some day on the Morro Castle the hope of the poor and suffering country for many generations in the past." (*The State*, Sept. 30, 1898.)

Actually, *The State* favored annexation of Cuba, but only if the Cubans wanted it. It favored commercial and economic relations of the closest kind while the Cubans organized their own political life, but believed that annexation to the United States was Cuba's "manifest destiny." (*Ibid.*, Sept. 20, 1898.) Despite this contradictory position, *The State* consistently defended the right of the Cubans to organize their own government, free of U.S. domination.

tutional Assembly, composed of representatives of all Cubans, would be called. The document ended on a note designed to overcome the fears of the American government regarding the revolutionists: "Past differences will be completely forgotten since genuine peace makes it necessary, and our people need a total and complete peace which would not be the case if a triumphant party instituted a regime of exclusion and vengeance committing the crime of giving new forms to a past fight."[32] Although the "Exposition" was ignored by McKinley, the Cuban revolutionary forces had at least put themselves on record as determined to play a role in shaping their country's destiny.

On October 24, the Cuban Assembly, composed of delegates elected by 31 corps of the Liberating Army, met at Santa Cruz del Sur. It was greeted with a message from Bartolomé Masó, President of the Republic in Arms. Masó pointed out that the Cubans had accepted the military assistance of the United States, "just as they would have accepted help from any country in their fight against Spain." He noted that under the Joint Resolution of Congress, "America came to our help to compel Spain to relinquish her sovereignty over Cuba in order that the Cubans themselves might be placed as promptly as possible in possession of the island and might assume the administration of its affairs and have a government of their own." He then recounted the efforts of the Cuban government and the Liberating Army to participate actively in the war effort after U.S. intervention and to achieve, if not full recognition, at least a friendly attitude on the part of the American military authorities so that the Cubans could play their part in the organization of the island's affairs after the surrender of the Spaniards. He noted, however, that this reasonable request had been rejected, "and the Liberating Army found itself in the dishonorable position of having to enter cities and towns still governed by authorities representing Spanish colonial domination." Masó urged the Assembly to insist on Cuban participation in the organization of political and economical life following the withdrawal of Spanish authority, and to remind the American government that the Joint Resolution of Congress had made it clear that the United States "will not perform acts of sovereignty, dominion or administration over Cuba, limiting its actions to pacification over the island, in order to hand over to the Cuban people the free direction of its affairs." Masó closed by appealing to all Cubans "to show true patriotism," and, while offering every expression of gratitude to the United States, to make sure that Cuba was governed by its own people, and "to make prompt arrangements for paying off the Cubans in arms and for getting the country into working order." [33]

After the Council of Government had formally dissolved itself in favor of the Assembly, the delegates turned to the appointment of a Commission to Washington to gain some idea of the intentions of the United States toward Cuba, to explore the possibility of obtaining funds to pay off the Liberating Army so that it could be discharged, and funds to liquidate the accumulated debts of the Cuban Republic. The Assembly instructed the Commission to inform Washington that it was ready to disband the Cuban Army entirely, unless the Americans wanted part of it to remain under arms to help keep order, but that no soldiers could be discharged until they were paid for their services as they had been promised. The Commission was to point out that the men who had fought for independence could not be sent home without resources to sustain themselves until the country could be reorganized and they could find the means by which to live. The group was to ask the United States to advance a "reasonable" sum for this purpose. The Assembly did not specify what was a "reasonable" sum, leaving it for the Commission to determine this.[34]

Obviously if the provisional government would have been allowed to collect the revenues of the island it could have paid off the troops itself. But as the United States was collecting these revenues, and would continue to do so for an indefinite period, the Assembly logically looked to Washington for the necessary funds.

The Cuban Commission to Washington was headed by Calixto García. It included, besides García and several other prominent commanders of the Cuban troops, Gonzalo de Quesada, the chargé d'affaires in Washington, and Horatio S. Rubens, the lawyer for the Cuban *Junta*. Although the Commission came in the name of the Cuban Assembly, it also spoke, through Quesada and Rubens, for the *Junta* in the United States. While Máximo Gómez was not included on the Commission, he had already announced that he regarded the Assembly as the only body with authority to disband the Liberating Army. Moreover, García was Gómez's principal lieutenant, and shared his views on many of the issues with which the Commission would deal.[35]

Washington had been worried about the convening of the Cuban Assembly, but Gonzalo de Quesada hastened to asure the Administration that the body would take no position "antagonistic to the policy at Washington but ever in sympathy with the execution of that policy." He also made it clear that his role on the Commission would be that "of preventing friction" between the United States and Cuba.[36] When the Administration learned that a major purpose of the Commission was to discuss paying off the Cuban Army and then disbanding it, it was pleased. "Since this body represented the only tangible threat to American rule in Cuba," notes David F. Healy, "the Americans wanted to get rid of it as quickly as possible."[37] *The Coming Nation*, a Socialist paper published in Tennessee, had observed as early as August 20, 1898 that the newspapers and politicians who charged that "the 'Cubans won't fight' show an overly anxious desire that the Cubans should lay down their arms and go home and let the monopolists take peaceful possession [of Cuba]." The reports from Cuba that elements of the Cuban Army were ready to take to guerrilla warfare to obtain the independence of Cuba certainly convinced Washington that action should be taken as quickly as possible to disband it.

The fact that Calixto García was head of the Cuban Commission did not alarm Washington in November as much as it might have in July. The Administration had gone out of its way to soothe García's anger over his treatment by Shafter. When García entered Santiago with his troops on September 23, he was met outside the city by a delegation led by General Wood and General Lawton and escorted with honors through the streets thronged with cheering thousands of Santiagans. Responding to the occasion, García expressed gratitude to the United States which he described as "a grand nation." "A grand nation it must be," he went on, "when sons of millionaires, who had nothing to gain in Cuba but a soldier's glory, should come here to die side by side with Cubans." He closed by assuring the United States that nothing would ever diminish Cuba's gratitude.[38]

A few days later, García gave the Santiago correspondent of the New York *Herald* an interview in the course of which he announced bluntly that "there is no government in Cuba of Cubans. I do not recognize any government on this island save that of the United States. From the moment the American troops landed on this soil but one government is represented in Cuba."[39] Naturally, most American newspapers were delighted. The Washington *Post* gleefully announced that García had all but demolished "the ridiculous opera bouffe government which, for the past two years, has been flitting about from one hiding place in eastern Cuba to another on the back of some sure-footed mule." It was even reported that García advocated annexation, and this made such a big splash in the American press that the Cuban general was forced to deny the report. While he conceded "the necessity for temporary occupation of the island," he still advocated independence.[40]

García's statement that no Cuban government existed was, of course, consistent with his stand throughout the war, for he always had ridiculed the provisional government as a nonentity. But it was one thing to express this point of view in private letters to Estrada Palma or Gómez, and quite a different matter to do so publicly at a time when the Cubans were striving to establish the right to rule their country. Little wonder that some patriots accused García of having been bought out by the United States to reduce the influence of the provisional government.[41] Of course, this was nonsense, but *The State* was correct in criticizing García for his statement, noting that it "plays into the hands of the enemies of Cuban independence."[42] At any rate, García's appointment as head of the Cuban Commission was certainly not displeasing to the McKinley administration.

Early in December, 1898, McKinley invited the Commission to the White House for an interview in which the main topic was the payment of the Cuban Army. (The Cubans were received merely as citizens of the island and not as representatives of a government.) The Commission came to the interview split over what was a "reasonable" sum for the Army. The majority favored floating a loan, to be advanced by the United States and to be secured by the future revenues of Cuba, big enough to pay the Army monthly wages from the beginning of the war in 1895. But García, reflecting Gómez's views, felt that such a large loan would cripple the Cuban Republic before it even got started, and might even be used as an excuse by the United States to postpone the day of Cuba's independence. Hence he favored payment of an amount sufficient to enable the soldiers to return home and tide them over temporarily until they could find work.[43]

There was more to the idea of a loan from the United States than the amount of money involved. Juan Gualberto Gómez, the Negro patriot from Oriente, had advanced the idea of a loan in the Cuban Assembly before the Commission had left for Washington. Gómez argued that a loan would achieve two purposes in addition to providing a reasonable sum for each soldier upon his discharge: it would force the United States to recognize the Cuban Assembly as the legal spokesman for the whole island, and, to make certain that the loan would be repaid by a Cuban government, the United States would be forced to hasten the establishment of an independent Republic.[44]

Evidently McKinley understood the implications of a loan, for he quickly informed the Commission that a loan was out of the question, being prohibited by the Constitution. What the United States was prepared to offer was an outright gift. The only question was how much was required to disband the Cuban Army. García promptly replied, "Three million dollars." The other Cubans just as promptly protested, but the die had been cast. McKinley, taking advantage of the split in the Commission, insisted that the United States would only consider the three million dollar figure. The subsequent negotiation with McKinley's representative, Robert P. Porter, produced nothing better. The Cubans, overriding García's objections, tried to raise the amount for the Army, but no matter how hard they insisted, the answer was always the same: three million dollars. The accumulated debts of the Cuban Republic could be thrown into the pot together with the money for the Army, even though this by itself amounted to between two and a quarter and two and a half million dollars. But all there was was three million dollars, and the Cubans could take it or leave it.[45]

To add to their disappointment, the Cubans found little support for their position on this and other issues among members of Congress. Indeed, Senator John T. Morgan, Democratic member of the Senate Committee on Foreign Relations, who had been an advocate of the extension of belligerent rights to the Cuban Republic prior to the declaration of war against Spain, read the Cubans a long statement in which he dismissed all Cuban objections to indefinite military occupation by the United States. Sovereignty in Cuba during this indefinite period must lie with the United States alone. Most ominous of all was Morgan's casual denial that the Teller Resolution had any significant relation to the future of Cuba. He conceded that the Resolution was morally binding on the United States, but it "is not an agreement with anybody, nor is it a decree or a law." It would be carried out as the United States saw fit, "in such a manner and at such time as the competent authority in the United States shall provide." When the time came for establishing a permanent government which would replace American military rule—a time to be determined by the United States alone—the military authority should have the responsibility of framing it. To be sure, they should act "with reference to the wishes" of all the Cuban people, but the decisions would be American, not Cuban.[46]

Shocked by such a blatant expression of imperialist designs by a man whom they had regarded as a friend of Cuban independence, the Commission, in a written reply signed by Calixto García, vigorously attacked Morgan's presentation. Rejecting the theory that the Future of Cuba was "at the discretionary power of the American Government," the Commission insisted that the Teller Amendment was "a law like any other law, and was legally as well as morally binding upon the actions of the United States." The Cuban people, the Commission reminded Morgan, would not passively accept being robbed of all they had fought for. While this did not mean armed resistance against the United States, it would mean a refusal to cooperate with it. The Commission announced its intention to withhold approval of any American government which violated Cuban aspirations. In such a case, "we will see the necessity of standing to one side, of not cooperating in the work of the government and policy of the American military authority, leaving to it the most absolute responsibility for the results. . . ."[47]

This defiance of American imperialism was García's last act in behalf of the independence and freedom of the Cuban people. On December 11, 1898, after a brief siege of pneumonia, the hero of the first and second wars for independence, died suddenly in Washington.* With García's untimely death, the work of the Cuban Commission came to an abrupt close. After the funeral, the rest of the Commission returned to Cuba.

In its formal report, the Commission recommended that the Cuban Assembly accept in principle the three million dollar offer to pay off

---

* After an impressive funeral in Washington, attended by Secretary of State John Hay and a number of American generals and officials, García was temporarily buried in Arlington National Cemetery. (New York *Tribune*, Dec. 12, 14, 1898.) *The State* contrasted the official honors now paid García in Washington with the fact "that two years ago he was a pestiferous filibuster who was arrested by the United States after two unsuccessful attempts to take expeditions to Cuba and forfeited his bond to the government when he made his third and successful endeavor." (Dec. 14, 1898.)

the Liberating Army, but that they continue to work to increase the amount. On the question of the policy to be followed by the United States in Cuba, the report was most discouraging:

> It was absolutely impossible for the commissioners—in spite of their determination and their insistence—to obtain any explanation but only vague manifestations, and even phrases more or less evasive, either from the President or the Secretaries, or from other persons who they consulted . . . ; although everyone declared that they were resolved to comply faithfully with the resolutions of Congress of 19 April, 1898, they never let a word escape regarding the means they would adopt to obtain this result, nor the duration of the occupation of the island, as if they really had no definite political program. . . . [48]

As if to underscore the Commission's observation that the United States would not commit itself to a specific statement as to "the duration of the occupation of the island," McKinley's message to Congress in the same month, December, 1898, emphasized that there was no time limit to the forthcoming occupation: "Until there is complete tranquility in the island and a stable government inaugurated, military government will be continued." [49] A number of American newspapers were quick to point out that this left it up to the United States alone to judge whether Cuba ever was fit to be independent. The London *Standard* noted that McKinley had defined the qualities which Cuba must possess to be free and independent "on such a Utopian model, that the day of emancipation from military tutelage may be indefinitely postponed." [50]

The failure of the Cuban Commission to Washington on the eve of U.S. miiltary occupation was the death blow to the revolutionist hopes of American cooperation in securing immediate independence and self-government.

Tragically, the mission itself had contributed to this development. For one thing, the United States had been made aware, through the Commission, that the Liberating Army was shortly to be disbanded. This meant that the one force which might have challenged unlimited American domination over Cuba would soon be removed from the scene. Naturally, this strengthened the United States' determination to move full speed ahead with its policy regardless of Cuban objections.

Then again, the open split in the Commission over the amount to be asked for the Cuban Army enabled the United States to limit its contribution to the meager sum of three million dollars, and the Cubans were in no bargaining position to raise the amount. In a broader sense, the split alerted the United States to the fact that a cleavage had developed in the ranks of the revolutionists, a fact already pointed up by García's statement about the non-existence of a Cuban government, and Gonzalo de Quesada's assurance to Washington that the Cubans would not really challenge the Administration's policy toward Cuba. As we shall see, American imperialism knew well how to use this split for its own purposes.

The truth is that the revolutionists' ranks were becoming weaker as the situation became more critical for Cuba. In December, 1898, at the initiative of Estrada Palma, the Cuban Revolutionary Party, founded by José Martí, was dissolved, and with it the local revolutionary clubs which had played such an important role in supporting and advancing the War for Independence.[51] The justification for the dissolution of the Party was that its work had been accomplished. But the facts, as revealed by American policy since the surrender at Santiago, proved that the need for the revolutionary organization was as great as ever if real independence for Cuba, as envisaged by Martí, was to be achieved. Moreover, the dissolution of the Party severed the links connecting the Cuban workers in Tampa, Key West and other cities in the United States with those in the island.* The separation between the most radical elements in the Cuban struggle weakened revolutionary unity at a time when such unified activity was most needed.[52]

---

* The need for such unity was repeatedly emphasized by the emigres. Gualterio García, a young secretary of the Cuban Revolutionary Party in Southern Florida, wrote to Gonzalo de Quesada in April, 1898: "Are we finished with the tasks we assumed when we formed the Cuban Revolutionary Party? To my mind, no. . . . I believe that all men of good will have a patriotic duty to return to Cuba to . . . put their minds to the most difficult task of rebuilding our devastated native land, to do everything possible to see that the government that we constitute is a government of strength and honor without tyranny." In June, García, fearing that while the war against Spain had been won, the peace might be lost for Cuba, wrote again to Quesada: "What are we doing? What is the program of the Party for the future of Cuba? What line of conduct should we follow with the emigres? Should we travel to Cuba en masse or not?" (Gualterio García to Quesada, Tampa, April 22, June 26, 1898, Gonzalo de Quesada y Miranda, editor, *Archivo de Gonzalo de Quesada, Epistolario*, I, II, Havana, 1948, 1951, vol. I, pp. 179-80, 187.) Unfortunately, the leaders of the Party in the United States ignored such appeals.

## CHAPTER XVIII
# The Treaty of Paris

THE PROTOCOL ending hostilities between the United States and Spain declared that the peace commission should meet in Paris on October 1, 1898, to draw a treaty. On that day, following the exchange of credentials, the commission took up its task. The American commissioners were William R. Day—who resigned as Secretary of State and was succeeded by John Hay—Senator Cushman K. Davis of Minnesota, an ardent imperialist and chairman of the Senate Foreign Relations Committee, Senator William P. Frye of Maine, also favorable to expansion and a member of the same committee, Whitelaw Reid, editor of the New York *Tribune* and one of the leading spokesmen for imperialism,* and the lone Democrat, Senator George Gray of Delaware, an opponent of expansion. Thus the commission was heavily weighted in favor of emerging American imperialism.

The Spanish commissioners were Eugenio Montero Ríos, Buenaventura de Abarzuza, José de Garnica, W. R. de Villa-Urrutía, and Rafael Cerero, jurists or diplomats. The Cubans were not invited to send any representatives to the conference; the exclusion practiced by Shafter at Santiago was continued in Paris. The United States was not prepared to permit any Cuban interference with its plans, and Spain took pleasure in exacting revenge upon her former subjects by agreeing to the exclusion.[1]

One thing was clear even before the conference opened: the United

---

* On the eve of the peace conference, Reid advocated unlimited American expansion. "We must hold Cuba, at least for a time and till a permanent government is well established for which we can be responsible; we must hold Porto Rico, and we may have to hold the Philippines." (Whitelaw Reid, "The Territory With Which We Are Threatened," *Century Magazine*, vol. XXXIV, Sept. 1898, pp. 788-89.)

States was in the driver's seat and could get all it wanted. Spain was financially bankrupt and helpless. All it could offer at Paris was resistance of tongue and pen. Nor was the United States concerned about any of the European powers coming to Spain's assistance. On September 30, Day wrote to McKinley from Paris: "Our best advices are that we need look for no European intervention, and that we will be permitted to make this settlement with a free hand."[2]

Besides the disposition of the Philippine Islands, the most important question before the commission was the so-called Cuban debt. Having accepted the loss of Cuba and Puerto Rico as inevitable, the Spanish commissioners turned their whole attention to avoiding payment of the debt. It took four weeks before this issue was settled.*

In the second session of the conference, the American commissioners proposed the following article: "The Government of Spain hereby relinquishes all claim of sovereignty or title to Cuba." The Spaniards offered a counter-proposal that the Spanish government would relinquish its sovereignty over the island to the United States, which in turn, if it so desired, could give it to the Cuban people. (The Spaniards argued that Cuba could not receive its sovereignty from Spain, and since the Americans contemplated a military occupation of the island until it was pacified, it was automatically forced on them.) The sovereignty thus relinquished would include all prerogatives, powers, and rights which Spain had exercised in Cuba, and all obligations and charges which the crown of Spain and Spanish authorities had contracted prior to the ratification of the treaty. These charges were to include the salaries of the civil officials and of the clergy, but most important of all, the huge Cuban debt. The total debt which Spain wanted either the United States or Cuba to pay, amounted to about $455,710,000 plus the accrued interest.

The Spanish commissioners argued strenuously that this debt represented expenses and obligations arising from Spain's government of Cuba and relating solely to that island, and that it should therefore pass from Spain along with Cuba. Since Spain would no longer receive revenue from Cuba, it should no longer be obligated to pay Cuba's

---

* There was some discussion of the Puerto Rican debt, but since Spain herself had reported in 1896 that the island had no "public debt," and no Puerto Rican bonds had been issued, the matter was quickly disposed of. (*Senate Document* 62, 55th Congress, 3rd Session, p. 103.)

debts. In other words, island and debts must go together. The American commissioners replied by reciting the origin and history of the so-called Cuban debt. They proved that Cuba had had no part in contracting the debt; that a large part of the total represented the cost of putting down rebellions in the island, particularly the cost of the long Ten Years' War and the revolution which began in 1895,* and that the debt was not really a Cuban debt but a national debt of Spain, allocated to Cuba for payment. In short, the Cubans had received nothing from the huge expenditures, and the debt should not constitute a further burden upon the Cuban people.[3]

The Spaniards tried to reduce their losses by proposing that sovereignty over Cuba be transferred directly from Spain to the United States "unconditionally," the latter accepting "without express obligations to transfer to Cuban people," but agreeing to assume the obligations of Spain in Cuba. (It became clear during the conference that the Spanish commissioners preferred to have the United States annex Cuba rather than have an independent nation established in their former colony.†) Although Senator Gray favored "accepting sovereignty unconditionally thus avoiding future complications while pacifying Cuba," McKinley rejected it. "We must carry out the spirit and letter of the resolution of Congress," he instructed Hay to wire Day.[4] Upon learning this, the Spaniards retreated slightly and proposed that the United States assume sovereignty over Cuba without adding "unconditionally" to the transfer, but when sovereignty was later transferred to the Cuban people, the Cuban debt should go along with it, and the

---

* By 1868 when the Ten Years' War broke out, Cuba had acquired a debt of about $18,000,000; in 1880, when the cost of suppressing the revolution was added to the charges against the Cuban treasury, the debt had risen to $170,-000,000. (*Senate Document* 62, 55th Cong., 3rd Sess., p. 48.) U.S. Consul General Williams estimated in March, 1896 that there was an increase in the Cuban debt of $131,010,075 in the first year of the war. (Williams to W. W. Rockhill, March 16, 1896, State Department Dispatches, Havana, NA.)

† Undoubtedly, the Spaniards felt that their interests would be better preserved in a Cuba owned by the United States than one ruled by the Cuban people. In fact, as early as July, 1898, the Madrid correspondent of the London *Times* wrote: "The growing dissensions between the Cuban insurgents and the American authorities are noted here with great satisfaction, and on all sides I have heard it said: '*If we must lose Cuba, it is better that the island be annexed by Americans because the traitors would thereby be punished and the enormous Spanish interests in the island would be protected.*'" (Reprinted in *The State*, July 25, 1898. Emphasis in original. P.S.F.)

United States should remain as guarantor of the debt. But the Americans refused either to assume sovereignty over Cuba or to recognize the Cuban debt. "We insist on transfer as agreed on in protocol and refuse assumption of Cuban debt," Day wired McKinley on October 14. "If the Spaniards must break with us upon these propositions, so much the worse for them. We can maintain our position both upon the agreement of the protocol and the right and equity of the matter." [5]

Bickering over the debt continued until the American Secretary of State, in reply to a request for instructions, informed the commission on October 25 that the President would refuse any proposal for the assumption of the Cuban debt, and that the "United States would never induce a subsequent government of Cuba to assume it." Following Hay's instructions, the American commissioners stated that the United States would refuse to assume or to pass on to Cuba any debt charged by Spain. Finally, in desperation, the Spaniards proposed that Cuba retain responsibility for "all debt not peninsular but properly and peculiarly Cuban," the amount to be determined by a mixed commission. This plan for assumption of part of the debt was also rejected, and on October 27, the Spaniards accepted the American position.[6] The problem was resolved by neither the United States nor a Cuban government being required to assume the Cuban debt, a debt which had not been made by Cuba and from which Cuba had not benefitted. To have saddled Cuba with the debt would, of course, have made it impossible for the Cuban people to have attended to the most needful services of the island.*

The next problem for consideration was the disposition of the Philippines, which the protocol of August had left to be settled by treaty. This issue was to be settled without any representative from the Filipino people allowed to be present. In September, Aguinaldo appointed Felipe Agoncillo as "Minister Plenipotentiary and Extraordinary" to represent the Philippine Republic, whose independence had already been proclaimed on June 12, 1898, as "Minister Plenipotentiary and Extraordinary" in Washington and Paris. Agoncillo saw McKinley

---

* In April, 1896, when it estimated the Cuban debt at over $300,000,000, *La Discusión* of Havana pointed out that Cuba would have to pay $18,000,000 annually as interest on the coming of peace if the debt were assumed. "When peace comes," it warned, "the labor of the Cuban people must not go toward paying the debt." (April 25, 1896.)

early in October, and pleaded (through an interpreter) for representation on the American peace commission. McKinley brushed aside the suggestion, and the Filipino had to settle for sending a memorandum urging that the existing government of the Philippines have a say in the disposition of the country. The document was received by McKinley, but never acknowledged. When he went to Paris, Agoncillo was not allowed to represent his government at the peace conference, and his warning that any resolutions agreed upon which did not recognize the independence of the Filipino people would not be valid, was ignored by the commissioners of the United States and Spain.

There was some division among the American commissioners on the Philippine question; Senator Gray opposed annexation, while Day favored only the acquisition of some of the islands. But McKinley, unconcerned about the views of these commissioners, instructed the delegation: "The cession must be of the whole archipelago or none. The latter is wholly inadmissable, and the former must therefore be required." [7] In the session of October 31, the American commissioners presented a proposal for the annexation of the Philippines. The Spaniards were astonished by the demand; at most they had expected to lose not more than one or two islands. But they had not realized how American appetite had grown,\* how American business interests had their eyes on the Philippines for its own market and as a gateway to the growing China market, both of which would be a partial solution to the problem of surplus good and capital. "The capacity of the American people for consuming the articles of their domestic manufacture has already been far outstripped by the productive capacity of American factories and workshops," the New York *Journal of Com-*

---

\* McKinley himself described how his appetite had grown. He told a group of ministers that at first he had thought of retaining only Manila, then Luzon. After much prayer, he had decided he had but four choices: he could not return the Philippines to Spain, "that would be cowardly and dishonorable"; he could not turn them over to another power, "that would be bad business and discreditable"; he could not leave them to themselves, for they were unfit for self-rule; "there was nothing left for us to do but to take them all, and to educate the Filipinos and uplift and civilize and Christianize them. . . ." Then he went to sleep and slept soundly. (*Christian Advocate,* Jan. 22, 1903.) But as Timothy McDonald points out: ". . . the decision to keep Manila and its environs had been made long before McKinley informed the Almighty and his fellow Mid-Westerners of his plans for the Philippines." ("McKinley and the War With Spain," *Midwest Quarterly,* Vol. VII, Spring, 1966, p. 234.)

*merce* editorialized on the eve of the peace conference, urging the commissioners to keep this fact in mind when they took up the question of the Philippines. And the *United States Investor* reminded the commissioners that they must "recognize the fact that in certain parts of the world—the Far East especially—the volume of trade is going to be enormously increased in the future. . . . The nation that obtains the greatest hold upon them will be the great world power of the future." [8]

It is not surprising then that the American commissioners were adamant in the demand for the Philippines, and Spain had no alternative but to yield. After negotiations of an extended nature, the conference agreed to the transfer of the islands to the United States for the consideration of $20,000,000. The Spanish possession of Guam was also transferred to the United States.

There is considerable dispute as to whether the $20,000,000 was paid as a purchase price for the Philippines. Actually, the payment was linked to the Cuban debt issue. During the conference, the Spanish Ambassador to France met privately with Whitelaw Reid, pleaded that Spanish public opinion would not tolerate a complete surrender of both the Philippines and the debt, and urged that some concession be made by the United States. Senator William F. Frye suggested paying the Spaniards $20,000,000 on general principles in order to enable the treaty to be ratified by Spain. On learning of the transaction, *The State* declared angrily:

> The Spaniards do not have the Philippines to sell. One city the American arms have won—the rest of the islands the Filipino insurgents have won. . . . Spain has no rights in the Philippines; the Filipinos have. Yet President McKinley proposes that we shall buy 8,000,000 Filipinos from Spain, ignoring wholly the protests of the people whose independence is thus sought to be bargained away. Russia would have as much right to sell us the possessions of the wild tribes of Borneo, and we would have as much right, decency and good sense in buying them.[9]

There was only one error in this statement. The only city "won by" "American arms"—Manila—had actually been won by Filipino and American arms.

At the last session of the peace conference, held December 10, the commissioners signed the draft treaty. Apart from those which ceded Puerto Rico, Cuba and the Philippines to the United States, the articles dealt with Cuba. The first article stated that "Spain relinquishes all claim of sovereignty over and title to Cuba," and provided that since "the island is, upon its evacuation by Spain, to be occupied by the United States," the latter would be responsible for Cuba's international obligations during the period of her occupation and for the protection of life and property. In Article Seven, the United States and Spain mutually relinquished all claims for indemnity "that may have arisen since the beginning of the late insurrection in Cuba," while in Article Eight, Spain relinquished all property of the crown in Cuba. Articles Nine through Thirteen dealt largely with the rights of Spanish subjects in Cuba and the ceded areas. Such subjects had the option of staying where they were or of leaving, in either case retaining all property and freedom of activity. They could preserve Spanish citizenship by making an official declaration of such intention at any time within a year of the ratification of the treaty; in default of such declaration, at the end of one year they would be held to have adopted the nationality of the territory in which they remained. They were to be allowed the free exercise of their religion, were to be subject to the same laws and courts, and have the same legal rights as the citizens of the country in which they resided. The last article, Article Sixteen, stated: "It is understood that any obligations during the period of her occupation and for the obligations assumed in this treaty by the United States with respect to Cuba are limited to the time of its occupancy thereof; but it will upon the termination of such occupancy, advise the Government established in the island to assume the same obligations." [10]

The draft treaty was to be submitted to the two governments for ratification and exchange as soon as possible.

During the war, McKinley had jotted down the following note on a scrap of paper: "While we are conducting the war and until its conclusion, we must keep all we get; when the war is over we must keep what we want." The Treaty of Paris embodied the principles of this imperialist policy. The work of the American commission, Day rejoiced in a wire to the President, had brought the United States "a goodly estate indeed." [11]

While American capitalists in general shared Day's joy, many would have preferred outright annexation of Cuba, and felt that McKinley should have taken the island "unconditionally" when offered it by Spain, and should have forgotten all about the Teller Amendment which, in their eyes, having been "hastily passed by all parties in Congress, at an excited hour, was an error." [12] It was well known that the Spanish peace commissioners had advised the American delegation that Spain was ready to accept "absolute independence or independence or an American protectorate, or annexation to the United States, preferring annexation." [13]

But annexation, in the first place, would have been very expensive. The United States could not assume sovereignty over Cuba without assuming a debt of $400,000,000. "It fortunately costs something to be dishonest and greedy in this matter," *The State* noted.[14] More important, perhaps, outright annexation of Cuba in the peace treaty would have been fatal to the Administration's "large policy" of imperialism. As it was, the treaty was going to face great difficulty in obtaining Senate ratification. As early as November 19, 1898, Day had wired McKinley from Paris: "Whatever the treaty we get here, I suppose will meet with considerable opposition in the Senate." [15] To have disregarded the Teller Amendment on top of the annexation of Puerto Rico, Guam, and, most important of all, the Philippines, would have doomed the treaty to defeat and probably also guaranteed the defeat of McKinley and his party in the presidential election of 1900.[16] * Many Americans opposed the imperialist policy of their government. Their opposition took organized form even before the close of the Spanish-American War, as it became clear that the war was now openly one for conquest.

The organization through which this opposition was expressed was the Anti-Imperialist League, born on June 15, 1898, at a mass meeting in Boston's Faneuil Hall, site of numerous historical meetings in the

---

* Another reason cited for the decision not to annex Cuba was that "Admission to the Union on an equal basis with the other states . . . was politically unfeasible because of the race issue. Southern Democrats because of racial prejudice . . . opposed statehood for the new American conquest on the ground that its racially mixed population was unassimilable." (Theodore P. Wright, Jr., "United States Electoral Intervention in Cuba," *Inter-American Economic Affairs*, vol. XIII, Winter, 1959, p. 51.) However, a student who has made a study of this subject notes that the imperialists felt that "Cuban assimilation to the United States institutions was entirely practicable. . . . The Spanish inhabitants of the American Southwest had been assimilated." (Philip Wayne Kennedy, "The Concept of Racial Superiority and U.S. Imperialism, 1890-1910," unpublished Ph.D. thesis, St. Louis University, 1962-63, pp. 172-73.)

American Revolution and the anti-slavery struggle. Moorfield Storey, President of the Massachusetts Reform Club and Civil Service Reform League, and President of the American Bar Association, declared: "We are here . . . to insist that a war begun in the cause of humanity shall not be turned into a war for empire, that an attempt to win for the Cubans the right to govern themselves shall not be made an excuse for extending our sway over alien peoples without their consent. . . ." The audience adopted protest resolutions against the war of conquest, declaring that it would be time enough to think of governing others "when we have shown that we can protect the rights of men within our own borders like the colored race of the South and the Indians of the West, and that we can govern great cities like New York, Philadelphia, and Chicago." The meeting selected an anti-imperialist committee of correspondence to contact "persons and organizations throughout the country." [17]

The Anti-Imperialist League did not have to wait long to find work cut out for it. Taking advantage of the war fever, the advocates of the annexation of Hawaii pushed for realization of their objective so long withheld from them. Avoiding the treaty requirement and over the protests of the vast majority of the islanders, the McKinley Administration pushed the annexation of Hawaii through Congress in the form of a joint resolution requiring only a majority vote. Ostensibly it was a measure for the employment of Hawaii as a naval base to prosecute the war against Spain, but no one was fooled. As the annexation resolutions were forwarded to President McKinley, the legislature of Hawaii sent a protest to Washington pointing out that the "joint resolution has not been passed upon by the people of Hawaii, nor by their representatives in Legislature assembled, and called upon the people of the United States "to refrain from further participation in the wrongful annexation of Hawaii." The petition was ignored, and Hawaii was annexed against the wishes of its people. Moorfield Storey, speaking in behalf of the Anti-Imperialist League, noted that "the governed were not asked whether they approved the Constitution or the rulers under which they lost their liberty," and predicted a dismal future for blacks in the United States as a result of the brutal imperialist seizure of "a friendly state":

> We have said that the native population of Hawaii was not entitled to vote upon the vital question which we decided against

their will, that by reason of their color, or race, or ignorance they may be governed without their consent. It will be far more difficult hereafter to insist that the colored voters of the south are entitled to rights denied to the colored voters of Hawaii, so that equality of rights, which is the first of rights, is jeopardized within our own border, and problems which thought the Civil War had settled are reopened to fresh and dangerous controversy.[18]

The American Anti-Imperialist League, whose first president was the 80-year-old Republican George S. Boutwell, former Senator from Massachusetts and former Secretary of the Treasury under President Grant,* did not oppose the Spanish-American war as such, but insisted that since it had been undertaken as a war of liberation, it should not be turned into one for empire. The League and its local affiliates spearheaded the drive to influence the U.S. Senate to reject the Spanish peace treaty. Through meetings, protests, speeches, articles and petitions, the League protested to the Senate "against any extension of the sovereignty of the United States over the Philippine Islands. In accordance with the principles upon which our Republic was founded, we are in duty bound to recognize the right of the inhabitants to independence and self-government." Although they were called "traitors" by the imperialists, the anti-imperialists gained in influence as the nature of the treaty became clear. Small wonder Henry Cabot Lodge, leader of the imperialists in the Senate, wrote to his jingo colleague, Theodore Roosevelt on February 6, 1899, "We are going to have trouble over the treaty." The treaty was finally passed by only one vote more than the two-thirds necessary for ratification.† Thirty-three Senators stood firm in opposition.‡ Lodge, breathing a sigh of relief, described the

---

* The League's 41 vice-presidents included ex-President Grover Cleveland, his former Secretary of War, William Endicott, and former Secretary of the Treasury, Speaker of the House Carlisle, Senator "Pitchfork" Ben Tillman, President David Starr Jordan of Stanford University, President James B. Angell of the University of Michigan, Andrew Carnegie, Samuel Gompers, President of the American Federation of Labor, and Congressmen, clergymen, professors, lawyers, and writers. Booker T. Washington and W. E. B. Dubois, Negro leaders, the novelist William Dean Howells, and the great American novelist, humorist, and social critic, Mark Twain, were members of the League.

† The Spanish-American War was formally ended on April 11, 1899 with the exchange of ratifications of the peace treaty by the United States and Spain. President McKinley issued a proclamation declaring that the war was at an end.

‡ When William Jennings Bryan called upon two Democrats in the Senate who were vacillating to vote for the treaty, he guaranteed the final vote. Later,

struggle for ratification as "the closest, hardest fight I have ever known." An ardent advocate of annexation of Cuba, he conceded that had this been in the treaty, it would have gone down to defeat.[19]

While the activity of the Anti-Imperialist League played a large part in blocking the annexation of Cuba in the treaty, the movement did not concern itself with the fact that the people of the island were being denied the right to govern themselves and forced to endure military occupation by the United States. Indeed, a number of anti-imperialists used the argument that the Cubans were not fit to participate in government as a reason for opposing the annexation of the island. "There are multitudes of Americans," declared Carl Schurz, former cabinet member and Senator and one of the leaders of the Anti-Imperialist League, "who say now that if they had known what a sorry lot the Cubans are, we would never have gone to war on their behalf. However that may be, the same Americans should at least not permit those same Cubans to take part in governing us." Andrew Carnegie, the multi-millionaire iron and steel tycoon and a leading figure in the League, opposed annexation of Cuba on the ground that it would mean the addition of a large Negro population to the American Union. He added: "Should Cuba be largely settled by our own people in the course of time, the chief objection to incorporation in the Union would be removed."* Other anti-imperialists insisted that the

---

Bryan explained: "I thought it was better to ratify the treaty and correct the mistake by an act of Congress than to fight the treaty, continue the war and correct it by diplomacy." (William J. Bryan to Mrs. O. S. Wissler, May 20, 1900, William Jennings Bryan Papers, Library of Congress.) However, Senator George F. Hoar accused Bryan of urging ratification of the Treaty in order to keep the issue alive in the campaign of 1900 when he would certainly again be the Democratic choice for President. (George F. Hoar to Bryan, May 15, 1900, *ibid.*)

The deciding vote was cast by Senator John L. McLaurin of South Carolina, and Senator Tillman accused his colleague of having sold his vote to the Administration in return for federal patronage. (*The State*, Fab. 26, 1902.)

* Although he exaggerated the freedom and equality enjoyed by Cuban Negroes, Booker T. Washington, the American Negro leader, made a telling point when he declared: "My general feeling is that Cuba ought to be left to govern themselves [sic]. In bringing Cuba into our American life we must bear in mind that, notwithstanding the fact that the Cubans have certain elements of weakness, they already seem to have surpassed the United States in solving the race problem, in that they seem to have no race problem in Cuba. I wonder if it is quite fair to the white people and the colored people in Cuba to bring

United States had the right to maintain stable conditions in Cuba even if this meant delaying the time when the island would become independent or qualifying its independence. Edward Atkinson, a fiery anti-imperialist on the subject of the Philippines, argued that annexing Cuba would be a "moral outrage," but went on to propose that the United States establish a protectorate over the island. Andrew Carnegie went so far as to maintain that even the annexation of Cuba would not be imperialistic since it would be accomplished peacefully. "Cuba need not trouble us very much," he wrote in an article. "There is no 'Imperialism' here—no danger of foreign wars."[20]

A few voices in the anti-imperialist movement were raised in opposition to military occupation of Cuba by the United States. "Shall the Liberty Cause in Cuba be thus betrayed and sacrificed without a determined resistance by liberty men and women everywhere?" asked Charles G. Baylor, the Rhode Island Negro leader. "I ask the question because the American Negro cannot become the ally of Imperialism without enslaving his own race."[21] When, in November, 1898, Negroes were shot and killed in cold blood in cities throughout North Carolina in a white supremist drive to capture the governments of the cities and the state, protest meetings of Negroes in New York and Washington called upon President McKinley to remove the troops occupying Cuba and send them to North Carolina.[22]* In an address to

---

them into our American conditions and revive the race antagonism so that they will have to work out anew the race problem that we are now trying to solve in this country." (Indianapolis News, April 15, 1899 in "Cuba Annexation. Newspaper Clippings compiled by Robert P. Porter," scrapbook in New York Public Library. Hereinafter cited as "Cuba Annexation.")

* In July, 1899, Antonio González Pérez advanced the argument that Negroes in the United States favored the annexation of Cuba so as to be able to flee there "to escape extermination at the hands of Southern whites." (Chicago Tribune, July 13, 1899.) There is no evidence that Negroes in the United States favored annexation of Cuba, but as early as November, 1898, there was a report of the importation into Cuba of Negro colonists from Kansas. The Bandera Cubana, a weekly paper published in Santiago de Cuba, said that they would be welcomed: "Negroes have made equally patriotic efforts with the whites to secure the liberty of Cuba, and consequently no objection should be made to the coming of good Negro colonists." (Reprinted in The State, Nov. 27, 1898.) For proposals in favor of American Negroes settling in Cuba, see "What Cuba Offers to the Negro Who Will Take Advantage of the Opportunity," and "The Negro's Canaan," The Recorder, Feb. 18, July 8, 1899. The Recorder, a Negro weekly, was published in Indianapolis.

the Chicago Peace Jubilee, October 18, 1898, Samuel Gompers, President of the American Federation of Labor, demanded that "freedom and independence to which she is entitled, be immediately given to Cuba." "What has become of our paens of praise for the brave Cubans?" he asked. "Was our charge against Spain in her refusal to give the people of that island freedom and independence, baseless? . . . Is it not strange that now, for the first time, we hear that the Cubans are unfit for self-government; that whether they protest against it or not, they must be dominated by us, annexed by us or become a dependency of ours?" Gompers explained this development as the product of American imperialism:

> There are some Americans— our money makers—whose only god is the almighty dollar, whose only human or divine trinity is dividend, interest and profit. They have come to the conclusion that if poor, suffering Cuba can be handed over to their tender mercies, their diety and their deviltry can hold full sway. To these gentlemen, when there is a question between liberty and profit, present or prospective, liberty is thrown to the dogs as a wornout and threadbare thing of the past.[23]

For once *The People,* organ of the Socialist Labor Party, agreed with Gompers (whom it usually attacked as a "labor lieutenant of the capitalists"), and urged the American people to rise up in protest against the Administration's Cuban policy, under which "we merely displace the Spanish Captain General for the American one, and the [American] volunteers will be called upon to 'preserve peace' much the same way as the Spanish troops have 'preserved peace.'"[24] The Socialist Labor Party of the State of Washington, at its annual convention, announced that it should be "left to the Cubans, Puerto Ricans, and Philippines to establish their own government without any outside interference."[25] Almost alone among daily newspapers, *The State* opposed the provisions of the treaty of peace regarding Cuba. On February 4, 1899, it declared:

> The majority of Cubans want as soon as possible the independence they have made such sacrifices for, and do not see the need of all this American dry nursing, which is a reflection upon their capacity, integrity and humanity. In this we agree with them. No people in the world fit for freemen would relish this assumption of their unfitness to govern themselves without long foreign

tutelage. We would despise any people who did. . . . The Cubans have striven half a century and fought fourteen years for independence and they do not like to be kept out of it.

But the anti-imperialist movement in general was concerned with the Philippines (and to a lesser extent Puerto Rico) and paid little attention to the Administration's Cuban policy. At a mass anti-imperialist meeting in New York City on January 22, 1899, addresses were made by Grover Cleveland, William Jennings Bryan, and W. Bourke Cochran, but the only mention of Cuba was in the criticism of the inconsistency of the United States in going to war to free the Cubans and of denying the same freedom to the Filipinos. Not a word was said about the military occupation of the island.[26]

Probably many anti-imperialists felt that all of their efforts were required to defend the Filipino independence movement, in existence for thirty years and for which many had fought and suffered prison, exile and death. But while this was understandable, the result was that the only forces in the United States which could, with some effort, have protested the refusal of the Administration to allow the Cuban people "to establish their own movement without outside intervention," were silent.[27]

What was even worse was that some of the earlier champions of Cuban sovereignty and self-government now began to retreat from their principled position. We have already mentioned the role of Senator Morgan during his interview with the Cuban Commission, but the most significant example was that of Senator Henry M. Teller, father of the Teller Amendment. On September 8, 1898, Teller made a speech at Colorado Springs in which, negating the essence of his own resolution, he came out for territorial government for Cuba which would be controlled by the United States. The most important thing was "to put a strong hand on them and give them good government."[28] This was but the prelude to an even more shameful retreat Teller made on the floor of the Senate. He rose on December 20, 1898, to speak against the Vest Resolution, introduced by Senator George Vest of Missouri, which declared that "under the Constitution of the United States no power is given to the Federal Government to acquire territory to be held and governed permanently as colonies."[29] Teller not only attacked the general principle of the Vest Resolution, but he vigorously justified the Administration's policy toward Cuba. "It is not necessary," said the Colorado Senator, "that we should have a concession from Spain to say that Cuba is ours . . . if we choose to assert our right" to hold it. And he asked: "Who else can govern Cuba today but the United States?" Not the Cubans, for they were not ready to govern themselves. Indeed, insofar as international relations were concerned, Teller doubted that the Cubans would be capable of managing matters for a long time. "In all their international relations I believe, for many years to come at least, the Government of the United States must speak to the world for Cuba." Even in Cuban internal matters, the United States had to be supreme. It certainly was "not necessary . . . that we invite every man in Cuba to participate in the government that we there establish." The "unstable and unsafe elements" of the population —i.e., the people who had fought the Revolution—had to be excluded from political participation, if not by the Cubans, then by the United States authorities. But if the Cubans were able to maintain themselves a government "of the character I have mentioned . . . then we should let them do so in all their local affairs." [30]

This, of course, was a far cry from the Joint Resolution of Congress, which had renounced "sovereignty" and "control" over Cuba. The "character" of the government Teller now envisaged for Cuba was simply a United States protectorate. Foreign affairs would be under the complete control of the United States and all the Cubans would enjoy would be local self-government, and even that only after they had disenfranchised a large part of the population and complied with other conditions set by the authorities in Washington.

Teller did not base his arrogant stand on the Treaty of Paris. We had acquired possession of Cuba "by right of conquest," and it was ours to do with as we pleased.[31] This essentially was the position of the Administration. The formal military occupation of Cuba by the United States had begun over a month before the treaty was ratified, and it was based, said McKinley, on the right of conquest. But this position was challenged by a number of outstanding Americans. Although he still favored a U. S. protectorate, Edward Atkinson, industrialist, economist, and a leading anti-imperialist, argued effectively that the United States had no legal right to occupy Cuba:

> By the signing of the treaty [of peace] Cuba has become a free and independent state. . . . I ask, by what authority of law

are United States troops kept to do the police duty for Cuba at the expense of the taxpayers of this country? By what authority of law do officials of the United States collect taxes in Cuba, . . . By what authority of law can they [American troops] remain in charge; Cuba being an independent state?

The exercise of power by the President of the United States in maintaining these conditions is either that of an autocrat assuming powers for which there is no constitutional or legislative basis, or else we have no more right to keep our forces in Cuba than we had to keep them in Mexico after the treaty of peace (at Guadaloupe Hidalgo) had been signed.[32]

Senator J. B. Foraker, who played a leading role in framing the Joint Resolution of Congress, argued that there was nothing in this Congressional declaration which authorized the United States to occupy Cuba after peace was declared:

When the last Spanish soldier was driven out, the power conferred by the resolution of intervention was exhausted, and when peace was declared the war power of the President was at an end. Since the declaration of peace, he has been without authority to maintain troops in Cuba and our acquiescence in his action has not invested him with such authority. It has been my opinion that the island would be pacified as soon as the Spaniards were gone, and that at once we ought to allow the Cubans to enter upon the work of establishing their own government.

Why was this not done? Senator Foraker answered:

In order to secure the granting by this government *under the usurped authority which it is proposing to exercise in Cuba*, of all kinds of rights and privileges, electric light, gas, street railroads, interurban and steam railroads, etc. Aside from the immediate results of such franchises to those interested in them was the further ultimate purpose to so entangle us with the island and so saddle upon the government responsibility for the safe enjoyment of these franchises as to make our withdrawal from the island an impossibility." [33]

## CHAPTER XIX
# Military Occupation: The Brooke Administration

DECEMBER 1, 1898 WAS THE DEADLINE for the Spanish withdrawal from Cuba, but in response to a request from Spain, McKinley extended this time until January 1, 1899. The President also chose Major-General John R. Brooke, a sixty-year-old career soldier as Military Governor of Cuba. In a letter instructing him about the policies he should follow, dated December 22, 1898, McKinley offered "a few unofficial suggestions." United States authority in Cuba, he wrote, was derived "from the law of belligerent right over conquered territory." Brooke would rule as the direct representative of the President until the Cubans had established a government "stable enough" so that the United States could "deem it safe" to withdraw its forces. The military government of occupation was "not in the interest or for the direct benefit of this country," but rather that of the Cubans, and those who had "rights and property" in Cuba. Although Brooke headed a military government, it should function in a non-military manner: ". . . let your government be a government of laws, not one of military force."[1]

McKinley's letter thus placed no time limit on the American occupation. The United States would be the sole judge of when it was "safe" to withdraw American forces.

To carry out its program of pacifying Cuba, the United States sent a military force "larger than the entire body of men who engaged in fighting in Spain." Fifteen regiments of infantry volunteers, one of volunteer engineers, and four battalions of artillery were sent to Cuba between December 13, 1898 and February 17, 1899. At the beginning of the Occupation, U.S. forces numbered about 24,000 officers and men; by March, 1899, this number reached almost 45,000.[2] However, before Brooke took over the government from Spain, the Cuban army actually functioned as an interim government in large parts of the island. As the Spanish army withdrew from the interior in the closing months of 1898, Cuban army units replaced them and took charge of evacuated regions. General Brooke later testified that the Cuban army had performed police and other duties well. Indeed, even during the opening weeks of the American occupation, while the U.S. army extended control to all parts of the island, the Cuban army continued to do valuable work.[3]

In the latter part of December, 1898, American troops entered the outskirts of Havana in readiness for the transfer of sovereignty from Spain. At the same time, the revolutionary patriotic committees of Havana were preparing a great victory celebration, hailing the end of Spanish sovereignty and the joint Cuban-American triumph of arms which had made this possible. The long-awaited event was to be celebrated for five days with banquets, speeches and balls, and on the very day of the transfer, the Cuban army would parade through the city.

The revolutionary celebration was never held. General Brooke notified the Cuban leaders, through General William Ludlow, the designated miilitary commander of Havana, that no Cuban soldiers would be allowed in Havana at the time of the transfer of government. The Cubans could not be trusted to maintain good order, and fighting between Cuban and Spanish troops might break out. The revolutionists of Havana visited Ludlow and offered to make themselves personally responsible for the soldiers' behavior during the celebration. General Máximo Gómez announced that he would not come to Havana unless he could be received there by the army of which he was commander-in-chief. Brooke refused to budge.

This arrogant stand aroused protests from indignant Americans, many of whom criticized Brooke for caring so little for the feelings of the Cuban people and "for the decent courtesies of life."[4] Senator Teller wrote to McKinley that Brooke's order was unfair to our Cuban allies, and "will create a false idea of what our course is to be in dealing with them, and our difficulties are quite great enough without any additions."[5] (Teller conveniently overlooked the fact that ten days before, on the floor of the Senate, he had advocated a policy toward Cuba which gave the Cubans a fairly clear idea of "what our course is to be in dealing with them.") Despite these protests, McKinley backed Brooke's stand.

At Brooke's invitation, eight Cuban generals were present at the transfer of government ceremony on January 1st. But the Cuban army which had fought so long and so hard to achieve the end of Spanish rule, and Máximo Gómez, its chief, were absent. There was, furthermore, no great victory celebration in Havana. Perfecto Lacoste, chairman of the Havana Committee, voiced the feelings of many Cuban revolutionists: "For years we have suffered only to see, at this hour, our emotions changed from pleasure at the departure of the Spaniards to apprehension at the arrival of the Americans." And Gómez wrote in his *Diary* that "the Americans have embittered, with their tutelage imposed by force, the joy of the victorious Cubans." [6]

On January 1, 1899, in the throne room of the Salon at the Palace of the Captain-General, the Spanish General Adolfo Jiménez Castellanos turned over the island of Cuba to the government of the United States. The flag of Spain came down and the Stars and Stripes was hauled up in its place.* General Brooke then announced the inauguration of the United States Military Government of Cuba and issued a proclamation addressed "to the People of Cuba." He had come as the representative of the President of the United States to further the humanitarian purposes for which "my country intervened to put an end to the deplorable conditions of this island." He continued:

> I deem it proper to say that the object of the present Government is to give protection to the people, security to the person and property, to restore confidence, to encourage the people to resume the pursuits of peace, to build up waste plantations, to resume commercial traffic, and to afford full protection in the exercise of all civil and religious rights.
>
> To this end, the protection of the United States Government will be directed, and every possible provision made to carry out these objects through the channel of civil administration, although

---

* The people of Havana had their own way of celebrating the departure of the Spanish troops. They tore down the statue of "good Queen Isabella" of Spain, and in its place erected a monument to the leaders of the Revolution. (Charles T. Andrews to the Seneca *County Courier* (1899), in book clippings, "Cuba and Porto Rico, 1899," Charles T. Andrews Papers, Cornell University Library.) Andrews had been appointed Electorial Commissioner for New York State to visit American army units in Cuba and Puerto Rico, and his letters include reports of his observations during his trip.

under military control, in the interest and for the benefit of the people of Cuba, and those possessed of rights and property in the island.

The new governor promised that the civil and criminal codes existing at the end of Spanish sovereignty would remain in force, except for such modifications as he might find necessary "in the interests of good government." He invited and urged the Cubans, "without attention to their former affiliation," to cooperate with the new government, and to show "moderation, conciliation and good will toward one another." Brooke closed by announcing that he would be pleased to receive citizens who wished to consult him on matters of public interest.[7]

To carry out this program, General Brooke organized the machinery of the Occupation Government. This was a dual structure composed of two separate organizations, one civil and one military, with the Military Governor as head of both. The Military Governor was supreme, his powers being limited only by the President of the United States and the Secretary of War. Only the Postal Service was independent of the authority of the Military Governor, being under the supervision of the Postmaster General of the United States.

The framework of civil government was at first largely taken over from the Spanish regime. At the bottom was the municipality, consisting of a town or village and the surrounding country, and governed by an *alcalde* (mayor) and municipal council. Above the municipalities were the six provincial governments, each headed by a governor. The provincial governors supervised municipal administration in their areas, kept public order, granted permits for meetings and parades, and titles to mining and timber rights, and handled many other details of administration.

At the top, General Brooke organized a civil government of four departments: Department of State and Government, Department of Finance, Department of Justice and Public Instruction and a Department of Commerce, Agriculture, Industries and Public Works. Each department was headed by a Cuban Secretary: Domingo Méndez Capote as Secretary of State, Pablo Desvernine as Secretary of Finance, José Antonio González Lanuza as Secretary of Justice and Public Instruction, and Adolfo Saenz Yanez as Secretary of Agriculture, Commerce, Industries and Public Works. The four Secretaries, in addition to administering their respective departments, formed an advisory body which soon came to be known as the Cuban Cabinet.[8]

Of the four departments the most important was that of State and Government under Domingo Méndez Capote. It had general supervision of the provincial governments and of municipal administration within the provinces as well as of the administration of the civil service. This made the Secretary supervisor over six governors for the six civil provinces and 128 *alcaldes* and municipal councils. On the other hand, the Department of Finance was limited in authority and functions, since the bulk of Cuban government revenue during the Occupation came from customs duties, collected by a Customs Service independent of the Department of Finance. This Customs Service was managed by the United States Army and was headed throughout the Occupation by Colonel Tasker H. Bliss. It turned over its receipts to the North American Trust Company, which acted as Fiscal Agent for the Cuban Government. The Cuban Secretary of Finance had supervision over the meager internal revenue.[9]

During the early period of the Occupation, the military command system was superior to the civil government and dominated all phases of activity in the island. The military command system was divided into seven departments corresponding to the six provinces and the city of Havana. Each of the departments was commanded by an American general who exercised authority over provincial and municipal administrations, had general supervision of the jails, charities, public works, and sanitation, and was in charge of all United States troops in the command area.

The commands at first were: Havana Province—General Fitzhugh Lee; Pinar del Río Province—General George Davis; Matanzas Province—General James H. Wilson; Santa Clara Province—General John C. Bates; Puerto Principe Province—General Luis Carpenter; Santiago Province—General Leonard Wood; Havana City—General William Ludlow. During subsequent months, the departments were coupled together: the first two named above under Lee, the third and fourth under Wilson, the fifth and sixth under Wood, with the city of Havana remaining under Ludlow. Thus the military departments were reduced in number to four.[10]

General Wilson urged Brooke to use the following as a basic rule for appointments of Cubans to civilian offices: "the officers of the successful revolution should have preference for civil employment over those who had supported the Spanish Government or stood neutral between it and those who were contending for independence." [11] Unlike General Wood, who filled most offices in Santiago with Spanish and conservative Cubans,* Brooke did follow Wilson's rule to a certain extent. Two of the Secretaries of the four departments—Méndez Capote and Lanuza—resigned from the Cuban Assembly to accept the post from Brooke;† and of the six provincial governors appointed by Brooke, all but one were ex-generals of the Cuban Army.[12] But a large number of the local officials were men noted for their "extreme devotion to the fallen regime," and in Las Villas even former members of the Spanish guerrillas were appointed to office.[13] Moreover, Negroes complained that they were discriminated against in appointments to civilian offices, and in the municipal government of Havana, with its large working class population, only lawyers, doctors, engineers, and other professionals as well as industrialists and bankers were appointed, while no member of a trade union was deemed fit to serve in the administration.[14]

It is estimated that under Brooke 97 percent of the officials in the operation of the civil government were Cubans.[15] While the United States proudly paraded this fact as proof of the Cubans' cooperation with the Occupation, many people in the island had a different point of view. José María Céspedes noted ironically: "The hypocrisy of the intervention is illustrated in the fact that the Americans use Cubans to do their dirty work." [16] Actually, many Cubans found government jobs under the Occupation the only way of earning a living in the devastated island, and were eager to take advantage of United States' patronage. ("We are growing to be a nation of petty office seekers," complained General Enrique Collazo as early as February, 1899.[17]) Still others felt that the quickest way to end the Occupation was to cooperate with the military authorities and use their positions in the civilian administration to put the country on a stable foundation. To

---

* *The State* criticized Wood for this policy, reminding him that "the United States intervened in Cuba to help its suffering people and not to help their oppressors. It would be to defeat the object of intervention to allow the Peninsulares, who have done Spain's bloodiest work for years, any voice in the government of Cuba." (Aug. 13, 1898.)

† Méndez Capote was president of the Cuban Assembly at the time of his resignation.

a great extent, they succeeded in achieving this condition in Cuba much earlier than had been anticipated in the United States, but they soon learned to their dismay that this did not bring with it an automatic end to the Occupation.

The appalling condition of Cuba after the war was still evident over most of the island when the official American Occupation began. In fact, it was made worse by the retreating Spaniards. They looted public buildings, destroyed plumbing and lighting fixtures, and choked up drains; stripped whatever they could take with them to Spain and destroyed much of what could not be removed. Estes G. Rathbone, the new Director-General of Posts, wrote: "The Spanish government on retiring left no records for my guidance, and not one stamp of any denomination, nor a cent in money. In fact, about all that was found was a great quantity of undelivered mail matter, some of it dating back as far as the year 1891; a disreputable old post-office building in very bad sanitary condition, and a miserable post-office outfit."[18]

Havana was full of sick and starving people, the streets littered with dead horses and dogs. The conditions in the provinces were no better, except, as we have seen, in parts of eastern Cuba, where relief had been furnished and the population had started to rebuild the ruined economy. An American passing through Matanzas Province, where it was estimated the war had cost the lives of one-third of the population, wrote early in the Occupation:

> It was substantially a wilderness. . . . Every few miles, indeed, we could see the bare walls and wrecked machinery of the sugar mills, and occasionally the straggling cane that was growing wild in the sites of the plantation which the Revolutionists destroyed. The huts in which the peasantry had lived had vanished with their occupants. In the villages, it is true, a few remained, and once in a great while we saw a cottage that had been erected since the war, and the little patches of bananas, corn, sweet potatoes and cocoa trees from which the dwellers sought subsistence. Occasionally a farmer was out with the wooden plow and bull team, and sometimes we could see them working with hoe or machete—but the aspect of desolation brooded over all, and betokening it the buzzards were sailing, sailing everywhere.

Not all Cubans in Matanzas had suffered as severely as the peasants, for the same writer reported that he attended "a ball given . . . by the

Cuban Club, at which the elite of Matanzas were present with many of the American officers and such of their ladies as were in the city. . . . We found [Cuban] gentlemen and ladies richly clad in evening dress. Some of the latter were indeed elegant." The American noted proudly that these "richly clad" Cubans were the ones most eager to cooperate with the occupying forces.[19]

To alleviate the effects of hunger and disease, Brooke quickly organized an emergency relief program. He ordered food suplies shipped to all major towns, and to many interior points, for free distribution by the army. From the 1st of January to the end of November, 1899, a total of 5,493,000 free rations were distributed in Cuba by the United States. (A ration was enough food to feed one adult for one day.[20]) Most of this food was paid for from the island's revenues. The Customs Service turned over revenue to the government, and these funds were used to pay for rations for the poor.[21] The general impression in the United States, however, was that the government was using American taxpayers' money to feed the Cubans and reconstruct the island. The money used by the authorities throughout the Occupation came from Cuba's export and import duties and taxes.

By the summer of 1899 it was possible to give up the wholesale distribution of rations; after the first of July, few free rations were distributed except to hospitals and asylums. Many Cubans had returned to the land and had begun to feed themselves by growing sweet potatoes, yams, bananas, beans and peas.[22] It required time, of course, to produce these crops, and in the meantime, the rations, paid for by Cuban revenues, had kept the people from starving.

At the same time, the new government began vigorous sanitation measures. Army medical officers and Cuban doctors throughout the island took over appropriate buildings and began treatment of the diseased. In Havana, where a quarter of a million people lived, 114 physicians made house-to-house inspections, and large crews were put to work disinfecting houses at the rate of 25 per day.[23] In some towns it became necessary, as a sanitation measure, to burn the thatched houses, so permeated were they with disease. The owner was usually paid about fifty dollars if he would go into the country and take up rural life.[24]

The reconstructive work done in Havana by General Ludlow was fairly typical of the whole program. Ludlow immediately set all branches of work into motion; divided Havana into districts for the distribution of rations and medicines, and organized a house-by-house inspection system for reporting the case of need in each district. A citizens' committee helped the Army to administer relief and to direct it where it was needed. The city water supply was overhauled; street cleaning begun, a system of disposing of refuse instituted, and hospitals and asylums established. A native police force was set up and General Menocal of the Cuban Army made chief of police.[25]

The same sort of work done in Havana was carried out in the provinces on a smaller scale. Though each need not be described in detail, it is sufficient to note that by the end of six months, starvation and disease had been largely checked. (Yellow fever, however, was not conquered until 1900.) General Lee reported in September, 1899 that brigandage in his province had been stamped out, many houses had been built, lands put under cultivation, and that property values had increased due to the rise of general confidence.[26]

It can be said that under General Brooke the hungry were fed, disease fairly well eliminated, and order restored. Municipal governments and local finance systems were reorganized; the marriage laws were reformed and the fee required for that ceremony was reduced; the tax laws were revised, all unpaid Spanish taxes due under former Spanish law in the island were cancelled, the rates of taxes were changed and inheritance taxes were adopted. The empty treasury of Cuba could show $10,000,000 of collected revenue by September, 1899. On the basis of a school law drawn up by the Cuban scholar Enrique José Varona, a decentralized school system was inaugurated under Alexis Everett Frye which marked the real start of popular education in the island. The need for this was clear. Robert P. Porter reported that the situation in 1898 so far as education was concerned was simply deplorable. The few public schools were not worthy of the name, and only a small portion of the children attended even them: Illiteracy abounded throughout Cuba.[27]\*

Early in 1899, Brooke made an allowance of $50 per schoolroom

---

\* A census of Cuba taken on the basis of an order issued on August 19, 1899 showed that the number of children under ten who had attended school was only 40,559, and the number who had not attended was 316,428. Of the persons ten years or over only 433,670 could read and write while 690,566 could neither read nor write.

to the municipalities for the establishment of such schools as could be opened prior to the inaugugation of a new system. In November he created the office of Superintendent of Schools, and appointed Frye to the position. Many schools were then organized; too many and too rapidly, it was charged, since Frye could not provide them with equipment. But a beginning of publication had been made.[28]

Yet to General Brooke and to Washington, the greatest achievement of his administration was the liquidation of the Cuban Army. The presence in Cuba at the beginning of the Occupation of armed Cuban soldiers, well-experienced in guerrilla warfare, was a nightmare for Washington. As Senator Foraker warned, the great danger was an armed clash between Cubans and Americans similar to what had happened in the Philippines. ". . . if there should be a clash . . . there will be serious trouble here at home as well as in the Island, particularly if we do not speedily get to the end of the difficulties in the Philippines. . . . In my opinion the moment the American soldiers pull the trigger on the Cubans, if they ever do, the mischief will be to pay generally, and the Administration at Washington will have to pay it, and I predict there won't be funds enough on hand for the purpose."[29]

Foraker's reference to the Philippines had real significance for American imperialism. When they received news from Paris in November, 1898 that the treaty of peace would cede the Philippines to the United States, the Filipinos had warned that they would "fight to the bitter end for their rights and freedom."[30] But the Administration and most of the American press ignored this announcement, although the Atlanta *Journal* did observe: "The outlook now is that we will have to fight both the Cubans and the Filipinos. . . . This is the programme of the imperialists."[31]* Then on February 6, 1899, the same day the Treaty of Paris was ratified, newspapers all over the United States carried the news that war had broken out in the Philippines.

At 8:30 P.M. on Saturday night, February 4, 1899, an American sentry, of the Nebraska Volunteers, fired on and killed a Filipino soldier trying to cross a bridge in San Juan del Monte, a Manila

---

* The pro-imperialist Indianapolis *News* openly called for a war against the Cuban revolutionary forces at the same time that similar steps would be taken against these forces in the Philippines. "We can not abandon Cuba, any more than we can abandon the Philippines, to anarchy," it argued. (Reprinted in *Public Opinion*, March 23, 1899, p. 356.)

suburb. The war was on, and Americans and Filipinos engaged in battle on a line extending two miles. Immediately General Aguinaldo announced that the Philippine Republic was at war with the United States. In his proclamation he included the following statement: "I deplore very much this rupture and hostilities. I have a clear conscience for I have tried to prevent it and have attempted with all my power to maintain friendship with the American army, although we suffered certain humiliations and sacrificed many rights." [32] The battle was joined and a new Filipino fight for independence was under way.

"We have annexed a war," bitterly observed an anti-imperialist paper.[33] For it soon became clear that the United States faced a national uprising that could be subdued only by a major war.* The uprising in the Philippines was difficult enough for the United States to handle. But what if, in addition, the Cubans should take up arms, like the Filipinos, to expel United States forces from the island? "The thought of another Manila at Havana sobers even an army contractor," wrote Henry Adams from Washington on February 26, 1899.[34] When this was written, the Cuban Army was still in possession of its arms and still not disbanded. It is clear, then, that continued American occupation of Cuba was dependent on disarming and disbanding the Cuban army. For if the United States was forced to fight a war on two fronts simultaneously, the entire imperialist policy of the Admiinstration, as Foraker correctly noted, would go down to defeat. The American people, already concerned by the war in the Philippines, would simply not tolerate armed conflict between American and Cuban soldiers.

In January, 1899, the Cuban Assembly met to hear the report of the Commission it had sent to Washington. When it learned that McKinley's offer was only three million dollars, the Assembly voted to reject this as utterly inadequate, and to prepare its own plan for dealing

---

* In what was undoubtedly his wisest observation, Shafter wrote to H. C. Corbin of the War Department: ". . . let me tell you, that you will find that about twenty-five or fifty more regiments will be needed before you get through with this Filipino business. That is my calm judgment about it, based upon the character of the people who are fighting out there and don't know when they are whipped; who thrive as well in time of war as in time of peace, and when only a small portion of them are so far in arms." (W. R. Shafter to H. C. Corbin, Nov. 1, 1899, H. C. Corbin Papers, Library of Congress.) As we shall see, the Filipino people did *not* thrive as well during the war with the United States as in peace.

with the future of the Cuban Army.[35] Many of the delegates still hoped to force or induce the United States to place the civil administration of the island immediately into the hands of the Cubans rather than American military officials. To accomplish this, they counted on the necessary support of Máximo Gómez and the Cuban army. With Gómez and the army behind them, the Assembly could force the Americans to make concessions. At least so these delegates believed.[36]

The McKinley Administration, determined to brook no interference with its rule over Cuba, moved to apply a technique which all imperialist powers have found useful in maintaining their rule over subjected peoples: divide and conquer. The only individual in Cuba who had the prestige to oppose the Cuban Assembly was Máximo Gómez. The commander-in-chief of the Cuban army was the central figure of the revolutionary movement, and his popularity was so great in the island that his every word was regarded almost as gospel. As early as August, 1898, the Administration was advised that if it wished the American Occupation to be "smooth, it would be wise to consult with Gómez who has been quoted as saying that he would permit no interference with the plans of the United States. To ensure harmonious action a concert with Gómez is the proper thing." [37] In short, with Gómez's backing, the Cuban Assembly could be forced into oblivion.

It was well known in Washington that Gómez had had little regard for the Revolutionary civil government during the war and that he retained this scornful attitude after peace was achieved.[38] At the same time, Gómez remained in his headquarters in Las Villas without showing the slightest disposition to come to agreement with the Occupation authorities. Actually, Gómez was extremely suspicious of United States policy towards Cuba, and the refusal of General Brooke to allow the Cuban Army to enter Havana at the time of the transfer of Spanish sovereignty had only increased his doubts. "The Americans," he confided to a colleague, "are not thinking of independence. Even if finally they give it to us, it will be as a gift, while we have earned it with continuous efforts during more than half a century. I am obliged to be grateful to the Americans, but only when they fulfill their promises, and if they fulfill them with decency and without aggravation to the Cubans. The Cuban army cannot dissolve itself unless I receive the assurance, honorably promised, that independence will be given to

Cuba and that it will be given as the just reward of Cuba's efforts, suffering, constancy, and spilled blood." [39]

Publicly, however, Gómez was more conciliatory towards the American Occupation. On December 29, 1898, from his camp at Narciso, two hundred miles from Havana, he issued a proclamation to the People of Cuba and the Liberating Army in which he noted that Cuba was "not yet free or independent" and that "for that reason we must dedicate ourselves to bring about the disappearance of the causes for American intervention." This should be done by peaceful cooperation to restore constitutional government and prosperity, for the sooner these were attained, "the sooner the Occupation will terminate." To this, Gómez added that the Cuban Army could not be disbanded until it had been paid. "Until this is settled, I shall remain waiting in a suitable place. If ever I am needed, I shall be at the service of the people of Cuba, to conclude the work to which I have dedicated my life." [40] Although the concluding statement was not very explicit, it meant that the Liberating Army would continue its organized existence, with Gómez in command, and that an armed clash with the occupation forces was not out of the question. But Gómez was worried about the very needy condition of the troops. The soldiers were poverty-stricken and without means of support, enduring suffering which, Gómez wrote in his *Diary,* could not be born as well in peace as in war, when victory sustained his men. "I decided," Gómez noted, "to send a plea to President McKinley explaining the situation to him. Conill took the message to Tomás Estrada Palma or Gonzalo de Quesada on the twenty-ninth [of December, 1898]." [41]

To the Administration, Gómez's message was a godsend; here was the opening it was looking for to split the ranks of the revolutionists and get the Cuban army out of the way. Near the end of January, 1899, McKinley sent Robert P. Porter to Cuba to meet Gómez and deal directly with him on the question of the Cuban army, bypassing the Cuban Assembly which was the only body with legal authority to handle the problem. Gonzalo de Quesada, assigned by Estrada Palma for the mission, accompanied Porter. In an interview with a reporter from the Havana newspaper, *La Discusión,* Quesada praised the good intentions of the United States and urged cooperation of all classes of Cubans with the Occupation. He warned: "To fire a single shot in our fields would be to prolong indefinitely the realization of our ideals and satisfy the desires of our enemies because the resolution of last April [the Joint Resolution of Congress] says that the government of the Island will not be turned over to us until peace has been assured. We must look upon the Americans as our real friends and trust them. In this way, Cuba will be happy and prosperous." [42] It is obvious that Quesada was the right man to help Washington weaken Cuban resistance to the military occupation of the country. And this was the man called the "spiritual son of Martí." [43]

Estrada Palma took the same position. He too expressed "absolute confidence in the good faith of the American people and the present administration in regard to the fulfillment of the pledge in favor of Cuban independence." Like Quesada, he warned against any hostility to the occupying forces. "Should they [the Cuban people] have occasion to protest against too long a continuance of the military occupation of the island, I am sure it will be in some dignified and orderly way, which will appeal to the good judgment of the American people, and not in a hostile or turbulent form. . . . I repeat I have entire faith in the American people and the government." [44] This was from the man who had replaced Martí as the Delegate of the Cuban revolutionary government!

There is little doubt that Gómez was greatly influenced by the fact that both Estrada Palma and Quesada, with whom he had close relations, were confident that the United States would soon turn over the island, free and clear, to the Cuban people, and that cooperation, not hostility, to the Occupation authorities was in the best interest of Cuba. As Albert G. Robinson, correspondent in Havana for the New York *Evening Post*, noted after an interview with Gómez: "He has faith in the honor and integrity of the United States. He is ready to disband his army. . . . But he clings and doubtless will cling to his ideas of Cuban independence." [45]

On February 1, Porter and Quesada visited Gómez at Remedios, where the commander-in-chief now had his headquarters. Porter stressed McKinley's strong desire to achieve the disbandment of the Cuban army, and offered the same sum of money to achieve this as he had held out to the Cuban Commission in Washington—three million dollars. This money, however, was not to be regarded as part payment of the back wages owed the Cuban soldiers, but only a fund to achieve demobilization. The United States, Porter made it clear, was not accepting responsibility for any Cuban revolutionary debts. Finally, he stressed the benefits Cuba would gain from the return of the soldiers to useful occupations. He also held out the possibility in the future of using members of the Cuban army for a national police force, pointing out that General Wood had recruited the Rural Guard from the Cuban army for the purpose of suppressing banditry in Oriente Province.[46]

To Porter's delight, Gómez's response was on the whole favorable. He agreed that it would be desirable to return the Cuban soldiers to peaceful occupations so that they could help the reconstruction of the country. He approved of the idea of using Cuban soldiers to assist in the work of the Occupation; he himself believed that Cuban regiments should be added to the American occupation forces.* He favored a moderate payment for the army, scornfully rejecting the idea, advanced by the Cuban Assembly, of raising huge sums by loans. However, he felt that three million dollars was inadequate. At this point, Quesada urged Gómez not to quarrel about the sum for the army, but to accept what was offered and not delay demobilization any longer. Gómez then agreed that since the smallness of the amount was not his fault, he would do the best he could with it. He refused, however, to be personally responsible for the money, and insisted that it must be in charge of General Brooke rather than himself.[47]

Porter had brought with him a letter from Brooke inviting Gómez to Havana for a conference about paying the Cuban army. Gómez not only agreed to confer with Brooke, and sent the General a cable indicating his intention of coming "soon" to the capital, but at Porter's suggestion, dispatched the following cable to McKinley: "It has afforded me great pleasure to have conferences with your commissioner Porter, introduced by my friend Quesada, and I am informed of and satisfied with your wishes. In order that all may run smoothly, following your advice and gladly contributing to the reconstruction of Cuba."[48]

Delighted at having so completely won over the outstanding Cuban leader to the American policy, Porter returned to the United States, leaving Brooke to handle the actual negotiations when they should began. Gómez, on his part, made a triumphant march through Las Villas and Matanzas, arriving in Havana on February 24. Although U.S.

---

* Porter, however, made it quite clear that civil rather than military duties were envisaged for the Cuban soldiers who would assist the Occupation.

officials were worried at Gómez's delay in getting down to business with Brooke, they were impressed by the enthusiasm with which the people in the various towns along the route to Havana greeted the old commander-in-chief. Gómez, it was clear, had captured the hearts of the people as no one else in Cuba had done. Nor was this surprising. "With Martí and Maceo dead," notes Sergio Aguirre, "only the great Dominican remains to receive the testimony of the enthusiastic gratitude of the people he has served with supreme courage, warm and singular disinterest throughout the wars of independence. Máximo Gómez is independence itself." In Havana, the American commanders received Gómez with full military honors, and even allowed Cuban troops to parade in the city for their leader.*

On February 24, 1899, the fourth anniversary of the beginning of the Second War for Independence, Gómez entered Havana at the head of a *mambi* cavalry. The entire city was waiting to greet him; it is estimated that 150,000 people were in the streets. Gómez reviewed 2,500 of his soldiers from the balcony of the governor's palace. Before the ceremonies were over, he received the solemn thanks of the municipality for his contributions to Cuban freedom.[49]

During the next few days, Brooke and Gómez worked out the details of the plan to pay off the Cuban army. Actually, there was little to discuss, since Gómez in the conferences with Porter had already agreed in principle to the demobolization, in return for the distribution to the soldiers of three million dollars by the American government. He and Brooke now simply decided that each Cuban soldier should receive $100. They would make the official rolls of the Cuban army the basis of payment, the money would be disbursed by a mixed Cuban-American commission named by Gómez and Broke.[50]

To the Cuban Assembly, the news that Gómez had agreed to dis-

---

* The honors accorded Gómez were also an attempt to overcome the bad taste left at the funeral of Calixto García in Havana on February 11. Although the Military Government had allotted places in the funeral procession to the Cuban army and the Cuban Assembly, the Cubans were pushed out by an American cavalry unit. When a protest to Brooke failed to restore them to their places, the Cubans—troops, Generals, and Assembly—withdrew from the procession, and at the cemetery, only Americans were left to conduct the ceremony. The incident aroused great resentment throughout the island, especially in Havana. (Rafael Martínez Ortiz, *Cuba: Los Primeros Años de Independencia,* París, 1929, vol. I, pp. 44-45.)

band the army for a mere three million dollars came as a bitter disapointment, especially since the delegates had visions of getting a huge sum through a loan from private bankers. A certain C. M. Coen, representing a group of American bankers, had come to Cuba early in March to meet a committee of the Assembly. At the request of the committee, he had submitted his proposals to the Assembly, in writing, in behalf of "C. M. Coen of self and Associates." The proposal was to give the Cubans $12,400,000 in return for Cuban bonds valued at $20,000,000, which were to pay five percent interest and to be redeemed at face value within thirty years. The money which the Cubans received must be used solely to pay off the army, and for no other purpose; and the contract must be approved by the President of the United States, or it would be null and void. Coen undertook to secure this approval through his associates, but the Assembly was also to send a commission to Washington to ask the President's permission for the loan. Meanwhile, the contract was to remain secret.[51]

For three days the Assembly, meeting at El Cerro, near Havana, debated Coen's proposal. Most of the delegates favored accepting the plan, arguing that it was the only way vast sums of money could be procured for the army. But a number of delegates pointed out that the terms of the loan were highly unfavorable, since Cuba would be receiving $12,400,000 and would be required to pay back $20,000,000 plus five percent interest on the loan, dating from the time they received the money. In other words, they would receive only 62 cents on the dollar. Then again, who was Coen and who was behind him? Nobody knew, and Coen refused to tell.*

The vision of obtaining a large sum of money overrode these objections, and on March 9, the Assembly, by a large majority, voted to approve the Coen contract. That same day, the Assembly, at the suggestion of Manuel Sanguily, sent a committee to Gómez with the demand that he adhere to the decision to hold out for more money and lend his approval to the loan. Gómez replied that he had already made an agreement with the American authorities, and that he would not

---

* The Cuban paper *El Reconcentrado* reported simply that "a representative of an American syndicate including Senator Hanna is now here [in Havana] with a view of making a loan to the assembly." (Reprinted in *The State*, March 16, 1899.) Mark Hanna, Senator from Ohio, a leading American capitalist, was a close friend of President McKinley.

go back on his word. He also indicated strong opposition to the loan, pointing out that it would cripple the Cuban Republic financially.

Up to this point, Gómez had ignored the Cuban Assembly. Now he had openly defied it. In their rage, the delegates passed a resolution dismissing Gómez as General-in-Chief of the Cuban army. It achieved this by the simple expedient of abolishing the army grade of General-in-Chief, which it called "unnecessary and prejudicial at present." (That this was merely a device is seen in the fact that Bartolomé Masó, who supported the Assembly, was shortly appointed to replace Gómez as General-in-Chief.) The Assembly also removed Gonzalo de Quesada as chargé d'affaires in Washington, because of the part he had played in the Porter mission.[52] Quesada was immediately appointed by the McKinley Administration as representative of Cuba in Washington at a salary of five thousand dollars a year. Salvador Cisneros Betancourt, formerly twice president of the Cuban Republic, denounced Quesada as "the pliant tool of the Military Government for their own purposes," and charged that the position he now held in Washington was "the reward" for his role in convincing Gómez to yield to the terms offered by the United States.[53]

The "document of justification" for dismissing Gómez, adopted by acclamation, reviewed at great length the negotiations with Porter and Brooke, and accused Gómez of insubordination in accepting Porter's offer and in closing a deal with Brooke without consulting the Assembly. It declared that the three million dollars was insufficient and that Gómez's actions threatened to ruin negotiations for the loan which promised a larger sum. However, Sanguily put the case more clearly and briefly when he said that until he accepted Porter's proposal, Gómez had acted in the best inteersts of Cuba, but that from that moment, "he went over to the side of the United States neglecting Cuba." General Mayía Rodríguez, claiming to speak for the army, agreed with Sanguily. "We would a thousand times prefer to march to our homes clad in misery and honor, than to stain the last four glorious years by a single act of insubordination, or the acceptance of a reward unauthorized by the Assembly which is our supreme authority and to which the army owes obedience because it is the guardian of our interests and honor." [54]

Gómez replied to the Assembly in a calmly-worded statement. He informed the Cuban people that his removal was due to his opposition to the loan and that he had taken this stand because he was convinced that it was in the best interest of the emerging nation. He acknowledged the right of the Assembly to remove him, and noted that although he was a foreigner, he had not come to Cuba as a mercenary and therefore nothing was owing to him for his past services. He thanked the Assembly for making it possible for him to return to his home in Santo Domingo, and closed with a promise to the Cuban people that no matter where he might be they could always count on him as a friend.

The news of Gómez's dismissal stunned the Cuban people. A wave of protest swept the island. Members of the Assembly were burned in effigy and crowds gathered outside Gómez's home to cheer the old warrior. Telegrams of support poured in to Gómez, and letters to the press denounced the Assembly for ingratitude toward a man who had sacrificed so much for Cuba. It was clear that the Assembly had lost all popular support and that its authority had all but vanished.[55]

The United States authorities moved quickly to take advantage of the conflict between Gómez and the Assembly. Brooke announced that he would continue to recognize Gómez as the only representative authorized to speak for the Cuban army, and that "the United States will not recognize any obligations incurred by the body known as the Cuban Assembly." Washington soon afterwards added a further blow by notifying the "so-called Assembly or any part of it will not receive recognition by this Government under any conditions whatever." Nevertheless, the Assembly passed a conciliatory resolution, introduced by Sanguily, which expressed the gratitude of the army and people of Cuba "for the magnanimous assistance with which the people and the Congress of the United States strengthened the cause of the independence of our country, hastening and assuring its triumph," for the assistance given by the U.S. government "to the political and economic reconstruction of the country as well as the establishment of order and the Cuban nationality in a devastated island, exhausted by war," and for the offer of three million dollars for the disbandment of the soldiers. The resolution then pointed out, again in a conciliatory tone, that the Assembly, having more "exact knowledge of the character and needs of our army and the agricultural and economic situation of our country," considered that this sum, "which for our honor we cannot accept as a gift, but as a loan," was "insufficient and useless," and therefore, asked President McKinley for authorization "to raise the funds which are indispensable and which will be exclusively applied to the Cuban troops so that they can be disbanded without difficulties or apprehension, so that a definite and lasting peace may reign in the island of Cuba." In the final resolution, the Assembly appointed a committee to deliver this declaration to McKinley.[56]

The committee, made up of José R. Villalón and A. Hevia, went to Washington and managed to get an interview on March 31st with John Hay, the Secretary of State. Speaking for the President, Hay told the committee that it was absolutely impossible to authorize any loan to the Assembly, or to add to the three million dollars to pay off the Cuban army. The emissaries wired Cuba that "the Assembly can hope for nothing from the American government." The three million dollars offered by McKinley was the only plan that would be approved, and no action of the Assembly would change it.[57]

Leading American papers, like the New York *Tribune*, criticized the Administration for delay in "dispersing the so-called Cuban Assembly," denounced men like Sanguily as "nothing but rebels against all proper authority," and expressed hope that "the authorities would soon find a way to put an end to the scarcely disguised insurrection against all existing authority." In the Senate, Morgan of Alabama declared that the stand of the Cuban Assembly proved that it was "dangerous " for the United States to think of an early end of the Occupation, and he called on the Administration to dissolve the body immediately and "take a firm stand" against revolutionists on the island.[58]

The Administration shrewdly waited for the Assembly to pass out of existence. It was fully aware that the body was completely isolated, and that Gómez's prestige far outweighed that of the Assembly. Washington had only to wait for the inevitable. It came on April 4, when the Cuban Assembly voted to disband the army, to dissolve itself, and to turn over the rolls of the Cuban army to Brooke so that he and Gómez could go ahead with their arangements. Only one vote was cast against these motions that of Salvador Cisneros Betancourt. There was, however, a heated discussion before the motion was passed which recommended that the officers and soldiers of the Cuban army should turn over their rifles and ammunition to their commanders, who in turn would deliver them to the city councils, where they would "be subject to the disposition of whatever permanent government shall eventually be established in Cuba." A number of delegates favored disbanding the army, but insisted that the soldiers retain their arms. "The Americans did not disarm the Spanish Volunteers who were their enemies," argued General Rafael Portuondo, "and there is no need to disarm the Cubans who are their friends. The arms should be left as souvenirs of war."* But many delegates, including Sanguily, argued that such an outcome would not be acceptable to the United States, and that the return to peace should be complete. If, after the soldiers had surrendered their rifles, the Cuban people should need arms to protect their freedom, they would get them. "We had none in 1894, but we got them, and we could get them the same way again." [59]

In the closing moments of the final session, Sanguily likened the members of the Cuban Assembly to a "band of faithful workers devoted to Cuba's good, but finally vanquished by uncontrollable conditions." General Fernando Freyre de Andrade, president of the Assembly, ended the session with the moving statement: "As the shadows of night fall over our city, we finish our work. So is Cuba's future clouded and dark. I take leave with sorrow, and my last words are: May Cuba some day be free and independent." [60]

The news that the Assembly had passed out of existence received prominent space in the American press, and Gómez was hailed as the real hero of the Occupation. Reports from Havana featured the news that "the military administration would like to compliment Gen. Maximo Gomez in some substantial way. His services have been and are exceptionally useful to the Americans." [61] But on April 19, 1899, *El Reconcentrado* printed a caricature of Gómez trampling the flag of Cuba while holding aloft the American flag. The caption asked: "What next?"

What was next was equally disturbing. Gómez's agreement with Brooke, it will be recalled, had provided for payment of $100 to each Cuban soldier. But when the rolls showed that 48,000 veterans were to be paid, it was clear that three million dollars would not cover them. Brooke and Gómez then agreed to reduce the amount per man from $100 to $75, and to eliminate payment of all Cuban veterans who

---

* Even *La Lucha*, the pro-Spanish paper published in Havana, conceded: "The rifle represents to each soldier more than dollars." (May 22, 1899.)

held paying jobs in the Military Government. They also agreed that at the time of payment, the Cubans would have to surrender their arms to the mixed Cuban-American payment commission. But many Cubans objected to the idea of the soldiers turning over their arms to a commission made up of Americans, despite Gómez's acceptance of this arrangement. In fact, none of the Cuban officers named by Gómez to the mixed commission would accept the duty, and the Veterans of Independence unanimously resolved not to surrender any arms to any body on which Americans would be represented.[62]

Faced with the danger that the deal worked out with Gómez might blow up, and pressured by Washington to get the Cuban army business disposed of before the Philippine war grew even more serious, Brooke ordered that the arms should be deposited with the mayors of the municipalities in which payment took place, rather than directly to the payment commission. But Secretary of War Alger held out for having the arms turned over only to American authorities, which prompted *La Lucha* of Havana to ask on May 19, 1899: "His attitude raises the question, what does he want? Does he desire a war here similar to that in the Philippines?" The answer was obvious, and Brooke's plan was finally accepted. On this basis, payment of the Cuban army began in June, 1899, and by the late summer, the officers and soldiers had been paid off and disarmed. Not all veterans, however, accepted the payment and turned in their arms. Many of the men who fought under Antonio Maceo went home with their arms, refusing to accept money from the United States.[63]

Ironically, not all of the three million dollars was used up in the end. Brooke and Gómez had agreed that in such an event the remaining money should be paid to disabled officers from a list drawn up by the Cuban general. But this list was never prepared, and the surplus funds were finally returned to the U.S. Treasury.[64] So the removal of the threat of an armed rebellion in Cuba cost the United States even less than the meager sum it had bargained for!

On June 7th, after the plan for the payment of the soldiers had been completed, Máximo Gómez issued his farewell manifesto to the Liberating Army. He was leaving to visit his native land, Santo Domingo, but before embarking, he had a parting word "to the people for whom I have sacrificed thirty years of my life." The time had come for Cubans to put the war behind them. "Now we no longer want soldiers, but men for the maintenance of peace and order, which are the basis of Cuba's welfare."* Cubans should be grateful for the role the United States had played in terminating the war, but this did not mean that they should be satisfied with the policy it had followed since peace. On the contrary, "none of us thought that this . . . would be followed by a military occupation of the country by our allies, who treat us as a people incapable of acting for ourselves, and who have reduced us to obedience, to submission, and to a tutelage imposed by force of circumstances." Nevertheless, Gómez warned against resistance and urged peaceful cooperation with the Americans in a task "which is as disagreeable for them as for ourselves." Cubans should help the Americans to complete the "honorable mission" which circumstances had forced on them. "This work was not sought by those rich northerners, owners of a continent. I think doubts and suspicions are unjust." Today there were no longer autonomists or conservatives in Cuba—"only Cubans." The thing for Cubans to do was to unite, organize politically, and "make useless the presence of a strange power in the island," and the immediate task was for them to form "a committee or club, to be the nucleus of a government." [65]

For Gómez the Cuban Revolution was obviously over. But for the poor peasants and the workers it had really just begun. During the war, Gómez had understood that there were conservative, wealthy Cubans who opposed the Revolution and that the humble people had supported it in the hope of a better future. But under the Occupation with which he advised cooperation, it was the people who had opposed the Revolution who were coming into power under American tutelage, while the poor who had made the most sacrifices were reaping none of the benefits of victory. It is strange, too, that Gómez had only words of praise for the United States and gave the impression that the Americans were content to be only "owners of a continent." He was a man who had

---

\* Gómez stressed the same theme in many of his proclamations and manifestoes. He repeatedly emphasized that Cuba "must not have government by the sword but government by law . . . neither soldiers nor fortifications in our cities. . . ." The Liberating Army must not become a mercenary army, living off the people, but must make its contribution "to the reconstruction of the public wealth, principal source of the well-being which should be enjoyed by all cultivated society." (Emilio Roig de Leuchsenring, *Máximo Gómez, el Libertador de Cuba y el primer Ciudadano de la República*, La Habana, 1959, pp. 10-13.)

frequently proclaimed the international struggle for freedom and independence. Yet Gómez now had nothing to say about the imperialist annexation of Puerto Rico or the war waged against the Filipinos, a people who, like the Cubans, wished only to govern themselves.

Gómez issued several statements justifying his collaboration with the American authorities. At first he declared that to have aided the Cuban Assembly in its effort to raise loans "would compromise the greatest financial and political interests of Cuba," and that he was motivated by the desire to keep "the nation's honor spotless." Later he said bluntly: "I do not think it is a disgrace that Cuban soldiers should receive, from a government which is able to pay, sums that will relieve their immediate needs." But he finally declared that there was really only one justification for the course he had pursued—there was no other real alternative. As he put it when he accepted the proposal of the Cuban generals who, after the dissolution of the Cuban Assembly, asked their former commander-in-chief to represent the army in any negotiations with the United States military authorities: "We must recognize that the only power today in Cuba is the power of those who have intervened, and therefore for the present, thoughts of a Cuban independent government can be no more than a dream." [66]

The role Gómez played in the disbandment of the Cuban army is one which most Cuban historians have discussed with some reluctance, for they have been unwilling to criticize a man who made such tremendous contributions to the freedom and independence of their country. Recently, however, historians like Sergio Aguirre, Julio Le Riverend, and Euclides Vázquez Candela have taken the position that while he was personally incorruptible and influenced primarily by a desire to help the country for which he had sacrificed so dearly, Gómez lacked the political sagacity to understand clearly how his position served the interests of American imperialism.[67] Heretofore, however, most Cuban historians followed the line that while Gómez was theoretically insubordinate in defying the Cuban Assembly (the legal representative of the Cuban people), and in weakening its power and prestige in a critical period, he was realistically correct in pursuing this policy. For one thing, he was correct in refusing to support the grandiose scheme for a loan which would have caused Cuba grave financial problems, and would have economically retarded the country for years to come. In helping to frustrate this deal, Gómez had made a great contribution for the cause for which he had fought. As for his cooperation with Porter and Brooke in the disbandment of the army, the historians point out that Gómez really had no choice: the needy condition of the troops demanded a speedy demobilization. Finally, the military occupation was a fact, and in urging cooperation with it, Gómez was being realistic. A different policy, one challenging the Occupation, ran the risk of an armed clash between the Cubans and the Americans and would have given the United States a good excuse to continue the Occupation indefinitely, if not to annex the island outright. Gómez had kept his army intact and disciplined, and thus proved that the Cuban revolutionists were not a lawless, predatory mob, but were amenable to reason. The most important problem was to get the United States out of Cuba and an independent government established, and this could only be achieved through peaceful cooperation.[68]

There is much justification for the position taken by these historians. One might also add that Gómez did not act out of personal ambition. Unlike too many others who had been active in the Revolution, including generals of the Cuban army, he did not sell himself to the United States for a lucrative post in the Occupation, and he could have had any one he wanted. Gómez did not, like too many other Cuban generals, hasten to attend the lavish receptions General Brooke and General Ludlow held in Havana for veterans of the Revolution, as part of a well-designed plan to wean them away from an anti-American position. (As M. Márquez Sterling points out, it was with "fiestas and receptions that the military chiefs of the American Occupation sweetened the foreign regime."[69]) Finally, there is considerable justification for the viewpoint that it was important to prevent an armed clash between Cuban and American armed forces so as to frustrate the plans of annexationists in the United States, who were itching for such an event.

Yet when all this has been said, the fact remains that Gómez's actions had strengthened the hold of American imperialism over Cuba, for he deepened the split in the Revolutionary forces and enabled the United States to get precisely what it wanted: unconditional liquidation of the Cuban army. Gómez was correct in opposing the loan scheme —apart from imposing a heavy burden on the Cuban people, it would open the door to a vast amount of graft and corruption—but he *could* have cooperated with the delegates in the Assembly who wished to use the disarming of the army as a means of forcing concessions from the United States in ending the occupation of the island. By agreeing to the conditions advanced by Porter and Brooke without even consulting the Assembly, Gómez cut the ground from under those who were anxious to negotiate a better deal for the Cuban people from a financial and political point of view.

The truth is that Gómez was naive in his evaluation of American policy in Cuba. He understood that the Occupation robbed the Cubans of what they had fought for and was reducing them to a status of servility. But he failed to understand that this was part and parcel of a policy to dominate Cuba in the interests of the United States. He revealed this not only in his farewell message—note his reference to the Occupation as an "honorable mission" which had been forced on the United States by circumstances—but in an interview with Gonzalo de Quesada published in the New York *Journal* of February 26, 1899. Here Gómez expressed complete confidence that the United States would shortly carry out the principles of the Joint Resolution and leave Cuba to govern itself, free of all American interference. If American politicians dared to prevent the establishment of a Cuban Republic in the very near future, Gómez was certain that the President, the American people, the press and Congress would defeat them. On the subject of future economic relations between the Republic of Cuba and the United States, Gómez expressed confidence that it would be a relationship of equals, and that the latter would assist Cuba to become economically as well as politically independent. He had no fear of investment of American capital in Cuba; on the contrary, he welcomed it, and he wanted American capitalists to understand that they would find in Cuba "a splendid return and also perfect security"—in fact, "magnificent profits."

Of one thing Gómez declared he was certain: the Americans would grant the Cubans full self-government. "For an American to think in any other way, it would be necessary for him to think that Spain was right in keeping us subjected and that the United States had committed an error in going to war with Spain to liberate us." Later, Gómez was to concede that he had been mistaken in expressing such confidence in the good intentions of the United States towards Cuban independence, but he had no doubts throughout the period of negotiations for the disbandment of the Cuban army. In late May, 1899, Brooke informed the War Department that he found "a deep-seated suspicion in the minds of the Cubans" toward the U.S. Government.[70] But Gómez was not among those referred to, for he kept assuring the Cuban people that such "doubts and suspicions are unjust." Events, unfortunately, were to justify the doubters, and were to demonstrate that while he acted in what he honestly considered the best interests of Cuba, Gómez failed to understand the real nature of American imperialism and how it used him for its own purposes and against the best interests of the people for whom he had sacrificed so many years of his life.

It is interesting to contrast Gómez's evaluation of the course of events in Cuban-American relations with that of General Enrique Collazo. In a letter to the *Herald* of Havana, early in June, 1899, Collazo defended the Cuban Assembly, criticized Gómez's conduct, but directed his main attention to clarifying the real issues involved in the whole question of disbanding the Cuban army. It is worth quoting his interpretation at some length:

> A good deal of the discussion now in progress shows that the real situation is misunderstood. Both the Americans and the Cubans desire the independence of the island, the Americans because they are pledged to it, and the Cubans because of patriotism and political considerations. *Between the two stands the Washington administration, representing the important business interests involved. There is no doubt that the beauty and rich possibilities of Cuba have aroused in many of our visitors a greed which is responsible for the attempts to excite the notion that the country is warlike whereas the fact is that the Cubans are so docile that even the desperation of hunger will not lead them into wrongful action.*
>
> The offer of charity affronts the dignity of our people and the gratuity of $3,000,000 insults them. The United States government if it intends to free the island, should pay what is due the army, in the form of a loan to Cuba, which the Cubans would gladly and easily repay. We do not want gifts, and the course hitherto followed discredits the American government among us. It inspires distrust. The Cubans have been deceived for four centuries, and it is only logical that they should be suspicious now. . . .
>
> The Cubans are starving while hundreds of thousands of dollars are spent upon palaces for the American commanders, who apply the military of the Spanish law, as their whim suggests. Charity, such as is offered, must be in any event useless, because inadequate. Cuba will not recuperate without $50,000,000 to finance her agriculturists and without paying the army what it

deserves. In this way, recuperation can be accomplished. All that is necessary is the good will of the American administration.[71]

Collazo understood the plans of American imperialism for Cuba. Gómez did not, and this failure led him to weaken the revolutionary unity needed if Cuba was to end the Occupation, and end it with meaningful independence.

In an article in the *Review of Reviews,* on the eve of the formal American occupation of Cuba, a writer urged the American officers bound for the island "to learn something of the real history of the island, particularly since about 1825. The American officer who professes ostentatiously that he has no sympathy with the Cubans and considers them a mongrel lot, unworthy of their independence, unfit for self-government and only fit to be ruled arbitrarily by Spaniards or somebody else, may be a good soldier; but this ignorance disqualifies him for helping to reconstruct the island of Cuba after four years of warfare." [72] But it is the nature of imperialism that precisely such men as the author warned against should be its agents and administrators, and the American occupation of Cuba was no exception to the rule. A number of Cuban historians have praised the Brooke administration as honest and efficient, a point of view shared by most American historians.[73] Yet Brooke himself conceded that "we are working against the habits and thoughts and actions of this people," [74] and he and his officers showed a propensity for ignoring Cuban traditions and experience, and ruling by legislative fiat and decrees. Brooke shocked the religious element by his order in May, 1899 that only civil marriages should be legally valid. Charles T. Andrews reported that Cuban teachers were angry because of Brooke's decree requiring them to go to the capital of their provinces to get their pay. "In the case of those of Cienfuegos, this would mean an expense of $15 on railroad fares to get $40 in wages." [75]

In Havana, the ringing of church bells was banned, gambling was proscribed for the Cubans (not for the Americans), and Puritan laws were enforced. The prominence given to English in the schools angered Cuban patriots who protested: "It has always been the custom of conquerors to impose their language on the conquered." [76]

Too often American officers and soldiers treated Cubans as inferiors, lorded it over them in trains and other public conveyances,* and ordered restaurants and cafes to bar dark-skinned patrons. Reporting that "We cater to white people only" signs were going up in Havana cafes, the New York *Tribune,* although fully supporting the Occupation, condemned American officers and soldiers for insisting on such displays, telling Cubans that "theirs must be a white man's country and that the United States means to make it so. . . . They have, there is grave reason to fear, succeeded in alarming many black Cubans, and arousing among them the fear that the old Spanish sport of bullfighting may presently be replaced with what they understand to be the favorite American pastime of 'nigger lynching.' " [77]

American soldiers aroused much hostility by marching intoxicated through working-class districts, waving money and shouting that they were looking for prostitutes. Cuban historians emphasize that while prostitution had existed in Cuba since the early days of the Spanish regime, it never flourished as openly and widely as from the beginning of the American occupation.[78] Drunkenness among American soldiers was frequently reported by correspondents. "There have been hundreds of instances in Habana," wrote the correspondent for the New York *Tribune* as early as April, 1899, "in which drunken soldiers have resisted arrest and committed all sorts of offenses against the municipal law, and such conduct has been aggravated by the common feeling among the troops that the local guardians of the peace had not the courage to use their arms against offenders in American uniforms." [79]

When these distasteful features of the Occupation were criticized in the Cuban press, Brooke's reaction was swift. He appointed a press censor in Santiago de Cuba and Havana to whom all editorials had to be submitted for approval prior to publication. When Ricardo Arnauto, publisher of *El Reconcentrado* of Havana, denounced this action, as he had previously attacked press censorship by Weyler and had had his press assaulted by Spanish soldiers, General Ludlow, with Brooke's approval, issued an order on August 1, 1899 closing down the paper,

---

* An American wrote as early as February, 1899, following his return from Cuba: "The people of this country are not aware of what the Cubans have to put up with from the American soldiers. Many . . . are constantly dominating over and bullying the poor Cubans, the provost guards, in particular, and if they resent it, they are either jabbed with the bayonet or arrested." (Philip B. Harvey in *The State,* Feb. 14, 1899.)

confiscating its press, arresting Arnauto and the editors, and warning that this decree "is not solely against this newspaper [*El Reconcentrado*] but also against any other obscene publication . . . in the jurisdiction of Havana."[80] A few newspapers protested this dictatorial action, but did so mildly, probably fearing reprisals. In the United States, newspapers which should have been the first to condemn interference with freedom of the press in Cuba, conceded that the restrictions imposed by the military were "harsh," but viewed them as "necessary for the establishment of American authority in Cuba."[81]

We shall see below how the Cuban labor movement was severely restricted under General Brooke, but we have already seen enough to appreciate Margaret Leech's estimate that the Brooke administration "in spite of great benefits, was obnoxious to the inhabitants."[82] As the Cuban poet, Bonifacio Byrne, put it:

> Returning from distant shores,
> With my soul saddened and somber,
> Longingly I sought my flag,
> And saw it waving beside another.[83]

CHAPTER XX

# Military Occupation: The Wood Administration

IN REMOVING SOME of the occupying troops in March, 1899, the U.S. War Department announced that it was "confident of a continuation of the prevailing peace and good order in Cuba."[1] The confidence was merited. It was clear by the summer of 1899 that Cuba was as pacific as anyone could desire. General Wilson informed Senator Foraker in July that now that the Cuban army was disbanded, he was convinced there was no further need for American troops in the island. Foraker replied:

> My advices are also not only from you but from many others who are in the island, and who know what they write about, that there is no need whatsoever to keep an army longer in the island for the purpose of pacification, for the simple reason that the island is already pacified. This being true, I think the President should get us out of the island as quickly and decently as possible, and he should take the first step by announcing without any further delay that the Cubans can proceed in some proper form to set up a government.[2]*

No one knew better than General Brooke that Foraker was correct. Indeed, he conceded that not only was the pacification phase of the

---

* Both Wilson and Foraker felt that it had been a mistake to pass the Teller Amendment to the Joint Resolutions, but that since it had been done, it was necessary to abide by its provisions. Wilson, who favored annexation of Cuba, believed that the best solution was a permanent American protectorate; but Foraker, while hoping that Cuba would want annexation, and favoring some limitations on a Cuban government, came out for immediate independence. (Wilson to Foraker, May 12, 1899; Foraker to Wilson, May 22, 1899, James H. Wilson Papers, Library of Congress.)

Occupation completed, but the civil departments had taken over the duties pertaining to them from the military "until the civil departments are now nearly complete in all the provinces, and the affairs of Cuba may be said to be conducted through the channels of civil administration, although under military control, except the department of customs." The great bulk of the work was done by the Cuban cabinet officers and their departments.[3]

It was quite logical for the Cubans to ask why there was a need for continuation of United States authority in their country. The time had come for the United States to leave and permit the island to govern itself. As José Miguel Gómez, civil governor of Santa Clara Province, told Charles T. Andrews in the summer of 1899: "Cuba is ready and able to govern itself." [4]

This position received backing from many Americans. In the summer of 1899, the American Anti-Imperialist League urged the end of the Occupation and the beginning of self-government for Cuba. In this plea, the League was joined by its affiliates in Chicago, Cincinnati, Philadelphia, San Francisco, Detroit, St. Louis, Portland, Oregon, New York and Washington, D. C.[5] Late in June, 1899, a broad coalition that included Socialist Eugene V. Debs, Social Reformer Jane Addams, Populist "Sockless' Jerry Simpson, Reverend Lyman Abbott, A.F. of L. President Samuel Gompers, former Illinois Governor John P. Altgeld, Negro leader Booker T. Washington, and author and reformer Henry Demarest Lloyd, met and drew up an "Address to the People of the United States," in which "our continued government of Cuba by armed forces and the military grants of Cuban franchises and special privileges" was denounced. In words that have a truly modern ring, the sixty-seven-year-old statement declared: "A nation cannot deny the capacity and violate the right of another nation to liberty and self-government without losing faith in the capacity of its own people for self-government, and in the right of its own people to liberty." [6]

But there were also other voices in the United States. The imperialist press featured reports that although the Cuban army was disbanded and the Cuban Assembly dissolved, the island was still not really pacified. The revolutionists had been weakened, but they were still organized and able to stir up trouble. They were even threatening that "if Cuban independence is not acknowledged and the government transferred to the Cubans, the torch is to be applied to one end of the island to the other, by which means all foreign investment will be destroyed."[7] Such reports, of course, frightened American imperialists. On July 10, 1899, Theodore Roosevelt, who with Senator Lodge was an outstanding spokesman for this group, wrote to Leonard Wood that McKinley did not seem to be aware of the dangers still present in the Cuban situation and on the contrary, thought that things were satisfactory in the island. "I told him plainly that I did not think so, and that I did not think they were growing better. . . ."[8]

To the Roosevelt-Lodge group was now added Elihu Root who, on August 1, 1899, formally replaced Russell A. Alger as Secretary of War.* A prominent corporation lawyer in New York City, closely associated with the leading finance capitalist in the United States, J. P. Morgan, Root shared Roosevelt's anxiety that Cuba be made safe for investment of American capital. As Secretary of War, he was in a position to fulfill this objective. He helped to formulate the colonial policy of the United States, and his part in modernizing the American military command bore early results in the more effective operations against the Filipinos. Root, in short, was highly efficient in furthering American imperialism.[9]

In Cuba itself, the man who was part of this coalition was the military governor of Santiago Province—General Leonard Wood. Wood was convinced that General Brooke was too weak a man to promote American interests in Cuba effectively. On July 12, he warned Roosevelt that Brooke was endangering American control over the island by placing too much power in the hands of the Cuban Cabinet, without realizing that this body was plotting to bring an early end to American occupation. "Their hope is that Cuban discontent will be of such character that there will be a general expression of disapproval and that the 'Mugwumps' [anti-imperialists] at home will side with the discontented people in asking for the withdrawal of our occupation." He predicted that if Brooke continued in command another six months, American authority in the island might be completely disrupted. Hence action had to be taken immediately to remove Brooke; "the system of civil government which is being developed here is got to be uprooted and

---

* Roosevelt felt that Alger, because of his general incompetence, was a liability for American imperialism. "While Alger is in the Cabinet I always have a feeling of uneasiness about Cuba and the Philippines," he wrote to Lodge on April 27, 1899. (Theodore Roosevelt Papers, Library of Congress.)

suppressed entirely in the end and every day makes it more difficult to do without more or less trouble." Wood urged Roosevelt to show his letter to Elihu Root, the newly-appointed Secretary of War, "not for any purpose of furthering my advancement or anything else, but simply as a statement of conditions which actually exist." [10]

Although Brooke was not relieved of command until December, 1899, it was already clear by the preceding summer that his policy did not suit the pro-imperialists. To be sure, Brooke was not in favor of withdrawing the American army and leaving Cuba to govern itself. ("From what I can learn," he wrote to McKinley on September 26, 1899, "from those whose opinion is valuable and from my own observation, I do not think the time has yet arrived when this people can establish a stable government."[11]) Nevertheless, he was not aggressive enough in organizing the Occupation in a way that would suit American business. What was really wanted was set forth most clearly by Henry Clews, a Wall Street banker who spoke for American investors and potential investors in Cuban properties. Clews said that these men favored most of all outright annexation of Cuba, but knew that there were difficulties in attaining this objective. They were willing to settle for a stable, independent Cuban government under the protection and domination of the United States. Such a government "will be one from which American investors have nothing to fear." [12]

But only a strong military governor could push such a scheme down the throats of the Cuban people, and Brooke was obviously not the man for the job. There was some talk of General James H. Wilson for the post, for the favored setting up an independent Cuban government, tied to the United States by a treaty which would establish a virtual United States protectorate over Cuba, and by tariff agreements which would tie the Cuban economy closely to her North American neighbor. All this would be a prelude to eventual peaceful annexation of the island.[13] Wilson's Cuban policy was attractive to American business, but it was weakened by his firm belief that the Occupation should be ended forthwith, that the Cubans be permitted to call a constitutional convention at the earliest moment and establish their own government—subject, of course, to the limitations he proposed. Wilson assured Roosevelt in July, 1899 that under his plan, the Occupation could be ended "in 48 hours" while Cuba would continue in reality under American domination.[14] But this was rushing things too fast to suit American imperialism.

What finally eliminated Wilson from consideration was that there was a much better candidate to do the job for American imperialism— Leonard Wood.* For one thing, Wood was strongly in favor of continuing the Occupation indefinitely. He claimed, moreover, that this approach reflected the real desires of the Cuban people. "The sentiment for our remaining here forever is becoming very strong in this part of Cuba," he wrote to McKinley in April from Santiago, "and I think we shall have hard work to get away."[15] Interviewed by a reporter for the New York *Times* in June, while on a visit to the United States, Wood came out openly for annexation, and again maintained that he was voicing the desires of "the people" of Cuba. However, this time he was more specific about whom he meant, for he listed "the propertied classes, and all the foreigners in Cuba, including the Spaniards" as favoring annexation, "because they realize that we can give them a stable government."[16] By September, Wood was assuring McKinley that prolonged occupation, to be followed by annexation, would win universal support in Cuba. "The people who are talking 'Cuba Libre' and the total withdrawal of the American Army in the daily press represent at most not over five per cent of the Cuban people."[17]

Wood favored a firm policy in handling the Cubans, whom he contemptuously described as "a quiet people, without enough force of character to be seriously troublesome if we can only keep them moderately busy." What Cuba needed was "a firm and stable government in the hands of men who would not hesitate to use severe measures should the occasion arise."[18] Wood had already demonstrated in Santiago what this meant. He had threatened to shoot the editor of a paper who dared to criticize his policies. He had organized the Rural Guard not only to stamp out banditry, as was commonly asserted, but also to put down "the agitators who began to grow restive at the presence of the Americans."[19] He had surrounded himself with Cubans and Spaniards who were mainly of the propertied classes, men who frequented the Conservative San Carlos Club and who had opposed the Cuban Revolution. With his usual high hand, he trampled upon

---

* An additional factor operating against Wilson was that he was too close to Senator Foraker, a bitter opponent of the Administration's Cuban policy.

the courts of justice whenever their decisions did not suit him, replacing recalcitrant judges with men who were ready to do his bidding. "Such an abominable state had never been known in Cuba even in the most nefarious time of Spanish domination," wrote a Cuban of Wood's administration of justice in Santiago.[20]

It is not difficult then to understand why Wood easily pushed Wilson aside as the replacement for Brooke. Roosevelt noted to Lodge in July, 1899, that as between Wood's policy of indefinite military occupation and Wilson's policy of ending the occupation but continuing control through treaty and tariff arrangements, McKinley "is inclined to Wood's policy." This is hardly surprising, since Foraker, after talking to McKinley, concluded that the President's policy, such as it was, was "to hold on by military force to the control of the Island, including Customs Houses and all other sources of revenue." [21]

On December 13, 1899, Leonard Wood was assigned to the command of the Division of Cuba in place of General Brooke, and took over the command of the Cuban Occupation seven days later. "I know you were pleased by the appointment of Wood in Cuba," Root wrote to Roosevelt.[22] Most pleased of all were American capitalists bent upon controlling Cuba for their own profits.

General Wood retained most of the structure of the Occupation as it had existed under Brooke. Of the seven provincial governors appointed by Brooke, six remained in office until the end of the Occupation, while most of the lesser officials stayed at their posts.[23] However, Wood immediately reorganized the civil administration of Cuba. He increased the four civil departments to six, separating Justice and Public Instruction, and dividing Public Works from Agriculture, Commerce and Industries. He then appointed new heads of the six administrative departments. Brooke's Cuban Cabinet had resigned, and Wood informed Root he was glad to get rid of them.[24] He had criticized Brooke for giving the Cuban revolutionists too much influence in the civil administration, and he had indicated that when he was placed in command, he would choose mainly men "who are in sympathy with American ideals." [25] This he proceeded to do. Only two of the civil administrators were revolutionary leaders and veterans of the Cuban army: José Ramón Villalón, Secretary of Public Works, and Juan Riuz Rivera, Secretary of Agriculture, Industry and Commerce. Moreover,

Wood made the Cuban Secretaries do his bidding, and deprived them of much of the authority they had enjoyed under Brooke.[26]*

Wood, however, tried to use his patronage to neutralize the old Cuban leaders and further split the ranks of the revolutionists. "I propose," he wrote to Root, "to put General Gomez, General Rodriguez and possibly one other of the old generals on a committee to look after the old and crippled soldiers of the war, giving General Gomez a salary of $5,000.00 a year, Rodriguez $3,600.00 and any other associate $2,400.00. *These men have great influence with the army and great influence with the people.* They are practically starving, at least are living on what is given them by their friends."[27] But this effort to bribe the revolutionary leaders into accepting continued American occupation failed. In a letter written in broken English, Gómez refused Wood's offer, stating his unwillingness to limit his "political purety." His only remaining mission, Gómez wrote, was "helping with neither interest for the liberty of this country."[28] Wood's plan was still-born: the committee on veteran's welfare was never established.

Wood was no more successful when he tried to allay the suspicions of other revolutionary leaders as to his purposes in Cuba. On January 1, 1900, he called together the old leaders of the Cuban army, including General Bartolomé Masó, ex-president of the Cuban Republic, and urged them to support American policy toward Cuba. But the Cubans accused Wood of favoring permanent United States control in Cuba, and one of the generals, José Miró, who had been Antonio Maceo's chief-of-staff, charged Wood with planning annexation instead of Cuban independence. Wood denied this, but the Cubans who knew the American general well from his role in Santiago, remained unconvinced.[29] Wood, however, had one consolation. "The Spanish element is very friendly," he assured Root.[30]

As military governor, Wood extended many of the projects begun under General Brooke. Havana and other cities were modernized; yellow fever was suppressed; jails and prisons were reformed; the judicial system was overhauled; municipal government reorganized; sanitary campaigns were pushed with vigor; roads were built, harbors dredged,

---

\* General Rivera resigned as Secretary of Agriculture, Industry and Commerce in April, 199 because the U.S. government refused to set a limit for the occupation of the island. (*The State,* April 23, May 5, 1900.)

sewers installed, streets paved and telegraph lines strung. Finally, and perhaps most important of all, public education became a reality in Cuba. Again, as under Brooke, all of the funds for these campaigns, including the expenses of the United States troops and the building of camps and barracks, were paid from the Cuban treasury. "This is a fact that is hard to get into the heads of some of our imperialists," noted *The State*. "They cherish the theory that the United States is paying out money for Cuba's rehabilitation." [31]

Under Wood, a school law was promulgated, nationalizing the educational system, with a hierarchy of inspectors, culminating in a cabinet officer, and providing for the national payment of all costs, and the election of local school officials.[32] Schools were opened all over the island—within six months the number increased from 635 to 3,313— and better equipped than they had been under Brooke. Enrollment increased tremendously; indeed Wood's administration marked the high point of education in Cuba for years to come.* In 1900, slightly more than $4,000,000 was spent for education—or one-fourth of the national budget. In the summer of 1900, Harvard University raised funds by voluntary contributions to bring nearly 1,400 Cuban teachers to Cambridge for a summer's instruction in teaching methods.[33] In 1901, similar sessions were organized at several places in Cuba, while a selected group of 200 was again sent to Harvard University.

Under Wood, higher education was also reformed, provided by the University of Havana and six "Institutes" or high schools, one in each province. The University, founded in 1734, was in 1899 a decadent diploma mill, with 381 students and 107 faculty members. It was thoroughly reformed and re-equipped, as were the high schools, and commercial schools were established. By the end of Wood's administration, there were 3,800 public schools with a total enrollment of 255,000 and an average daily attendance of 160,000. Before the war, only 33,000 had been enrolled, and by the time the Spanish left, there were

---

* Number of Cubans attending school per 100 population

| Year | Number | Year | Number |
|------|--------|------|--------|
| 1900 | 75     | 1924 | 32     |
| 1920 | 50     | 1932 | 12     |

(Carleton Beals, *The Crime of Cuba,* Philadelphia, 1932, p. 297)

no longer any high schools, nor a school house, nor any significant school attendance.[34]

Probably the most widely publicized achievement of the Wood administration was the stamping out of yellow fever. However, there were plenty of critics who pointed out that the campaign to eradicate yellow fever was designed to prevent it from killing Americans, not Cubans, who were immune to the disease. One commentator even claimed that Cubans "regarded the disease rather kindly because it rid them of Spaniards."[35] However that may be, the fact is that in 1901, a Yellow Fever Commission came to Cuba to discover the causes of the tropical disease. Operating under Major William Gorgas, the Commission included both Cuban and American doctors, among whom Doctors Reed, Lazear, Carroll and Agramonte were outstanding. These four men decided to abandon the generally accepted theory that yellow fever was a filth-generating disease, and to test the theories of a Cuban doctor, Carlos Finlay, that the yellow fever organisms were transmitted by the *Stygomyia* mosquito. After an exhaustive series of tests during which Lazear and Carroll died, martyrs to the cause, Finlay's theory was found to be correct. Now it was possible to take proper precautions against the dread disease. By March, 1901, the city of Havana was entirely free from yellow fever, the first time it was without the disease since June, 1899.[36] The Insular Department of the U.S. War Department reported in March, 1902, without mentioning the name Carlos Finlay*: "It has established the fact that yellow fever is only

---

* It was Major Gorgas, in his report, who paid tribute to Dr. Finlay's contribution. He referred glowingly to "Dr. Finlay's theory of the mosquito," and noted that *"the theory of Dr. Finlay . . . was proved as no other theory in medicine has been in the course of one year. . . . I do not know of any theory advanced by any man of science which has been proved so rapidly and brilliantly."* (Report of Major C. W. Gorgas in *Civil Report of General Leonard Wood for the Period from January 1 to December 31, 1901*, Washington, 1902, vol. I, pp. 6-8. Emphasis in original.)

Actually, not until Major Gorgas revealed the fact in his report did most Americans even know that Dr. Finlay was a Cuban. Whatever mention had been made of him was as Dr. Carl Finlay and it was assumed he was British or American. (*The State*, April 17, 1901.)

In his own comment on the elimination of yellow fever, Dr. Finlay modestly made no mention of his own contribution. Instead, he wrote: "To Colonel W. C. Gorgas of the American Army who was head of the Sanitation of the Island until May 20, 1902, falls the glory of having been the first to eradicate yellow fever in Havana; a triumph which he achieved in the space of seven months

transmitted by a certain species of mosquito, a discovery that in its power for preserving human life is only excelled by Jenner's great discovery, and as time goes on it will stand in the same class as that great boon to mankind." [37] Not only Cuba but other areas of the world, including the Southern cities of the United States, became safer to live in as a result of the joint efforts of the medical profession of Cuba and the United States.

The degree of success Wood's administration achieved in general has been a source of controversy. His supporters, both American and Cuban, maintain that "he gave Cuba the best government the island had ever had." [38] Wood's laudatory biographer, Herman Hagedorn, even asserts that as a result of Wood's policies "in a period of scarcely more than two years, the Americans had lifted the Cuban people out of a state of physical desolation and political chaos . . . into a condition of order, stability and contentment." [39] Lord Cromer, who knew imperialist administration from his experience in Egypt, said of General Wood's work in Cuba that it was "the greatest piece of colonial administration in all history." [40]

While agreeing that there were many important achievements, especially in the areas of sanitation, education, and public works, Wood's critics dispute the assertion that his admiinstration was truly successful. Albert G. Robinson, one of Wood's severest contemporary critics, charged that "we have mistaken philanthropy and sanitation for statesmanship. . . . Street cleaning and school administration are ineffectual substitutes for broadly constructed illustrations of stable and satisfying self-government." Robinson pointed out that the government was characterized by "military absolutism" just as bad as that of the Spanish rule. Cubans, he wrote, had little to say in the policies adopted by the military government under Wood. But the most serious fault, Robinson maintained, was that the government "ignored all of Cuba's past history, and . . . essayed political and administrative reform, when what was needed imperatively was industrial and economic prosperity." It

---

ending in September, 1901, through the strict observance of the fundamental laws stressed above. To eliminate yellow fever in Havana meant its disappearance in the whole country, since there did not exist in the whole Island any other population center with a number of non-immune inhabitants sufficient for maintaining itself as a permanent epidemic center. . . ." (Carlos J. Finlay, *Obras Completas*, Academia de Ciencias de Cuba, La Habana, 1965, Tomo I, p. 69.)

did little good to open schools when many poor children could not attend regularly because of lack of food, clothing and shoes. Robinson charged that Cuba, after three years of American rule, was poorer than "at any other time within the last eighty years." [41] This last point was corroborated by Leland H. Jenks who, writing in 1928, noted: "The island was certainly not so well off economically in May, 1902 [when Wood's administration ended], as it had been in February, 1895." [42] We shall discuss the reasons for this situation below, but as to the truth of these statements there can be little doubt.

One fact cannot be disputed. The military government, especially under Wood, in the words of Carleton Beals, "ignored the Cuban revolution." It "elbowed aside" the patriots who had fought for Cuba's independence—that is, those whom it could not win over by patronage —and "turned chiefly to the Tories . . . the people who had looked with apprehension upon a free Cuba." These were the Spaniards and the Cuban conservative property owners who had opposed independence, and now openly favored annexation to the United States.[43] Wood conceded that pro-United States sentiment was strongest among planters, merchants, and the upper classes generally, while he attributed Cuban nationalism chiefly to the revolutionists, the peasants and the working class. He also was frank in acknowledging that he based his administration on the former group.[44]

Herminio Portell Vilá expressed the viewpoint of many recent Cuban historians when he contended that the Wood regime was arbitrary in its methods, inclined to engage in political intrigue, and determined to Americanize the island, that is, to re-establish the colonial economic system under American domination.[45] On the question of Wood's determination to Americanize Cuba there is no longer any doubt. David F. Healy puts it well: ". . . the Americanization of Cuba, remained one of the governor's basic goals, and is visible in the background of many of his reforms." [46] To be in favor of Cuban nationalism was a crime in Wood's eyes. Thus Alexis E. Frye was forced to resign as superintendent of schools in Cuba because he showed himself "too fervent for early Cuban independence." Wood conceded that Frye was very popular with the Cuban people, and that this popularity "is based on affection." But as he explained to Root, this did not count, because the American educator was spreading "the most intense radicalism as to the future relations between Cuba and the United States." [47] The New York *Evening Post* pointed out:

> One who has the affection and sympathies of the Cuban people is worth more as a governing force than ten regiments. There was no secret about Mr. Frye's popularity. It sprang from his hearty entering into the hopes and aspirations of the Cubans. He did not, like the rest of official America, cease cheering for "Cuba Libre" the moment the war was over and as soon as the island began to appear as a very fruitful Naboth's Vineyard for us to seize upon. Mr. Frye always spoke, and spoke openly, as if the United States intended to keep its solemn promise, and as if Cuba were to be launched as an independent nation. This made him popular with the Cubans. It appears to have made him unpopular with the American miiltary government.

The entire Cuban school system under Wood, vast improvement though it was over what had existed under Spain, was modelled closely upon the United States system in order to inculcate American principles. Wood replaced Brooke's school law with one written by Lieutenant Matthew E. Hanna, an ex-Ohio school teacher, and based on the laws of the state of Ohio. As Elihu Root proudly reported: "The courses and methods of instructions are those most approved in this country. The text-books are translations into Spanish of American text-books." [48] No attempt was even made to have these books relevant to the experience and traditions of Cuban children, who while they had much to learn from the lives of Washington, Jefferson and Lincoln could have benefitted immensely from learning about José Martí, Antonio Maceo, Ignacio Agramonte, and other martyrs of Cuban independence.

While Wood rejected the plan of some ardent annexationists in the United States to send American teachers to Cuba to man the new schools and thereby "Americanize the children," [49] he thought highly of the plan to "Americanize" the Cuban teachers. This, after all, was the main purpose of sending Cuban teachers to Harvard University to learn American teaching methods.\* A similar purpose was behind the

---

\* Shortly before the Occupation ended, Lieutenant Hanna negotiated a long-term contract with a New York normal school, providing for the training in the United States of thirty Cuban teachers a year. After the Occupation was over, opposition to the contract was so strong in Cuba that the new Republic was compelled to abandon it.

activity of the Cuban Educational Association, which directed Cuban youths to institutions of higher learning in the United States. These students were expected to return to the island, upon completion of their studies, thoroughly "Americanized." The Association found, however, that only certain Cubans were considered fit to be "Americanized." Darker skinned Cubans could not gain admission to a number of American universities and colleges. The President of the University of Missouri advised Gilbert K. Harroun, Secretary of the Association that while "there is no law forbidding Negroes to enter our university, if one should attempt to do so, he would surround himself with no end of trouble owing to the status of public opinion in the state. You understand therefore that the offer is not extended to the Cubans that may be Negroes." [50]

Evidently this aspect of "Americanization" increased during Wood's administration, for as early as April, 1900, a delegation of Cubans protested, in a petition to the Governor General, that official documents used such terms as "mulatto, colored and brown which distinguish a man by his color." The petitioners urged Wood to issue a decree making illegal the use of such terms, and ordering that only the word "citizen" be employed. "The colored race has already proved its value and capability, and the continuance of the use of such descriptive epithets only tends to perpetuate the barrier between the black and the white." Wood, who believed that the Cuban Negroes would prove their capacity to turn their country "into another Hayti" if allowed to exercise influence in political affairs, ignored the petition.[51]

Contemporary critics of Wood's administration pointed to the fact that the cost of the Occupation was entirely excessive, and that there had been an extravagant use of funds for sanitation, public works and for building barracks for American soldiers. Some critics even charged that the Cubans were being forced to pay excessively for the sole benefit of the Americans, "to house an unnecessary army and to suppress the yellow fever to which the Cubans are immune." [52] In August, 1900, Salvador Cisneros y Betancourt, twice President of the Cuban Republic, visited President McKinley in Washington to protest abuses inflicted upon the Cuban people during the Occupation, especially under General Wood. His *Appeal to the American People on Behalf of Cuba* was published in the United States following this visit, and embodied what he had told the President.

Cisneros charged that the military authorities "have been arbitrary in their proceedings; that they have disregarded the rights of the people of Cuba; that they have often acted as conquerors in a conquered land rather than as representatives of a free people helping those who had struggled for freedom; that, in utter ignorance of the language, customs and traditions of the people, they have deeply wounded their feelings and dignity." Specifically, he accused the military authorities of having "unlawfully discriminated against the Cuban people" in favor of their friends from the United States; of having "used patronage at the expense of the public treasury to gain supporters"; of having done little, if anything, to revive the Cuban economy; and of having done all within their power to suppress the Cuban desire for independence. Cisneros conceded that much had been achieved in the way of sanitation, but criticized the fact that so much had been spent for this purpose, and caustically noted that more had been spent for the protection of American troops against yellow fever than for the Cubans since the islanders were immune to the disease anyway. He accused American officers, soldiers, and functionaries of "generally assuming an air of offensive superiority and acting as if the people had no rights which the Military Government was bound to respect," and insisted that General Wood set the example for this obnoxious conduct by his own overbearing attitude toward the Cubans and his practice of overriding all laws which stood in his way.[53]

Wood dismissed Cisneros' complaints. The American Occupation had only one purpose: to achieve a "stable government" in Cuba, and the Cuban people had to be forced, rather than persuaded, to do what was necessary to achieve that goal. When asked to define what he meant by a "stable government," he wrote:

> The people ask me what we mean by a stable government in Cuba. I tell them when money can be borrowed at a reasonable rate of interest and when capital is willing to invest in the Island, a condition of stability will be reached.[54]*

By this criterion, Wood's administration was a great success. For, as we shall now see, American capitalists not only invested in Cuba, but by the time the Occupation was over, were well on the way to dominating its economic life.

---

* Wood had still another definition: "When the people ask me what I mean by stable government, I tell them 'money at six per cent'. . . ." (Wood to Root, Feb. 6, 1900, Elihu Root Papers, Library of Congress.)

## CHAPTER XXI

# U.S. Economic Penetration of Cuba During the Occupation

SHORTLY AFTER THE OUTBREAK of the Spanish-American War, an American newspaper editor predicted that victory for "Cuba Libre" would benefit the United States more than Cuba, for "the Americans will make the money."[1] About the same time, the New York *World* predicted "a new invasion of Cuba" following the war. It would not be an invasion of soldiers and sailors, but of United States businessmen and investors. It predicted, too, that "whatever may be decided as to the political future of Cuba, its industrial and commercial future will be directed by American enterprise and stimulated with American capital."[2] In his book, *Our Island Empire,* published in 1899, Charles Morris wrote: "To the United States, among the chief advantages of the liberation of Cuba will be a commercial one." Cuba now offered rich fields for investment and greatly expanded markets.[3]

These predictions were to come true. Even before the Spanish flag was down in Cuba, U.S. business interests set out to make their influence felt.* Merchants, real estate agents, stock speculators, reckless ad-

---

* Fitzhugh Lee, it will be recalled, had urged American capitalists to invest in Cuba even before the United States intervened. Once the war was over, he called for speedy action by his associates before other American capitalists gobbled up the best franchises. In December, 1898, he wrote to Daniel S. Lamont: "There is more money along there now than any place I know of, and does not seem to have attracted the attention of any one. . . . If a *few* of us can pick up these [real estate] properties now, and build the trolley line, there are millions in it. Do give this prompt consideration and let me hear from you. . . ." (Fitzhugh Lee to Daniel S. Lamont, December 3, 1898, Daniel S. Lamont Papers, Library of Congress.)

To get in on the ground floor even when there was still no immediate prospect for profits, motivated P. D. Armour, G. F. Swift, Nelson Morris, and

venturers, and promoters of all kinds of get-rich schemes flocked to Cuba by the thousands. Seven syndicates battled each other for control of the franchises for the Havana Street Railway, which were finally won by Percival Farquhar, representing the Wall Street interests of New York. Thus simultaneously with the military occupation began what an on-the-spot observer in Cuba called "another occupation—that of commercial occupation. Spokesmen for the McKinley Administration not only conceded this was taking place, but predicted it would bring about the annexation of Cuba. "As American capital and American enterprise make their way over the island, the Cubans will be bound more closely to this government and this will lead to a desire for admission to the Union of the States." [4]

Even American businessmen who stayed at home were assured that they would benefit from the military occupation of Cuba. The American army in the island, General Brooke proudly announced, was an advertiser for American products. In a letter to the National Business League, he pointed out that the army made known American products just as the distribution of American supplies to the needy Cubans made "many people . . . accustomed to a number of American products they never heard of before; and naturally, a demand for these products may arise." The fact that all discriminating duties in favor of Spain had been removed during the Occupation and Spanish monopolies abolished, Brooke added, opened the door for American products which "will most quickly gain a foothold and continue in demand." [5]

Most of the American businessmen, financiers and speculators who came to Cuba early in the Occupation were seeking franchises and contracts. The War Department had at its disposal franchises, grants, and all kinds of concessions, and the man at the head of the Department, business-minded Secretary of War Russell A. Alger, was inclined to dispose of them with a free hand.* In Cuba, this policy had the support of most of the military commanders, especially Leonard Wood.

---

Thomas J. Lipton jointly to seek to erect "immense cold storage plants in Santiago and Havana." As one packer put it: "While the natives of Cuba do not as yet require very much meat, we hope to educate them so that they will require some of our products and then we shall have attained the end we desire and created a demand for our goods." (Springfield *Republican*, Dec. 14, 1898.)

\* In the Philippines the military government began in September, 1898 to issue licenses to American firms.

The military governor of Santiago openly encouraged the invasion of American capitalists. One American reporter related after an interview with Wood: "He regards the future of Cuba as most promising. Its mineral wealth in copper, iron, asbestos, manganese, petroleum, coal, and possibly gold, has been little suspected; while its forests and arable lands offer large returns to wise investors." [6] The *Lumbermen's Review*, organ of the American lumber industry agreed with Wood's evaluation of the importance of the forests of Cuba, and, as early as June, 1898, observed: "The moment Spain drops the reins of government in Cuba and trade relations are re-established with the States, the moment will arrive for American lumber interests to move into the island for the products of Cuban forests. Cuba still possesses 10,000,000 acres of virgin forest abounding in valuable timber . . . nearly every foot of which would be saleable in the United States and bring high prices." [7]

By the second week of February, 1899, barely six weeks after the formal opening of the American Occupation, the process of disposing of franchises, railway grants, street car line concessions, electric light monopolies and similar privileges in Cuba to American financial syndicates and individual capitalists was about to begin in earnest. "The franchise carpetbaggers are knocking at the doors of the War Department, where they have somehow the notion that everything yields to political 'pull,' " reported a keen student of American business.[8] The War Department had created a new board for this purpose, headed by General Robert P. Kennedy of Ohio, and the group was set to leave for Cuba to look over the situation and then fill applications for concessions.[9] (Puerto Rico was also to be surveyed for the purpose of granting applications by American investors for concessions in that island.) Even before it departed for Cuba, the board was engaged in processing applications. On February 10, 1899, the Washington *Evening Star* broke the story that members of the board "were busy to-day with a number of clerks, classifying and filing applications and concessions and receiving personal calls with these matters . . . [such as] the sale or gift of franchises, either local or interprovincial; railway grants, street-car line concessions, electric light and other municipal monopolies."

When this scheme to divide up Cuba's resources came to the attention of Senator J. B. Foraker, he decided to act. The Ohio Senator, it will be remembered, was convinced that the Occupation of Cuba— which he considered illegal and unwarranted—had the domination of the island by American capitalists as its main purpose, and that if the plan to allot franchises to these interests proceeded without interference, it would "make our withdrawal from the island an impossibility."[10] He therefore decided to interfere and to tie the two issues together: prohibit franchises and end the Occupation, leaving Cuba free to determine its own destiny economically and politically. On February 28, in the Senate, Foraker introduced an amendment to the current army appropriation bill: the first section forbade the granting of "franchises or concessions of any kind whatever" in Cuba, by the United States or its authorities, for the duration of the American Occupation; the second part declared that, "the pacification of the island of Cuba having been accomplished," the President was authorized to withdraw the army and "leave the government and control of the island to its people."[11] The second part was eliminated by the Senate Committee on Appropriations so that the Senate only considered the section relating to franchises or other concessions.

Defending his measure in the Congressional debate, Foraker argued that if the plan of granting franchises got under way and American economic penetration obtained a solid foothold, "it means that the United States will not get out of Cuba in a hundred years." Even though his proposal to accomplish this had been eliminated, the Ohio Senator came out for a speedy end to American Occupation and early self-government for the Cubans. Most Administration spokesmen, led by Orville H. Platt and Mark Hanna, urged defeat of the Foraker Amendment, arguing that it was unnecessary, since there was never any intention of giving away franchises in Cuba; and to say otherwise, through a Congressional measure, would reflect on the honor of the Administration. This did not carry much weight since the Kennedy Board had been appointed by the Administration for the precise purpose of granting franchises.

Foraker received the support of anti-imperialist Republicans and Democrats, and of the politicians, like the pro-imperialist Henry Cabot Lodge, who feared public reaction if they openly supported giving away franchises in Cuba. While Senator Teller did not agree with Foraker that the free grant of franchises would indefinitely delay the end of the Occupation, he was convinced "that such franchises could outlive our military occupation," and, on that ground, supported the Amendment.[12]

The Foraker Amendment, passed by the Senate by a vote of 47 to 11, stated that "No property franchises, or concessions of any kind whatever, shall be granted by the United States, or by any other military or other authority whatever in the Island of Cuba during the occupation thereof by the United States." [13]

Foraker noted that his sponsorship of the anti-franchise measure led to bitter attacks upon him by "a lot of thieves . . . [who] were put off by this amendment from designs they had in the island." [14]* But they were only temporarily "put off." On December 19, 1900, a Cuban visitor to the United States reported that American capitalists "evade the Foraker law by various tricks." Cuba was being taken over economically by United States business interests who, "without boldly violating the letter of the Foraker law are contemptuous of its spirit." [15]

The Foraker Amendment did cut short many plans by fly-by-night speculators for great wealth. But it did not prevent leading American industrialists and financiers from taking over railroads, mines, and sugar properties, nor did it stop the military government from aiding them in these ventures. The military government held that mining claims were not concessions, and that there was no objection to a person or company buying land or building a railroad. The Amendment prevented neither the cancellation of a dock franchise granted by the Spanish government and the turning it over to American capitalists, nor the validating of a contract between the Pan-American Express Company, an American-dominated corporation, and the Cuban railroads. It did not stop the military government from letting contracts for public works to Americans, pushing aside all other bidders, nor the grant of a ten-year monopoly to the Jai-Alai Company which sought to introduce into Cuba a professional type of handball.[16]

While he was military governor, Wood was a strong partisan of making as many concessions as possible in spite of the Foraker Amendment. "I am disregarding it," he wrote to Root on December 22, 1900. Nevertheless, he complained that he was liimted in the number of

---

* Foraker referred especially to a series of attacks upon him by Herman H. Kohlsatt, editor and publisher of the Chicago *Times-Herald,* accusing the Ohio Senator, among other things, of having received bonds from the Cuban *Junta* to lobby for recognition of the Cuban Republic prior to the declaration of war against Spain. (Chicago *Times-Herald,* June 4, 1899.) Foraker replied, calling the charge "a tissue of falsehoods." (*Ibid.,* June 9, 1899.)

"concessions" he could grant American capitalists, and urged repeal of the Amendment. "The Foraker Resolution must be revoked if possible." [17]

Even with the Foraker Amendment, at least $30,000,000 in American capital was invested in Cuba during the military occupation.[18] Viewing this development, the American historian John Clark Redpath commented in the summer of 1899 that "the idea that we are in Cuba on a philanthropic and humane mission has gone to join the other misplaced, absurd and hypocritical pretexts which history has flung with a lavish hand into limbo near the moon." [19]

Shortly after the end of the Spanish-American War, Gonzalo de Quesada spoke at a banquet in New York City attended by leading American politicians and capitalists. He emphasized the great prospects Cuba held for the investment of capital, and stressed the need for developing the Cuban railroad system, particularly in the eastern part of the island, culminating in a railroad uniting East and West. Present at the banquet was an American-born, naturalized Englishman, Sir William Van Horne, builder of the Canadian Pacific Railroad. On the return trip to Washington, Van Horne and Quesada struck up a conversation, and the railroad magnate promised to look into the subject the Cuban had raised at the banquet.[20] In February, 1900, having retired from the presidency of the Canadian Pacific, Van Horne went to Cuba on a vacation, accompanied by George B. Hopkins, an American business man. Van Horne was immediately reminded of Quesada's appeal for a railroad line in eastern Cuba.* He found that while the western end of the island had a fairly adequate network of tracks, east of the city of Santa Clara there were only a few short and disconnected lines. Crops had to be taken over wretched dirt roads, which in the rainy season became rivers of mud. The taking of the crops to market overland from eastern Cuba was prohibitive.

On March 14, 1900, Hopkins wrote to Senator Spooner of Wisconsin:

---

* In 1909, Van Horne wrote to Quesada that "it was because of you that I was for the first time attracted to Cuba." ("Archivo de Gonzalo de Quesada, Epistolario I," *Academia de la Historia de Cuba*, La Habana, 1948, p. 82. For an uncritical treatment of Van Horne, see Herminio Portell Vilá, "Van Horne, el Creador del Ferrocarril Central de Cuba," *Bohemia*, 28 de diciembre de 1952, pp. 104-13.)

> Both Sir William and myself were struck favorably with the fine opportunity offered for building a trunk line Railroad right through the middle of Cuba down to Santiago with several lateral branches to the northern and southern seaport towns. . . . If not as a commercial proposition it should be done immediately for military purposes.
>
> As soon as we returned to New York we put the matter in shape and found no difficulty in interesting capitalists to furnish the money provided Sir William Van Horne who retired from the Presidency of the Canadian Pacific last year would build the Road, which he has agreed to do and invest largely in it of his own money. The others interested are such well known men as James J. Hill, John W. MacKey, General Dodge, E. J. Benvind, Samuel Thomas, Levi P. Morton, and other names equally well known in finance. . . . *Our company is purely an American affair. We were strongly urged to go to London with it, but declined because we believed that American capital should build this Road and that it could easily be raised here by the proper parties.*
>
> *We mean business and not a thing in Cuba should be allowed to get away from Americans.* It is by far the most valuable piece of land that I have ever seen. . . . Commercial interests now and always must favor annexation. *Carry the present conditions, or any decent conditions along for comparatively a short time and commercial interests will have become so powerful that they can dictate and will dictate the final policy of the whole people.* . . .[21]

It is clear that so far as leading American capitalists were concerned, not only would the proposed railroad provide lucrative profits, but also greatly increase American influence in Cuba, stimulate further investment and trade, and pave the way for outright American economic and political control of the island.*

"Cuba's Railroads to be Controlled by Syndicate of American Capitalists," blared the headlines of many American newspapers in the summer of 1900.[22] Formed in April, 1900, under a New Jersey charter, the Cuba Company began the surveys for the railroad and starting acquiring right-of-way property. Van Horne and his associates had thus far not bothered about the Foraker Amendment, since they had operated on the basis that the measure did not forbid the buying of

---

* General Brooke was frequently criticized in the American press because he was said to have allowed English and other European capitalists to get concessions in Cuba. (Cf. *Boston Advertiser*, July 1, 1899 and other newspapers in July, 1899 in "Cuba Annexation.")

land and building a railway on it without a franchise. Van Horne told a reporter for the New York *Sun* in Havana that though he had "no concession to build the line," he expected "no opposition" from the Administration.²³* Actually, Van Horne had been assured, after a personal interview with McKinley, that it was perfectly legal to build a railway without a franchise. But, under the Foraker Amendment, it would be necessary to get governmental authority to cross public roads and bridge streams and rivers. As was to be expected, General Wood came to the rescue. An enthusiastic partisan of the railroad as a means of furthering American control of the island, he appealed to Elihu Root for assistance. Root hit upon the idea of the "revocable permit"; the company would be issued such permits authorizing it to cross roads and bridge streams. Furthermore, Wood was authorized to use the power of eminent domain to condemn lands for the railroad.²⁴ Foraker also agreed to the "revocable permit," although he would not accept Wood's proposal that, in the interest of the railroad syndicate, the Amendment bearing his name be repealed. The Cuba Company would have to go ahead in the hope of getting a regular franchise from the Republic of Cuba when the independent government was set up.²⁵

Since most of the Van Horne group doubted that there would ever be a Republic of Cuba, the Cuba Company went full speed ahead. (The *New York Times* reported that Van Horne and his associates "do not undertake to say what the probabilities are of Cuban independence or of annexation," but that most of them "are betting on annexation."²⁶) The Cuba Central Railroad began to operate in December, 1902, just two years after the work commenced. The railroad was of considerable importance to Cuba, since now for the first time land communication existed between Santiago and the West, and bulk crops could go economically to market from the interior of the eastern province. But, as Hopkins had predicted to Senator Spooner, the railroad also faciiltated American economic control over Cuba—for the shippers of bulk crops were chiefly a few powerful sugar companies owned or controlled by American capitalists.²⁷

As might be expected, the principal objective of United States control was the Cuban sugar industry. The process was facilitated by

---

* The *Sun* headlined the interview, "Road Without Franchise." (Dec. 8, 1900.)

the war. Many Cuban farmers, planters and mill owners were forced to abandon their rural properties in favor of cities because of destruction, misery, danger, and the reconcentration policy. Subsequently, many of them lost not only possession but even title to their lands. Others were forced to sell at any price they could get. In September, 1898, Henry Clews notified American investors that "the numerous owners of ruined estates [in Cuba] will be in the market as sellers of their properties."[28] All this cleared the way for foreign investors, principally American, to create huge concentrated holdings.[29]

A second factor in this development was the absence of agricultural credit for many who still held possession of their land. Cuba had few banks; farm loans were impossible to obtain, and the interest rates were prohibitively high.[30]

The entire economic and social history of Cuba after the War would have been different if the miiltary occupation had followed a policy of assisting the small farmers and planters to resume production. As early as November, 1898, an agent for the Cuban Relief Committee emphasized that such a policy was the key to the reconstruction of the Cuban economy. "With seeds and farming utensils and some cash to buy work horses or cattle, the problem would be solved in a very short time," he predicted.[31] But nothing was done, and the Cuban agriculturists, planter and peasant alike, were left to their own devices.[32] However, in May, 1899, General Wilson urged Brooke to appropriate $20,000 a month to each province to be used for loans to enable small farmers to purchase tools, seed and work animals. The loans would be limited to $400 to any one individual, and the funds would come from Cuban revenues. Brooke rejected the proposal, arguing that the loans would never be repaid and that agricultural credit was no field for the government to enter. Rather than involve the government in the loan policy, he favored giving supplies to the farmers as "an outright gift." But Washington turned thumbs down on the idea of gifts to Cuban farmers. The result was that nothing was done during Brooke's administration to solve this crucial problem.[33]*

---

* Albert G. Robinson regards this as the most serious mistake of the first year of occupation. (*Cuba and the Intervention*, New York, 1905, pp. 87-100, 130.) After he returned home from Cuba, he wrote angrily: "Those of us who have seen Cuban peasants scraping a shallow furrow in the ground with a piece of bent iron barrel hoop in order to plant a little seed, and have seen the

Wood, too, rejected Wilson's plan of extending small government loans to needy farmers and planters. Not even the most pro-American planters were to be assisted financially. This led Perfecto Lacoste, the Cuban Secretary of Agriculture, Commerce, and Industry, to accuse the military government of ignoring the most pressing need of large numbers of the population. Writing in an official report in the spring of 1901, he noted that Cuban planters had tried repeatedly to get the government of intervention to help them rebuild their war-devastated properties, but they had failed.* Whatever had been "accomplished in the way of reconstruction" was "due exclusively to the personal efforts of the planters." Lacoste pointed out that there was not a single credit institution in Cuba to meet the needs of the planters, and concluded that "up to the present time nothing has ever been done toward the improvement of our agricultural situation by the Military Government." [34]

Wood was unimpressed by this critical analysis. He continued to turn a cold shoulder to all proposals to assist Cuban small farmers and planters through government loans. "There has been considerable thoughtless talk in Cuba about making loans to aid agriculturists," he commented coldly in 1902. "It is not believed that any such policy is either wise or desirable." [35] Thus the military government which spent $9,700,000 for sanitation and $5,800,000 for public works during the

---

patient endurance with which, destitute of resources and facilities, the Cuban people have been laboring for maintenance, know where lies the credit for what they have accomplished." The United States deserved none of this credit, for it had done nothing to assist the Cubans to reconstruct their economy. (*The State*, June 5, 1902.)

* On September 28, 1899, Perfecto Lacoste, as President of the Association of Landowners and Agriculturalists of Cuba, petitioned General Brooke to authorize the military government to distribute "oxen and farm implements in the aid of agriculture." On October 7, Brigadier-General Chafee replied for Brooke, informing Lacoste that the proposal was "impracticable." He added: "The owners of large estates have in their properties an amount of wealth on which credit may be obtained for supplying all needful cattle and farm implements. This is not so with the small farmers, and if it seemed possible to the Military Governor for action to be taken in this matter, it could be done only in favor of the poorer class of small proprietors and responsible tenants, all of whom should be men having a family to support." (A. Chafee to Perfecto Lacoste, October 7, 1899, Records of the United States Military Government of Cuba, National Archives.) This touching solicitude for the welfare of the small, poor farmers of Cuba meant very little since the military government decided not to assist any agriculturists no matter how desperate the need.

Occupation[36]—money derived from Cuba's revenues—would not spend a single penny to aid the needy farmers and planters even though these funds, too, would come from the island's revenues.

There is an explanation for this contrast. Robert Porter had reported in 1898, following the study of conditions in the island for the Administration, that manufacturing in Cuba was very limited and could not be widely extended until the sanitary conditions of industrial centers were improved. American capital would not invest largely in these centers until the danger from epidemics was eliminated.[37] To a man like Wood who defined a stable government in Cuba as one under which capital was willing to invest in the island, money spent on sanitation was perfectly reasonable. But money spent to aid needy farmers and planters was a different matter.

In criticizing the military government's refusal to aid agriculturists, the Planters' Association of Cuba declared bitterly: "Cuba should be for the Cubans, but Cuban lands will now pass into the hands of foreigners."[38] It was an accurate prediction. Farmers and planters, impoverished by the war, facing bankruptcy, and lacking capital to reconstruct their property, were forced to sell their land for a pittance —seven and one half cents an acre.[39] Much of this land was not put to immediate use but held either for speculative purposes or for future exploitation. William Van Horne, hoping to populate Oriente and Camagüey with small farmers, to guarantee profits for the Cuba Central Railroad, watched this development with alarm. He asked Wood to institute a system of land taxation which would be "the best safeguard against holding lands in disuse for speculative purposes."[40] But this advice was ignored. Wood advocated large land grants and the cultivation of sugar in particular.

On board a ship bound for Cuba in 1899, Charles T. Andrews met Congressman R. B. Hawley of Texas. Andrews noted that Hawley, "the lone Republican representative of the Lone Star State . . . represents New York capitalists in establishing sugar plantations in northern Cuba."[41] After he left Andrews, Hawley met with Mario García Menocal, a Cornell-trained engineer who had served with distinction in the Liberating Army and had recently been appointed chief of Havana's police department by General Brooke. At García Menocal's suggestion, Hawley bought up 66,000 acres of land in the vicinity of Puerto Padre, a harbor on the north coast of Cuba for himself and the New York capitalists he represented. At Puerto Padre, the syndicate built the largest sugar-mill that had been constructed in Cuba up to this time, the first 12-roller mill in the island, with an initial capacity of 200,000 bags of sugar. (This was ten percent of the entire Cuban crop in 1900.) On March 24, 1901, the Louisville *Courier-Journal* headlined the following news:

## MAMMOTH SUGAR PLANT TO BE ESTABLISHED IN CUBA

*Americans Will Control. May Be First Step Toward Large Combination. Big Contracts Awarded.*

The story underneath the headlines told of the formation of the Chaparra Sugar Company of Cuba, with offices in New York City, with former Congressman Hawley as president, and in which H. H. Howell & Co. and Theodore Havemeyer were largely interested. "The company has acquired 66,000 acres of land in the eastern portion of Cuba. Nearly 10,000 acres of this land are under cultivation, while on the rest the work of planting sugar cane will be immediately begun. This enormous planting is without precedent in the history of Cuba."

The mill of the Chaparra Sugar Company began operation in 1902, under the management of García Menocal, who remained in charge of the Hawley interests in Cuba until his election as president of the Cuban Republic in 1912.

Hawley and his New York capitalist associates also formed companies to restore two other sugar properties: Mercedita, a mill on Cabanas Bay, sixty miles west of Havana, and Tinguaro, a 7,000-acre estate in Matanzas province. In 1901 the Hawley syndicate added a refinery at Cárdenas, the only one remaining in Cuba, to their holdings. The Hawley group spent about $7,500,000 in their Cuban enterprises. In 1906 all of the mills were consolidated into the Cuban-American Sugar Company and listed in the New York stock market.[42]

While the Hawley group's operations were the most extensive during the Occupation, they were not the only ones. Under the headline, "Big Investment in Cuba," the *Daily People* of August 5, 1900 carried the following dispatch from Baltimore:

> The United Fruit Company of this city, according to report, has invested $300,000 in sugar land and the machinery necessary

to manufacture centrifugal sugar in Cuba. This is the largest investment made in the islands since Americans became interested in its development.

Ten thousand acres of land have been purchased in the vicinity of Sama, Banes and Gibara, part of the province of Santiago, in the northeastern section of the island.

Many tons of machinery have been sent to the island, and more will be forwarded at once. Foundations for the cane-grinding mills have been built by American workmen near the coast. Wharves will be erected and vessels chartered or built to bring the sugar to the United States.

In 1901, a syndicate headed by United Fruit Company's president, Andrew W. Preston, bought 1,900,000 acres on Nyre Bay, at a cost of $400,000. While the company was planting bananas elsewhere in the Caribbean, in Cuba it was raising sugar cane.[43]

The Francisco Sugar Company was founded when the McCahan sugar refining interests of Philadelphia joined the Rionda family in 1901 in developing the 80,000 acre estate, Francisco, on the southern coast of Cuba. Toward the end of 1901, an American company, backed by Stuyvesant Fish, a railroad financier, bought the central Constancia near Cienfuegos and combined it with the Gramercy refinery in Louisiana.[44]

Meanwhile, the Atkins property of Soledad had recovered from the war and increased its operations. Atkins was an influential figure in the American Sugar Refinery Company, the Sugar Trust;* and Henry D. Havemeyer, president of the Trust, was already the owner of a *central* in Trinidad, and had interests in the sugar factories at Cappawa and Santa Cruz.† The Sugar Trust had an interest in the

---

* The American Sugar Refinery Company, which came to be known as the Sugar Trust, was originally organized in 1887 as a result of a merger of all the important refining interests in New York and Brooklyn, controlling fifteen plants in all. Henry D. Havemeyer, its president, was closely linked to Wall Street.

† In his study of the Sugar Trust, Jack Mullins writes: "Henry Havemeyer and the Sugar Trust began investing large sums after 1898 in a number of firms which controlled Cuban plantations or imported sugar from Cuba. The Trust early acquired control of Zaldo and Company and the Havana firms of 'Almacenes de Depósito' and 'Almacenes de Hacendados.' They also followed the customary practice of American investors in Cuba of furnishing Cuban companies and planters with supplies and cooperage materials on credit. They also lent money at high rates of interest, with the sugar crop as collateral. As

McCahan refineries of Philadelphia which, as we have seen, controlled the Francisco Sugar Company. Already, moreover, the Sugar Trust was the principal purchaser of Cuban raw sugar since little of it was now refined on the island.[45]

It is impossible to determine the place of American capital in the sugar industry of Cuba by the end of the Occupation. But in 1905 there were 29 mills owned by American citizens, producing 21 percent of the sugar.[46] With the exception of the Atkins properties at Soledad, and a few others which had existed before the war, most of these figures are accounted for by American corporations which had entered the Cuban field during the military occupation. Large mills were costly to build and run—the great sugar mills cost from $250,00 to $1,000,000 —and even wealthy Spaniards and the few well-to-do Cubans lacked the capital. Corporate enterprise, foreign-owned and managed, provided temporary relief. Soon long-term financing brought American bankers into the picture. They purchased properties and merged them with others they had taken over during the Occupation.[47]

Complete American dominance of the sugar industry was thus on the way to becoming a reality. Already, too, the latifundium which Ramiro Guerra y Sánchez calls "Cuba's tragedy" was becoming a reality. Guerra wrote in 1927:

> For four centuries the Cuban people had been settling the country little by little, clearing it and making it a healthy place to live in. They imported its principal commercial crops; they adapted cattle and domestic livestock to its climate; they found suitable locations for towns and cities on its coasts and in its interior; they courageously defended the island against invasion; they allotted and divided its land among farmers; they laid out and built its modern railways as well as its old but useful country roads; they fought for liberty and independence in the hope of establishing a vigorous republic that would be shared by and would serve all; and, thanks to the genius of a Cuban—Finlay—not only Cuba but the whole world was freed of one of its worst plagues.
>
> When all this toil of centuries seemed to be almost completed and fruits could at last be enjoyed by their children, the sugar latifundium, which had ruined the West Indies with its two formi-

---

early as 1895, the Trust executive committee authorized loans of $500,000 each to two companies." (Jack Simpson Mullins, "The Sugar Trust: Henry O. Havemeyer and the American Sugar Refining Company," unpublished Ph.D. thesis, University of South Carolina, 1964, p. 182.)

dable instruments, foreign capital and imported cheap labor, invaded the island. Its appearance marked the beginning of the wholesale destruction of our small and medium-sized properties and the reduction of our rural landowners and independent farmers, backbone of our nation, to the lowly condition of a proletariat being stifled by that economic asphyxiation which afflicts the country today from one end to the other.[48]

This was the legacy of American military occupation and the refusal to permit the use of the funds belonging to the Cuban people to assist the small farmers and planters to retain their land and rebuild their properties, damaged or destroyed during the Revolution.

Behind the slogan "Let us Americanize Cuba," there began a takeover of Cuban land which, Leland H. Jenks points out, "reproduced upon a limited scale, all the phenomena which characterized population movements in our own West."[49] Large haciendas for raising cattle were purchased, as were tobacco *vegas*. But the greatest expansion was in agricultural settlements, promoted in the United States by speculators who promised the immigrants of Cuba that "after a few short years of slight hardships and trifling deprivations, a life of luxurious comfort lay before them."[50] On September 27, 1898, even before the American occupation of Havana began, the "Island of Cuba Real Estate Company," a U.S.-owned corporation, opened business to deal in country lots.[51] Soon after the occupation began, notices like the following began to be featured by the American press:

> The great estates of "Tinguaia" and "San Rafael" in Manzanillo, Cuba, have become the property of a United States Senator. . . . It is said to be the intention of this senator to improve the estates and colonize many American families on this land.
> The vast plantation of "Carbonica" in Holguin has been sold to an American company which in a few days will begin the work of constructing many modern buildings for the purpose of bringing down from the United States several hundred American families.[52]

These reports led the Rochester (N, Y.) *Democrat-Chronicle* to warn the Cuban people to cease being "indolent" or else they would find their country taken over by "the energetic American."[53] It failed to add that the Americans were most "energetic" in picking up land at low prices from people who were without means, and for whom the

Occupation government refused to provide loans so that they could develop their property. Although Manuel Sanguily, the Cuban patriot, warned against permitting Cuban land to pass into the hands of the Americans, predicting that there would follow "the inevitable influence of the attrition, discrediting, and adulteration of our language and, finally, of the legislation and the ultimate destiny of the Cuban nation,"[54] many poverty-stricken farmers and small planters had no choice but to sell. By 1903, there were 37 American agricultural settlements in Cuba—in all the provinces except Pinar del Río—and between seven and ten percent of the entire area of the island, the most fertile part, was owned by Americans.[55]

The biggest American land scheme involved the Isle of Pines, an island a few miles off the southern coast. Much of the land here was taken over for a trifling sum by American development corporations. Having resold land to Americans, one United States company on the island even promoted a revolution in 1905, hoping to win annexation to the United States and free access to its market. Although nothing came of the venture, it served to recall how so much of the land of Cuba was taken over by Americans during the Occupation.[56]

"The American tobacco trust has large interests in the island of Cuba and is now building the largest factory in Havana," a visitor returning from the island reported in the fall of 1900.[57] Formerly a Spanish monopoly, the tobacco industry came, during the Occupation, under the domination of the U.S. tobacco monopoly. In 1899 the Havana Commercial Company, organized in New York City, bought up 12 cigar factories and one cigarette factory in Havana. The American company then took over the leaf-importing business of F. García Brothers and Company, bought a number of tobacco plantations, and by December, 1900, had advanced up to $1,300,000 to Cuban planters. Its success and huge profits stimulated the Tobacco Trust in the United States—the American Tobacco Company—to invade the Cuban cigar business through its cigar affiliate, the American Cigar Company. When the Havana Commercial Company was absorbed in May, 1902 by the Tobacco Trust, after it had gained control of the Henry Clay and Block Co. Ltd., 90 percent of the export trade in Havana cigars was concentrated in the hands of the American Cigar Company. This comprised nearly one half of the entire manufacture of cigars and cigarettes in Cuba.[58]

Before the Spanish-Cuban-American War, much U.S. capital had gone into Cuban mining. The first occupation troops landed on the site of American-owned manganese and nickel mines which had supplied material for the armor plate of the invading vessels. When General Wood was in command in Santiago, he arranged for Charles M. Dobson, a mining expert, to examine the metalliferous deposits of the province. Dobson found deposits of manganese sufficient to supply forty percent of the demand of the United States, as well as deposits of lead, copper, zinc and other minerals of commercial importance. The production of Bessemer ore, moreover, promised particularly rich rewards. For more than 130 miles to the foothills on each side of the Sierra Maestra mountains, there were continuous deposits of iron ore of varying quality and volume. Dobson reported that the deposits of Bessemer could be exploited profitably, but it would require corporations equipped with the necessary capital to open the ore deposits, build railroads, and import equipment for the transportation of the ore to the seaboard.[59]

The report naturally aroused great interest among American capitalists, particularly the Bethlehem Steel Company of Pennsylvania, already operating in Cuba. In 1899, the Juragui Iron Company, controlled by Bethlehem Steel, acquired possession of the iron deposits of Daiquirí. Bethlehem shortly also took over the Spanish-American Iron Company, and aided by concessions from the military authorities, acquired valuable iron ore deposits in Santiago province.

In 1899 the Boston manganese mines in the Christo district were bought by the Standard Manganese Company of New York. The Isabelita manganese mine in Oriente was taken over by a group of New York capitalists, the Ponopol Mining and Transportation Company in the eastern Sierra Maestra by a Philadelphia syndicate, and the Augusta Luis Manganese mines by a New Jersey corporation. The Caridad manganese mines were in the hands of the Federal Steel Company, an American corporation.

By the end of the Occupation, at least 80 percent of the export of Cuba's minerals were in American hands, the greatest part in the control of the Bethlehem Steel Company.[60]

Under Spanish rule, no effort had been made to establish an adequate banking system in Cuba. The Banco Español de la Habana (later Banco de la Isla de Cuba) was established in 1850, but was principally a Havana bank and not of sufficient size to be useful except locally.

This left the door open during the Occupation for foreign banking interests. During Wood's administration, the North American Trust Company of New York was brought into Cuba to act as the occupying government's fiscal agent, and it assumed some banking functions. In July, 1901, this company began to operate under the name of Banco Nacional de Cuba. Its unique position as fiscal agent for the Occupation authorities enabled it to expand throughout the island. Soon after it was established, the Banco Nacional organized branches in seven principal cities, and contracted with correspondent institutions in the others. American banking houses were later to exercise full control over Cuba's economic life, but a real beginning toward that role had already been made during the Occupation.[61]

In general, American economic penetration of Cuba during the Occupation was only a prelude to what was to come later. But even then the foundation had been laid down. Indeed, some of the men who came with the Occupation army were to return after their discharge, and together with other American enterprisers in Cuba, gain increasing control over the island's economic affairs.* In any event, the Occupation enormously accelerated control of Cuba's economic life by American capitalists. True, much of the capital invested by Americans helped to develop the island. But it is a tragic fact that, as a Foreign Policy Association study pointed out, in winning political freedom from Spain, "Cuba lost control over its economic resources." [62]

---

* One of the best examples of this group was Frank Steinhart. He came to Cuba in charge of the headquarters of General Brooks, as his private secretary. Later, he became chief clerk to General Wood. After his discharge in Havana in 1903, he was immediately appointed U.S. Consul General in Cuba and held the post until 1907. He became engaged in various enterprises, including the Havana electric railway, which later absorbed the Havana electric light system, and the Spanish bank, as well as other corporations in Cuba. (Leland H. Jenks, *Our Cuban Colony*, New York, 1928, pp. 166-74.)

## CHAPTER XXII
# The Cuban Labor Movement During the Occupation

IN SEPTEMBER, 1899 a manifesto appeared in Havana signed by a group of Cuban working class leaders. It opened: "As soon as the war in Cuba was over, the workers in this island thought that emancipation was a reality, and they believed this because they had kept constantly in their minds and hearts the words of the man whom the Cubans call 'The Apostle' [José Martí] who was the architect of liberty. Unfortunately, as everyone knows, the Spanish and Cuban workers continued to be only workers, enslaved after the emancipation as they had been before it."[1]

There was full justification for this bitter complaint. The Cuban working class which had contributed so much to the independence of their country received little recognition from the American Occupation. The same military leaders who were so lavish in disposing of Cuba's resources to American capitalists, and so ready to fill the public offices with men who had collaborated with Spain during the Revolution, looked with contempt on the working class. Leonard Wood reported that the Cubans were not good workers—sloppy, careless, without pride in their work, with exaggerated ideas of their own importance.[2] Since Wood consorted mostly with the employers—Spanish and Cuban—it is hardly surprising that he reflected their attitude.

The 1899 census revealed that the labor force in Cuba was 678,000 out of a total population of 1,572,797, or 43 percent. (This compared with the 1846 figure of 431,258 out of a total population of 896,294, or 41 percent.) Of this number, those in agriculture, fisheries and mining were 336,271: 330,271 in agriculture, 5,000 in mining, and 1,000 in fisheries. The urban working class population of 342,301 was divided into the following categories: manufacturing and mechanical industries, 97,703; trade and transportation, 81,918; professional services, 8,768, and domestic and personal services, 151,912. In order of numerical importance, the occupations were: clothing trades, tobacco trades, building trades, transportation, metal workers, foods and liquors, leather workers, printing trades, brick-masons and potters, and wood workers. The clothing trade was still largely cottage-industry. Actually, the tobacco workers was the dominant force in urban labor.

One other point about the Cuban labor force revealed by the 1899 census is worth noting: the ratio of Negro and white workers.[3]

|  | Urban | Rural |
|---|---|---|
| White | 196,647 | 198,230 |
| Negro | 117,750 | 100,967 |

Since the census of 1846, the urban labor force had increased by nearly 200,000—from 150,919 to 342,301, but the Negro labor force had only increased from 92,113 to 117,750, a decline of one third in ratio to the total labor force. In the rural labor force, the decline was even more startling: 225,835 Negroes as compared with 54,504 whites in 1846 and 100,967 Negroes to 198,230 whites in 1899. However, these statistics may not be entirely revealing, for there was a tendency in census-taking to register as white any person who could "pass for white" (*pasar por blanco*).[4] Nevertheless, it is clear that the rural labor force was now composed of nearly twice as many white as Negro workers, where previously the Negro had outnumbered the white agricultural worker in the ratio of four to one. However, while the agricultural economy was no longer based mainly on the labor of the Cuban Negro, the Negro still occupied an important place in it; and in the urban labor force, he was of considerable importance.

Unemployment was widespread when the Spanish-American War came to an end. Only a handful of industries functioned in the cities: tobacco (cigars and cigarettes), shoes, alcohol, wood, and several others. With the exception of tobacco which, unlike the sugar industry, revived quickly after the war, they employed only a few hundred workers. Unemployment, however, dropped during the early months of the Occupation, partly because of the numbers employed in sanitation and public works, and partly because of the slow but steady recovery of the economy in the island.[5] While employment improved, conditions of work did not. There were many shops in which workers labored from dawn until ten or twelve at night, with only thirty or forty minutes permitted for meals, and with only one day off every two weeks. Workers often slept where they worked, in ill-ventilated barracks completely lacking in sanitary facilities. Wages were "barely enough to furnish food to keep the workers in a state of being able to work." Apprentices were kept working for months, even years, without receiving any pay at all.[6]

In the rural areas, conditions were even worse. Living conditions for field laborers and mill workers were deplorable. Wages were often paid in scrip, redeemable only at stores operated by the employers. "The store system prevails on many plantations," went a contemporary report, "and is often so manipulated as to keep the field laborer in debt to his employer."[7] The working day was still from sunup to sundown. Unemployment was the lot of farm workers for several months of the year, for after the sugar harvest there was little work available. "He is free to give his time to other employment," noted a contemporary study, "but as this period of leisure coincides with the dull season for agricultural labor, he derives little practical benefit from this advantage."[8]

Spain left nothing that could be characterized as social legislation dealing with conditions of work. The military government did not concern itself with this problem. "There have been no laws enacted for Cuba, either by the Spanish or by the military government relating specifically to labor," Victor S. Clark observed in 1902, in a bulletin published by the United States Department of Labor.[9]* Hence the employers had a free hand in exploiting workers, and they did so, confident that they would meet with little resistance. The vast majority of the workers' organizations had been suppressed by the Spanish authori-

---

* However, General George W. Davis, military governor of Pinar del Río province, did issue an order in January, 1899 that all who worked in industry and commerce in that province "should have one day of rest a week for their own affairs." (José Rivero Muñiz, El *Movimiento Obrero durante la primera Intervención: Apuntes para la historia del proletariado en Cuba*, Universidad de Las Villas, 1961, p. 41.)

ties during the war.* Only three trade unions survived the persecution —all belonging to the tobacco industry—and they were in weakened straits.[10] Indeed, so feeble was the status of the labor movement at the beginning of the Occupation, that American capitalists planning to invest in Cuban industry were assured that there was "little organization, little class spirit among her working people." [11]

Before long, there was a change. Soon American newspapers were complaining that Cubans refused to work for rations, and were demanding money from the occupying authorities. They complained too, that "after they [the Cuban workers] passed beyond the danger of starvation they developed labor agitators." [12] Some of the workers were Cubans returning to the island from Tampa and Key West, with trade union experience in the United States, men who had participated in strike struggles. Almost from the beginning of the Occupation, strikes broke out in Cuba. The first work stoppage occurred on January 10, 1899, nine days after General Brooke took office, when the dockyard workers in Cárdenas walked out, demanding that in the future, instead of the Spanish gold dollar, they should be paid two U.S. dollars daily. The speculation in currency had so drastically reduced the value of the peso that the workers were finding it impossible to live on their wages,† especially since their employment was tied to the sugar harvest

---

* For information on the Cuban labor movement before the outbreak of the Second War for Independence, see Philip S. Foner, *History of Cuba and Its Relations with the United States,* (New York, 1963, vol. II, pp. 136-48, 300-04.)

† Prior to the Spanish-American War, Cuba was part of the Spanish monetary system. But as was the case of several Latin American countries, coin of other realms circulated at various and varying values relative to Spanish currency. During the American Occupation, the dollar was added to an already confused monetary system, when it was declared the only tender acceptable in payment of governmental accounts. An official rate of exchange was declared for the dollar vis-à-vis the Spanish centén and the French luis, both gold coins in wide circulation, which slightly overvalued the dollar ($4.78 for the centén and $3.83 for the luis). Only the dollar was accepted in governmental payments; the luis and centén were the mediums of exchange in the wholesale trade, and the various silver coins served as means of payment in the country for small payments, and in the retail trade.

The chaotic monetary system was a source of handsome profits to thousands of exchange houses which operated in the island and caused considerable losses to the unwary public. (Henry Christopher Wallich, "Cuban Monetary Experience, 1914-1942," unpublished Ph.D. thesis, Harvard University, 1943, p. 5; Willis Fletcher Johnson, *The History of Cuba,* New York, 1920, vol. IV, pp. 363-64.)

in the province of Matanzas, which gave them work only for three months during the year. Although the employers held out for a few days, hoping the American occupying army would come to their assistance, they were compelled to settle. While the workers did not get all they asked for, they did win wages of one and one and a half dollars in American money, which represented an increase of 100 percent in the daily wages they had been earning.[13]

Stimulated by this victory, workers throughout the island began to demand payment of wages in American money. But without organizations to back their demands, most of the efforts, even when they resulted in strikes, were not successful.

Not all of these early strikes were for payment of wages in American money. On January 16, the port workers in Havana walked out and the ferry operatives joined the strike. They demanded: wages of two pesos for a day's work which would begin at 6 in the morning and end at 5 in the afternoon; 25 centavos per hour overtime; and double pay on Sundays, holidays, and for working during the night. Since the majority of the workers were employed scarcely two weeks out of each month, the demands could hardly be called excessive. But this did not prevent General Mario García Menocal, who had just been appointed police chief of Havana, from attempting to break the strike, and only the intervention of General Brooke himself kept the former hero of the Liberating Army from succeeding in his purpose. The strike ended when the employers promised to revise the wage scale. This promise was fulfilled several months later.[14]

General Menocal was more successful as a strikebreaker a few weeks later. Early in February, 1899 the dockworkers petitioned for wages of 17 centavos gold per hour. The employers rejected the demand, and discharged the workers' leaders who had presented the petition. When the others struck, the employers called in the police. Menocal urged his men "to give the club to those who refuse to go back to work." The strikers were beaten back to their jobs, but Menocal was denounced in the Cuban press.* *El Yara* commented bitterly: "Never did any man who joined the Cuban Army think when offering

---

* In contrast to Menocal's strikebreaking role, General Rafael de Cárdenas. second in command of the police, intervened to settle a strike on the United Railways in February, 1899, with assurance of an increase in wages. (Rivero, *op. cit.*, p. 47.)

his services to the Revolution that the day would arrive when one of its chiefs, justly famed for his intelligence and valor in the difficult days of the war, would command them not to make an admirable assault of the forts as in [Victoria de] Las Tunas, but to assault, in the manner of the formers soldiers of the Spanish Army, the miserable posts of a few day laborers, who have only the strength of their uncoerceable right to esteem their personal labor." [15]

Thus, early in their battles, the Cuban workers learned that they would have to fight against not only employers and foreign rulers, but even some of the men who had fought for the independence of the island. As far as the foreign rulers were concerned, their role was quickly revealed. When the street laborers in Matanzas went on strike in March, 1899, Major Cartwright delivered a speech warning that he was continuing the operations with strikebreakers and that if any strikers interfered, "those persons would be courtmartialed and shot." [16]* In April, the railroad workers in the shops of the United Railways at La Ciénega asked for higher wages and threatened to strike if the demand was not met. General Ludlow, military governor of Havana, immediately announced that he would not "tolerate in any manner the planned interruption." The strike never occurred, and wages remained unchanged.[17]

Despite such threats, strikes continued to break out in various cities almost every day. Mostly they were for a small raise in daily wages, although some, especially among the tobacco workers, took place because employers threatened to move their shops to other communities if the workers did not accept a wage cut. In any event, most of these strikes were quickly settled with some gains for the workers.[18] Still, it was clear that without effective organization, Cuban labor could not make much headway. Short, spontaneous, unorganized and poorly-prepared strikes could not bring lasting benefits.

Gradually, the labor organizations which had been forced to suspend activity during the war reappeared, and a number came into existence for the first time.[19] If anything, there were now too many individual unions and insufficient centralization of organization. The

---

* Major Cartwright did not confine his strikebreaking to Cuban workers. When teamsters imported from the United States struck for higher wages than $40 a month and rations, the Major at once discharged them and replaced them with Cubans at $25 a month and rations. (Charles T Andrews, op. cit.)

cigar rollers of Havana, for example, were not in a single organization; there existed as many societies as there were shops, each one working by itself.[20]

Two new organizations emerged during this period: the *Partido Socialista Cubano* (Cuban Socialist Party) and the *Liga General de Trabajadores Cubanos* (General League of Cuban Workers). The Cuban Socialist Party, founded by Diego Vicente Tejera, a poet and intellectual with influence among the workers, announced its birth in a manifesto addressed "To the People of Cuba," distributed throughout Havana on March 29, 1899. The Party declared that it hoped to contribute to establishing the future Republic as "a model nation, such as was imagined by the valiant combatants who gave their lives and homes for it, a nation which, as the 'Apostle' [José Martí] was to proclaim as a slogan around the star of the new flag, the new phrase, the synthesis of love and priority: 'With all and for the good of all!' " To achieve this goal political independence was not enough. It had to be "followed immediately by social and economic advances," and eventually by "a radical transformation of the entire society"—in short, the establishment of Socialism. How was this to be accomplished: "Through propaganda and discussion, persuading and demonstrating, we will multiply our legions and the day will arrive when our ideal will be embodied, without force, by the vote of the Cubans."

Meanwhile, until Socialism was achieved, there was much work for the Cuban Socialist Party. There were injustices which had to be eliminated from Cuban society, and the miseries which cried out for alleviation. There was a crying need for the passage of laws which would "remove from the neck of the unhappy proletariat the iron hand of the exploiter, which is choking him," for the protection of women and children, the achievement of a peaceful old age for those who worked in the shops and factories, indemnification for families whose breadwinners were worn down by sickness and death, for the reduction of the hours of labor so that the worker "should not only have sufficient time to care for and enjoy his family, but also for recreation and cultivation of his mind so that he can enjoy society and life. In a word we must exalt the humble ones, raising them in dignity and well-being to the level of the privileged ones of today."

It was an ambitious program, one which correctly combined the struggle for immediate demands with the ultimate goal of a Socialist society. However, the Cuban Socialist Party made it clear that its struggle would always be a peaceful one, based on propaganda, discussion and political action by the Cuban masses once they had gained the right to vote. "We do not wish and we will not initiate class war; we are convinced that violence does not produce triumphs as complete and lasting as those produced by reason and love." Just how "the privileged ones" were to be convinced by "reason and love" to surrender their privileges was left unsaid.

"The Socialist Party is born. Long live the Socialist Party," the manifesto closed. But the Cuban Socialist Party had only a short life. It was condemned by the press despite its disavowal of class warfare and violence. Some of its leaders succumbed to the influence of the anarchist and anarcho-syndicalists, while others were weaned away by offers of positions in the occupation government. Nevertheless, the very existence of the Party, the first Socialist Party in Cuban history, was an indication of the growth of Socialist thought.[21]

On September 1, 1899, at a meeting in Havana, the General League of Cuban Workers was formed with Enrique Messonier as president and Pedro A. Navarro as secretary. (Diego Vicente Tejera was designated honorary president in recognition of his contributions to Cuban labor.) The program of the organization stressed five issues:

1. "That the Cuban workers in general should enjoy the same advantages and guarantees enjoyed by foreigners in different industries in this country."

2. "To achieve employment in all workshops of Cuban emigres forced to return to the island."

3. "To initiate a campaign in behalf of the moral and material interests of Cuban women workers."

4. "To provide for the welfare of all orphans (whether or not they were children of the Liberators) who were crowding the streets in great numbers."

5. "To be prepared for defense against every harmful element which tries to place obstacles in the path of the advance of the Cuban Republic."

The first issue grew out of a long-standing grievance: discrimination against Cuban workers in favor of Spanish immigrants. Equality for all workers was a demand which reflected a deep feeling among

Cuban workers. It was also reflected in the demand for improvement of conditions of Cuban women workers. Not only were they paid miserable wages in the occupation in which they were employed— washing trains, rolling cigarettes, and domestic service—but they were forbidden entrance into many trades. The issue concerning orphans grew out of the inadequate number of asylums, resulting in large numbers of orphans being forced to live in the streets and parks. The final demand was directed against the Cuban annexationists who favored indefinite continuation of the American occupation, and saw it terminating not in a Cuban Republic but in annexation to the United States.

Plans were set to establish branches of the League in various *barrios* (neighborhoods), and a committee was appointed to draw up a manifesto and present it to the public. It was issued on September 14, 1899, under the heading, "Al Pueblo de Cuba" (To the People of Cuba). The League, the manifesto pointed out, was "an association born of the heat of necessity, deeply felt by the Cuban worker," out of conditions which violated the principles of "justice and equity," and which it would be "oppressive and humiliating to tolerate any longer without appealing, as honorable men, to the public conscience." Thus:

> The Cuban worker in several of the most important industries of the country is denied work in favor of foreign elements who monopolize employment for their own advantage. Does any reason exist to justify this situation? We believe not.

Cuban workers had demonstrated their capacity for hard work and competence in many foreign countries, yet in their own land these qualities remained unrecognized, and they were the victims of discrimination. The manifesto listed not only the different departments of the tobacco industry to which Cubans were denied entrance, but cited other occupations in which they could only obtain the worst and least remunerative jobs. This, it insisted, was a distinct hangover of the colonial regime; the old element of Spanish *integrismo,* having lost the war, sought to continue to dominate "the social and economic field." After listing and discussing the other issues drawn up at the League's founding meeting, the manifesto closed:

> The fundamental causes for which we came into public life now being expressed, something remains to be said with regard to

our line of conduct. Legality will be our norm. In the development
of the political life of our country, we will never be an obstacle.
On the contrary, the League declares solemnly that in the achievement of the ideal of absolute independence of this beautiful land,
drenched with the blood of thousands of its sons, there will be, on
its part, only the firmest support. For this we have sacrificed
ourselves and are ready for new sacrifices. . . .[22]

While this expression of Cuban working class aspirations and
demands were being prepared, events of a far-reaching nature were
beginning to take place. Since August 27 the masons of Havana had
been on strike for higher wages and an eight-hour day. On September
7, General Juan Luiz Rivera, civil governor of Havana, made an effort
to settle the strike, but got nowhere with the employers in the building
trades. The latter, having received public assurances from General
Rafael de Cárdenas, now chief of police, that the forces under his
command were ready to protect *rompehuelgas* (strikebreakers), were in
no mood to grant the strikers' demands, especially the eight-hour day.
Meanwhile, the masons' battle was winning wide support in working-
class circles; indeed, in late August, Major Tasker H. Bliss, Collector
of Customs for Cuba under the Occupation, wrote worriedly to General
Adna R. Chaffee, Chief of Staff in Havana, that "other trades may
join in this strike out of sympathy." Bliss feared that laborers and
lightermen "who practically have the entire commerce of this Port at
their mercy," would join the strike, and he recommended abolition of
the lighterage system and the construction of landing piers "which will
enable every vessel to discharge immediately upon the wharves."[23]

On September 16, representatives of the principal labor organizations in Havana met to discuss a general strike to help the masons.
Speakers emphasized that the masons' demand for an eight-hour day
was clearly justified, and that a victory for these workers would pave
the way for a shorter working day for all Cuban workers. (At this
time, a movement for early closing of establishments and stores, many
of which stayed open twelve to fourteen hours, reflected the workers'
interest in the shorter working day.) A meeting was scheduled at the
*Círculo de Trabajadores* (Workers' Circle), to which the presidents of
all unions were invited. The purpose was to plan a general strike!

On September 19, representatives of all labor organizations in Havana, meeting at the Workers' Circle, voted unanimously to call a

general strike to begin the following morning at 6 A.M. A resolution ordering the general strike in sympathy with the masons, referred to the action as made necessary by "the constant contempt for their rights displayed by the arrogant bosses, and the indifference of the authorities to the abuse of a class which constitutes a most important part of the Cuban population, but realizes only hunger and misery." Two days later, the reasons were more fully set forth in a printed manifesto circulated throughout Havana and pasted to the walls of many buildings.* It was signed by Francisco de Armas López, Sarafín del Busto, Evaristo Estenoz, Simón Camacho, José Fraga and Juan Aller, and began with the bold statement:

> A country lacking workers is no good to anyone. The capitalists and the rich landowners need the workers, and they owe them a decent life. But this is not the case in Cuba, and as such a state of things cannot continue, we have determined to promote the struggle between the worker and capitalist. For the workers of Cuba will no longer tolerate remaining in total subjection.

Then followed the demand for the eight-hour day and a historical analysis of the movement for it, especially the struggle in the United States in the 1880's, climaxed in the Haymarket Affair of 1886:

> From the time that in Chicago seven martyrs offered their lives when they raised the red flag which inspires all the workers, we also have to raise the same symbol for this country, a country for which so many loved ones and noble companions died. . . .†

---

\* There does not appear to be in existence a copy of the original leaflet in Spanish, and even Cuban historians have had to use the English translation appearing in the report on the strike submitted to Washington by General Ludlow, military governor of Havana. (*Annual Report of Brigadier-General William S. Ludlow, United States Army, Military Governor of Havana,* "Strikes," Oct. 4, 1899, pp. 184-85.)

† As a result of a bomb explosion during a labor meeting for the eight-hour day in Chicago on May 4, 1886, eight men were arrested and sentenced to death or imprisonment. Four were hanged, one committed suicide, and three went to prison, later to be pardoned as having been, like the others, innocent. The men were tried for their opinions—they were anarchists and anarcho-syndicalists—and not for their actual connection with the actual bomb throwing. (Philip S. Foner, *History of the Labor Movement in the United States,* vol. II, New York, 1955, pp. 105-15.) Latin Americans were familiar with the Haymarket Affair because José Martí had written extensively on the subject while he was still in the United States (*See* "El proceso de los siete anarquistas de Chicago, 2 Septiembre 1886," and "un drama terrible, 13 Noviembre 1887," in *Obras Completas de José Martí,* La Habana, 1946, pp. 1736-41, 1842-63.)

And why should we not do this? Already the workers of a Republic which is a model for us and our neighbor have achieved the eight-hour day, and the totality of the right which all men should enjoy.* And if we, sons of the new America, know what a Republic is and know the rights which the workers should have, shall we consent to be the mockery of all the workers of the world? No!

How then to avoid this? By all the workers uniting in one compact body, destroying the yoke of servitude, and beginning to enjoy the life of a free and happy people.

The demand for the eight-hour day, the manifesto continued, was not a new idea even in Cuba. "But death has taken the men who have established the demand for the eight-hour day." Those who wished to change the existing situation were urged to attend a mass meeting on September 24 at the Little Square Balboa. The manifesto closed: "Workers! Come to the meeting on which depends the life or death of the workers of Cuba." [24]

Even before the manifesto was released, some workers were going out on strike in sympathy with the masons. The first to do so were the cart-drivers who, on the morning of September 20, stopped driving their carts to the wharfs in order to transfer merchandise from the docks to the different warehouses of the city and the railroad station of Villanueva. Other workers, especially those on the cars between Havana and Vedado, also joined the walkout. However, the strike at this point was far from general. Business continued as usual, and the tobacco workers, who were usually ready to show their solidarity with other workers, were still debating whether to join the strike. Only one cigar factory stopped work at this stage—"Suárez Marías"—but when the workers in this establishment met to vote on whether to join the general strike, the police moved in and broke up the meeting. The truth is that the general strike had been called with insufficient advance preparation; the General League of Cuban Workers had barely come into existence, and was hardly in a position to unite the various unions behind the masons. The manifesto was not published in any of the daily

---

* This was an exaggeration. Actually, only a small percentage of American workers by this time had gained the eight-hour day. The majority still worked nine to ten hours and many twelve hours a day. The steel workers worked twelve hours a day, seven days a week. (See Philip S. Foner, *History of the Labor Movement in the United States*, vol. III, New York, 1964, pp. 18-20.)

papers, all of which usually found space for the most trivial announcements, so that many workers still had insufficient information about the struggle shaping up.[25]

Between 4,000 and 8,000 workers gathered in the Little Square Balboa Saturday afternoon, September 24th, in response to the manifesto, making it the largest meeting held in Havana for many years. A bevy of trade union leaders addressed the gathering, urging an effective general strike in support of the masons. Finally, a committee was elected to direct the general strike—Francisco de Armas, César García, Simón Camacho, Serafín del Busto, José González Pintado, Juan Aller—and a declaration was adopted, without a single dissent, affirming the determination of the workers "to go out immediately on a general strike."

> We the workers of Havana, realizing from the first moment, the significance of the step toward progress taken by our brothers, the masons and their aides, believe it is a duty of working class solidarity to help them to sustain themselves effectively in the position in which they are placed, lending them all financial aid. Seeing, moreover, that in spite of the time that has elapsed, they have not achieved their goals, we therefore believe it necessary to offer them our further help, launching ourselves into a general strike to uphold the principle of the eight-hour day. With this efficient help which we lend them, we hope to crown the struggle with a victory for the eight-hour day, a triumph which will be written in bronze letters in the pages of the history of the working class.[26]

The action taken at the meeting revealed that support for a general strike was spreading rapidly. Indeed, on the evening following the meeting, many unions which had heretofore stayed apart from the movement, voted to walk out the next morning, among them the machinists, the firemen of the Havana ferries, the bakers and butchers, and the workers in the offices and warehouses of the railroad station. This would result in tying up a great part of the city's life.[27]

When news of this development reached General Ludlow, he immediately went into action to break the strike. Up to now, the U.S. military authorities had anxiously watched the developing struggle, but had refrained from interfering directly, believing the general strike would quickly collapse. But the tremendous gathering at the Little Square

Balboa, the militant stand in favor of a general strike unanimously adopted by the thousands at the meeting, and the decision of new groups of workers to join the walkout, caused them to abandon the wait-and-see attitude. In the early hours of September 25, General Ludlow sent a communication to the Mayor of Havana, notifying him that forces were joining together to carry through a general strike, that "seditious and disorderly language" had been used in the public meeting at the Balboa Square, and "seditious publications" distributed throughout the city. In view of these circumstances, Ludlow ordered the Mayor to arrest eleven trade union leaders and detain them until "the formulation of the proper charges against them." Mayor Perfecto Lacoste immediately jumped to do the American general's bidding, and at his order, the police proceeded to arrest all eleven of the men listed by Ludlow.[28] Thus the man who, it will be recalled, had complained that the American occupation might turn out to be worse than the Spanish regime, was doing his part to make this come true.

Many trade unionists did not dare visit their homes for fear of being arrested. Nevertheless, the jailing of the strike leaders did not succeed in stopping the workers from joining the general strike. Nor did the fact that Havana was placed under a siege, with U.S. troops occupying the railroad stations and the docks, with the police moving through the city attacking and breaking up gatherings of workers and preventing meetings at various workers' clubs. Economic activity in the city came to a halt; even the theaters were empty.[29] Forty-five tobacco shops voted on September 26 to join the movement, and the printers went on record as ready to walk out "as faithful soldiers of the proletariat." Obviously, more arrests were necessary. At the request of General Ludlow, C. V. Casiero, Adjutant General, notified Mayor Lacoste immediately to arrest the leaders of the bakers' union. Perhaps then Havana would get bread. At the same time, General Ludlow himself ordered the civil governor of the province to prohibit "political meetings, processions or demonstrations of any type which have as their object to support the strike."[30] And Ludlow ordered all newspapers immediately to publish a proclamation which he had written, addressed "To the People of Havana."

It was an amazing document. It began with an explanation for the proclamation which made it appear that the general strike was the result of a handful of "irresponsbile and seditious individuals" rather than the expression of the will of thousands of Cuban workers. Ludlow then went on to remind the Cubans that the United States had "guaranteed to establish in the island of Cuba a firm and orderly government," and that it did not intend to allow the few "irresponsible and seditious individuals" to prevent it from carrying out its obligation. He then proceeded to contradict his interpretation of who was behind the general strike by noting that "the workers of Havana" were involved in the strike, but attributed this to the fact that they were "seduced" into becoming involved. Then followed a blunt warning that if these workers continued to carry through the general strike, they would be responsible for making "the exercise of liberty and the enjoyment of the rights of man recede for an indefinite period." In other words, the Occupation would be indefinitely extended unless the general strike was immediately terminated! Ludlow at last came to the reason for the strike:

> The alleged motive consists of the demand to reduce the working day to eight hours. In reality, such a petition has not been formulated. No employers' group has been petitioned to reduce the working day to eight hours; no request of this nature has been directed to the municipality; no communication has been sent to the American authorities.

This was an obvious distortion of the facts. It was well known that the masons had repeatedly petitioned their employers for the eight-hour day, and had refused to settle for anything less. As for a request directed to the municipality or to the American authorities, there was not the slightest reason why the workers should have done so. Their battle was with the employers, and they had good reason, as Lacoste's and Ludlow's actions had demonstrated, to stay clear of the municipality and the American authorities.

Ludlow continued:

> At the instigation of a few self-seeking demagogues, backed by a more numerous element that prefers idleness to labor, and excitement of any kind to the calmer life of thrift and protection of the family, the workingmen of Havana are urged to forego all labor; to extinguish the lights that protect property and discourage crime, to close the bake shops that furnish food, and, if that could be accomplished, to cut off the water supply. Meanwhile, the trades and occupations are to be abandoned, industry is to perish and food is to fail.

Since the "element that prefers idleness to labor" were working at this time twelve hours a day, to label them as not willing to work was to reveal a total contempt for the problems facing the Cuban workers. Ludlow then issued his final warning:

> No man can be compelled to work against his will. But if he can work yet will not, he is only a vagrant and a burden, and he must take the responsibility for his own acts and the needless and innumerable sufferings which he imposes upon his kindred, as well as upon the public.[31]

Translated into specific language, this meant that while the United States authorities could not compel any man to work, it would do so just the same.

As was to be expected, *El Diario de la Marina,* the newspaper formerly most loyal to Spain, hailed Ludlow's proclamation, praised him for his courage in facing up to what it called "a revolutionary, subversive threat to the country."[32] But what was surprising was that *Patria,* the journal founded by Martí as the organ of the Cuban Revolutionary Party, and edited after his death by Enrique José Varona, should have defended General Ludlow. Varona argued that Ludlow had only acted because of "the unprincipled conduct of a few" who had "conspired against the legitimate aims of the workers of Havana." "We do not wish anyone to abdicate his rights," *Patria* concluded, "but violence provokes only violence."[33] Not a word about the well-known fact that it was the police and not the strikers who had initiated the violence by attacking peaceful meetings of workers, dispersing union gatherings, and beating defensive strikers. How was it possible for the voice of the Cuban Revolution to charge that a desire for an eight-hour day was a conspiracy against "the legitimate aims of the workers?" Truly, the strike was revealing that not all who had fought for Cuban freedom believed that the working masses should enjoy the benefits of victory over Spanish despotism.

Ludlow also received support from still another unexpected quarter: the leadership of the General League of Cuban Workers. The League remained aloof from the strike, but the attitude of its leadership was expressed in a manifesto addressed "To the Workers," supporting Ludlow's proclamation, attacking the strike leaders as "enemies of order and of the country," and warning the workers that if they joined in the general strike, they would "lead the country to the abyss." Although the manifesto carried only the signature, "The Workers Who are Friends of Order and of the Country," it was widely attributed to the League, especially its president, Enrique Messonier. It was common knowledge that Messonier was involved in negotiations with leaders of political groups in Cuba who were ready to offer him a prominent place in their councils if he would repudiate the general strike, and he was publicly accused of having "betrayed" the cause of the working class."[34] Unfortunately, Messonier was not the only working class leader to betray that cause.

Ludlow's proclamation appeared in the Havana press on September 27. That same day his threats became a reality, as mounted police and units of the Rural Guard moved through the streets attacking workers, headed by a worker carrying a white flag with the number 8 printed in the center, was attacked, the demonstrators beaten and 150 of them arrested.[35] That same afternoon, crowds of workers gathered before the police headquarters to protest police brutality towards the strikers and demand the release of hundreds of strikers, men and women, who were in jail. To the amazement of the workers, they were confronted by the strike leaders who had been arrested at Ludlow's command. Estenoz and Tenerio, two of the men arrested, addressed the crowd, and urged them not to condemn the police or the U.S. authorities, assuring them that there was no need to continue the strike since the arrested leaders were "already at the point of solving the problem and achieving the eight-hour day." The crowd dispersed, but there was a growing suspicion that a conspiracy was under way to betray the strike.[36]

There was justification for these suspicions. What had happened was that the arrested leaders had been brought before General Ludlow who offered them the opportunity to go free as soon as each signed two joint letters: one repenting for their actions, and the other urging the workers to end the strike.* If the strike leaders rejected these

---

\* According to another version, Pedro Roca, president of the Estivadores' [Longshoremen's] Union was seized at his home by an armed guard, brought before General Ludlow and threatened with indefinite imprisonment unless he called off the strike. Roca argued that he had no authority to do so, but agreed to visit the imprisoned men and urge them to call off the strike. Under guard, Roca was taken to the jail where he consulted with the imprisoned men, and told them that unless they issued a manifesto recommending to the workers of

terms, they would be turned over to the courts and remain in prison indefinitely. Estenoz and his colleagues asked for time to consider the proposal. The following day, all agreed to sign the letters and to ask the strikers to end the general strike.

In the first letter, addressed to the Mayor, the arrested strike leaders declared that "it was never our intention to produce disturbances of public order; that we have not wished to create obstacles in the path of authorities nor to embarrass the progressive march of this country, so that we could enjoy the Constitution of our native land which we are all legally bound to serve." They denied that they were anarchists; regretted the turmoil caused by the strike, and promised to operate within the law. The letter closed with a plea that "we be restored to complete liberty . . . and that this favor be extended also to all in a similar situation."

The second letter, also addressed to the Mayor, was signed only by Domingo García Punto as Secretary of the Masons' and Day Laborers' Union and Evaristo E. Estenoz as member of the Administrative Committee. It stated: "We promise you to use our good offices with our worker comrades to put an end to the present strike of the union. We hope that in view of this promise, you will take similar measures, together with others which might be appropriate, to return us to liberty." [37]

Even after the issuance of these declarations, the strike leaders remained in jail for another three days. Then they were released, and other strikers in prison were also set free. Confused and demoralized by what they openly denounced as the "cowardice" of their leaders, and facing the danger of new arrests and imprisonments, and in the case of the Spanish workers, deportation to Spain, many strikers slowly drifted back to their jobs. Some of the masons, however, continued to hold out, and in a public manifesto, boldly asserted: "Our strike, peaceful and orderly, continues and we will not yield to the intervention of the authorities." Others were encouraged to hold out longer by a cable received from General Carlos García, son of Calixto García, who wired Diego Vicente Tejera from Washington: "I place my person

---

Havana that they call the strike off, they would remain in prison "during the Governor's pleasure." (Samuel Gompers, "A Trip to Cuba," *American Federationist*, vol. VII, March, 1900, pp. 61-62.)

at the disposition of the long-suffering working class with whom I sympathize and whose heroic effort for the conquest of its legitimate rights I applaud.

But by this time the strike was over. On October 3, General Ludlow sent congratulations to Mayor Lacoste, expressing his gratitude for the Mayor's cooperation and for that of his police force in breaking the general strike. "The disappearance of the danger," Ludlow wrote, "is due principally to the tact and firmness with which you have conducted the matter and to the discretion and viligance of the police under the capable direction of General Rafael Cárdenas." [38] The "discretion and viligance" of the police had consisted of trampling down the rights of the workers, attacking them wherever they gathered, breaking up their meetings, and arresting and imprisoning hundreds of strikers!

The workers who returned to their jobs had not fought courageously for nothing. For one thing, the masons did force their employers to grant the eight-hour day and thus become the first workers in Cuba to win a working day of eight hours. Then again, in order to prevent new working-class uprisings, many employers throughout the island began to reduce the working day from twelve to ten hours. Moreover, General Brooke urged the municipalities to heed the warning of the strike and reduce hours in public establishments to ten hours a day, and this was shortly carried into effect. "Thus," writes José Rivero Múniz, "the general strike, notwithstanding its relative failure, contributed to the benefit of the workers." [39]

The general strike had widespread and significant repercussions. It hastened the rapid decline of the General League of Cuban Workers from a membership of 10,000, most of them cigar makers, at the beginning of the strike, to about 300 at the end. Messonier and his colleagues had so completely alienated the workers by their stand against the strike and their dealings with the authorities, that few wished to associate with an organization they headed. It would take a long time before the League regained its prestige and recovered these losses.[40] One other effect of the strike was to encourage police brutality against labor. Having been assured of support for this policy by the Occupation authorities, the police did not hesitate to use force to break up gatherings and meetings of workers. Even as innocent an event as the funeral of the typographer-liberator, Enrique Creci, the working-class hero of the Cuban army who had been killed in action against Spain, was marked by police brutality. His remains were brought to Havana on November 19, 1899, for a mass funeral attended by thousands from all over the island, representing every trade union in Cuba. When the funeral cortege, bearing a red banner and led by the aristocratic and patriotic Salvador Cisneros Betancourt and the Negro patriot Juan Gualberto Gómez, moved to the cemetery, it was savagely attacked by the police and many workers were cruelly beaten.[41]

A number of anti-imperialists in the United States pointed to the breaking of the strike in Cuba as evidence of what militarism held in store for workers everywhere if American power became dominant. "Doubtless strikes are grievous things," *The Public,* an anti-imperialist weekly, noted on October 7, 1899. "But there are more grievous things than strikes, and one of them is military power in time of peace and over the industries of a people. Yet this power has made itself felt more effectively in Cuba under the American flag than in Germany under the flag of that empire; and if imperialism and its twin sister of evil, militarism, progress as they have since the army limit was raised from 25,000 to 100,000 men, it is a power that will soon be felt in the United States itself."

The general strike in Cuba also had repercussions in the labor movement of the United States. Many American unions adopted resolutions condemning General Ludlow for breaking the strike, and a mass meeting of trade unionists in Chicago, demanded his immediate recall from Cuba. In his report to the U.S. government, Ludlow cited these protests against his strikebreaking policy as proof that the Cuban strikers had received "expert guidance from abroad." The greatest denunciation, he noted, came from "a labor organization in Chicago, showing how close was the connection between the two localities." He boasted that he had broken the general strike which he described as having been precipitated by "certain professional agitators," aided by subversive elements in the United States.[42]

The labor and Socialist press in the United States was filled with denunciations of Ludlow's role. *The Carpenter,* organ of the powerful Brotherhood of Carpenters and Joiners, protested that Ludlow's policy "struck at the fundamental rights of labor." The *Coast Seamen's Journal,* voice of the Sailors' Union of the Pacific, denounced Ludlow for having "deprived the Cuban workers of one of the basic principles for which they fought against Spain." "Are not the workmen of Cuba free agents and can they not work when they will and be idle at their pleasure?" asked the *Labor Advocate* of Oshkosh, Wisconsin. "Now, then, what in Hail Columbia is it Ludlow's business to stick his nose where it is not wanted." [43]

*The People,* spokesman for the Socialist Labor Party, was even more vehement. It called Ludlow "a military tool of the capitalists" for having taken it upon himself "to terrorize the Cuban workingmen into submission . . . to protect the American and, incidentally, the few Cuban capitalists in their right to squeeze the life out of their wage slaves." Ludlow had, however, accomplished one good thing: By his action, he had "brought out the true class character of the war [against Spain] and . . . made clear to the uninitiated what the Socialists have maintained all along, that it was a war waged in order to bring a strange people within the speedy grasp of the American capitalists." [44]

The Knights of Labor held President McKinley and his Administration responsible for the Ludlow policy. The President had not disavowed it nor had he reprimanded the General, although he was urged to do so by "prominent labor leaders," Congressmen and United States Senators.* For that reason, the convention of the Knights of Labor, held in Boston, November, 1899, resolved that workingmen should use their votes to defeat McKinley in the election of 1900.[45] At the convention of the American Federation of Labor, held in Detroit, December, 1899, the delegates applauded President Gompers for lashing out at the U.S. military authorities who had broken the strike in Cuba. Gompers declared in his presidential report to the convention that the Cuban workers had full justification for having sought "to secure some of the advantages resultant from modern civilization; that is, a reduction in the hours of daily toil," and they had "exercised their natural and legal right to cease work" when their request was denied by the employers. He then condemned Ludlow's proclamation, describing it as "containing the most offensive and unjustifiable attacks and abuse of the workers who sought an amelioration in their conditions, and relief from burdensome toil." Ludlow, Gompers told the delegates, had even threatened to arrest the strike leaders if the workers did not immediately return to their jobs, and as a result, the general strike was

---

* Just which Congressmen and Senators protested was not mentioned, and as far as can be determined, there were none. Of course, many labor leaders did protest.

broken. He then commented bitterly on the effect of the U.S. military occupation on the Cuban working class:

> It may be that the wealth possessors of Cuba enjoy as large or larger liberty of action since the Spanish authority has been driven from the Pearl of the Antilles, but no surprise need be felt that Cuba's workmen are not boiling with an ebulition of joyous enthusiasm over the change which has taken place. Cuba's toilers enjoyed the right under Spanish domination to quit work, either singly or jointly, to remedy wrongs and grievances, to enforce their rights, their demands, and their hopes. Under the military rule of our country these rights have been denied them.

Gompers warned American workers not to make the mistake of thinking that the events in Cuba did not concern them. "It is not difficult to imagine that it is but a step from military rule applied to Cuba to the territory constituting the present United States. We have already seen ... the attempt made in the Couer d'Alene district of Idaho and elsewhere." [46] Every American worker knew what the reference to Idaho meant. In the spring of 1899, federal troops had been called in to break a strike of the Western Federation of Miners at Couer d'Alene.[47]

Gompers soon learned that he had underestimated General Ludlow's strikebreaking activity. In February, 1900, following an accident caused by a collision with a trolley car, Gompers went to Havana to recuperate. He decided to use the opportunity to investigate labor conditions, the labor movement, the rule of the military, and the full part General Ludlow had played in breaking the general strike. He soon discovered that he had been mistaken when he told the A.F. of L. convention that Ludlow had only threatened the leaders of the general strike with arrest. "I learned," he wrote to the *American Federationist* from Havana, "that they were not only 'threatened,' but really were arrested, and this too without any shadow of a cause or excuse. I have it upon the most reliable authority that there was no disorder, no semblance or even the suspicion of disorder, connected with the Havana 8 hour strike; that the employers who would have been compelled to yield to the just demands of the men successfully induced General Ludlow to arrest 'the leaders' of the strike." [48]

Gompers had interviews with Governor-General Leonard Wood

and other American authorities for the purpose of protesting the action of General Ludlow. Later, he reported to the A.F. of L. convention: "Without at all attempting to take or attribute credit to ourselves or to anyone, it can be stated that within a few weeks General Ludlow was removed from his command as governor general of Havana."[49] Ludlow's office was abolished on May 1, 1900, and the General was transferred later to the Philippines. But his removal from Havana was due more to Wood's desire to get rid of him than to Gompers' influence, or to the part he had played in the general strike. Hermann Hagedorn, Wood's biographer, notes that Ludlow acted independently and "followed Wood's lead with reluctance when he followed it at all."[50] Wood was not one to tolerate such conduct.

Gompers addressed several meetings of workers while he was in Havana, urging the need for organization along the lines of the American Federation of Labor. He also reported that he had been instrumental in settling a strike of 14,000 cigar makers. The workers had walked out four weeks before Gompers' arrival in the island because of the refusal of their employers to hire Cuban youth as apprentices, or to promote Cuban cigar makers to positions of superintendents or foremen, filling these places with Spaniards. According to Gompers, he obtained an agreement from Gustavo Bock, representing the employers, that in the future there would be no discrimination against Cubans in employment as workers, apprentices or foremen. Thereupon, Gompers wrote, the cigar makers voted to end their strike and returned to work.[51]

No Cuban historian of the labor movement in his country refers to this activity on Gompers' part.* Indeed, Rito Estaban, referring to Gompers' visit to Havana, writes: "Mr. Gompers . . . in conformity with his reactionary position, collaborated with the North American imperialists, abandoning his duty, which should have been to aid in the liberation and complete independence of the Cuban people."[52] This was hardly fair, for Gompers had been playing a distinguished role inside and outside of the American Anti-Imperialist League to bring

---

* In his study of the history of the Cuban labor movement, Charles Page reports that he interviewed Manual Muñiz Rivero and Antonio Pechet, active labor leaders of the time, and that neither recalled any such action by Gompers. (Charles Anson Page, "The Development of Organized Labor in Cuba," unpublished Ph.D. thesis, University of California, 1952, p. 46.)

about an early end to the occupation of Cuba and the achievement of self-government by its people. What Estaban may have been referring to was what Gompers wrote from Havana: "There can be no doubt but that General Wood is regarded with favor in Cuba. It is believed that he is sympathetically inclined toward Cuban independence."[53] If there is one thing every Cuban patriot knew, it was that Wood was not regarded "with favor" by the friends of independence and that he was not "sympathetically" inclined towards Cuban self-government.*

Gompers also portrayed Wood as a friend of the Cuban workers and their aspiration for higher wages, shorter hours, and improved working conditions.[54] But the following article in the Brooklyn *Eagle* of February 28, 1900, soon after the A.F. of L. president returned from Cuba, cast considerable doubt on the accuracy of Gompers' report. Under the headline, "Why We Are Needed in Cuba," the article stated:

> An incident in Cienfuegos gives a suggestive intimation of what might be going on all over Cuba if the Cuban republic for which sentimental Americans used to agitate, had been established. There was a strike among the freight handlers of the port. True to the Cuban instinct for revolution the Mayor and the local police sided with the strikers and stopped other men willing to work from taking the vacated places. . . . General Wood heard what was going on, promptly deposed the Mayor and ordered American troops to protect every man who wished to work. . . .
>
> We are apt to forget that the Cubans and most tropic races are where our ancestors began well back in the last century. . . . Fortunately, General Wood and his soldiers will see that the local governments do not promote anarchy, such as would now be reigning in Cienfuegos if the General had not interfered.

---

\* Gompers' reputation really sank in Cuba when it was learned that he had played an important part, together with the International Cigar Makers' an A.F. of L. affiliate, and the cigar manufacturers of Tampa, Florida, in wrecking *La Sociedad de Torcedores de Tampa y Sus Cercanías*, popularly known as *La Resistencia*, a trade union formed by the cigar workers, mainly Cubans, of that city. When cigar workers in Havana sought to prevent scabs from leaving Cuba to help break the strike called by *La Resistencia*, General Wood jailed 150 of them. For a discussion of this episode in 1900-01, see Durward Long, "La Resistencia: Tampa's Immigrant Labor Union," *Labor History*, Vol. VI, Fall, 1965, pp. 193-213; Philip S. Foner, *History of the Labor Movement in the United States*, Vol. III, pp. 260-62.)

The *Eagle* failed to mention that the employers of Havana had just agreed to increase wages for stevedores, to pay double wages for night, Sunday and holiday work, and to pay wages in American money. This agreement, worked out with the military authorities, stimulated the dock workers in other cities to seek improvements in their conditions.[55] The *Eagle* also failed to mention that the 635 dock laborers at Cienfuegos, 350 lightermen, 200 stevedores, 110 longshoremen, and 75 cartmen had gone on strike because of the unwillingness of the employers to raise wages; instead they had imported foreign labor to unload vessels. It also did not mention that Mayor Frías informed General Wood that the strikers were "entirely pacific," and that there were "no disorders, in marked contrast to similar labor movements in other countries," and that there was absolutely no need for American troops. "Order is entirely guaranteed," he wired Havana.[56] But Edwin F. Atkins, the American sugar capitalist, carried more influence with Wood. He complained that "the civil authority is timid," and urged troops be sent, warning: "Business situation is very serious and estates must positively shut down within a few days." The troops were sent, and the strikers were forced to return to work, leaving it to an arbitration committee to decide the workers' demand for higher wages. In the end, the workers received only a slight increase.[57]

General Wood also took action to break a strike of stevedores, warehouse laborers, and sugar handlers at Cárdenas. When these workers struck early in January, 1901 for more wages and shorter hours, Wood sent two cavalry troops and justified this action with the announcement: "Unreasonable demands should not be acceded to. Acts of this kind are serious menaces to the commercial prosperity of the country. Every effort should be made to suppress demonstrations of this nature." To the commander of the cavalry troops, Wood wired: "Make every effort to bring outside workers and to resume business." Business was resumed with strikebreakers, and the strike was broken.[58]

Wood's strikebreaking activities did not go unnoticed in the United States. *The People* denounced Wood for "following in the footsteps of Ludlow and the officials in Puerto Rico who imprisoned the labor agitators."[59]* The *National Labor Standard*, in an article entitled

---

* When the leaders of the Free Federation of Workmen of Puerto Rico called a general strike in the summer of 1900, after their demand for wages in American money, weekly pay and the eight-hour day, was rejected, the

"Despotism in Cuba," accused Wood of acting to guarantee the profits of American and Cuban capitalists. This attack on the Cuban workers had to be denounced. "He [Wood] should be repudiated by all true Americans and his deposition and recall demanded. Therefore, the American Federation of Labor, the State Federations and all the local trade unions and reform associations throughout the United States should take prompt action against the infamous action of an infamous despot." [60] Unfortunately, the American Federation of Labor and its leadership remained silent. Gompers had been outspoken in condemnation of Ludlow's policy as a strikebreaker, but he said nothing at all about the fact that Wood was pursuing the same policy. Indeed, following his return from Havana, for the duration of the American occupation, Gompers never mentioned Cuba again; neither in the *American Federationist*, which he edited, nor in his presidential address to the 1901 A.F. of L. convention did he refer to events in the island or American policy toward Cuba.* Perhaps, having assured the American workers that Wood was a friend of the Cuban labor movement, he was not anxious to eat his words in public. More likely, his return from Havana coincided with his (and other A.F. of L. leaders') close association with the National Civic Federation, an organization founded in 1900 for the purpose of promoting peace and harmony in the industrial world and achieving collaboration between the leaders of big business and the leaders of organized labor, particularly those in the American Federation of Labor. Associating with Mark Hanna and with representatives of the House of Morgan, Gompers lost interest in combatting American imperialism, which was being promoted by the same industrialists, financiers and political leaders who were active in the National Civic Federation.[61]

Meanwhile, Wood's strikebreaking activities continued. When the laborers loading coal in tugs at Matanzas went on strike in February,

---

American military authorities arrested between thirty and one hundred trade union officials, including Santiago Iglesias, the president of the Free Federation. The Puerto Rican labor movement was denounced by the American military authorities as consisting of "revolutionists" and "anarchists." (*Proceedings, American Federation of Labor Convention*, 1901, p. 160; *National Labor Standard*, Oct. 11, 1900.)

* During the meetings of the A.F. of L. Executive Council, February 17-20, 1901, nothing was said about events in Cuba. (*See American Federationist*, vol. VII, March, 1900, pp. 112-120.)

1901 for higher wages and shorter hours,* Wood notified Colonel Noyes that the strikers were halting "military work, and nothing must be allowed to interfere with it." Colonel Noyes hired strikebreakers, and boasted to Wood: "I have arrested the chief of the strikers for interfering with our laborers [the strikebreakers] this morning. Have notified the laborers union that I will will release him if they promise no more interference." The union agreed; the strikebreakers continued to do the work of the strikers, and the strike ended in defeat.[62]

Encouraged by the role played by the American military authorities, the employers in Havana repudiated their agreement with the stevedores. Wood refused to interfere even though he had influenced the workers to accept an agreement calling for less than they had demanded. But when the stevedores struck, in March, 1901, to compel the employers to live up to the agreement, he was not so indifferent. On the contrary, Wood proceeded to arrest and imprison the officers of the union on the charge of "sedition." The men were finally released after an outburst of protests from trade unions in which General Carlos García joined. Urged by a number of political leaders to submit the issue to arbitration, the union agreed. But when General García, who was championing the strikers, broached this subject to Wood, urging him to support arbitration, he was turned down. Wood even refused to receive a committee of the strikers accompanying General García.

In a letter to the labor and Socialist press in the United States, Secundino Toral, secretary of the union and one of the men imprisoned early in the struggle, bitterly denounced the "brutal interference of the military government." Despite Wood's efforts in behalf of the employers, the strikers were holding firm. "The strike movement is very strong and absolute solidarity prevails throughout the labor organizations of Havana. We have received demonstrations of fraternal sympathy from federations of Cardenas, Matanzas, Cienfuegos, Barbacoa, Batabacoa, and Santiago de Cuba, and from other ports. The importance of the movement to all laborers is evident." Eventually, a Board of Arbitration was appointed, and the strike ended after it handed

---

* "They complain that they are compelled to work overtime, often thirteen hours, and they are not paid for their work," reported an American investigator. (Lt. W. W. Wallace to Adjutant General, Matanzas, Feb. 14, 1901, "Strikes in Cuba," Records of the United States Military Government of Cuba, Selected Documents Concerning Strikes in Cuba, 1899-1908, National Archives.)

down its findings that the workers were justified and that the employers should abide by the original agreement. General García hailed the decision, but in a public statement, declared that no thanks were due to General Wood for the workers' victory. The Governor General, the son of Calixto García charged, had proved himself an agent of the most backward employers.[63]

Beginning in February, 1901, a series of strikes broke out among the workers constructing the Central Railway of the Cuban Company. The American workers received higher wages than the Cubans, and were paid in American money, while the Cubans were paid in Spanish. When the Cubans protested, the company reported that it "cannot pay the Cuban Laborers the same wages as to the Americans because the former do not render the same work as the latter." [64] At first when the Cuban and Spanish laborers walked out, the Americans continued working. But on March 10, at Santa Clara, Cuban, Spanish, and American laborers went on strike together, demanding payment for all workers of one dollar per day in American money. On March 13, at General Wood's order, the Rural Guard arrested 51 "Spanish, Cuban and American strikers." [65] These strikers spent several weeks in prison, but work stoppages continued. In July, 1901, a call was issued from Ciego-de-Avila in Sancti Spiritus for a general strike on the entire line. This time, in addition to payment of one dollar a day in American money, the demand was for an eight-hour day instead of ten. At the request of R. G. Ward, manager of construction for the Cuban Company, the three men who had signed the call—José Rodríguez López, Ramón Puertas, and Juan Rodríguez Martinez—were denounced by the American military authorities as "bandits," arrested by the Rural Guard, and imprisoned on the charge of mutiny. Ward demanded the severest punishment for "[José] Rodríguez and his associates," warning that otherwise "we will have serious difficulties in this vicinity." His warning was heeded. Rodríguez, the chief leader of the railroad construction workers, was sentenced to eight years penal servitude.[66] Writing to the editor of *El Combate,* the father of Ramón Puertas, one of the "bandits," pointed out that the only crime his son and his two companions were guilty of was "seeking to improve the conditions of their fellow workers of the Cuba Company. . . . These are the terrifying bandits of the region of Ciego de Avila! . . . They are all children of Labor, for their ages run from 18 to 30 years. So you will see for yourself upon whom the guilt really rests." [67]

All the strikebreaking actions during the Wood administration described above were public knowledge. But what was not known was that as soon as Wood assumed office as Governor General, he had the "*Sección Secreta*" (Secret Section) of the Havana Police Department compile lists of "leaders of agitation" among workers and "leaders of the disturbing elements." These lists were kept for use in case it was necessary to move in swiftly to cripple a strike. It is interesting to note that the men on these lists were also described as "bitterest to the Government of the Intervention." [68] When one considers the way strikers were dealt with during the Occupation, it is hardly surprising that militant Cuban labor leaders should have had been bitter, even apart from their anxiety to see an independent Republic. In fact, so anxious were most Cuban workers to see the Occupation ended that many refrained from engaging in struggles for better conditions in order not to give the Americans the excuse that "anarchy" required the continued presence of U.S. troops.[69]

Cuban labor had entered the period of the Occupation with its trade union shattered or dispersed. During the four years of the Occupation, Cuban labor organizations reappeared and grew in number and strength. Through the efforts of Diego Vicente Tejera, progressive elements who believed in Marxist ideas were brought together. But the attempt to form an effective central labor body did not get far. One group of workers—the masons of Havana—gained the eight-hour day, and many had their daily hours reduced from twelve to ten. The stevedores of Havana increased their wage scale. All of these achievements came because of militant struggle, which gained notice outside of Cuba and resulted in strengthening the links of solidarity between Cuban and American labor.

Apart from these achievements, Cuban labor gained little from the Occupation. Many of its strikes were broken by the military authorities, and the police and Rural Guard acting under orders of these authorities. Writing in 1902, Victor S. Clark noted that wages in 1805 in Cuba were "nearly as high as those prevailing in Habana at the present time. . . ." [70]* In his book, *Legislación social de Cuba,*

---

* Clark lists the following as typical daily wages in 1902: mining, quarrying, and day working—$2 a day in American money; carpenters (Habana)—

published in 1936, José R. García Pedrosa wrote: "The first North American intervention [1898-1902] left us only the unfortunate General Immigration Law and an ineffective Order prohibiting the garnishing of the salaries of public employees." [71] José Rivero Muñiz concludes his study of the Cuban labor movement during the Occupation on the following note: "The state of misery of the majority of the proletariat at the end of the Occupation was depicted by the way in which it lived, dressed and fed itself. Working class families were housed in miserable dwellings and ate miserable food. The children were half-nude, and many workers had no more to put on than their trousers and shirts. Their shoes were of the worst quality. The women were often clothed in sacks." [72]

Still the years of the Occupation had proved one thing: Cuban workers did not accept exploitation without protest. As the Socialist *Daily People* put it: "The capitalists who thought that owing to centuries of Spanish rule the spirit of Cuban labor had been entirely broken, are much disappointed to find that the workers kick against the greater exploitation now imposed upon them." [73]

---

$2 and $2.50 in Spanish silver; $1.40 and $1.75 in American money; bricklayers—$2 to $3 a day in Spanish silver; $1.40 to $2.10 in American money; hod carriers—$1 in Spanish silver; 70 cents in American money; tobacco workers—skilled—$2 to $3 a day in Spanish gold; $1.80 to $2.70 in American money; sorters—$100 a month; wrappers—$5 or $6 a week in American money. (Victor S. Clark, "Labor Conditions in Cuba," *Bulletin of the Department of Labor*, No. 41, Washington, July, 1902, p. 725.)

## CHAPTER XXIII
# Failure of the New Annexationist Drive

IN FEBRUARY, 1901, MARK TWAIN, formerly a fervent suporter of the Spanish-American War but now increasingly disillusioned by its results, wrote ironically in his most famous anti-imperialist work, "To the People Sitting in Darkness" that a strong movement was afoot "to slip out of our Congressional contract with Cuba. It is a rich country and many of us are already beginning to see that the contract was a sentimental mistake." [1] What Twain had in mind was clearly set forth in an editorial of July 28, 1900 in the *United States Investor*. Denouncing the Teller Amendment to the Joint Resolution of Congress, the leading Wall Street journal commented that the United States had "made a grand mistake when we promised to give the Cuban people independence. The American people, unfortunately, are impulsive and indiscreet. The promise ought to be broken because it is our interest to break it. To retire from Cuba would be a crime which would not be justified by a promise made in ignorance to the Cubans." The spokesman for American imperialism closed with a specific demand that the United States proceed to annex Cuba and be done with the problem of what to do with the island.

The idea that the Teller Amendment had been "a grand mistake" which should be remedied by annexation did not begin in the summer of 1900. Actually, a year before this, a surge of annexationism swept a large part of the American press. It was kicked off by the publication in June, 1899 of Robert P. Porter's *Industrial Cuba*. Porter, a personal friend of McKinley, had been sent to Cuba right after the surrender of Santiago de Cuba, as the President's "Special Commissioner." He had studied Cuban trade, currency, banking and tariffs, and had published his *Report on the Commercial and Industrial Conditions of the Island of Cuba,* in which he stressed the importance of the island for

American trade and investment. In his book, Porter came out strongly in favor of annexation of the island, and recommended that the United States work closely with the Cuban annexationists. Since Porter was a close personal friend of McKinley, it was generally assumed that he voiced the Administration's attitude.*

Porter quoted at length in his book from Cubans he had interviewed in the island, all of whom favored annexation to the United States, and concluded that the only real hope for Cuba's economic development and future stability lay in "complete union with the greater Republic."[2] This phase of Porter's book received wide attention in the American press, and it was further highlighted by interviews with Porter in which he harped repeatedly on the theme that "all the moneyed interests [in Cuba] favor annexation to the United States."[3] Suddenly, from one end of the country to the next, identical articles began appearing in many newspapers which opened:

### CUBA'S FUTURE

Robert P. Porter Says It Is Annexation

*Only Solution of the Problem is Americanization*

A quotation from Porter's book followed which read: "The future in Cuba, in my opinion, can only lie in annexation and the longer the Cubans in Cuba and the anti-expansionists in the United States continue to deceive themselves and the people by suggesting any other solution the longer capital and enterprise will be held back from the island."[4]

Porter's bold assertion in favor of American imperialism received immediate backing from General Leonard Wood, then in Santiago de Cuba, and new headlines began to blossom forth reading: "Wood Says

---

* One reason why the McKinley Administration had refrained from becoming associated with the annexationist drive before this was probably the desire not to disillusion the leaders of the Filipino independence movement. Aguinaldo appears to have been convinced that the United States' pledge to give Cuba its independence was assurance that the same policy would be applied to the Philippines, and open support of the annexation of Cuba would have had the effect of alerting the Filipinos to what was in store for them before the McKinley Administration wanted it so understood. *See*, in this connection, Teodoro A. Agoncillo, *Malolos: The Crisis of the Republic* (Quezon City, Philippines, 1960), pp. 145-50.

People of Cuba Favor Annexation. Calls Porter's Analysis Correct." This was followed by Wood's opinion that the people of Cuba were "contented under American rule," and if given a choice would overwhelmingly favor annexation. "I am firmly convinced that annexation would be carried four to one in Santiago." [5] The imperialist press in the United States praised Wood's acumen and vision. "It is a growing impression that Cuba will eventually be annexed to the United States," remarked the Chicago *Tribune* on August 1, 1899, "and, of course, General Wood would be given much credit for stimulating annexation sentiment."

Now the press began to feature reports from correspondents in Cuba, or from local citizens who had just returned from the island all emphasizing two themes: the first was that "the feeling in Cuba in favor of annexation grows at a rapid rate. But one class, a noisy one, is said to oppose it, and that is the cafe politicians." The second was that independence would bring into being another Haiti. The following appeared in scores of newspapers in August, 1899, each paper carrying the same headline:

### FEARS A BLACK REPUBLIC

> A leading Havana merchant, a Cuban who claims to be well posted regarding affairs in the island, said today that universal suffrage would mean a black republic in the near future, and that the only means of preventing it will be the incorporation of the island as a possession of the United States, as a State, Territory, or Colony, leading to American immigration. In his judgment Cuba is otherwise doomed to become another Hayti.[6]

It did not require much imagination to understand what was happening. The demand for annexation had formerly been raised on the eve of the Spanish-American War, during the war, and immediately afterwards. But it had been advanced in a scattered way, and its adherents had emphasized that it was necessary even though the Cuban people did not favor it, they were simply not fit for self-government, and that the United States should take over the island regardless of the wishes of the inhabitants. This, it was argued, was simply the operation of "the law of the survival of the fittest." [7]

This initial campaign never really got off the ground because it flew squarely in the face of the commitment embodied in the Teller Amendment. The Cubans, the opponents of annexation argued, might not be ready for independence, but it was their country, to do with as they pleased, and the United States had pledged them this right, a pledge which had to be honored. With the American occupation of the island, a new argument against annexation came to the front: the Cubans were being trained to develop as a self-governing people, and should be allowed to organize their own government as soon as it was clear that they reached the point where they could take over from the occupying forces.[8]

Now a new factor was introduced into the drive for annexation. This is not to say that the emphasis on the Cuban's unfitness for self-government disappeared. But the greatest stress was placed on the argument that the Cubans themselves wanted to be annexed. Could anyone bring up the Teller Amendment if Cuba, of her own free will, were to voice the desire to incorporate herself with the United States? This theme was paraded in the press throughout the United States. The fact that the same articles began to appear simultaneously in different parts of the country did not escape notice. "A regular campaign in support of the annexation of Cuba has been undertaken and from an unknown source," a Massachusetts paper commented in August, 1899. "Newspapers are receiving printed sheets containing the argument that the Cubans want to be annexed from various publications favoring annexation."[9] Others were certain as to the identity of the "unknown source." This was a bureau set up in Washington which was "sending out literature by the car-load with a view of educating public sentiment in this country for the annexation of Cuba." The bureau was financed by "syndicates and monopolies who have acquired and hope to acquire still further interests in Cuba." One monopoly specifically mentioned was the Sugar Trust. The Trust received the largest part of its supply of sugar from Cuba, and stood to gain enormously if, by annexation, Cuban sugar could enter free of duty. "Besides, it is understood that some of the trust magnates have acquired extensive sugar properties in Cuba and thus, if annexation is accomplished, they would make profits both in producing and refining."[10]

There was considerable evidence to substantiate these charges. It was public knowledge, and openly reported in the press, that a group of New York business men, headed by Henry F. Havemyer and Edwin F. Atkins of the Sugar Trust, had set up a fund "to undo the mistake made by Congress last spring when the resolutions were passed in connection with liberating the Cubans from Spanish rule and establishing a free republic."[11] This fund was used to distribute articles favoring annexation to the press around the country. Since Robert P. Porter played an important role in this campaign, its links to the Administration appeared to be clear.*

The package of articles favoring annexation was entitled "The Future of Cuba: New York Business Men Advocate Annexation." Included were statements by New York merchants, bankers, capitalists, and industrialists, who deplored the fact that Congress had not confined itself merely "to the liberation of the Cubans from the oppressive rule of Spain," and who predicted "a great future for Cuba under the restraining influence of conservative American administration, and enormous revenues for American investors." Also included were statements by Cubans pleading for the United States not to permit people of the island "to establish a government. . . . The possibility of his [the Cuban] assuming charge is keeping lots of capital out of the island. It is too bad that such a state of affairs exists, for labor is now very cheap, and for that reason alone, if for no other there is at the present moment a fine opportunity for capital." But all this would vanish without annexation.[12]

But the annexationist drive encountered a formidable obstacle. The anti-imperialist press featured statements by Cubans condemning Porter and Wood, and pointing out that the Cubans who were said to favor annexation represented only the old autonomist elements or the openly pro-Spanish groups in the island.† Special attention was paid to a statement by General Carlos García in which he charged that Robert P. Porter had been greatly influenced by "the Marquis de Apeztezula who is a Spaniard who belongs to the American Sugar Trust, and who has all his life been opposed to the Cubans in their struggle for freedom. This man was the ardent spokesman of Weyler in Cuba, the worst enemy of Cuba today, a mercenary at heart, ready to yield his convictions to

---

* The book of clippings Porter kept entitled "Cuba Annexation" has several items indicating the key role he played in this campaign.

† It is not difficult to understand the feelings of Cubans when they read of recruiting appeals by the U.S. Army hung in post offices throughout the United States which urged young Americans to join "Uncle Sam's Personally Conducted Excursion to his new possessions Manila, Cuba and Porto Rico." (Springfield *Republican,* June 13, 1899; *La Discusión,* June 27, 1899.)

the highest bidder." García warned that the Cubans would not surrender their independence, and that if the United States went ahead with plans to annex the island, it would meet with armed resistance.[13] The anti-imperialist press urged the Administration not to take this warning lightly. "Annexation will lead to a rebellion like that in the Philippines. This nation has one war on its hands now, and one at a time is enough."[14]

Evidently his words were not lost on the annexationists. The campaign to take over Cuba tapered off by the end of the summer of 1899. But not for long. From October through December, 1899, scores of newspapers began to beat the annexationist drums once again. They played up the statement of the Cuban Commercial League delegation which, on arriving in Washington, told the press that Cuba had but one future—annexation to the United States.[15] The emphasis now, however, was mainly on the argument that annexation was the best solution of the Cuban problem. "Surely they [the Cubans] must see that annexation would be a blessing to them," declared the Chicago *Times-Herald,* but the United States was urged to annex the island whether the Cubans saw this or not. Similar editorial sentiments, many identically worded, appeared in the press of Boston, St. Paul, St. Louis, New Haven, Cleveland, Memphis, Dallas, Boise, Portland, and many other cities.[16]

Supported by this vociferous demand for annexation, the Administration made the first open move to achieve this goal. Reports began to circulate in the press, during the fall of 1899, that Leonard Wood would head a permanent United States civil government instead of a supposedly temporary military government. Annexation would be accomplished by making Cuba an American colony. It was reported that the Administration was putting out a feeler to see how the Cubans would react to this plan.[17] There was more to this, however, than rumor. Senator Foraker wrote to General Wilson on November 20, 1899: "As to a Civil Governor, I think as you that the President has decided to appoint one, and that he will select General Wood. Everyone here [in Washington] is of this impression."[18] Foraker had a special reason to be concerned, for it was also reported that under a civil governor his bill prohibiting the granting of franchises would become null and void since it applied only to the military occupation of Cuba.

When news of this plan to establish "a sort of colonial administration of Cuba" [19] reached the island, the reaction was immediate. The Cuban press raised a loud cry of protest, charging that the Occupation was being transformed from a temporary to a permanent status. A typical comment was voiced on November 14, 1899 by *La Discusión* of Havana: "To us the constitutional argument is unanswerable: Cuba is not American territory, is is not a State, nor a conquered country like Puerto Rico or the Philippines, which was ceded to the United States without reserve condition or restrictions. Regarding Cuba Spain did nothing but renounce its sovereignty and titles." The plan for a civil governor, it emphasized, was "a snare prepared by annexationists of both here and there." *La Discusión* asked every Cuban who wished to see his country independent to speak out in protest against the proposed plan.

On November 19, *Patria* issued the warning: "Alert! Be on Your Guard!" It denounced the civil government plan as a device to annex Cuba eventually and meanwhile to annul the Foraker Act, thereby relegating the island "to the feudal control of wealthy American capitalists and monstrous trusts which would distribute among themselves as booty of the Intervention, the fertile soil of our country. . . ." Like *La Discusión*, *Patria* called for protests, and urged "all worthy and high minded Cubans to come forward to the energetic defense, by all peaceful and lawful means, of Cuban independence, against the astute tricks of American politicians and those Cubans who place the material benefits that would accrue to them by the absorption of Cuba by the United States, above the dignity and future of their country. Therefore —Be on Your Guard!"

On November 26 the Council of the Veterans of Independence telegraphed President McKinley, warning that the creation of "an American Civil Covernment . . . will alter the noble aims of the intervention of the United States in our struggle with Spain." Rather than alter the form of government, the Council urged the President to "hasten as much as possible the creation of elective organisms, that are to constitute the stable Cuban government, to whom, according to the Joint Resolution of April 19th, 1898, the Island, independent and sovereign, should be delivered. Any alteration that does not lead to that end will create ill feeling and alarm in this country, which hopes always to find in the United States a great and generous friend."

In behalf of the Council of Veterans of Independence, General Menocal urged all municipalities and townships in Cuba to inform the United States authorities of their opposition to the proposed civil government. This appeal was endorsed by Máximo Gómez, who declared himself in favor only of a civil government "elected by a Cuban National Convention. Under an American Civil Government, we would have to deal with the Government in Washington, and this is not in accordance with the purposes of the Revolution." [20]

The response was not slow in coming. Telegrams denouncing the change to a civil government began to pour into the headquarters of the Military Government from scores of mayors, municipal councils, Cuban army veterans' organizations, civic clubs, and civil governors of the provinces.. The majority of the telegrams from the mayors and municipal councils endorsed the position taken by the Council of Veterans of Independence, and urged that "rapid and efficient steps be taken to guarantee that independence will be ultimately established." The Mayor of Cienfuegos wired:

> An imposing demonstration has just taken place, the American and Cuban colors being carried in the procession and the bands playing the Cuban and American hymns. The object of the demonstration was to make known their opposition to the establishment of the Civil Government. The crowd then went to the Mayor's Office, huzzaing the Civil authorities and delivered their petition requesting that it be forwarded to McKinley. The merchants closed their stores as a token of sympathy.

The Mayor of Madruga wired that the people of his municipality had asked him "to acquaint you with their opposition to any Civil Government not originating in the popular suffrage and whose object should be other than the accomplishment of the independence of the country." The Municipal Council of Cacagua telegraphed President McKinley requesting that:

> Far from changing the character of the Military occupation, it be upheld as provisional and temporary; that the proposed civil government be not established as it would seriously threaten the legitimate aspirations of the Cuban people; that steps be shortly taken that would serve as means to carry out the noble purpose of the generous American Nation in regard to constituting a

strong, stable government for the Cuban Republic, a promise on which Cuba and the whole world rely because of the fitness of our people and the conditions of the country. Besides, Generals and Chiefs of the Liberating Army and inhabitants numbering over 500 persons have sent their protest to the President of the "Centro Veterano de Matanzas" against the establishment of the civil government.

All over Cuba, between November 29 and December 7, a series of rallies and protest meetings were held, at which resolutions were adopted protesting the plan for a civil government, calling for the speedy end of the Occupation and the formation of an independent Cuban government. Daily demonstrations against the proposed policy of the United States occurred in cities, towns, and villages, at which thousands of Cubans clamored for "Independence or Death" and "Cuba Libre." [21]

*La Discusión* was well satisfied with the results of its appeal for protests. "We do not need to express how much this movement pleases us," it declared joyfully. Now Elihu Root and other Administration leaders who had been led to believe by certain Cubans in Washington that a civil government paving the way for annexation would be welcomed in Cuba, would know that these men spoke only for themselves.

> They are the ones who devilishly defended Spain's sovereignty, obtaining in exchange, favors, positions and influence. They are the ones who sanctioned all the acts of said sovereignty, including those perpetrated by Weyler. They are the sworn enemies of the cause of Cuban independence, who consider themselves lost by its triumph, and, therefore, spare no efforts to induce the Americans to violate their promises and be divorced from the Cuban people.
>
> They should understand this in Washington. Those who joined the Americans at San Juan and El Caney, who were their allies and helped them take Santiago de Cuba, are opposed to that strange thing, obscure and incomprehensible, that calls itself *American Civil Government,* while they are encouraged to carry out the scheme by those who cursed them during the struggle with Spain, those who were then their enemies and ours.
>
> We have just emerged from a cruel war, during which we exhibited the most irrepressible heroism, holding in check an army of over two hundred thousand men, well equipped, with all kinds of arms, abundantly supplied with ammunition, holding the forts and arsenals of the country, and masters of the sea. During the war we showed the whole world that we knew how to fight to

obtain the independence of our country. And now, in peacetime, we unanimously respond to the call of the Veterans, expressing our protest by all legal means, defending in the press and in the tribune what we deem our rights, while asserting our ability to govern ourselves.[22]

Having been led to believe by Porter and Wood and by the pro-annexationists in the island that the Cubans were burning with a desire for continuation of the American presence leading to annexation, the Administration was both surprised and alarmed by the wave of protests against the idea of an American civil government. It quickly beat a retreat and announced that there was "no immediate intention" of establishing a civil government in Cuba. Even Wood, who was in Washington conferring with McKinley on Cuban affairs, and who was itching for the post of civil governor, denied that such a plan was afoot. Nevertheless, he attributed the opposition to it in Cuba to a small group of "unprincipled agitators," and criticized the Cubans for having misunderstood the term civil governor, which did not necessarily "mean permanent American government for the island." [23] Since this was precisely what Wood wanted for Cuba and since this was the interpretation placed on the plan by the annexationists in the United States and Cuba, it was hardly surprising that the vast majority of Cubans had viewed it in this light. Estes G. Rathbone, in charge of Cuba's post office, wrote Elihu Root from Havana that the Cubans, in the main, regarded the civil governor plan "as meaning a postponement of the time when the Island will be turned over to them, and they be given absolute independence." The ultimate outcome, they feared, would be annexation, and while "those who own business, property, or money, desire annexation pure and simple," this class was "in the minority. Others want independence." Rathbone warned that it would be a mistake for Washington to shape its Cuban policy on the aspirations of the annexationists in the island, for this would only lead to a clash between Cubans and Americans. Not even the Rural Guard could be trusted in such an event. "Many Cubans are revolutionists by inheritance and training; . . . to put arms in the hands of any considerable number of them would be risky." [24] One can only imagine what Rathbone would have written if the Cuban army still possessed its arms!

It was clear that to move ahead toward annexation in one form or another would be extremely dangerous for the United States, already deeply involved in the war against the Filipinos. The manager of the Havana Commercial Company, which owned large plantations in Pinar del Río province, reported in alarm that "the spirit of dissaffection is spreading and is liable soon or late to burst into flame." [25] To prevent the "flame" from bursting forth, the Administration had to assure the Cubans that there was no foundation to the reports that they would be deprived of their independence. Thus it was that on December 1, 1899, the War Department released the text of the Annual Report of the Secretary of War. In this document, Elihu Root set forth the steps to be taken in Cuba. He opened with a statement of general principles:

> Our temporary occupation of the island of Cuba involves a very simple plan of operation, with some difficulties in its application which are apt to be overlooked by those who are impatient for immediate results. The control which we are exercising in trust for the people of Cuba should not be, and of course will not be, continued any longer than is necessary to enable that people to establish a suitable government to which the control shall be transferred, which shall really represent the people of Cuba and be able to maintain order and discharge its international obligations. . . . Our present duty is limited to giving every assistance in our power to the establishment of such a government, and to maintaining order and promoting the welfare of the people of Cuba during the period necessarily required for that process.

Root then laid down the formula for the steps by which Cuba was to be given independence. First, the Cuban Census which had just been taken would have to be tabulated and totalled, in order to give correct information upon which to base suffrage and representation for municipal elections "which will place all the local governments of the island in the hands of representatives elected by the people. . . ." No elections could take place anyway until after April 11, 1900, for on that date the year of grace allowed by the peace treaty would expire, the year during which the residents of Cuba could elect whether they would be Cuban or Spanish citizens. When the local governments had been established, the next step would be taken: "the formation of a representative convention to frame a constitution and provide for a general government of the island, to which the United States will surrender the reins of government. *When that government is established the relations which exist between it and the United States will be matter for free and uncontrolled agreement between the two parties.*"[26]

Root's announcement appeared at first glance to deliver a death blow to the annexationists. The anti-imperialists in the United States even hailed it as proof "that the Administration intends to carry out the pledges which the country gave when that island's cause against Spain was made our own."[27] In Cuba *Patria* announced joyfully that Cuban independence at long last appeared safe. Other newspapers, however, were not so optimistic, pointing out that there was still no date set for Cuban independence, and much might occur before all the steps outlined by Root were carried through.[28]

Those who were skeptical found their suspicions justified by McKinley's annual message for 1899, which went to Congress on December 5th. While affirming that the pledge of the United States as to Cuban independence "is of the highest honorable obligation and must be sacredly kept," the President left the door open to indefinite control of the island, on the excuse that the mission of the United States there was "not to be fulfilled by turning adrift any loosely framed commonwealth to face the vicissitudes which too often attend weaker states whose natural wealth and abundant resources are offset by the incongruities of their political organization and the recurring occasions for internal rivalries which sap their strength and dissipate their energies." He also left open the door for annexation, by emphasizing that the new Cuba "must needs be bound to us by ties of singular intimacy and strength," and then added the meaningful sentence: "*Whether these ties shall be organic or conventional, the destinies of Cuba are in some rightful form and manner irrevocably linked to our own, but how and how far is for the future to determine in the ripeness of events.*"[29]

One anti-imperialist paper tersely summed up the section of McKinley's message dealing with the political future of Cuba: "If it were his policy to keep up the profession of good faith and yet stimulate a revolt on the island and then make the revolt the excuse for conquering and annexing it he could not have framed his sentences more provocatively."[30] General Wilson shared this interpretation of McKinley's intentions, for he wrote to his friend Goldwyn Smith, the anti-imperialist historian, that he had advised the Cubans with whom he came in contact to be quiet and not cause disturbances. Otherwise, "they will be guilty of just enough violence to play into the President's hands, and cause an indefinite postponement of the return of our forces to the United States."[31]

As was to be expected, the annexationists took heart from McKinley's message and began a new drive for an American take-over of the island. Once again, pro-annexationist articles, couched in identical language, began to appear in newspapers. Once again, headlines like "Annexation Declared to Be The Island's Only Hope"; "Cuban Wants Annexation," appeared above these articles.[32] Not all Cubans, it was now conceded, desired annexation, but those who counted did. "If a vote could be had," the *New York Times* acknowledged, "the majority for independence would be enormous. But the majority is not the class to whom Cuba's commercial importance is due. . . . Substantial interests, with business to lose or property to suffer, hope for complete American domination." The New York *Sun* put it more bluntly: "The attitude of the people of Cuba toward annexation seems to be this in brief: the wealth and intelligence of the island are generally in favor of it, and the agitators and their tools, the ignorant Negroes, are opposed to it."* America should base its policy on the desires of "the wealth and intelligence" of Cuba.[33]

In the *Atlantic Monthly* of March, 1900, Richard B. Olney, Cleveland's Secretary of State, Wall Street lawyer and financier, spokesman for America's leading business interests, wrote that Cuba was already annexed to the United States since "the Spanish War ended in the acquisition of Cuba by the United States." This was true despite the Teller Amendment which Olney called "ill-advised and futile at the time of its passage, [and] if now influential at all, is simply prejudicing the interests of Cuba and the United States alike." Congress should forget the Joint Resolution which, in any case, should not be "allowed to impede the natural march of events," and make "Cuba in point of

---

* On his return from Cuba in the fall of 1899, Charles M. Pepper, Cuban correspondent of the New York *Tribune* and the Washington *Star*, let it be widely known that the black population of Cuba was bitterly opposed to annexation to the United States because of fear of facing the type of discrimination imposed upon blacks in the North American country. "The colored race in Cuba," Pepper declared, "has reached a pretty unanimous decision that its future is not promising if the island become a State in the Union. That is the present sentiment, and it is in itself powerful enough to dampen any annexation movement." (*The Literary Digest*, Dec. 9, 1899, p. 696.)

law what she already is in point of fact, namely United States territory." Olney was certain that "such a consummation would be favored by practically the entire body of the intelligence and wealth of the Island."[34]

Olney's imperialist call was widely reprinted in the American press.[35] By May, 1900, the annexationist drive was again in such full swing that Senator Edward Hale of Maine declared "that a conspiracy exists in this country with the object of inducing the United States to violate its pledge of independence to the people of Cuba." He did not speak in generalities, but pointed to the specific source from which the conspiracy emanated:

> I think there are very powerful influences in this country—largely located in New York City, largely speculative, connected with money-making corporations—that are determined we shall never give up Cuba. I think that is the dangerous cloud in the sky.... There are very powerful influences—commercial, mercantile, financial and political—that are opposed to our ever withdrawing from Cuba.[36]

Unfortunately for the annexationists, the Cubans would not allow themselves to be taken over by the United States. The hoped-for outburst of mass support in the island for annexation, so optimistically predicted in American newspaper headlines, never materialized. In March, 1900, a sub-committee of the United States Senate, made up of Senators Orville H. Platt, Nelson P. Aldrich, and Henry M. Teller, visited Cuba. According to General Wilson, Senator Platt went to Cuba to prove that the United States would be justified in disregarding the Teller Amendment. "Platt came down to Cuba—told my officers—more than one of them, that the troops would not be withdrawn and that we should 'never relinquish Cuba.'"[37] All Platt needed was concrete proof that the Cubans wanted annexation. But on its return, the committee reported, to the dismay of the annexationists, that only a minority of the Cubans favored annexation. "It can be said of all classes in Cuba that they are looking to the establishment of an independent government, a Cuban republic."[38]

There was still one hope—the coming municipal elections in June to elect mayors (*alcaldes*), members of city councils, municipal treasurers, municipal and correctional judges for a term of one year. The

American annexationists knew that pro-annexation sentiment in Cuba was strongest among planters, merchants, and the upper classes generally, while they attributed the desire to independence to the revolutionists and to the propertyless working class in the cities and in the rural districts. If the suffrage could be restricted, then the elections would be won by the pro-United States elements, and could be held out as proof that the Cubans favored annexation.[39] In his article, "United States Electoral Intervention in Cuba," Theodore P. Wright, Jr. puts it this way: "If there had to be elections, they might be arranged in such a way as to prevent the poor, uneducated and unruly mass of the population from bringing in full weight of number to bear." Wright concedes that the aim was to cut down "anti-American majorities."[40] Naturally, the public justification for restricting suffrage in the Cuban elections did not reveal its real purpose. At first, it was defended as necessary "in order to prevent Cuba from being reduced to the level of Haiti, since with a dominant Negro population, under any approach to manhood suffrage the Negro ingredient of the population of Cuba would be in the majority."[41]* But when the Cuban Census was made public in Washington in April, a new justification was found. The Census revealed that the whites greatly outnumbered the Negroes: 57.8 percent white Cubans, 9 percent foreign white, and 32 percent Negro and mixed races.† "The official figures of the Cuban Census . . . ought to enlighten the minds and close the mouths of those who from one motive or another but ever in the choisest spirit of nincompoopery, have been insisting that independence of Cuba means negro domination of the island," observed *The State,* as it called for universal suffrage in the forthcoming elections.[42]

Not so fast, retorted the annexationist press. The Census had disclosed that 66 percent of the population was illiterate! "There is something worse than the 'black republic,'" argued the New York *Tribune.* "It is an illiterate republic, and that with a vengeance, is

---

* At a reception held in his honor in New York City, Brigadier-General William Ludlow, governor of Havana, declared that under universal suffrage, Cuba would "drift to a Haiti No. 2." (*The Literary Digest,* Dec. 9, 1899, p. 695.)

† The census revealed that the population of Cuba was 1,572,845, broken down according to provinces as follows: Havana, 424,811; Matanzas, 202,462; Pinar del Río, 173,082; Puerto Príncipe, 88,237; Santa Clara, 356,537; Santiago, 327,716.

what Cuba would be today if it were made independent and endowed with universal suffrage." Municipal elections dominated by an illiterate electorate would prove only that the "real voice" of Cuba could not really express itself.[43] But the Washington *Bee,* a Negro weekly, charged that the entire scheme was to disfranchise the blacks of Cuba, and it commented bitterly in an editorial on January 13, 1900:

> In other words, the men who have furnished the brawn and sinew of the many wars which have been fought for Cuban independence must accept under the benign influence of American policy to be relegated to the rear and denied the privilege of participating in a government to secure that which cost the blacks so many lives that they had to offer upon the sacred altar of liberty. The excuse that the blacks are illiterate is the same blarney which comes up from the South today. . . . If after the blacks of Cuba have done so much toward securing their independence of Spain, they are to become the victims of the American prejudice and have their manhood rights taken from them, it had been far better that they had remained under the Spanish yoke. . . .

Even before the Census was made public, Washington had already prepared its plan "to qualify the suffrage."[44] As drawn up by Elihu Root, it would be based on literacy, property-ownership and past service in the Cuban army. Originally only the first two qualifications were included, but Root and Wood agreed that this would be impossible to put across, and that by enfranchising all Cuban army veterans, many of whom were Negroes, the argument that the suffrage law was racially discriminatory could be overcome. In addition, it would win over "General Gomez and the old soldier element." "Giving the vote to the ex-soldiers has removed the only element which would be in any way dangerous," Wood wrote to Root early in 1900. There was still "some talk of universal suffrage," but the "best people" in Cuba ("the educated classes") were happy because they now felt relieved of the fear that the masses "would be allowed to dominate the political scene. Giving the vote to this element means a second edition of Haiti and Santo Domingo in the near future." Wood was happy because "eight out of ten people" eligible to vote under this plan would be "our friends: by our friends I mean the friends of good government and of what we are doing."[45]

The electoral law of April 18, 1900,* was basically Root's plan for a restricted franchise. Potential voters must be male, over twenty-one years of age, and citizens of Cuba according to the terms of the Treaty of Paris. In addition, they must fulfill at least one of three alternative requirements: be able to read and write; own property worth $250 in United States gold; or have served in the Cuban army prior to July 18, 1898, with an honorable discharge.[46] Apart from the suffrage provision, the election machinery had been worked out by a commission consisting of thirteen Cubans and two Americans. The latter, James E. Runcie and Horatio S. Rubens, "were both trusted agents of Wood who were included in the group to safeguard Wood's policies." The minority report, favored by Runcie and Rubens and only two Cubans, was accepted by Wood.[47]

The annexationist press in the United States waited anxiously for the returns of the municipal elections to be held June 16, confident that with the "unruly masses" ineligible to vote, other than the Cuban army veterans, the conservative, pro-annexationist forces—"the Spanish-descended, the rich, the cultured, the landowners"—would score a stunning victory.[48] But the result was a stunning defeat for annexation. For one thing, the election went off quietly, "A Model of Order," without the riots predicted by those who questioned the Cubans' "fitness for self-government."[49] For another, the returns revealed that annexationism had no real following. In Havana and most of the municipalities, the Cuban National Party, the party of the old revolutionary element, the party most prominent in opposing annexation and in demanding early independence, won. In several cities, particularly in the eastern section of Cuba, the Republican Party, also running as opposing annexation and urging early independence but containing a larger proportion of Negroes, was victorious. The Democratic Union Party, made up mainly of former autonomists, Spaniards, and the moneyed class, and openly favoring continued American occupation and annexation, found,

---

* Wood wanted to publish the suffrage regulations early, but Root urged waiting until the Census report was completed when it could be used as an argument to justify the restricted suffrage. (Root to Wood, Feb. 28, 1900. Leonard Wood Papers, Library of Congress.)

In a speech delivered before the Union League Club of New York early in 1903, Root declared that Negro suffrage in the United States had failed because the Negro was not suited for it. (*New York Times*, Feb. 7, 1903.) It is not difficult to imagine his attitude toward Negro suffrage in Cuba.

soon after its organization, that its cause was hopeless, and did not make a straight contest in any city.[50] Wood wrote sadly that the result was a victory for "the extreme and revolutionary element," but Root comforted the General with the thought that the result would have been even worse had not the restriction of the franchise excluded "so great a proportion of the element which have brought ruin to Haiti and San Domingo." [51]

The annexationists tried to dismiss the results as of no real consequence. "So far as the question of annexation is concerned," the Baltimore *American* argued, "nothing definite can be learned from the elections. There was a huge stay-at-home vote which had it been cast would have favored annexation." [52] It did not mention that there was a huge stay-at-home population which was not allowed to vote by edict of the United States, and that this vote, had it been cast, would have produced an even greater disaster for the annexationists.

A week after the municipal elections, J. C. Carlington, a Southern editor, returned from Cuba, and urged the annexationists in the United States to stop whistling in the dark:

> It will not do for the United States to dream of annexation. It cannot be. The Cubans demand independence and they will have it. But, as one very intelligent Cuban remarked, "While nothing short of a Republic of Cuba will meet the case, we all realize that we will get independence with a string tied to it." [53]

Carlington's analysis was correct on both counts. First, annexation was impossible. To be sure, the desire for it was overwhelming among the business groups in the United States. "Commercial interests now and must always favor annexation," George B. Hopkins, Wall Street banker, business leader, and co-organizer, with William Van Horne of the syndicate to build the Cuban Central Railroad, wrote to Senator Spooner on March 14, 1900.[54] But there was only one way in which this desire could have been realized: if the Cuban people had favored it. Short of that, it was difficult if not impossible for the United States to violate the letter of the Teller Amendment. Senator Orville H. Platt, who longed for annexation, made this clear to Edwin F. Atkins when this spokesman for annexation suggested this as the best way to advance American interests in the island. "I think annexation is absolutely out of the question," wrote Platt sadly. "In the first place that foolish

Teller resolution stands not only in the way of that, but all other action which we might take if it had never been passed. I think I know enough of Congressional sentiment to know that it is regarded as a pledge of the government against annexation."[55]* It was "a great pity," as the annexationists repeatedly pointed out, that the Teller Amendment had been passed, but passed it had been. The annexationists tried to get around it by picturing the Cubans as favoring annexation, but every time this campaign got under way, the Cuban people forced it to retreat by indignant protests and clear demonstration of their desire for independence. This is not to say that there were not those in Cuba who favored annexation after the war just as there were Cuban annexationists long before the war. In fact, there were probably more annexationists in Cuba after the war than before: the American business colony which owned stores, saloons and boarding houses and other businesses in leading cities; American speculators with options on lands and other properties, and seekers of franchises; owners of sugar estates and makers of cigars and cigarettes who longed for special privileges in the American market if Cuba became part of the United States; and conservatives in general, many of them Spaniards, who feared that an independent Cuba might be too radical.[56] The McKinley Administration was frequently accused of postponing the announcement of a date for the end of the Occupation in order to give the Cuban annexationist forces time to rally popular support behind them, and thus present annexation as a widespread demand.[57] But time did not help the annexationist cause. It was clear at all stages of the Occupation that the annexationists constituted a distinct minority in Cuba. The vast majority of the Cubans insisted on independence. This had been their aspiration for half a century, and for this they had made untold sacrifices, They insisted, too, that the United States live up to its promise. This expression of the will of the majority of the Cuban people doomed the effort in the United States to undo the Teller Amendment. In the end, the annexationists had to concede that their goal was impossible to achieve.

---

* Platt was incorrect, however, when he wrote to Leonard Wood: "If we had made no promises there would be, I think, a strong annexation sentiment among the business people of the United States." (Platt to Wood, June 1, 1900, Leonard Wood Papers, Library of Congress.) It would have been more correct to indicate that there was a strong annexationist sentiment among the business people despite the promises.

Yet Carlington's second observation was also correct. Many Cubans realized that while the annexationist drive had met defeat, the "powerful influences" which Senator Hale referred to—"commercial, mercantile, financial and political"—were not giving up the idea of annexing Cuba indirectly. Cuba, as we shall now see, was to get its independence, but the "string tied to it" would make it a virtual colony of the United States.

## CHAPTER XXIV
# The Cuban Constitutional Convention

IN FEBRUARY, 1900, Leonard Wood had assured Washington that there was no need to worry about announcing an early end to the military occupation because the Cubans were quite content to let matters continue as they were. "The agitators are growing less numerous," he wrote to Root, "and their influence over the people is decreasing daily. The Cuban people, as a whole, realize very fully well that they are not ready for self-government and the only people who are willing for it are those whose antecedents and actions demonstrate the impossibility of self government just at present." [1] But the municipal elections demonstrated that many Cubans did not in the least believe that they were not ready for self-government. On the contrary, the triumph of the nationalist forces indicated that they favored immediate independence. Immediately after the elections, General Alejandro Rodríguez, one of the leaders of the National Party, sent a victory telegram to McKinley: "The Cuban National Party, victorious in the election, salutes the worthy representative of the North American Nation, and confidently awaits an early execution of the Joint Resolution." [2]

It was time to stop the stalling and get on with the business of allowing the Cubans to set up their own government. Apart from the rising demand for this island,* there was the coming presidential election to consider. In January, 1900, George S. Boutwell, President of the American Anti-Imperialist League, had declared that "the only question of importance before the country" in the presidential election

---

\* Even the ultra-conservative *El Diario de la Marina* conceded that Washington's "fast and loose policy" toward Cuba had produced "a continuous state of unrest and excitement" in the island. Neither conservatives nor independents knew where they stood, since the Administration refrained from informing the people when the Occupation would end, if ever, and a "depressing and disturbing influence" abounded. (Reprinted in New York *Evening Post*, Feb. 7, 1900.)

would be the issue of "Republic or Empire." "Allow Cuba, allow Porto Rico, allow the Philippine Islands," said Boutwell, "to set up governments for themselves free from any dictation by us." [3] Speeches of other members of the League stressing the same theme followed Boutwell's within a month. While fire was concentrated on the Philippines, some attention was paid to Cuba, and the general emphasis was that the time to end the American occupation was long overdue.[4] At any rate, imperialism was freely conceded to be "the paramount issue" in the election of 1900. All other issues paled in comparison with it, there being, in the eyes of the anti-imperialists, "no second or third issues in any contest." [5]

The danger for the Republicans that the occupation of Cuba could become a major issue in the approaching presidential campaign emerged sharply in the spring of 1900, with the disclosure of widespread corruption in the American administration of the island. In February, the *North American Review* published Major James E. Runcie's article, entitled "American Misgovernment in Cuba." While it was filled with praise for Wood's policies in Santiago, where Runcie had served, and concentrated wholly on the inadequacies of Brooke's administration,* it alerted public attention to the fact that there was something wrong with the Administration-sponsored publicity campaign picturing the American occupation as a model of efficiency, the showplace of benevolent American rule of a people supposedly not yet fit to govern themselves.[6]

But Runcie's article was only the prologue. In May, a serious scandal in the Cuban postal system came to light. Large-scale embezzlements were reported in the Havana post office, with shortages of at least $100,000. Charles F. Neely, a minor postal official, was at first held mainly responsible, but it soon became evident that the entire body of American officials in the postal service was involved, including Estes G. Rathbone, Director-General and a political protege of Senator Marcus A. Hanna of Ohio. While McKinley ordered Joseph L. Bristow, the Fourth Assistant Postmaster General of the United States, to conduct a sweeping investigation which would "shield nobody who has committed a wrong," [7] the scandals were seized upon in the anti-

---

* Brooke accused Wood of having inspired the attack on his administration so as to build his own prestige. (Brooke to Adjutant-General of the Army, Feb. 15, 1900, copy in Leonard Wood Papers, Library of Congress.)

imperialist press as evidence of the evils inherent in imperialist domination. "Thus the art of good government and the blessings of civilization which a policy of imperialism seeks to foist upon a people no better off by being freed from Spanish robbers, are made paltry and contemptible," declared the *Social Democratic Herald* of Chicago, in an editorial entitled "Republican Looters in Cuba." [8]* Even Republican papers, ordinarily lavish in their praise of the Occupation, were forced to eat their words. The Philadelphia *North American* observed with justifiable irony:

> Had the management of Cuban affairs been entrusted to the people of the island at the close of the Spanish war the development in their postal services of a scandal like the Neely robberies would have been regarded as proof of Cuban unfitness for self-government and probably would have been settled upon as sufficient excuse for assuming guardianship over Cuba and filling her offices with able American instructors in the science of impeccable statecraft.[9]

On May 16, 1900, Augustus O. Bacon of Georgia, a leading anti-imperialist Democrat, arose in the Senate to deliver a scathing attack on the entire Cuban occupation. He began with the postal scandals which he characterized as sufficient to bring "the blush of shame to the cheek of every American citizen," and went on to charge that they exemplified a policy under the Occupation of stealing "large amounts belonging to the people of Cuba." He accused the Military Government of playing fast and loose with the resources of the Cuban people, spending many times more for the comfort of American soldiers in the island than would have been the case had they been quartered in the United States. The Cubans received no real benefits from this extravagant and wasteful use of their money. "These expenditures are mainly on American account—to house an unnecessary army and to suppress the yellow fever to which Cubans are immune." American contractors had been favored in the dealing out of contracts for public works in Cuba, and a railroad had been built in violation of the Foraker Amend-

---

* The *Social Democratic Herald* pointed out that Neely "once made himself conspicuous at Muncie, Indiana, by trying to break up one of Eugene Debs' meetings." (May 26, 1900.) Eugene V. Debs was the American labor and Socialist leader who ran as candidate for president in 1900 on the Social Democratic ticket.

ment. Yet the United States had no right to spend the money of the Cubans "except for the purpose of pacifying the island and assisting them in organizing their own government."

The American army of occupation, Bacon continued, was not only "unnecessary," it was illegal. The United States had no right governing Cuba. The only just reason for the United States to exercise authority in Cuba was to carry out the terms of the Joint Resolution. Yet there had been peace for nearly two years, and a Cuban government had still not been erected. Why all this delay? Was it not in order to leave open the door for the annexation of Cuba in spite of the self-denying avowal in the Teller Amendment? That Amendment had in fact already been violated, for it denied the United States not only sovereignty in Cuba, but jurisdiction and control" as well. There was only one thing for the United States to do: erect a Cuban government and get out. "In my opinion, this session of Congress should not be adjourned until by act or joint resolution there is definitely fixed the early date when we will leave the control of the island to the Cubans." In the meantime, Bacon called for a resolution of inquiry into the collection and expenditure of public money in Cuba.[10]

It fell to Senator Orville H. Platt, chairman of the Committee on Relations with Cuba,* to defend the Administration. But in his defense, Platt was forced to promise that work to establish a government of and by the Cubans would be advanced as fast as possible. As he explained privately to Wood, the scandals in Cuba, added to the war in the Philippines, had brought to the surface widespread public discontent with the Administration's entire colonial policy, and there was a danger, first, that Congress might "take the bit in its teeth and say we ought to get out of Cuba,"† and second, that the Cuban question would become a key issue in the presidential election. The Administra-

---

* By precedent and right, the chairmanship of the Committee on Relations with Cuba should have gone to Senator Foraker. But his opposition to the American occupation, his belief that it should be ended swiftly and a Cuban Republic established, and his sponsorship of the amendment which barred franchises from being disposed of during the American stay in Cuba, led the Administration to pass him over for Platt, an ardent champion of imperialism.

† Platt revealed that he had planned to propose a modification of the Foraker Amendment, but "to tell the truth I do not dare to do it now," for it would give the Democrats an issue in the presidential campaign. It would have to wait until after the election. (Platt to Wood, June 1, 1900, Leonard Wood Papers, Library of Congress.)

tion, Platt felt, had no choice now but to give up the idea of annexing the island, and take steps to get a Cuban Republic established. He closed with words which were to have far-reaching significance: "It will be necessary to secure such relations with the new [Cuban] government as will safeguard and protect not only the interests of Cuba, but our own interests with relation thereto." [11]

Wood agreed with Platt that the situation in Congress and in the country at large required that a Cuban government be established. To Root he suggested that a Constitutional Convention be called for some time in the autumn. In the meantime, he would prepare a Constitution for Cuba, which would contain a provision for "certain definite relations and agreements between the United States and Cuba." The finished document would be "presented to the Assembly as a model for adoption," but even after this "model" had been adopted by the Cubans, the Occupation should continue with American troops remaining in the island and with the Military Governor retaining an absolute veto power over the Cuban government. Wood conceded that "such a form of government would not differ materially from the present," but at least it would give the appearance that the Cuban people had gained the right to make their own laws.[12] What Wood meant, of course, was that since there was now no chance of annexing the island in the immediate future, it was necessary to maintain American control by giving the Cubans a sense of self-government without relinquishing domination by the United States. Meanwhile, to allay Cuban suspicions that this was the Administration's real objective, Wood suggested to Root that on July 1, "it would be a good idea to quietly authorize the floating of the Cuban flag from all municipal and civil buildings occupied by local authorities." Even his own palace at Havana should fly the Cuban flag![13]

Soon Wood moved up the timetable for holding a Constitutional Convention, but not because of consideration of the desires of the Cuban people. Rather he was now anxious to get out of Cuba as quickly as possible. News from China excited the imperialist-minded Military Governor. The Chinese people, led by the "Boxers," had risen up against the territorial encroachments upon their country by foreign imperialists, and the division of the thirteen richest, most populous, and most desirable of the eighteen Chinese provinces into "spheres of influence." War was the imperialists' answer to the attempt of the

Chinese people, to keep their country for themselves,\* and while a patriotic American like Mark Twain could proclaim publicly that if he were in China, he would be a "Boxer," and that "my sympathies are with the Chinese,"[14] Wood was anxious to play an active role in a war to crush the Chinese uprising, divide up their country, and at the same time, advance his career. As he wrote to his fellow-imperialist Lodge, "the people going to China have the opportunity for the one thing which gives the man of the Army reputation." And to Root, he wrote longingly: "If there is going to be a war in China I want to go. . . . I do not want to be left here to fossilize."[15]

Now Wood beat the drums to "rush the establishment of civil government" in Cuba. He favored calling the Constitutional Convention "right away," reminding the Administration that further delay would "only give a cudgel to the Democrats" in the presidential campaign.[16] This last argument carried considerable weight. The Democratic Party, with William Jennings Bryan again its presidential candidate, was giving every sign of making "the failure of the Republican Party to fulfill the pledge given to the world as to Cuba" a major issue.[17] The Republican platform on which McKinley was re-nominated cynically boasted that "to ten millions of the human race there has been given a 'new birth of freedom'" as a result of the Spanish-American War, fully endorsed overseas expansion, and called for the suppression of the "insurrection" in the Philippines in order to confer the blessings of liberty and civilization on the Filipinos, rescued by American arms from a life of darkness and paganism. On Cuba it said only: "To Cuba independence and self-government were assured in the same voice by which war was declared and to the letter this pledge shall be per-

---

\* In June, 1900, an international fleet bombarded and captured the Tuku forts which commanded the approach to Peking, and the American Admiral Kempff cooperated in the attack. Although the slaying of 242 foreigners, chiefly missionaries, was the excuse for the war against China, the slaying actually did not begin until the opening days of July, three weeks after hostilities had started. Some 18,000 international troops of eight powers, including 2,000 American soldiers, attacked China, plundered the country, executed leaders of the anti-imperialist movement, and imposed a humiliating treaty of peace. At the Republican national convention at Philadelphia in the summer of 1900, Chauncey M. Depew, a leading Wall Street railroad capitalist and banker, declared frankly: "What are our armies hammering at the walls of China and marching through the jungles of the Philippines for? It is to find a market for our two billions of surplus products." (Philadelphia *Inquirer*, June 23, 1900. See also *Appeal to Reason*, Oct. 26, 1907.)

formed." It said nothing about when this pledge would be kept, not even intimating that this would happen soon. In contrast, the Democratic platform declared that the issue of imperialism which had grown "of the Spanish war" was "the paramount issue of the campaign," and was very specific in demanding "the prompt and honest fulfillment of our pledge to the Cuban people and the world that the United States has no disposition or intention to exercise sovereignty, jurisdiction or control over the island of Cuba, except for its pacification. The war ended nearly two years ago, profound peace reigns over all the island, and still the Administration keeps the governments of the island from its people while Republican carpetbag officials plunder the revenues and exploit the colonial theory to the disgrace of the American people." [18]*

Within a few days after the Democratic platform was adopted on July 5, Wood was on his way to Washington to confer with Root and McKinley about early action in calling the Cuban Constitutional Convention. He went back to Cuba—not to China which the President said was out of the question[19]—with instructions to call for an election to the Convention. On July 25 the Military Government published Civil Order No. 31 providing for the election of 32 delegates on September 3, the Convention to begin its sessions at Havana on the first Monday in November. It cited the establishment of municipal governments in Cuba, and noted that the Cuban people "are now ready to proceed to the establishment of a general government which shall assume and exercise sovereignty, jurisdiction over the island." [20]

The issuance of this order during a presidential campaign in which the opposition made "imperialism the paramount issue," and prompt adherence to the Teller Amendment as part of it, was not haphazard coincidence. Two months before, *The State* had predicted this outcome: "In the approaching presidential campaign the Cuban question will take its place along with the Philippine question, and McKinley, seeking re-election, will have to meet it. It would not be surprising if the

---

* The platform also contained a blistering attack on Republican policies of substituting methods of imperialism for those of a republic, and warned the American people "that imperialism abroad will lead quickly to despotism at home." It condemned the Administration's Philippine policy which had been dictated by "greedy commercialism" and had involved the nation in an "unnecessary war and destroyed the country's reputation as a champion of freedom."

Republican party, weighted by responsibility for the evil deeds of its agents in Cuba, should find it necessary to make declarations fixing a definite limit to the occupation of the island by our troops and our carpetbaggers." [21]* That McKinley fully understood the importance of the Cuban question in his campaign for re-election is evidenced by the following account offered by Horatio S. Rubens. As a member of the Committee on Taxation in Cuba, Rubens suggested a tax on land values. Following a protest on the part of the absentee landowners in the United States who had heard of the proposal, Wood told Rubens that he could not agree to the idea "because it would raise an immediate storm and McKinley, who was facing a campaign for re-election, had asked him to keep things as quiet as possible in Cuba." [22]

The initial enthusiasm in the United States and Cuba at the news that an order had been issued calling the Constitutional Convention was tempered with the release of the text. One sentence in particular aroused criticism. It declared that the duties of the Convention were: "To frame and adopt a Constitution for the people of Cuba, and as a part thereof, to provide for and agree with the Government of the United States upon relations to exist between that Government and the Government of Cuba, and to provide for the election by the people of the officers under such Constitution and the transfer of government to the officers so elected." [23] There were two immediate objections to this sentence, although both were interrelated. It was unprecedented for a Convention both "to *frame* and *adopt*" a Constitution. Adoption was ordinarily by the people of the country. Why not in the case of Cuba? The *New York Times*, ordinarily pro-Administration on all issues relating to imperialism, offered the following criticism:

> There are to be only 31 delegates in the Constitutional Convention. It would be said that we had influenced the nomination and election of the delegates, had packed the convention, and by craftily contriving that it should adopt and ratify the Constitution without submitting it to the people, had prepared the way for a bastard Constitution that would not establish a sovereign nation, but would leave the Cubans in vassalage to the United States.

---

* The word "carpetbagger" was identified with northerners who hastened with little more than a carpetbag of personal effects, into the South for self-seeking purposes. For evidence that the carpetbaggers were not all corrupt, *see* Kenneth M. Stampp, *The Era of Reconstruction, 1865-1877*, New York, 1965.

This suspicion would be made plausible by the direction of the order that as part of the Constitution, the convention "is to provide for and agree with the government of the United States upon the relations to exist between that government and the government of the United States." [24]

The foes of imperialism in the United States were especially critical of the last part of the order. *The Nation* reminded the Administration that "what we promised her [Cuba] was independence, not suzerainty." The wording of the order, the New York *Evening Post* charged, showed that "Cuba is not to be 'free and independent,' as the joint resolution of Congress declared. . . . She cannot set up a government and adjust her relations with us afterwards as a free and independent government might do. She cannot exercise her own choice about these relations even in the Constitutional Convention. They must be arranged by agreement with us. That is, the relations must be agreeable to us before any Cuban government can go into effect." [26] *The State* pointed out that not only the pledge in the Teller Amendment to leave the government of the island to its people had been officially and publicly repudiated, but the promise of the Secretary of War as well. For in his Annual Report of November, 1899, Root had said that when the new Cuban government was established, "the relations which exist between it and the United States will be a matter for free and uncontrolled agreement between the two parties." Finally, "even the pledges of the Republican convention had been cast aside within six weeks after their making." [27]* *The State* urged the Cubans to be on the alert, and not trust the Administration "one inch. They have to deal with a set of greedy and unscrupulous imperialists who would

---

* *The State* urged Bryan to make an issue of this betrayal in his speech of accepting the Democratic nomination (August 3, 1900), but the Democratic candidate ignored the advice. His only reference to Cuba was the proposal that if he were elected President, he would convene Congress for the purpose of clarifying the American position relative to the late war, and of drawing up a plan of "establishing a stable terminal government in the Philippines as in Cuba." ("Notification Speech," August, 1900, copy in William Jennings Bryan Papers, Library of Congress.) In his acceptance speech, McKinley boasted of the United States' accomplishments in Cuba since it took possession on January 1, 1899, and noted that the Constitutional Convention would meet "to frame a constitution upon which an independent government for the island will rest. All this is a long step in the fulfillment of our sacred guarantee to the people of Cuba." (New York *Tribune*, Sept. 10, 1900.)

openly rob them of their liberties if they dared, and who will cheat them if they can." [28]

The Cubans were scarcely in need of such friendly advice. A protest movement began, in which all political parties united, to ask for the removal of the clause fixing the relations to exist between the United States and Cuba as part of the Constitution. On August 27, seventeen delegates, representing nine political parties or the provincial branches of parties, met in Havana and drew up a telegram to President McKinley, asking him to announce that the Convention "will not be bound to discuss and approve the relations between Cuba and the United States, such relations being regarded as forming no part of the Constitution." The National Party (Partido Nacional), however, delayed action on sending the telegram when its delegates announced that they were not authorized to sign it but only to ask that the order convening the Convention be explained. It was finally decided to hold another meeting a few days later, the National Party delegates meanwhile consulting their party as to signing the telegram. For reasons which are not clear, this meeting was never held and the telegram never sent. One explanation for the refusal of the Nationalist delegates to sign the telegram was that they did not want the elections delayed.[29]

McKinley, however, was not unaware of the Cuban attitude to the order convening the Constitutional Convention. It was brought to his attention in person by Salvador Cisneros Betancourt, who afterward disclosed, in his pamphlet, *Appeal to the American People in Behalf of Cuba,* what he had told the President:

> Why should the members of a convention called upon to frame and adopt a Constitution for the people of Cuba and to provide for their election of Government officers be directed "to provide for and agree with the Government of the United States upon the relations to exist between that Government and the Government of Cuba?" These relations are not a Constitutional question, but should and will be properly determined as those with any other country, by the Government of Cuba when duly established. The arbitrary character of this provision needs no discussion, and the grave dangers with which it threatens Cuba are increased by the absurdly small number of delegates provided for in that order.... Thirty-one (31) delegates for the entire Island of Cuba is not by any means a sufficient number to organize a Constitutional Convention which shall be truly representative of the diverse interests

and opinions of the people of Cuba, and, therefore, there is imminent danger, already evident, of outside pressure from that same Military Government, in such a reduced number.

Cisneros objected also to the fact that the Convention was to meet on the very eve of the Presidential election in the United States, charging that the delay was caused by a deliberate scheme to prevent any opposition in the Convention to this "attempted usurpation" of the independence of Cuba from becoming "a factor in the Presidential election."* He went further and urged the end of the military occupation even before the Constitution Convention met:

> It should cease it Cuba. The people of the island appeal to the people of the United States not to allow its continuance. The people of Cuba, by their courage and sacrifices during two bloody wars and by their patience and self-control under difficult and trying circumstances since, have not only earned their independence, but deserve the confidence and respect of mankind.
> The people of the United States, as that of the rest of the world, can rest in complete security that the Constitutional Convention will adopt a constitution which shall efficiently safeguard public interests and afford ample protection to life and property.[30]†

Wood insisted to McKinley that in asking for the end of the Occupation before the Convention met, Cisneros was speaking for himself, and that all Cuban leaders really wanted the United States to delay the end of the Occupation as long as possible but did not dare say so. He conceded, nevertheless, that the tieing together of the Constitution and the question of Cuban-American relations looked to all Cubans like a form of coercion, and had "given the rabid Anti-Americans a chance

---

\* Albert G. Robinson agreed with this interpretation, noting that the date selected for the Convention to meet was "timed so as to keep the Cuban issue out of the American presidential campaign of 1900." (*Cuba and the Intervention*, p. 209.)

† Cisneros was not the only Cuban patriot to request this of the Administration. When Elihu Root was in Cuba during the summer of 1900, Juan Gualberto Gómez went to visit him to urge the Secretary of War to end the Occupation before the Constitutional Convention met. Root answered that the United States was anxious to bring its stay in Cuba to a quick end, but added that "This depends on the conduct of the Constitutional Convention." Gómez replied: "It will be conducted with the dignity of the Cuban people." (Leopoldo Herrego Estuch, *Juan Gualberto Gómez: Un Gran Inconforme*, La Habana, 1954, pp. 153-54.)

to howl from one end of the Island to the other." He therefore requested permission from Root to announce that the Convention would be allowed to consider the issues as two separate matters.[31] But Root remained silent on this request prior to the election of the delegates.

The *New York Times*' suspicion that the Military Government would try to "pack" the Convention proved to be well founded. On August 13, Wood began a tour of the island designed to promote the election of the "best men" as delegates to the convention, and he made it quite clear that he meant candidates favorable to the policies of the United States. If the Cubans sent "a lot of political jumping-jacks as delegates they must not expect their work will be received very seriously." In Santiago de Cuba, on August 26, he stressed that great care should be taken not to select "the disturber and malcontent to represent you in the convention." He gave two reasons for his advice: first, "to avoid making Cuba into a second Haiti," and secondly, to win United States approval of the Constitution. "Bear in mind that no Constitution which does not provide a stable government will be accepted by the United States." Later, he told a gathering at Puerto Príncipe that unless men of "science and experience" were elected "who would afford guarantee of stability to the Government elected, the United States would not withdraw from Cuba." Cisneros attacked Wood bitterly for this threat:

> General Wood, on the eve of an election in the United States, would not have dared to utter such words before a body of electors. Why should he, in Cuba, endeavor to restrict the free suffrage, insult the people, and wound their just sense of dignity and manhood by such a threat?[32]

Wood hoped that his tour would "bring representative conservative elements to the front" under the banner of the Union Democratic Party. But his efforts were unsuccessful. The Union Democratic Party had the stigma of opposition to independence and pro-annexationism attached to it, and most Cubans viewed it as an American puppet party. It came as no surprise, therefore, that the Union Democratic Party showed little strength in the elections. The National Party, whose candidates campaigned on a platform urging immediate independence, sent the most delegates to the Constitutional Convention. Indeed, all of the delegates, except one, Eliseo Giberga, represented the nationalist viewpoint. Among the delegates were former Generals in the Liberating Army, jurists, University professors, mainly men who had played distinguished roles in Cuba's long struggle for independence. Elected were men like Gonzalo de Quesada, General Emilio Núñez, Salvador Cisneros Betancourt, General Julio Sanguily, Alfredo Zayas Alfonso, José M. Gómez, Juan Gualberto Gómez, Manuel Sanguily, and Domingo Méndez Capote.[33] The *New York Times'* Havana correspondent reported that "in the main the delegates are capable men." However, a number of American newspapers characterized Sanguily, Cisneros, and Juan Gualberto Gómez as "Jacobins."[34]

Wood wrote to Root that he was both "disappointed" and "satisfied" in the composition of the Convention. He had hoped that "they would send their very best men"; instead, while some of these were elected, so too were "some of the worst agitators and political rascals in Cuba. I should say that we have about ten absolutely first class men and about fifteen men of doubtful qualifications and about six of the worst rascals and fakirs in Cuba." Still he was not unduly upset because not over 30 percent of the qualified voters had voted. "The sum substance of the whole thing is that the people of the Island are today enjoying more liberty than they ever had before and they are not, as a body, anxious to make another leap in the dark. In other words, they lack confidence in their own people."[35] Naturally, Wood failed to mention what a number of Cuban correspondents for American newspapers reported: that the inclusion of the clause on future relations with the United States as a part of the Constitution had led many Cubans to refuse to participate in the election.* On October 10, at a banquet commemorating the "Grito de Yara," which had begun the Ten Years' War for Independence, General Hernández had exclaimed: "My fellow-countrymen, they are preparing to cheat you!" *The Nation* reported that "speaker after speaker avowed his distrust of the United States," and observed that two things besides the order for the Convention were contributing to this continuing distrust. One was the assertion of Indiana's Senator Albert J. Beveridge, a foremost Republican spokesman for imperialism, that the Teller Amendment "was made in a moment of impulse but mistaken generosity . . . and it will not

---

* There were also reports that the conservatives tried to induce the Cubans to refrain from taking part in the elections in order to prolong the intervention. (*Daily People,* Aug. 29, 1900.)

be kept." * The other was that, in anticipation of continuing American control of Cuba even after a Republic was established, "the advance agents of American Imperialism are swarming to the island, to exploit land, mines, forests, public franchises." [36]

Of course, none of this entered into Wood's reports. On the contrary, on November 1, 1900, in an article in the *Independent,* he assured the American people that "there is no distrust of the U.S. on the part of the Cubans . . . they have perfect confidence that this country will redeem every promise it has made." [37]

The Constitutional Convention held its first session in Havana's Teatro Martí on November 5, 1900.† Long before the session opened, the area around the theater was jammed. "Many thousands were unable to gain admittance," the *New York Times*' correspondent reported, "and the streets in the neighborhood were blocked with people." [38] General Wood arrived, bringing with him instructions from Root, who had finally agreed to allow the Convention to consider the Constitution and the question of Cuban-American relations as two separate issues. Wood made this change in the Administration's policy clear. In Civil Order No. 115, he told the delegates after welcoming them, that: "It will be your duty, first, to frame and adopt a Constitution for Cuba, and when that has been done, to formulate what, in your opinion, ought to be the relations between the United States and Cuba." The Constitution would have to be adequate to secure a stable and orderly free government. When the delegates had formulated the relations "which, in your opinion, ought to exist between Cuba and the United States," the U.S. Government would "doubtless take such action on its part as shall lead to a final and authoritative agreement between the people of the two countries to the promotion of their common interests." He then wished the delegates "a speedy and successful conclusion" of

---

\* Beveridge made this statement in a speech on September 25, at the Marquette Club in Chicago. His actual words were: "The resolution hastily passed by all parties in Congress, at an excited hour, was an error which years of time, propinquity of location, common commerce, mutual interests and similar dangers surely will correct." (Copy of speech in William McKinley Papers, Library of Congress.) The New York *Herald* of September 26, 1900 headlined the statement: "Beveridge Says Cuba Must Be Ours. Calls Promise A Mistake. Annexation Quite Natural."

† The theatre was originally called "Irijoa." It was renamed in honor of Martí for the opening of the Convention.

their work, and left the theater.[39] He did not, as some had feared, try to impose a "model" Constitution on the delegates such as he had suggested during the summer. "The delegates," wrote a correspondent, "cheered for the United States and for free Cuba and independence." [40]

While Wood had not made clear what the role of the United States would be in determining the relations between Cuba and her neighbor, there was certainly nothing vague now about the question of the connection between future Cuban relations with the United States and the Constitution. Wood's revised instructions made it clear, first, that the Cubans were to keep these two issues separate, and second, that they were merely to express their opinion on the subject of relations as a basis for future negotiations. Yet later, as we shall see, there was much unwarranted criticism of Cuba in the American press for failing to include a provision for relations as part of the Constitution, even though Wood's Order No. 455 explicitly instructed the Convention to deal with this matter separately. Although Wood's second and revised order was not as widely reported in the American press as had been the first, even those newspapers which did publish it joined the chorus of criticism. The *New York Times,* for example, though it published Wood's speech of November 5 to the Convention, declared on February 8, 1901, that the Cubans "appear to have forgotten the terms of General Wood's Order." The article then quoted the original Order No. 301 of July 5 and not the revised instructions in No. 455! [41]

After Wood had departed, an oath was administered to the delegates in which they "publicly and solemnly renounced allegiance to, or compact made with, any State or nation, whether made directly or indirectly, swearing to the sovereignty of the free and independent people of Cuba and swearing to respect the solution this convention may adopt as well as the government established by the Constitution." Then Delegate Alemán, insisting that the Convention was "only a continuation of the fight for independence," moved that the regulations governing the Cuban Assembly of 1896 be adopted. The session adjourned so that the delegates might become familiar with these regulations.[42] Thus ended the first session of the Cuban Constitutional Convention.

On November 6, when the convention reassembled, it sent a telegram to McKinley saluting the President and the Congress of the United States, and expressing "sentiments of gratitude to the American people."[43] That same day, the American nation went to the polls, re-elected McKinley and gave the Republicans their greatest victory since 1872. The popular vote was 7,207,923 votes for McKinley, 6,358,135 for Bryan. In 1896 the vote was 7,111,607 to 6,509,052. McKinley (and his vice-presidential candidate Theodore Roosevelt) had been elected by 53 percent of the votes cast and with a greater margin than in 1896. The Republicans also swept both houses of Congress.[44]

Many Americans, especially the anti-imperialists, who had supported Bryan reluctantly—they were called the "Hold-your-nose-and-vote" group—denied that the election meant that imperialism had been accepted by the American people.* But the imperialists interpreted the election as a go-ahead signal for expansion and conquest. The Chicago *Inter-Ocean,* viewing the election returns, said ominously, "What the American people take, they will keep."[45] *The State,* mourning Bryan's defeat, predicted "that within a year the issue of imperialism will be more prominent with respect to Cuba than with the Philippines."[46]

The Cubans did not have to wait a year to feel the effect of the election returns. On the day after McKinley's victory, the Philadelphia *Ledger,* a Republican paper, called on the Administration to establish a protectorate over Cuba and continue military occupation indefinitely regardless of what the Constitutional Convention did. This would not even contradict America's pledge to the Cubans, for Congress had "declared its purpose to establish a stable and orderly government [in Cuba]. Are stability and peace in the island practicable with an absolute independent Cuban republic?"[47] The *Ledger* evidently had not even bothered to read the Joint Resolution of Congress, for it said noth-

---

* Although the Liberty Congress of anti-imperialists endorsed Bryan on August 16, and though he was lauded as "the only man in the country that could defeat the imperial policy of McKinley," many could not forgive him for having urged the ratification of the Treaty of Paris, and they supported him only half-heartedly. Socialists criticized the Bryan ticket for condemning the Republican Administration for not giving the people of Cuba, Puerto Rico, and the Philippines complete political rights while remaining silent about the fact that the followers of Bryan in a number of Southern states had by legal enactment "practically disfranchised" the Negro people. (*Daily People,* July 29, Sept. 4, 1900.) Thomas A. Bailey concludes, after a study of the election, that Bryan was defeated by "the fear that Bryan would destroy prosperity by overthrowing the gold standard and putting into effect his economic heresies," and that his anti-imperialist stand was not crucial in his defeat. ("Was the Presidential Election of 1900 a Mandate on Imperialism?" *Mississippi Valley Historical Review,* vol. XXIV, June, 1937, pp. 47-51.)

ing about a "purpose to establish a stable and orderly government in Cuba," referring only to the "pacification" of the island after which the United States would "leave the government and control of the island to its people."

As more and more Republican papers echoed the *Ledger,* the New York *Daily People* advised the delegates to the Constitutional Convention to pack up and go home and thus save the "trouble and expense of a Convention named 'Constitutional.'" If they continued, they would work for nothing, it predicted, for all they would get from the imperialist-dominated McKinley Admiinstration would be "a make-believe independent Republic. . . . The capitalist class of the United States does not intend to take any chances. It will have no monkeying with its vested interests in Cuba . . . hence, the Cubans will be permitted to establish a free Government with a rope to it." [48]

What the delegates thought privately about such advice is impossible to determine; the Convention continued. But the tone of the triumphant Republican press in the United States did not escape the notice of the Negro patriot, Juan Gualberto Gómez, delegate from the province of Santiago de Cuba. Alert to anything which threatened to infringe upon Cuba's independence, he felt that even the concession in Wood's speech to the delegates was not a sufficient guarantee of Cuba's sovereignty, and that the best way to insure this was to point out to the United States, in a polite but firm manner, that the whole question of relations between the two countries should be taken up *after* the Cuban Republic was established. But Gómez's resolution affirming this principle was voted down by the Convention, 22 to 4. Again and again at various points in the proceedings, Gómez tried to get the delegates to accept his proposal that the United States be informed that the question of relations would be negotiated only after independence was established, but each time he was voted down.[49] Evidently the majority of the delegates felt that such a stand would unduly antagonize the United States, and might lead to cancelling the Convention.

Most of the real work of the Convention was done in committee meetings, there being few planetary sessions. Several thorny questions were debated vigorously. One involved the question of separation of Church and State. In the Constitution of Guaímaro, the first fundamental charter of Cuba, drawn up by the revolutionary forces in 1869, the issue of Church and State was not dealt with. Article 22 guaranteed individual liberties, religious liberties being listed as one of them. Neither the second Constitution, that of Jimagüajú, adopted in September, 1895, nor the third, drawn up at La Yaya in 1897, tackled the question of Church and State, although the latter provided that Cubans and foreigners should be protected in their religious opinions and in the exercise of their respective worships as long as they were not contrary to public morality.[50]

During the conference in Paris to discuss a treaty of peace, Spain tried to influence the United States to maintain the status quo in Cuba with respect to the Catholic Church, offering the following provision: "The Roman Catholic Apostolic Religion, its institutions and ministers, shall continue to enjoy in all the territories which are subject of this treaty the liberty and the rights in the undisturbed possession of which they are at present. The members of this Church, whatever their nationality, shall continue to enjoy the same liberty and the exercise of their form of worship." But the American Commissioners stated that the United States could make no distinction as to religion, and proposed the following which was incorporated as Article 10 of the Treaty of Paris: "The inhabitants of the territory over which Spain relinquishes or cedes her sovereignty shall be secured in the free exercise of their religion."[51]

From the beginning of the American occupation of Cuba, the Church and State were separated, and none of the revenues collected by the military government were applied to the maintenance of the Catholic Church or any other Church, no matter what the religion.[52] Moreover, at the petition of the Cuban Cabinet, General Brooke decreed that hereafter only civil marriages were to be legal, ending the practice under the Spanish regime of recognizing only marriage celebrated according to the rites of the Catholic Church for those who professed that religion.[53] Later, bowing to opposition to this decree, especially from the Catholic Church and conservative forces in general, Wood offered a compromise in his Order No. 307 of August 8, 1900, which declared that marriage continued to be a civil contract, requiring the consent of the parties, in accordance with the terms of Brooke's decree. However, as to the form of celebration of the marriage, the new law authorized either the civil *or* the religious, both forms having the same legal effect, provided they were performed in conformity with the provisions of the order. The order thus again gave sanction to religious marriages as in the colonial epoch. The difference was that religious marriage was not imposed upon Catholics, as they might choose between religious and civil marriages if they desired.[54]*

This then was the background for the discussion on the question of Church and State at the Constitutional Convention, though one must add that the role played by most Catholic clergymen as firm supporters of the Spanish regime operated against establishing their Church as the state religion under the Republic. There was a spirited debate on the question of whether God's name should be mentioned in the preamble. Cisneros, among others, fought strongly against it. Manuel Sanguily, on the other hand, favored the idea, arguing that "if God is the symbol of the Supreme, from this merely abstract point of view I cannot understand that anybody may consider it humiliating and dishonest if we raise our hands toward Him and ask Him His protection." Cisneros' objections were overruled, and the following was adopted: "The Delegates of the Cuban people . . . agree and adopt, requesting God's favor, the following Constitution." [55]

However, the real battle took place over the proposal for a provision to read: "The profession of all religions is free, as well as the practice of all worship, without other limitation than that of respect to Christian morality and public order. The Church will be separated from the State, which may not grant a subvention, in any manner, to any religion." Juan Gualberto Gómez, a deeply religious man, led a movement to eliminate the second sentence. He argued that the people of Cuba were overwhelmingly Catholic and that the Cuban Republic should be founded on the basis of unity between the government and their Church. He insisted that a religious influence in government was essential if future disturbances were to be avoided. "Religious sentiment is for oppressed, unhappy, and enslaved people a refuge of consolation and tranquility." If the people were deprived of spiritual solace, the government would have to provide them with material benefits. "Since you have taken away their hope of enjoyment in the next world, you must then make certain that you give them the means to enjoy this one." This was indeed a strange position for a revolutionist, especially for a spokesman for a people who because of their color, faced

---

* Wood's Order brought a grateful letter from Bishop D. Sbarretti. (J. G. Holme, *The Life of Leonard Wood*, New York, 1920, pp. 155-56.)

The status established by Wood's Order remained in effect until July 29, 1919.

special problems in achieving benefits from the long struggle for independence. Were they to await the rewards for their sacrifices in the hereafter?

Manuel Sanguily took issue with Gómez, and criticized him for attempting to maintain a Church and State relationship as it had existed under Spain. He denied that the Cuban people were dominated by a strong belief in Catholicism, insisting that, on the contrary, the Church exerted little influence in the island. "The Cubans have always been the most disbelieving people on the earth." In Cuba, religion and ignorance had always gone hand-in-hand, and the Church, by its conduct, had alienated itself from the people, helping to make many of them irreligious.[56]

After a spirited debate, the Convention passed the proposed clause including the provision for a definite separation of Church and State and for the freedom of all religious groups in the island. All of the other Latin American republics had followed the custom of keeping Church and State together. But as Charles E. Chapman observes: "The Cubans rid themselves of an issue that has disturbed the politics of many of their sister republics."[57]

A prolonged discussion took place over the question of whether or not the public debt of Cuba which had accrued during the Spanish regime should be recognized by the new Republic. Then there was the question of qualifications for eligibility for the office of President. The issue revolved about Máximo Gómez who was a native of the Dominican Republic. If the original proposal that the President had to be a native-born Cuban had been adopted, Gómez would have been eliminated as a candidate. The anti-Gómez elements, still hostile to the veteran commander because of his role during the disbandment of the Cuban army, put up a strong fight against any change. (Seven of the Convention's 32 delegates, plus three of the alternates, had once been members of the Cuban Assembly.) But the pro-Gómez elements accused their opponents of ingratitude to a man who had contributed so much to Cuba Libre, and they finally won by one vote. The Constitution provided that to be eligible for the presidency, the candidate had to be a native-born or naturalized Cuban citizen. In the latter case, he must have served in the Cuban army for ten years.

A major issue revolved about the question of whether suffrage (male) should be universal. The conservative delegates, led by Gonzalo de Quesada, demanded that suffrage should be restricted by basing it on educational and property qualifications. They advanced two main arguments: first that universal suffrage raised the danger of creating another Haiti in Cuba, a direct plea to deprive the Negroes of a voice in the government; and second, that the United States would never accept a Constitution with universal suffrage. To include universal suffrage would play into the hands of those in the United States who wanted to prevent the establishment of a Cuban Republic, for they would argue that "it would be particularly hazardous to grant this island a government which might at some time be dominated by the blacks, and thus make a Haiti or San Domingo of it."

But the more radical delegates, led by Juan Gualberto Gómez (delegate from Santiago de Cuba), and supported by General José B. Alemán (delegate from Santa Clara), General José Lacret Marlot (delegate from Havana), José de Jesús Monteagudo (delegate from Santa Clara), and several of the delegates from Oriente, fought persistently and effectively for universal suffrage. They argued that the Cuban masses had been in the vanguard of the battle for independence for over thirty years, and that it would be a betrayal of all they had contributed, to restrict suffrage to the educated and the property owners. It would be a betrayal, too, of the principles of José Martí whose name graced the theater where the Convention had opened.[58] In the end, the radicals triumphed, and universal suffrage was provided for in the Cuban Constitution.

On January 30, 1901, the finished draft of the Constitution of the Republic of Cuba was published. It immediately became clear that basically the fundamental law of the Republic was modelled after the Constitution of the United States. Juan Gualberto Gómez, Manuel Sanguily, and Eliseo Giberga had favored a parliamentary system of government on the ground that this was more in keeping with Cuban traditions inherited from the Spanish era. But their advice had not prevailed. Probably the majority of the delegates felt that there was a better chance of having the Constitution accepted by the government of the United States if it followed the American document: the separation of powers, the electoral college, the bicameral legislature, and the power of judicial review. Many Cuban historians feel that some of Cuba's most serious political difficulties stem from these features, and that the Convention made a serious mistake in so closely following the provisions of the American Constitution.[59]

In describing the territory of the Cuban Republic, the Constitution included the island of Cuba and the "island and keys adjacent thereto, which are under the jurisdiction and control of the island of Cuba while it was a Spanish possession." (This included the Isle of Pines.) The Constitution declared that the people of Cuba constituted a State, sovereign and independent, and that the fundamental law was "framed and adopted" by the representatives of a "free and independent" people, by, under, and with the authority and instruction of, their temporary guardian.

The Cuban Constitution was at once a national Constitution, a State Constitution, and a general town and city charter. It provided, in the first place, for a central government with its legislative, executive, and judicial branches. This government consisted of a President and Vice-President, a Congress composed of a Senate and House of Representatives and a Supreme Court. The President and Vice-President were to be elected for four years by popular vote. The Senate was to consist of six members from each of the six departments—Havana, Pinar del Río, Santa Clara, Puerto Príncipe, Matanzas, and Santiago—elected for six years, one-third going out of office every two years, and were to be chosen by electors. The House of Representatives was to have one member for every 25,000 inhabitants or major fraction, to be elected for four years, and half the membership was to be changed every two years. The justices of the Supreme Court were to be appointed by the President, with the approval of the Senate, and were to hold office during good behavior. Although the government was not to be federal, the departments, while created by the national Constitution, were to have many of the powers of the American states. Each was to have a governor, elected for three years, and a departmental assembly, elected for the same term. The departments were treated as aggregations of municipalities which themselves had an independent existence, thus providing for a good measure of home rule. In fact, the Constitution expressly stated that the acts of the departmental assemblies should not be "antagonistic" to "that which pertains to the inherent rights of the municipalities." Finally, each town was to be governed by an "Ayuntamiento," composed of councilmen elected by direct vote. There was also to be a mayor elected in the same way. The towns were allowed to manage all their local affairs in their own way, subject only to the general restrictions of the Constitution.

The powers granted to the departments and cities were not accidental. For one thing, the Constitutions adopted by the Cubans in 1868 and 1895 recognized five distinct provinces which were to be erected into states upon the achievement of independence. Then again, the Western half of Cuba had about twice the population of the Eastern half which had contributed most to the two great revolutions against Spain, and suffered most as a result of these struggles. It would have been unfair to Oriente, Camagüey and Las Villas with their coffee, cattle, mineral and timber interests, to subject them wholly in matters of economic legislation to the sugar and tobacco interests represented by Matanzas, Havana and Pinar del Río.

As can be seen, the influence of the American Constitution was conspicuous throughout the Cuban document; indeed, the very words of the American Constitution were often used, as, for example, the first ten amendments known as the "Bill of Rights."* However, in several respects the Cuban Constitution went beyond the American. It required provision to be made for the necessary taxes for the payment of loans when the debts were contracted; it gave Congress express authority over telegraphs and railroads; it set high professional qualifications for justices of the Supreme Court; it gave the Supreme Court in explicit terms the power, which the U.S. Supreme Court had merely assumed, of deciding upon the constitutionality of laws; it protected local self-government; and it endorsed the principle of universal male suffrage. Nor did it, like the American Constitution, allow the states to determine the qualifications of voters, a device used in the United States to deprive Negroes particularly of suffrage.[60]

On February 11, 1901, the Cuban Constitution was adopted. Newspaper reaction in the United States was generally favorable. The Constitution, it was generally agreed, effectively answered the question

---

* Willis Fletcher Johnson, however, rejects the idea that the Cuban Constitution was modelled after the Constitution of the United States. He insists that the Cubans avoided making their Constitution too similar to the American fundamental law, first, to avoid being looked on as "an appendage" to the United States, and secondly, because an Anglo-Saxon Constitution would not suit a Hispanic-American Republic with Latin tendencies and background. (*History of Cuba*, vol. IV, p. 189.) One has but to read the American and Cuban Constitutions to realize that Johnson's thesis is without foundation.

whether the Cubans had the capacity for self-government. "If such a Constitution as this is presented to us," remarked the New York *Journal*, "we do not see how Congress can refuse to accept it. The only course open will be to submit it to a vote of the Cuban people, and if they approve it, to let them set up their government under it while we gracefully withdraw." [61] The *Daily People* commented that "although it is the product of the Radical element, the Cuban Constitution is a remarkably conservative document." The Socialist Labor Party organ explained that the Cuban radicals had leaned over backwards in order to assure the United States that there was every guarantee of "stability" as American capitalists interpreted that word.[62]

But it was the reaction of the United States government that counted. During the weeks when the delegates were framing the Constitution there had been no comment from Washington. McKinley had made only a passing reference to the Constitution in his annual message to Congress, December 3, 1900, merely noting that "when the convention concludes its labors I will transmit to the Congress the Constitution as framed by the Convention for its consideration and for such action as it may deem advisable." [63] However, it would appear that the Administration was generally satisfied with the Constitution. In commenting on the Cuban Constitution in his annual report of 1901, published in the fall of that year, Secretary of War Root stated:

> I do not fully agree with the wisdom of some of the provisions of this constitution,* but it provides for a republican form of government; it was adopted after long and patient consideration and discussion; it represents the views of the delegates elected by the people of Cuba; and it contains no features which would justify the assertion that a government organized under it will not be the one to which the United States may properly transfer the obligation for the protection of life and property under international law, assumed in the Treaty of Paris.[64]

"The imperialists," commented *The State* joyfully on December 28, 1900, "are unable as yet to get any helpful material out of the Cuban Convention." [65] But behind the scenes, the imperialists were working

---

* What these provisions were Root did not indicate, but *The State* reported that the Administration was upset by the inclusion of the Isle of Pines as part of Cuba, and the provision for universal suffrage. (Dec. 3, 30, 1900.)

out their plans carefully. In a widely-reprinted article in the *Review of Reviews* for December, 1900, entitled "The Cuban Republic—Limited," Walter Wellman, Washington correspondent of the Chicago *Record-Herald,* a journalist close to the Administration, predicted that these plans would result in making Cuba "nominally a sovereign state, but but actually a self-governing colony of the United States." [66]

## CHAPTER XXV

# Origin of the Platt Amendment

IN OPENING the Constitutional Convention, Wood had advised the delegates that, after they had framed and adopted a Constitution, they were "to formulate what, in your opinion, ought to be the relations between Cuba and the United States." But the Convention was not long in session before it became clear that the Administration did not want to wait until a Constitution had been framed and adopted before receiving specific guarantees on the issue of "relations." Washington, of course, preferred that the delegates should willingly concede all that the Administration wanted, and then it could be paraded before the nation and the world as the expression of the free will of the representatives of the Cuban people. To feel out Cuban thinking on such a possible solution, Wood had a long private conference in the opening days of 1901 with a group of delegates headed by Méndez Capote. He found, he informed Root, that "the conservatives will agree to anything we prefer," but that the radicals, who made up the majority of the group, were very much opposed to yielding to the United States on the general issue of Cuba's relations with her neighbor. He did not expect that there would be much trouble about getting a grant of naval stations to the United States, even though the radicals were "touchy" on this subject, and he felt that it might be possible to persuade the Convention to adopt a declaration that "no foreign negotiations in any way affecting matters of interest to the United States shall be entered into without our full consent and approval." To achieve more than this, the Cubans would have to be offered a substantial bribe in the form of tariff concessions for their products. Such concessions would "do more than all other things combined" to secure favorable action by the Convention. Wood also wrote to Senators Aldrich, Foraker and Platt urging them to try to get a 25 percent reduction "at least" in the import duties paid by Cuban sugars, and assuring them: "This will do more than anything else to make us masters of the situation here."[1]

Root advised postponing the whole question of tariff concessions until after the issue of relations between the two countries had been defined. Moreover, he doubted the possibility of securing favorable action from Congress on such a controversial subject, in view of "strong pressure on the part of the cane sugar, beet sugar and tobacco people." Finally, he was anxious to avoid the impression that the Cubans were being coerced into accepting what Washington wanted from them. "Of course," he wrote Wood on January 9, "you are taking special care not to permit anyone with whom you talk to have the opportunity to say that you are making demands, or even official suggestions. It seems to me important that the convention shall be required to take the initiative in stating what they want the relations to be, or to distinctly refuse it."[2]

But it soon became clear that the Administration was ready to drop the sham effort to get what it wanted from the Cubans of their own free will. On January 11, only two days after his lofty advice to Wood, Root wrote to Secretary of State John Hay asking him to consider "the advisability of *requiring the incorporation into the fundamental law of Cuba*," the following provisions:

"1. That in transferring the control of Cuba to the Government established under the new Constitution the United States reserves and retains the right of intervention for the preservation of Cuban independence and maintenance of a stable government, adequately protecting life, property and individual liberty.

"2. That no government organized under the Constitution shall be deemed to have been authorized to enter into any treaty or engagement with any foreign power which may tend to impair or interfere with the independence of Cuba, or to confer upon such foreign power any special right or privilege without the consent of the United States, and that the United States shall be entitled to be a party, in the first instance, to any negotiations having in view any such provision.

"3. . . . The United States may acquire and hold the title to land; and maintain naval stations at certain specified points.

"4. That all acts of the Military Governor, and all rights acquired thereunder, shall be valid and be maintained and protected."

Root requested the State Department to make a study of Great

Britain's policy of retaining a right of intervention in Egypt after she retired from that country, since "some good authorities were of the opinion that it would enable England to retire and still maintain her moral control." He pointed out that it was important now to "reach sound conclusions upon the scope and effect which the reservation of a right of intervention in Cuba would have."[3]

While the State Department was studying Root's proposal to require the Cubans to formulate future relations with the United States in such a way as to deprive them of much of their independence, the Supreme Court handed down an important decision which, it appeared at first, would put a stop to imperialist designs against Cuba. The decision grew out of the disclosures of the embezzlement of the postal funds of Cuba. C. F. W. Neely, a postal official in the Military Government, had fled to the United States, was arrested and kept in prison, and was awaiting extradition to Cuba where he was to be tried. His attorney appealed to the Supreme Court to halt the extradition on the ground that the requisition issued for Neely by the Military Government of Cuba was invalid. He argued that when the Treaty of Paris was ratified, the war with Spain had ended, and as no war had been declared against the Cuban Republic, all further justification under the war-making power to occupy Cuba ceased, and the President should therefore have withdrawn the United States army from Cuba. He claimed that the institution and maintenance by the President of a military government in Cuba was and continued to be without authority under international law and in flagrant contravention of the Constitution of the United States. The military government of Cuba was unconstitutional in that it was essentially a prosecution of war against the Cuban Republic, and since Congress alone had the authority to declare such war, the action of the President in occupying Cuba as Commander-in-Chief of the Army was a virtual prosecution of the war without the authority of Congress. The military government of Cuba, the argument continued, could be justified under the war power, but since the war power had no existence except in time of war which was authorized by Congress, the President could not constitutionally use the armed forces for the purpose of governing Cuba. Hence if the military government of Cuba was illegal, its requisition for Neely was invalid and could not be recognized by the courts of the United States.

It was recognized immediately that the Supreme Court, by accepting this interpretation, could end the military occupation of Cuba by declaring it unconstitutional. Hence the Administration heaved a huge sigh of relief when the Supreme Court, in a unanimous decision, held that Neely was subject to extradition and had to be surrendered to the military government of Cuba. Justice Harlan, speaking for the Court, held that the act of June 6, 1900, under which Neely was to be extradited, was constitutional; that there was no dispute that on the day that act became a law, Cuba was "under the control of the United States" and "occupied by this government." But the Court did not stop here. It held that Cuba was foreign territory even though it "is under a military government appointed by and representing the President in the work of assisting the inhabitants of the island to establish a government of their own which, as a free and independent people, they may control without interference by other nations. . . . As between the United States and Cuba that island is territory held in trust for the inhabitants of Cuba to whom it rightfully belongs and to whose exclusive control it will be surrendered when a stable government shall have been established by their voluntary action." [4]

To the American anti-imperialists the decision was a welcome one. For one thing, it effectively answered the argument of annexationists like Richard B. Olney that Cuba was already part of the United States as a result of the defeat of Spain. More important, it seemed to offer an insuperable barrier to the efforts of the Administration to rob the Cubans of real self-government by imposing terms "upon the people of Cuba incompatible with their retention of absolute sovereignty and independence." "We think," rejoiced *The State,* "we see in this decision the purpose of the Court to prevent the Washington administration from disgracing the country by evasion of the terms and a violation of the Joint Resolution. It was necessary for the Court to say all this. It could have confined itself to a mere declaration of the present status of the island, without indicating the course which the United States must adopt toward it. . . . We rejoice that it has spoken so clearly and so honestly. The redemption of our pledge to the Cubans may yet be somewhat delayed but it cannot finally be refused. The Republic of Cuba with its powers unrestricted, its full sovereignty unchallenged is a certainty." [5]

The Philadelphia *North American,* a pro-annexationist Republican paper, agreed that the decision had delivered a devastating blow to the Administration's plan to limit Cuba's independence. "The Supreme Court has declared that Cuba is a foreign country. Congress has no right to legislate for foreign countries, no right to dictate to their people what form of government they shall adopt, and therefore can neither ratify, reject nor amend the Cuban Constitution. The only question to be considered is, 'Does the Constitution provide for a stable government?' If it does, that ends American occupation and military control of Cuban affairs under the express form of the pledge given by Congress and confirmed by the Supreme Court." [6]

The author of the "pledge given by Congress," Senator Teller, announced that the Supreme Court decision had settled the issue of whether Congress had any power to modify in any shape or form the promise to Cuba of absolute and unrestricted independence. The Supreme Court had stated it clearly: Cuba was a foreign country. How, then, could Congress claim the right to pronounce on the form of the future Republic, or regulate its relations with the United States? Even a number of Republican congressmen agreed with Teller.[7]

But these appraisers of the Supreme Court decision underestimated the determination of American imperialists to achieve indirectly what they could not accomplish by direct annexation, and they were not to be deterred by legal niceties. Neither McKinley, Hay nor Root commented on the Supreme Court's decision, but Senator Orville H. Platt, chairman of the Senate Committee on Relations with Cuba, spoke for the Administration. In a perfect example of double-talk, Platt announced that he, too, agreed with the interpretation that under the decision, Congress had no right to accept or reject the Cuban Constitution or even to deal with it at all:

> In my view of the question, Congress has not the power to deal directly with the Cuban Constitution. That instrument, when finally completed and adopted by the regularly authorized body formed by proclamation of the executive authority of the United States to frame a Constitution, cannot be brought before Congress, the law-making power of this nation, and dealt with as if it were a bill enacted into law. My conclusion, therefore, is that we can neither approve, reject nor in any way amend or modify the Cuban Constitution by act of Congress. Why, the Supreme Court has explicitly and unequivocally declared that Cuba is a foreign country. Cuba, being a foreign country, is privileged to establish her own government without let or hindrance.

The next part of Platt's statement revealed that the imperialists had devised a way to get around the Supreme Court's decision. Congress could "neither approve, reject nor in any way amend or modify the Cuban Constitution." Then Platt unperturbably backpedaled from this firm assertion:

> But it should be borne in mind that this nation secured freedom for Cuba by act of Congress authorizing the President to intervene with the army and navy of the United States. That fact gives the United States certain rights and privileges in Cuba, and establishes minimal obligations which may be defined in a way or through a channel yet to be determined. For instance, Congress may, I think, declare upon what terms and conditions military occupation of Cuba may cease, and in doing that might express its opinion as to what necessary guarantees of our future relations should be embodied in its Constitution.[8]

Thus, while admitting the absolute independence of Cuba, the Administration had found a way to deprive it of that independence. It would simply retain the American army in the island until Cuba, which was conceded to be a foreign nation, would be coerced into giving the United States what it wanted!

Platt did not reveal that he and his imperialist colleagues in Congress were already engaged in nullifying the Supreme Court decision. Like Root, these men had hoped that the Cubans could be influenced to give the United States what it wanted without appearing publicly to have been forced to do so. Platt had suggested to Wood on January 18 that while tariff concessions on Cuban products could not be given before the Constitutional Convention had finished its work, the promise of such arrangements could be used to force the Convention to act quickly and in the right way.[9] Senator Lodge was even more explicit. The Cubans, he informed Wood on January 15, should be made to understand that "they will get no reduction on their products unless the provisions of their constitution are absolutely satisfactory to the United States." [10]*

---

* Lodge expressed the real yearnings of American imperialism when he wrote in the same letter: "The hope of Cuba lies in annexation which would give her immediate entrance into our markets." He found it "amazing" that the Cubans did not realize it. (Henry C. Lodge to Wood, Jan. 15, 1901, Leonard Wood Papers, Library of Congress.)

In spite of promises held out by Wood to the Cubans of rewards in the form of tariff concessions, the Constitutional Convention had failed by late January even to initiate a discussion of future Cuban relations with the United States. By the end of the month, the Administration learned that the Convention was about to complete its function of drawing up a Constitution without having even considered the question of relations. This type of procedure, the *Daily People* reported, "amounts to a slap on both cheeks of the Administration in Washington." Cuba had refused "to abdicate its sovereignty," and the Cubans could now expect "to be termed bandits, rebels and savages," and be made to do Washington's bidding.[11] On January 30, 1901, just as this prediction was being published, Platt, as chairman of the Committee on Relations with Cuba, sent a note to the Republican members of that body informing them that it was "very important" that they have an "informal conference."[12] The meeting was held at the Washington home of Senator William E. Chandler of New Hampshire. Nearly all present agreed that the time of waiting for the Cubans voluntarily to produce what the United States wanted on "relations" was over, and that they should now be told what to do. Chandler proposed, however, that one more device might be used to get the Cubans to agree to make the necessary concessions. They could be told that if they did not agree, the United States would demand $100,000,000 in four percent bonds as part payment of the costs of the war against Spain. This was finally rejected.[13] There was to be no more tempting the Cubans! They would have to bow!

On February 5, two days after his double-talking comment on the Supreme Court decision, Platt sent a note to Root informing the Secretary of War that the Republican members of the Committee on Relations with Cuba thought "that it would be advisable, without much delay, to formulate a resolution to discontinue the military occupation of Cuba whenever certain things shall have been agreed to and incorporated into the Constitution of Cuba, making it certain that results which we deem essential are assured. Of course the difficulty is to formulate the conditions in such a resolution, and I want to talk to you about it, and also with the President." The proposed resolution, Platt explained, would state the essential conditions which must be formally agreed to by the Cubans before the Occupation would end. It would be referred to the Committee on Relations with Cuba, and recommended by that group as an amendment to the Army Appropriation Bill. "It would at least be a notice to Cuba," Platt concluded, "which I think it is high time to give, as to what the United States is going to insist on." [14]

In the next few days, work went ahead rapidly on defining what the United States would demand from Cuba. On February 7th, Platt's committee conferred with Root and McKinley,[15] and on February 9th, the Secretary of War wrote a long letter to Wood outlining in detail the Administration's position on relations with Cuba. "The people of Cuba," he declared, "should desire to have incorporated in her fundamental law, provisions in substance as follows." What followed were the four proposals outlined by Hay a month earlier, along with a new one limiting the authority of the Cuban government to "assume or contract any public debt."

Root's justification for this reversal of his promise to the Cubans in his Annual Report of November, 1899—when the new Cuban government was established, Root had said, then "the relations which exist between it and the United States will be a matter for free and uncontrolled agreement between the two parties"—was that without these provisions in the Cuban Constitution, the war with Spain, from the standpoint of the United States, would have been in vain, though he coupled this hypocritically with Cuba's own welfare:

> It would be a most lame and impotent conclusion if, after all the expenditure of blood and treasure by the people of the United States for the freedom of Cuba, and by the people of Cuba for the same object, we should through the constitution of the new government, by inadvertence or otherwise, be placed in a worse condition in regard to our own interests than we were while Spain was in possession, and the people of Cuba should be deprived of that protection and aid from the United States which is necessary for the maintenance of their independence.[16]

Thus a leading spokesman for American imperialism conceded that the United States' "interests" and not the freedom and independence of the Cuban people had really motivated the war against Spain, and to protect those "interests," the Cubans had to give the United States what it wanted. All the extra talk about the Cuban people needing these provisions in their Constitution to maintain their independence was mere sugar-coating.

Root had another explanation for his demands:

> The preservation of that independence by a country so small as Cuba . . . must depend upon her strict performance of international obligations, upon her giving due protection to lives and property of citizens of all other countries within her borders, and upon her never contracting any public debt which in the hands of citizens of foreign powers, shall constitute an obligation she is unable to meet.[17]

It is interesting to compare the above with Root's comment on the Cuban Constitution, that "it contains no features that would justify the assertion that a government under it will not be one to which the United States may properly transfer the obligations for the protection of life and property under international law, assumed in the Treaty of Paris." In other words, the American government fully accepted the capacity of Cuba to carry out its obligations and protect life and property under international law. Therefore, the duty of the United States under the Treaty of Paris was at an end; ergo, no "special relations" between the United States and Cuba were necessary. But, of course, there were the "interests" of the United States that had to be protected!

It was now up to Wood to transmit Root's proposals to the Cuban Convention's Committee on Relations, a group chosen on February 12th. When Root's letter arrived in Havana, Wood and a friend were about to start on a crocodile hunt in Zapata Swamp, some distance from the capital. Not wishing to delay his trip, and according to his worshipping biographer, seeing "advantages in a discussion of Root's proposals away from the murky political atmosphere of Havana," Wood invited the committee to go along on his train.[18] In this undignified atmosphere, in a conference which took place during the railroad journey from Havana to Batabanó on the South coast, Wood proceeded to throw Root's instructions at the committee in a most perfunctory manner. He pointed out that Congress might desire additional conditions when it acted on the matter. The Cubans kept calm under the strain, but deeply resented the way in which Root's letter was, in the words of one member, being "pitched at" them.[19]

Martínez Ortiz, the Cuban historian, reports that the terms of Root's letter greatly distressed the members of the committee. Wood, as usual, was optimistic in his report to Root. Although he conceded that the

Cubans objected to the right of intervention and the leasing of naval stations, he expected "no serious objection to any of the conditions except . . . that in reference to Naval Stations." (He even urged Root to add his own pet proposal requiring the Cubans to continue the American sanitation program.) As for reports that the committee had been offended by having been summoned to discuss such serious questions on a railroad journey to an alligator hunt, they were spread by American reporters who were out to defeat the proposed provisions. The committee had thoroughly enjoyed the trip.[20]

On February 21, Wood sent an official letter to Dr. Diego Tamayo, president of the Convention's Committee on Relations, formally submitting the proposals which had been verbally transmitted the week before.[21] Soon he was complaining to Root that he was getting nowhere in trying to induce the Cuban committee to report Root's proposals as the basis of relations with the United States. Some of the committee members were ready to go along, but were simply afraid of the consequences to themselves personally. "The danger which confronts us is the moral cowardice of all these men, even as good ones as Tamayo. Their frankness is rather amusing. They will individually assure me that the relations proposed are just, with the possible exception of the naval stations, and ought to be accepted, without question; collectively they are timid." Some had told him, he reported, that "they are willing to accept pretty much whatever we propose if the United States insists on it," in which case they could avoid criticism. But a voluntary offer was impossible. Soon enough, then, the United States would have to show "the strong hand of authority."[22]

It is difficult to judge how accurate Wood was in reporting the views of the Cuban delegates—he always had a tendency to depict the Cubans as being on good terms with the United States and anxious to do its bidding—but that there were conservatives who would welcome the "strong hand" of the United States as a protector against the Cuban masses, goes without saying.* ("Our supporters are the [sugar] producers and the merchants," Wood pointed out.) Yet even these men were aware that public reaction to Root's demands, the nature of which

---

* In a dispatch from Havana, the correspondent of the *Daily People* wrote that Eliseo Giberga, a delegate from Matanzas, had argued that "every property holder" in Cuba would be safer if the United States' demands were accepted. (Feb. 18, 1901.)

had leaked out to the people, was so strong that it would be political suicide for them to propose them voluntarily as part of the Cuban Constitution. On February 21 when the delegates signed the Cuban Constitution, Cisneros had objected to sending a copy to the United States Congress. "Cuba is now independent," he insisted, "and I can see no reason for sending this Constitution to the United States for acceptance. The United States government has no right to pass upon it, for it is a distinctively Cuban document and was drawn up by this Convention which has assumed the responsibility of establishing a republic." Under no circumstances, would he agree to add to the Constitution any of Root's proposals, especially the right to intervene in Cuba. "The Americans," he told the delegates, paraphrasing Martí's famous remark, "are like the monkey. When the monkey closes its paw on a thing, it never wants to let it go."* Rather fight than surrender, he thundered, and he prophesied: "When the time comes to fight the Americans, we will fight them together." [23]

At meetings in Havana on February 24th to commemorate the sixth anniversary of the 1895 revolution, anti-American speeches dominated the proceedings. One Republic party speaker voiced approval of Cisneros' appeal to fight rather than surrender, told the wildly cheering audience that Cuba must be a truly sovereign nation, and that "sovereignty lies in the machete of its inhabitants." [24] "Cubans Aroused," American newspapers reported. Their correspondents in the island told of bitter opposition to the idea of giving the United States any of the proposals Root was reported to have demanded. "The Cubans who stand out for absolute independence say that they might as well accept annexation to the United States at once as to grant the concessions named. For what purpose, other than to overawe the island, does the United States want naval stations in this country, they ask." To allow the United States to establish naval stations would mean "practically giving up their independence." [25] Another correspondent wrote:

> The Cubans are in a smoulder of discontent, and it would not take much to cause the feelings to burst into flame. They all hope to get their rights peacefully, but, failing, are ready to fight for

---

* "Once the United States is in Cuba who will get her out?" was Martí's answer to those who favored United States' intervention to help Cuba achieve its independence from Spain.

them. Even the most optimistic cannot avoid the truth of the situation which is more and more apparent every day—the United States must redeem its pledge or prepare to meet a revolt.[26]

Wood, however, urged Washington not to take such reports too seriously. The firebrands did not have the support of the prominent politicians of all parties who took a moderate stand. Most important of all, Máximo Gómez and Estrada Palma favored the proposals for the future relations between the United States and Cuba. "Maximo Gomez," Wood wrote to Root on February 27, 1901, "came to me yesterday and repeated what I have already written to you and stated we must not think of getting out under any circumstances at present. He knows the people and knows that things will go to pieces if we move just now." Fortunately for the United States, men like Gómez and Estrada Palma were on its side. "These two men swing ten times the influence of the convention and they should be dealt with accordingly. With these men supporting our policy, we can hold the situation here absolutely without wavering." [27]

Even though one must view Wood's dispatches with caution, his report on Estrada Palma and Gómez had substance. Estrada Palma, of course, was a long-standing advocate of retaining American power to intervene in Cuba after independence and before ultimate annexation (which he really favored), as a means of keeping revolutionary action by the Cuban masses in check. It is not surprising, therefore, that he should have informed Cuban leaders to accept Root's proposals.[28] Newspaper dispatches from Cuba quoted Gómez as saying, "If Americans were to be withdrawn to-day, I would go with them." He was said to favor only one modification in Root's proposals: that the United States should lease land for naval stations instead of purchasing them.[29] Gómez indignantly denied these reports in a letter to the Cuban press, but Wood assured Washington that it need not be alarmed by this. He cabled Root: "No importance should be attached to Gomez's letter which he assures me personally is simply to retain his hold on the radical element." [30]

It is difficult to believe that Máximo Gómez would be guilty of saying one thing to the Cuban people and the opposite to the American Military Governor. Whatever might be thought of his political judgment, he was scrupulously honest and incapable of deceit. Moreover, he was certainly extremely anxious to have the American occupation end as quickly as possible. As he wrote to Sotero Figueroa about this time: "Never, not even when we were fighting Weyler with his 250,000 soldiers, did the Cuban fatherland undergo greater danger than in these moments. We have a stranger in the house." [31]* In his anxiety to get the United States out of Cuba and the Republic established, Gómez was prepared to accept most of what Washington demanded. It was his second political mistake during the period of the Occupation, the first having been made when he allowed himself to be used to destroy the Cuban Assembly.

On February 27th, the Cuban Convention in secret session received and approved the report of the Committee on Relations. (Juan Gualberto Gómez had insisted that the session be public to keep the people informed of these important developments, but his plea was rejected.) [32] The committee, in a dignified but firm way, tried in its report to keep the noose around Cuba's neck from being drawn tighter. The committee restated Order No. 455, which directed the Convention merely to state its opinion on relations. It then explained that it had expected its task would be an easy one, since all Cuban patriots desired the closest friendship with the United States, and there was no conflict between the legitimate interests of the two countries. "It seemed to all that in stating the desired 'opinion,' we could only declare that the United States and Cuba should forever maintain the ties of friendship most intimate and fraternal." But the Military Governor had "demanded a private interview," and then presented the Root proposals. This represented a change in their original understanding of their task, the committee complained; the Convention was instructed to formulate freely what kind of relations ought, in its opinion, to exist between Cuba and the United States, but now they were faced with specific proposals upon which to act.

While the Root proposals embodied only the opinions of the Executive branch of the United States government, they were entitled to "a careful consideration. . . . But we have a complete right to accept or reject them, to select from them that which we think fit, to add to them or to subtract from them others according to the dictates of our

---

* "Cuba fought against the dominion of Spain only to find herself under the heel of the United States," Gómez bitterly told an American reporter in the spring of 1900. (*Public Opinion*, May 3, 1900, p., 550.)

consciences, holding always before us our duty to reconcile all that may be a legitimate interest or a rational proposal of the people of the United States, with our own highest interest and sacred rights." The committee reminded the United States, "We are the delegates of the people of Cuba [and] . . . our primary duty lies in interpreting the will . . . of our people." Then came the forthright statement:

> The undersigned committee, while accepting the starting point of the American Executive—which provides that the independence of Cuba shall remain absolutely guaranteed—is of the opinion that some of these stipulations are not acceptable, inasmuch as they modify the independence and sovereignty of Cuba. Our duty consists in making Cuba independent of all other nations, including the great and noble American nation; and if we bind ourselves to ask the consent of the United States to our international treaties; if we allow them to retain the right to intervene in our country to support or displace administrations, and to fulfill rights which only concern the Cuban Government; and if, lastly, we concede to them the right to acquire and maintain any title over any lands whereupon they may establish naval stations, it is plain that we should appear to be independent to the rest of the world, but surely we should never be so with relation to the United States.

The Constitution which the Convention had just adopted, the committee pointed out, was sufficient to insure Cuba's independence, and there was no apprehension about the future behavior of the Cubans, since they had behaved so well in the past. Nevertheless, in order to strengthen the confidence of the United States in the new Cuba, the committee was ready to recommend a set of counterproposals which the future governmental authorities of the Republic of Cuba should adopt, "if they deem proper." There were five proposals:

"1. The government of Cuba will not make a treaty or agreement with any foreign power which may compromise or limit the independence of Cuba or which may permit or authorize any power to obtain, by means of colonization, or for military or naval purpose, or in any other manner, foothold or authority or right over any portion of Cuba.

"2. The government will not permit its territory to be used as a base for operations or war against the United States, or against any foreign nation.

"3. The government of Cuba accepts in its entirety the Treaty of Paris in which are affirmed the rights of Cuba, to the extent of the obligations which are explicitly indicated in them, and especially those which the international law imposes for the protection of life and property, and substitutes itself for the United States in the pledge, which they assumed in that sense according to articles 12 and 162 of the treaty of Paris.

"4. Cuba recognizes as legally valid all acts of the military government during the period of occupation, also the rights arising out of them, in conformity with the joint resolution and the Foraker amendment and the existing laws of the country.

"5. The government of the United States and Cuba should regulate their commercial relations by means of a treaty based on reciprocity, and with assuming ample special advantages in their respective markets." [33]

Although the committee had tried to avoid rejecting the American proposals outright, it had turned down Washington's three key demands: the United States' right of intervention in Cuba, the granting of naval stations, and a limit to the capacity of the Cuban government to contract debts. It had boldly included the tariff question in that of relations, while the United States had wished this question postponed until later. Finally, instead of writing the terms of the relations into the Constitution, the committee merely agreed to recommend such terms to the future government, which would still have full freedom to accept or reject them. Even so, the Convention by adopting this report took a more conciliatory stand than that of the more radical forces in Cuba who wanted to tell the United States that the question of relations had no place in the deliberations of the Convention, to quote Root's promise in his Annual Report of November, 1899 as justification for this position, and leave it at that. Let the United States then do whatever it wished.[34]

One thing the stand taken by the Convention clearly proved was that all of Wood's maneuvers to get the Cubans to surrender to the United States of their own free will had failed. No wonder the Military Governor was furious, and in forwarding the news of the Convention's action to Root, urged Washington not to give in an inch to the Cubans, even if were necessary to annex the island despite the Teller Amendment. "It is better to have it than to destroy the island by surrendering it . . . to the class of people whom I have always characterized as unprincipled and irresponsible." [35] Actually, Washington was in no need of such advice. There was no intention of yielding to the Cubans. Senator Platt, on being asked what he thought of the Convention's action, replied that there was no reason to be alarmed. "Cuba will come around, all right," he predicted.[36]

Platt had been busy for some time, of course, with a plan to coerce the Cubans. The Congressional resolution which he had discussed with Root, and which was to specify the minimum conditions necessary to end the Occupation, had taken shape in the same week that the Convention made its position clear. The sub-committee which wrote the resolution in close collaboration with Root and McKinley consisted of Senator Orville H. Platt of Connecticut, John C. Spooner of Wisconsin, Hernando de Soto Money of Mississippi, and Henry M. Teller of Colorado. These two groups—the Administration and the Senators—*decided to act without even waiting to hear from the Cuban Convention.* On February 25, 1901, Senator Platt introduced the finished resolution in the Senate, as an amendment to the Army Appropriation bill. The Platt Amendment which one historian calls "a document unique in the history of nations,"[37] but which was better characterized by a contemporary newspaper as "That Dreadful Document"[38]* read as follows:

> That in fulfillment of the declaration contained in the joint resolution approved April twentieth, eighteen hundred and ninety-eight, entitled "For the recognition of the independence of the people of Cuba, demanding that the Government of Spain relinquish its authority and government in the island of Cuba, and to withdraw its land and naval reserve forces from Cuba and Cuban waters, and directing the President of the United States to use the land and naval forces of the United States to carry these resolutions into effect," the President is hereby authorized to "leave the government and control of the island of its people" so soon as a government shall have been established in said island under a constitution which, either as part thereof or in an ordinance appended

---

* Another "dreadful document" introduced at this time was the Spooner Amendment to the Army Appropriation bill. This read in part: "All military, civil, and judicial powers necessary to govern the Philippine Islands . . . shall, until otherwise provided by Congress, be vested in such person and persons . . . as the President of the United States shall direct." (*Congressional Record,* 56th Cong., 2nd Sess., p. 3507.) The Spooner Amendment, the anti-imperialists charged, made the President, "the legislator, the judge, and executioner" of the Filipinos in violation of the first three articles of the Constitution.

thereto, shall define the future relations of the United States with Cuba, substantially as follows:

1. That the government of Cuba shall never enter into any treaty or other compact with any foreign power or powers which will impair or tend to impair the independence of Cuba, nor in any manner authorize or permit any foreign power or powers to obtain by colonization or, for military or naval purposes or otherwise, lodgment in or control over any portion of said island.

2. That said government shall not assume or contract any public debt, to pay the interest upon which, and to make reasonable sinking fund provision for the ultimate discharge of which, the ordinary revenues of the island, after defraying the current expenses of government, shall be inadequate.

3. That the government of Cuba consents that the United States may exercise the right to intervene for the preservation of Cuban independence, the maintenance of a government adequate for the protection of life, property, and individual liberty, and for discharging the obligations with respect to Cuba imposed by the Treaty of Paris on the United States, now to be assumed and undertaken by the government of Cuba.

4. That all Acts of the United States in Cuba during its military occupancy thereof are ratified and validated, and all lawful rights acquired thereunder shall be maintained and protected.

5. That the government of Cuba will execute and as far as necessary extend, the plans already devised or other plans to be mutually agreed upon, for the sanitation of the cities of the island, to the end that a recurrence of epidemic and infectious diseases may be prevented, thereby assuring protection to the people and commerce of Cuba, as well as to the commerce of the southern ports of the United States and of the people residing therein.

6. That the Isle of Pines shall be omitted from the proposed constitutional boundaries of Cuba, the title thereto being left to future adjustment by treaty.

7. That to enable the United States to maintain the independence of Cuba, and to protect the people thereof as well as for its own defence, the government of Cuba will sell or lease to the United States land necessary for coaling or naval stations at certain specified points, to be agreed upon with the President of the United States.

8. That by way of further assurance the government of Cuba will embody the foregoing provisions in a permanent treaty with the United States."[39]

Nothing was said in the Platt Amendment about commercial relations. Platt's original draft, however, contained the following article:

"Fourth, provisions to the effect that treaties with foreign nations shall only be made by the government of Cuba with the assent of the United States, and that simultaneously with the recognition of the independence of the government of Cuba a convention providing for the commercial and other relations to subsist between said government of Cuba and the government of the United States, acceptable to the President of the United States, shall be entered into and executed." But the second draft, likewise undated, omits all references to commercial relations.[40] It seems probable that Senators from the beet sugar states, with whom Platt conferred, warned him of the impossibility of pushing the Amendment through Congress if the promise of trade concessions to Cuba were included. Another possibility is that it was decided that the promise of trade concessions should be held in abeyance as a device to lessen Cuban opposition to the Platt Amendment if this became necessary. Platt himself later explained the omission on the ground that Cuba could not conclude a reciprocity treaty until she achieved status as a nation.[41]

The authorship of the Platt Amendment has been the subject of much controversy, with the dubious honor being given to three different men: Platt, Root, and General James H. Wilson. In response to a query from a friend who had seen a claim advanced by Secretary Root, Platt wrote in 1904: "It started with an original draft of four propositions by me, submitted to President McKinley and Secretary Root. It was the subject of many conversations with Mr. Root, and many consultations between the republican members of the senate committee, and its final draft was the joint work of myself and Senator Spooner. While these consultations were going on, Senator Root gave the orders to General Wood, stating what the president insisted upon, and that is all there is to it." [42] Among Platt's papers in the Connecticut State Library, there is a memorandum entitled "Proposition submitted to the President by me," which contained five of the eight articles of the Amendment. It is not dated, however.[43] At any rate, Platt conceded, "I am scarcely entitled to the credit of having my name attached" to the final Amendment.[44]

Root's claim was first presented by Walter Wellman in 1904 in an article published in the *Review of Reviews,* in which he asserted that only after the letter of February 9, 1901 was sent to Wood was it discussed with Senator Platt. Root, he insisted, "not only created, formed molded, trained . . . the Cuban nation, but wrote with his own hand its magna carta."[45] (Wellman showed an abysmal ignorance of both British and Cuban history.) Philip Jessup, Root's biographer, also favors the Secretary of War's authorship. He points out that Platt wrote to Root on February 5, 1901 that it would be advisable to formulate a resolution as an amendment to the Army Appropriation bill. This indicates, Jessup argues, that on that date Platt had not yet attempted to draft the Amendment.[46]

As for General Wilson, his claim is based on the fact that almost two years before, in his report of June 20, 1899 from Matanzas, he sketched out the provisions concerning the right of intervention and the grant of naval stations.[47] Actually, with unimportant changes of phraseology, five of the provisions of the Amendment (1, 2, 3, 4, and 7), were included in Root's letter to Wood, and four were in his letter to Hay. Article 5 was suggested by General Wood in a letter of February 19, and articles 6 and 7 were inserted by the Platt Committee. Thus the Platt Amendment is, in reality, a Root Amendment. But, in the words of Senator Joseph B. Foraker, "except only the provision to define *in their* [the Cubans'] *Constitution* the relations . . . there was nothing in the Platt Amendment that had not been discussed over and over again before the Committee on Relations with Cuba was created, and long before Mr. Root was made Secretary of War."[48] In other words, as soon as it was fairly clear that annexation was not possible, the imperialist forces began to devise the method to gain control over Cuba without actually annexing it. Or, as Senator Platt put it: "What difference does it make who wrote the Platt Amendment so long as it serves the purpose intended?"[49]

## CHAPTER XXVI

# Congress Adopts but Public Opinion Rejects the Amendment

ON FEBRUARY 25, 1901, when he introduced his amendment, Senator Platt remarked that he "hoped . . . there would be practical unanimity" of the Senate in its favor.[1] But he had barely finished expressing this hope when Senator John T. Morgan, Democrat of Alabama, objected to consideration of Platt's Amendment "under the state of information we now have." He pointed out that the Senate had not yet received a final copy of the Cuban Constitution nor the report of the Convention's Committee on Relations, and pleaded for delay until these documents could be studied.[2] But Platt refused to withdraw the Amendment.

The Senate debate that followed on this measure, certainly one of the most important in the history of American foreign relations, took only two days. The attack on the Platt Amendment, carried on mainly by the Democrats, began on the 26th with a major speech by Senator Morgan. "It is a piece of arrogant hypocrisy," he cried, "on the part of the Congress of the United States to make any such declaration, and in the same connection to say that we are executing the purpose and pledge of Congress that it [Cuba] shall be a free, sovereign and independent state." The Amendment was nothing but "an ultimatum, a legislative ultimatum to Cuba. . . . Take this and abandon your hopes of an independent . . . government." The terms clearly infringed Cuban sovereignty. The first article was "a perpetual covenant" abridging Cuba's sovereignty; the second indicated that the Cubans "should be treated like children." ("We must assume that they have intelligence enough to take care of themselves.") He went on article by article, showing how unless they were changed substantially or dropped entirely, they would rob Cuba of every semblance of real independence. Re-

578

ferring bitterly to the right of intervention, he declared: "You leave these words in there, and you compel Cuba at once to subordinate herself at all times to the visitation of the United States; to ascertain how she is dealing with her own people, not ours, whether she is protecting life and personal liberty and property there, according to our ideas of what she ought to do." Morgan closed with a statement that was to gain in significance with the passing years, predicting that the Cubans would be "absolutely irreconcilable to the United States" if the Platt Amendment were passed and they were forced to accept it.[3]

On the following day, the attack continued. Senator James K. Jones, an Arkansas Democrat, and Joseph B. Foraker of Ohio, long an opponent of the Administration's Cuban policy, tried to modify the terms of Article Three, which granted the United States the right of intervention. Both men introduced motions to delete "the maintenance of a government adequate for the protection of life, property, and individual liberty" as a ground for intervention, hoping thereby to limit intervention to purely external matters. Foraker, like Morgan, voiced a prophecy which was to become more meaningful as time passed. He prophesied that the intervention article would actually create more chaos in Cuba than it would prevent, for it would tempt the losing party in each election to raise such a furor as to necessitate American intervention and thus undo the result of the election:

> Suppose they have an election. One party or the other will be defeated. The party that is out is liable to complain, and with this kind of provision, it seems to me it might be very naturally done; it would be though by making objection, by making trouble, and creating difficulties, they could make a condition that would lead to an intervention of the United States to put the successful party out. It seems to me that instead of having a restraining influence, it would have an exciting influence and that the very result which the committee evidently sought to accomplish would be defeated . . . and the opposite would result.[4]

The attack on the Amendment concluded with speeches by a half dozen Senators. They charged the Administration with hypocrisy for violating the Teller Amendment, and Senator Benjamin R. Tillman of South Carolina said that the provision on the Isle of Pines "is the most apparent illustration of Anglo-Saxon greed for land ever presented in a legislative body." [5]

The proponents of the Amendment, certain of its passage, did not "waste time" in argument,[6] and those who spoke in its behalf did so rather apologetically. Senator Money, a Democratic member of Platt's sub-committee, defended most of the provisions as necessary and proper, but conceded that he did not like the form of the right of intervention in Article Three, for it obviously impaired Cuban independence. But it was better than keeping the troops in Cuba for another year. The main thing was to get the troops out of Cuba, and only passage of the Platt Amendment could do this.[7] Senator Teller also spoke for the measure, though he too conceded that he did not like Article Three, and regretted that something better could not be achieved.[8] Naturally, he did not repeat what he had told the press only three weeks before on February 3 at the time of the Supreme Court's decision:

> I resolutely hold that the [Teller] resolution means exactly what it says, and as it was adopted by both houses of Congress without question or a dissenting voice, it expressed fully and completely the national spirit and purpose. How we can get around it at this time without stultifying ourselves before the world, I am utterly at a loss to acknowledge. I agree fully with Senator Platt of Connecticut, that Congress has neither the right nor the power to touch the Cuban Constitution, but I am wholly at variance with his contention that it is within our province or duty to admonish the Cubans to amend their Constitution in any particular.[9]

Three weeks after making this principled declaration, Teller was advocating passage of a measure which would force the Cubans "to amend their Constitution" in the interests of American imperialism or face permanent occupation of their country by the United States!

Teller was not the only Senator prepared to stultify himself before the world by repudiating his former pledge. Senator George Hoar of Massachusetts, a leading anti-imperialist and heretofore a champion of unrestricted independence for Cuba, also spoke in favor of the Platt Amendment, calling it "eminently wise and satisfactory," having effectively "solved the difficult problem of our relations with Cuba."[10] His position, a good example of a fundamental weakness in the anti-imperialist movement,* was a God-send to the Administration.

---

* Hoar's speech reflected a common argument of quite a number of anti-imperialists that territorial acquisition was not necessary for the expansion of American trade and investment abroad.

The final vote in the Senate came on February 27th when the Amendment was carried unchanged by a vote of 43 to 20. Forty-two Republicans and one Independent (Kyle of South Dakota) voted for it, and 16 Democrats, 2 Populists, and 2 Independents voted against. Fourteen Senators who had voted for the Teller Amendment voted for the Platt Amendment! [11]

In the House, only two hours were allotted for debate on the entire Army Appropriation bill including the Platt Amendment. Here, however, the supporters of the Amendment, all Administration stalwarts, did not apologize for their stand. Republican Lacey of Iowa, ignoring any part the Cubans had played in their war for independence, cried: "Having, at a cost of millions of dollars and the sacrifice of thousands of lives, freed Cuba from her oppressors, we not only have the right, but it is our duty, to be sure that Spanish tyranny is not followed by anarchy in that island, and the assurances in this bill are both reasonable and moderate. They are in the best interests of Cuba and ourselves." [12] Following his colleague's line of reasoning, Representative Corliss of Michigan went a bit further, remarking: "I am unalterably opposed to the surrender of the sovereignty of the United States over Cuba." He continued with at least more honesty than those who talked about "the best interests of Cuba," saying: "I vote for the Amendment . . . because I believe that the adoption thereof will assure the continuance of our sovereignty over Cuba." [13]

Countering these Administration spokesmen, the House Democrats attacked the Amendment. One declared it contained "the most offensive and unconstitutional [provisions] . . . that were ingrafted, in my judgment, upon a bill presented to the American Congress." Another branded the measure "criminal," and still another declared that the Amendment was "clearly intended to perpetuate our control over the island and its inhabitants." Representative James R. Williams of Illinois warned: "If we pass this amendment against Cuba we advertise to the rest of the world what supreme hypocrites are in control at Washington. I would rejoice to see Cuba peacefully annexed to the United States, but I am not willing to steal it." [14]

One point emphasized by opponents of the Amendment in the House, which had been barely touched upon in the Senate was that the measure was a manifestation of "the bitter fruit of imperialism and commercial spirit." One member declared that the Republican Party and the Administration were acting on the usual imperialist principle "that there is profit in dishonor and money in crime." Another charged: "These amendments are not put in the army appropriation bill for Cuba's good, but to make excuse for keeping the soldiers of this country in Cuba to validate franchises procured by scoundrels while our army was in control there." Another member said that "the only excuse and justification [for the Amendment] . . . is that it will extend American trade and commerce, all at the instance of the great trusts and monopolies." Another sarcastically offered what he said should be the correct wording of the Platt Amendment: "Resolved that Cuba contains good stealing . . . and we intend . . . to boldly take the island and make of it a plundering ground for trusts and syndicates." [15]

At the end of the two hours allotted for debate, the House passed the Army Appropriation bill with the Platt Amendment as a rider, 161-137, and again the vote was exclusively on party lines.[16] The following day, March 2nd, President McKinley signed the bill and it became law. Two days later, in his second inaugural address of March 4, 1901, the President expressed satisfaction with the work of Congress, and declared that it expressed what "the legislative branch of the Government deems essential to the best interests of Cuba and the United States." [17]

Even though 20 of the 63 votes cast in the Senate and 137 of the 298 cast in the House were against the Platt Amendment, Root wrote to Wood on March 2 that it was "the subject of a most extraordinary unanimity in both parties in Congress." [18] Root was probably referring to the fact that the Democrats did not put up a real fight on the issue. For one thing, they could have, by filibustering in the Senate, prevented a vote on the measure before Congress adjourned in March, and forced an extra session by which time public opposition to the Platt Amendment could have been mobilized.* A filibuster had actually been threatened, but it quickly dwindled into face-saving speeches. The New York *Tribune,* a champion of the Amendment but anxious to lift the blame for its passage from the shoulders of the Republican Party, accused the

---

\* A vote on the Spooner Amendment to the Army Appropriation bill could also have been delayed by a filibuster. However, the Spooner proposal was somewhat changed by Senator Hoar's amendment which, like the Foraker Amendment in the case of Cuba, limited the power to grant franchises and other commercial rights in the Philippines.

Democrats of being "loudly virtuous talkers [who] took care to make their protests where they would be mere empty sound, and to avoid all action which might defeat the measure which they professed to oppose. It was perfectly within the power of the Democratic leaders in the Senate to have defeated the Cuban resolutions. Today they are as much responsible for the results as if they had openly spoken or voted for the measure. . . . The minority have practically abdicated opposition as a serious function of government and joined the Republican majority in responsibility for what is being done in Cuba." [19]

It was common knowledge that the leading Democrats in the Senate had been bought off so as not to stage a filibuster. They had been "soothed into acquiescence" by a generous River and Harbor bill and other special appropriations. Of the fifty million dollars to be appropriated for rivers and harbors, over half was to go to Democratic strongholds in the South. In addition, Congress had voted five million dollars of federal money to aid the forthcoming St. Louis Exposition, and this had won over Senator Francis M. Cockrell of Missouri. Senator Tillman had been persuaded not to stage a filibuster when his state (South Carolina) received funds in support of the Charleston Exposition and money for public construction elsewhere.[20] Bryan had tried to rally the Democrats against the Platt and Spooner Amendments, but the power of money was too great.*

The Senate Democrats denied they had been purchased. Their main defense was that it would have been political suicide to try to stave off a vote on the Army Appropriation bill and thus be accused of lack of support for the army, and they charged that the Administration had deliberately tied in the Amendment to the Army bill precisely for this reason. Hence there was no alternative but to let the vote go through. Tillman, who was severely criticized in his native state for not having started a filibuster against the Amendment, denied that he had been "bought off with the proposed appropriation of $250,000 for the Charleston exposition." But he put up a lame defense, placing the

---

* The New York *Tribune* reported that Senator William Allen of Nebraska had received a telegram from Bryan urging him to rally the Senate Democrats for a last ditch stand against the Platt and Spooner Amendments, even if they had to resort to a filibuster and even if it meant losing the River and Harbor Bill. Allen, according to the *Tribune,* made the effort, but Democratic leaders, especially Tillman and Cockrell, refused to heed Bryan's suggestion. (March 1, 2, 1901.)

blame for the failure to prevent "the proposed betrayal of Cuba," because Teller, a Democratic member of Platt's committee and "the author of our Cuban war pledge," had "acquiesced in a large measure with the legislation." [21] No one was really persuaded by this excuse, and the general opinion was that effective opposition to the Platt Amendment had been bought off. An anti-imperialist journal declared:

> The love of ease, the fear of an extra session, the danger of loss of the river and harbor pork, and last, but by no means least, the fear of incurring the displeasure of the Executive and thus cutting off the few crumbs of patronage which it generously pleased His Majesty [McKinley] to dole out to them, was too much to resist, and they [the Democrats] ignominiously surrendered, threw up their hands, and laid down.[22]

In his letter to Wood describing the Congressional vote, Root also emphasized that both houses, in passing the Amendment by "a most extraordinary unanimity," had so acted because they were "closely in touch with the people." [23] Of course, he failed to mention that the Platt Amendment had been swiftly enacted into law *before* public reaction to it in the country could be expressed. Now, however, the action of Congress aroused a bitter controversy. A few who supported the Amendment, like the Brooklyn *Eagle,* freely admitted that it was "in fact, a protectorate," but maintained that it was "as necessary as it was considerate." [24] Most of the supporters, however, were not so frank. They denied that the Amendment limited Cuba's independence. "All that we ask," Senator Platt wrote, "is that Cuba shall assent to our right to help her maintain her independence and protect her own interests." There was nothing really for Cuba to fear. "The United States will always be in a position to straighten things out if they get seriously bad." [25]

Coupled with this comforting but meaningless reassurance was the argument that the Cubans were incapable of stable self-government. "In many respects they are like children," wrote Senator Platt.[26] "Is it not our duty," inquired Senator Beverage, "to see that they are not destroyed by themselves?" Under the Platt Amendment, "land owners are not to be robbed; they are to be protected. Cities are not to be sacked; they are to be defended." [27] In short, supporters of the Amendment predicted that a state of anarchy would follow the withdrawal of

American troops, and that the peace that had reigned on the island for close to three years had been the result only of the presence of the U.S. Army. "The revolutionary and turbulent party," Platt asserted, "may attempt the destruction of Spanish and Cuban property." To prevent such anarchy, the Amendment was essential! This prompted correspondent Albert R. Robinson, who had spent years in Cuba, to declare that he found it unbelievable that Platt could be "so lacking in competent information regarding the Island and its people." [28]

The opposition to the Platt Amendment in the country at large was by no means limited to one party or to one region. It was expressed by all parties in all sections.[29] And it was expressed vigorously. The Philadelphia *North American* (Republican) declared that "the United States stands before the world dishonored." The Philadelphia *Public Ledger,* a fellow Republican paper, agreed. "This early demand for Cuban territory is repulsive." [30] The Boston *Herald* charged Congress with breaking its pledge, and warned that "in thus breaking faith it is inviting an armed uprising of the Cuban people." [31] The Buffalo *Express* pictured the United States as a conqueror: "The demands which we are making on Cuba are such as might properly follow successful war waged against the Cubans. They are the demands of a conquering, not of a liberating nation." [32] The New York *Evening Post,* which hammered away at the Amendment in almost daily editorials, called it "a melancholy spectacle," described it as providing for "government of Cuba by Americans and for the benefit of Americans," and declared that "the Army bill is just the place for an Amendment embodying the demands of the United States upon Cuba as they are an assertion of stark force." It warned: "If there is bloodshed in Cuba, the guilt of it will stain the hands of the men who have consented to sign away our fair fame as a truth-loving and honorable people." [33] The New York *World* asked: "If by a stretch of imagination we, the people of the United States, can put ourselves in the place of the Cubans, what do we think we would do in the present circumstances?" By way of answering its own question, the *World* fancied what the Revolutionary fathers would have said if France, having assisted materially "in securing our release from British tyranny, had proposed to the Colonies substantially the conditions which the administration, with the help of a subservient Congress, seeks to impose upon Cuba." It continued: "Americans would have told the French to get out," and this it hoped would be "what the Cuban patriots, who have fought so long and sacrificed so much for freedom and independence, will do." [34] The Boston *Post* agreed: "There is nothing of independence in the status which these orders give to Cuba. If this programme is forced upon the Cubans and they fight for the independence which has been promised and denied them, they will do just what we would do in their place." [35]

In the South, opposition to the Amendment was almost unanimous. *The State,* though not surprised,* was furious. The United States stood "disgraced among the nations by this scheme to rob Cuba of freedom." Indeed, it was even more worried about what the Amendment would do to the United States than what it promised to do to Cuba. "The action of the United States government in breaking its solemn pledge to the whole world as well as to Cuba, in putting a pistol to the head of its protege and demanding compensation for a volunteered kindness, will disgrace it in the eyes of civilization and mortify its own good citizens for generations to come. The loss and humiliation are ours. The penalty will be ours—the penalty of a national faithlessness which hereafter may well cause every people in the world to withhold all trust from 'lying America.'" [36] *The State* was bitter over McKinley's reference in his inaugural address to the fact that he was glad to be advised by Congress of the passage of the Platt Amendment, "a policy which the president himself formulated and forced through Congress by means which can be characterized only as bribery." It called this "an exhibit of Anglo-Saxon hypocrisy in its most loathsome form." [37]

Among the mid-western newspapers, only the Minneapolis *Journal* (Republican) was favorable. Its defense, however, was weak: "The United States has earned by her services to Cuba a right to have her relations to the Cuban government defined." [38] But all of the other papers in this huge region were forthright in their opposition. The Detroit *Free Press* characterized the Amendment as an "ultimatum"

---

* On the eve of the presidential election of 1900, *The State* had urged all friends of Cuban independence to vote for Bryan in whose victory "lies the only hope for Cuban independence." A McKinley victory would give Cuba only a "spurious independence." The Cubans would be kept "under a military government until they shall be driven to accept a condition of partially autonomous self-government as a relief from the rule of the soldier." (Oct. 30, 1900.) This proved to be an accurate prediction.

leading to a "benevolent assimilation" like that imposed upon the Filipinos.[39] The Chicago *Times-Herald* called the Platt Amendment "a shameless suzerainty," and declared that "the United States had no right to adopt any such conditions and hang them about the neck of Cuba."[40] But the Chicago *Chronicle* hit the nail on the head with a blistering attack:

> When Congress added the Cuban amendment to the army appropriation bill it was an avowal of the United States' intention to repudiate the pledge of Cuba's freedom and independence.
> That was bad; that was shameful. But it can be rendered worse and more shameful by affecting a hypocritical concern for Cuba's interests when all the world realizes that this nation seeks only to profit at the expense of the people whom it released from the Spanish yoke.
> When the President talks about securing justice, liberty, and assured order in Cuba his words cause a sensation of nausea, for it is of record in the United States Congress that we demand not justice and liberty, but coaling stations, supervision of Cuba's relations, and general suzerainty over the people whom we once declared to be free and independent.
> We are "out for the stuff." Let us be honest about it. The world has a certain respect for the freebooter who takes by main force and makes no pretense of of righteousness. It has only contempt for the snuffling hypocrite who steals everything in sight, rolling up his eyes and professing the greatest sanctity meanwhile.
> For heaven's sake, let us not add pharisaism to grand larceny.[41]

While the general press deplored the fact that the United States had violated its pledge to Cuba, the labor and Socialist papers said that this was exactly what should have been expected.* *The People* summed it up: "Pledges do not count for much with a capitalist government. Nor does the desire of the people of the island count for much." Only one thing counted: "material interest."[42] The *Journal of*

---

* The *American Federationist*, official organ of the American Federation of Labor and edited by Samuel Gompers, did not have a single word on the Platt Amendment during the winter and spring of 1901. As we have pointed out above, this was precisely the period when Gompers and other leaders of the A.F. of L. were uniting with the dominant figures in American industry and finance in the National Civic Federation, an organization whose chief function was to promote class collaboration between labor and capital.

the *Knights of Labor,* in an editorial entitled, "Shall Cuba Be Free or a Vassal," described the Platt Amendment as "an act of perfidy which has seldom been paralleled in the history of the world's worst despotisms in their treatment of weaker neighbors." But it, too, was not surprised. "It has all along been our belief that it has been and is the deliberate purpose of the leaders of the Republican party and the trusts which own and control them to permit no such thing as a Cuban republic; that from the moment of the landing of our troops in the island and the expulsion of the Spaniards, American authority was there to stay, and that eventually the Cubans would be accorded such measure of freedom as suited the benevolent purposes of the administration and Congress and their trust supporters." [43]

The *Railway Conductor* did not care if the violation of the Teller Amendment was inevitable under capitalism, as the Socialist press charged. It wanted the United States to keep its pledge. "The Cubans expect its fulfillment, and we are bound by our honor as a nation to grant them the terms it [the Teller Amendment] provides, without any strings attached to it." This meant scrapping the Platt Amendment, which reminded the labor paper "of the farmer who fed his chickens with one kernel of corn to which was attached a string, so that the kernel while fed might still be considered as being in the farmer's 'possession.'" [44]

The *Social Democratic Herald* of Chicago called the Platt Amendment "The Theft of Cuba," and said it was clearly the product of "the spirit of commercialism." Like the New York *World,* it made use of the experience of the American people in the Revolution: "The independence of this country could not have been accomplished without the aid of France, and we search in vain for a clause in our constitution giving the French any special rights." It predicted that "Cuba will not be free, and if she does not accept our terms we will never withdraw our troops, and the Philippines will not stand alone as new martyrs to the competitive system." [45] *The Challenge,* a Socialist paper published in Los Angeles, felt that Cuba could only gain its independence by fighting once again for it, and predicted "another war on the part of the Cubans, this time to secure freedom from what many of them consider the tyranny of the United States." [46]*

---

* "Cuba nur eine name" (Cuba only a name) was the heading over an article in the Socialist *New Yorker Volkszeitung* describing the Platt Amendment. (May 30, 1901.)

"Imperialism Now An Accomplished Fact," was the headline in one labor paper.[47] But the *National Labor Standard* pointed out that Platt Amendment represented a new and more subtle approach to imperialism. Instead of outright annexation, American imperialism had devised the protectorate. The Platt Amendment was to make of Cuba a virtual protectorate. Finding this protectorate device first useful in circumventing the Teller Amendment, the imperialists would employ it in embarking on a new wave of expansion. The labor paper called attention to a speech of the arch-imperialist Albert J. Beveridge, in which he hailed the protectorate as "the most important development of national power since the Constitution was adopted." Beveridge, said the *Standard,* had "let the cat out of the bag." Eventually this policy would include "the grasping of Mexico and other South American republics and possibly the whole of China and as many other countries that the great powers of the world may allow us to annex."[48] Who would benefit from "the new imperialism?" asked the *Railway Trainmen's Journal*. It answered: "Not the American workingmen, but the American capitalists will be the beneficiaries." It then observed: "Of what value will political freedom be to the Cubans, if under the Platt Amendment, American capitalists will have taken possession of the economic resources of the country?"[49]

In light of the widespread attacks on the Platt Amendment in the general, labor and Socialist press, one can see how ridiculous is H. Wayne Morgan's statement that "few Americans felt at that time that it was unjustified."[50] Most Americans felt that it was a betrayal of the cause for which, as they understood it, the nation had gone to war against Spain. As one man who had fought in the war wrote to the editor of *The State*:

> I wish to add a few words of protest to your own against this hypocritical treatment of Cuba on behalf of the American soldier who did the work of freeing her from Spain and who have a right to say whether the president and Congress shall dishonor them— degrading them from their proud position as champion of liberty to mere cats-paws in a game of national aggrandizement.
> If all we went through there and elsewhere was to give us a right to have a say as well as the president and the United States senators about what shall be done with Cuba, then have our sacrifices and our services been in vain. . . .

Grant that the temptation to hold Cuba is a powerful one, can we do it directly or indirectly without being false to our promises and bringing dishonor upon our land.[51]*

Ernest H. Crosby, social reformer and anti-imperialist writer,[†] summed up opinion in many parts of the country in his satirical poem, *Cuba Libre*. It read:

> When we sailed from Tampa Bay,
>   "Cuba Libre!"
> And our ships got under weigh,
>   "Cuba Libre!"
> As we floated down the tide,
> Crowding to the steamer's side,
> You remember how we cried,
>   "Cuba Libre!"
>
> When we spied the island shore,
>   "Cuba Libre!"
> Then we shouted loud once more,
>   "Cuba Libre!"
> As we sank Cervera's ships
> Where the southern sea wall dips,
> What again was on our lips?
>   "Cuba Libre!"
>
> These are foreign words, you know—
>   "Cuba Libre!"
> That we used so long ago;
>   "Cuba Libre!"
> And in all the time between
> Such a lot of things we've seen,
> We've forgotten what they mean
>   "Cuba Libre!"

---

* Edward Lehman Johnson of Columbia, South Carolina, the writer of this protest, urged that a petition be circulated among veterans of the Spanish-American War calling upon the President and the Senate "to give Cuba absolute and immediate independence." (*The State*, March 7, 1901.)

† Among Crosby's numerous anti-imperialist writings was the delightful, satirical novel *Captain Jinks, Hero* published in 1902. It satirized the war fever and the betrayal of the Cubans and Filipinos by the government.

> *Let us ask the President,*
>   *"Cuba Libre!"*
> *What that bit of Spanish meant,*
>   *"Cuba Libre!"*
> *Ask McKinley, Root, and Hay*
> *What on earth we meant to say,*
> *When we shouted night and day*
>   *"Cuba Libre!"*
>
> *But alas! they will not speak,*
>   *"Cuba Libre!"*
> *For their memories are weak,*
>   *"Cuba Libre!"*
> *If you have a lexicon,*
> *Borrowed from a Spanish don,*
> *Send it down to Washington,*
>   *"Cuba Libre!"* [25]

On March 28, 1901, the American Anti-Imperialist League gathered in a mass meeting at Boston's Fanueuil Hall at which the rallying cry was "Free America, Free Cuba, Free Philippines." All of the speakers denounced the Platt Amendment and were joined in this by a letter from Richard Harding Davis which condemned the measure as a betrayal of the Cuban people. Ex-Governor George S. Boutwell brought cheers from the audience when he said: "In disregard of our pledge of freedom and sovereignty to Cuba we are imposing on that island conditions of colonial vassilage." But the loudest applause followed the reading of a letter from Edwin W. Gayol in Havana "telling of the complete loss of faith by the Cuban people in the admiinstration's promise, but of their faith in the American people." [53]

This faith was also voiced by *La Patria* in Havana. In calling upon the Cuban people to mobilize all of their forces against the Platt Amendment, the journal founded by Martí declared:

> There is no room for doubt that the passage of the Platt Amendment results from the error that the Cuban people will accept it. It is incumbent upon us, therefore, to devote ourselves from this day on to energetically protest against this false supposition, because we entertain no doubt that once the American people become convinced of the real facts, they will retrace their steps, which will be equivalent to a return to the path of honor, as the good name and fame of the American nation are now subject to

mistrust, thanks to the policy of audacity, snares, cupidity, and shame which has been systematically carried out by its directors.

Reprinting this plea, *The State* urged the Cuban people to stand firm: "We believe that if the Cubans can hold out long enough the American people, on an issue fairly presented, will do them justice and give them that liberty which was pledged." [54]*

---

* Leonard Wood, enraged by the opposition in the anti-imperialist press in the United States to the Platt Amendment, accused it of encouraging Cuban opposition to the measure on the basis that the American people would force the next Congress to repudiate it if the Cubans refused to accept it. Theodore Roosevelt agreed, and called the editors of these papers "unhung traitors." (Wood to Roosevelt, April 2, 1901; Wood to Root, April 4, 1901; Roosevelt to Wood, April 17, 1901, Theodore Roosevelt Papers, Elihu Root Papers, and Leonard Wood Papers, all in Library of Congress.)

## CHAPTER XXVII
# Cuba Resists

ON MARCH 2, GOVERNOR WOOD transmitted the Platt Amendment to the Cuban Constitutional Convention. The first reaction of the delegates was one of utter dismay. Many favored dissolving the Convention, and Méndez Capote, President of the body, was reported as saying that "should we concede this, there will be born a government resting upon a supposition of incapacity."[1] Manuel Sanguily proposed calling a new election at which the people could vote their opinion on the question of relations with the United States and elect delegates to express their views on the Platt Amendment. While this was being decided it was agreed to appoint a committee to prepare the Convention's answer to the United States. The committee was composed of Juan Gualberto Gómez, Manuel R. Silva, Gonzalo de Quesada, Enrique Villuendas and Diego Tomayo—in other words, the same men who had made up the Committee on Relations, which had already presented the Convention's viewpoint on Root's original proposals.[2]

Meanwhile, Wood was keeping Washington informed of developments in the island. On March 2, he cabled Root assuring him that the "intelligent classes" were content, and predicted that there would be no serious popular excitement over the Platt Amendment. However, one could never be sure, and he suggested moving up the schedule for the Navy to visit Cuba. "Our squadron now on the Florida coast due here March 9th. Would not be a bad idea to have it here now." As for the action of the Convention, he could make no predictions because of the influence of the "extreme element" which was trying to induce the delegates "to dissolve and go home." In that event, all would still not be lost because "we have . . . the complete Constitution."[3]

Root must have thought that his subordinate in Havana was slipping. What was happening to Wood that he would even suggest the possibility of letting the Convention dissolve without ratifying the Platt Amendment! Root immediately wrote the Governor a stern letter of instruction. The members of the Convention must be made to understand that "they cannot escape their responsibility by a refusal to act," for in this event, the American authorities would simply convene a new Convention. They must be told there was no way to slip out of the noose. "Under the act of Congress they never can have any further government in Cuba, except the intervening Government of the United States, until they have acted." It did not matter in the slightest that the Cuban Constitution had been completed. It could not go into effect, Root insisted, until the Platt Amendment was accepted and became part of the Constitution. He suggested that the Cubans be informed that if they accepted it gracefully, they would create "a sense of kindliness" in the United States, but opposition would arouse bad feeling and make it difficult to get tariff concessions in the future.[4]

Wood promptly passed Root's threats to the delegates and they were sufficient to prevent them from dissolving the Convention and calling a new election. But Wood could do nothing to stem the tide of protest stirred by the news that the Platt Amendment had been enacted into law and must be accepted by the Cubans. Havana was the scene of a huge protest torchlight procession on the night of March 2nd. More than 15,000 Cubans, representing all classes and political groupings, descended upon the Convention, and while the majority waited outside the Teatro Martí, a delegation addressed the delegates, voicing approval of their stand in opposition to the American demands and urging them to continue to remain firm. Then the demonstration moved to the Governor's palace and delivered a petition to Wood condemning not only the contents of the Platt Amendment but the summary method in which it had been passed by Congress and presented to the Cubans. Taken aback by this tremendous outpouring of protest, Wood, as *La Discusión* reported, "with the deftness for which he is noted, tried to assure the Cubans that the Platt Amendment was not definitive, but that it only constituted a proposition which the delegates to the Convention could accept or reject; that if they did not adopt it, he understood that President McKinley would call Congress into special session and draw up a new plan." Wood, according to *La Discusión,* told the Cubans that he himself could not endorse any plan which infringed upon Cuban independence, "since upon accepting the post of Military

Governor, I did so with the explicit object of constituting a free, happy and orderly Republic. The establishment of any other government on this soil would signify the failure of my policy. I do not intend to let it fail."[5] Since most Cubans knew that Wood had desired anything but a Cuban Republic and had hoped to see the island annexed to the United States, his remarks were regarded as a maneuver to halt the rising tide of protest against the Amendment. Had they known that Wood was in possession of instructions from Root informing him that the McKinley Administration would tolerate nothing but complete acceptance of the Platt Amendment, the demonstrators might have told the Governor that he was lying when he said that the Cubans could accept or reject the measure.

New protest demonstrations occurred all over Havana on March 3rd. Meanwhile, outside the capital, *ayuntamientos* (municipal governments) were flooded with protest messages and resolutions; parades and meetings took place throughout the island, with Cuban flags flying and banners carrying inscriptions denouncing "*Enmienda Platt*" and proclaiming "*Nada de Carboneras*" (No Coaling Stations). Writing to McKinley from Santiago de Cuba, J. R. White, an American capitalist who was visiting Oriente to invest in sugar plantations, reported on a "great procession . . . composed of negroes of different shades of blackness" held the night of March 5th. "They halted at the plaza and several speeches were made, each speaker declaring that if the Constitution were not accepted by the United States, they would declare war against the Americans. They had fought for independence since 1850 and were ready to resume the field."[6]

"Fear Cuban uprising," blared the headlines in many American papers as reports from their Cuban correspondents reported opposition to the Amendment growing.[7] On March 28, the *New York Times* correspondent wrote that "it is doubtful if the Convention would accept the Amendment," so widespread was public opposition to it. About the same time, *La Patria* asserted that "all agree, even supporters of the Amendment, that it is a violation of independence . . . [a] flagrant, undeniable . . . non-fulfillment of the promise made by the United States government."[8]

Out of all the protests throughout the island emerged a moving and dignified appeal from the Cuban people to the American people. Cabled to American newspapers, it read:

## To the American People

The Cuban people raise their voices to the American people in a demand for justice. The vigorous arm and the vanquishing sword, which coming from the noble heart of the American people, helping decisively in the solemn moment of the glorious acquisition of their ideal of independence, will not shelter at this time a rapacious work of political ambition, but a sacred work of patriotic redemption. The Joint Resolution of April 20, 1898 was the voice of the great Washington proclaiming the austere purity of the strongest and most free of the democratic nations and the voice of Abraham Lincoln declaring respect for the liberty of people and the dominion of the rights of men.

The strict fulfillment of this solemn vote, the loyal execution of that mandate is what the Cuban people want today, and this is why we are appealing to American sentiment, justice and honesty. Absolute independence, complete sovereignty—without any limit, without restrictions—were and are the eternal, unquenchable and irreducible aspirations of the Cuban people.

In the name of gratitude for the past, and of peace and wellbeing for the future, Cuba entreats from the eternal greatness of the American people, the recognition of her right, the absolute independence of the country and the institution of her sovereign Republic.[9]

The attack on the Platt Amendment in Cuba was also expressed in satires and cartoons. Of the former, *Alma Cubana o Enmienda Platt* (The Cuban Soul or the Platt Amendment) is typical. In this pamphlet, Uncle Sam sells his soul to the devil in return for a promise of the Antilles and the Philippines. When he asks Satan to grant him a law giving him a monopoly on opium, the devil replies, "I will send you Platt." Satan teaches Uncle Sam Spanish so that he can win the heart of a beautiful Cuban girl. But even with the devil's assistance, Uncle Sam fails. The Cuban girl tells her mother that "the heart of a Cuban woman, like all legal documents, has a basic rule." "What is it?" her mother asks. "We do not admit cracks or amendments," the girl replies.[10]

The cartoons were much more devastating. One showed the "Cuban People," like Prometheus, bound to a rock labelled "Intervention," with an eagle labelled "Platt Amendment" eating at its liver.[11] But the most famous was the cartoon printed on the front page of *La Discusión* on April 5 (Good Friday) 1901. The cartoon, entitled "The Cuban Cavalry," showed a figure representing "the Cuban people" crucified between two thieves, who bore the faces of Leonard Wood and William McKinley while Senator Orville H. Platt stood by in the garb of a Roman soldier, holding a spear on the point of which was a sponge of vinegar labelled "Platt Amendment."* Infuriated when he saw the cartoon, Wood immediately suppressed *La Discusión,* closed and sealed its offices, and had both the editor and cartoonist arrested for criminal libel. The following day, however, yielding to the requests of members of the Convention, Wood ordered them released and allowed the paper to continue. *La Discusión* refused to be intimidated and continued to take the lead in voicing Cuban protests against the Platt Amendment.

While Republican newspapers in the United States pretended to be shocked by the cartoon, calling it "sacrilegious and insulting," the anti-imperialist press condemned Wood for his action against the newspaper and its staff members.† The New York *Evening Post* recalled that "Suppressed by Weyler" was the record long proudly displayed by *La Discusión,* and that it could now replace this with "Suppressed by Weyler and Wood."[12] (Actually, when *La Discusión* reappeared on April 8, it placed a new line under its title head, reading: "Suppressed by Weyler, October 23, 1896; suspended by Wood, April 6, 1901.) The Spartanburg (South Carolina) *Evening Journal* declared that Wood's conduct was "imperialism with a vengeance," and predicted that "it will not be long until these newspapers in the United States which print cartoons ridiculing the government will be treated likewise. Imperialism comes high, but we must pay the price."[13] But it was *The State* which made the most telling point:

> The columns of the imperialist press in the United States every day publish as insulting cartoons as this, aimed at the Cubans.

---

* The cartoon itself did not label Wood and McKinley as thieves, but the General was correct when he wrote to Root: "There is only one interpretation of this particular charicature [*sic*]—that the Cuban people are being crucified between two thieves." (Wood to Root, April 6, 1901, Elihu Root Papers, Library of Congress.) The cartoonist mistakenly drew a picture of Senator Thomas Platt of New York instead of the Connecticut Senator.

† The *Post's Havana* correspondent, Albert G. Robinson, reported that when the editor of *La Discusión* was brought before Wood, the Governor raged that "in the United States people had been lynched for lesser offenses." (New York *Evening Post*, April 16, 1901.) If the Governor meant Negro people, he was correct.

Republican cartoonists are fond of representing Cuba as a negro endowed with every attribute to create contempt and derision. . . .

Americans may insult Cubans as much as they will; they may break their pledges to them and rob them of their independence, but the Cubans may not resent it with the weapon of a cartoon. They must be humble and grateful and submissive under all the contumely heaped upon them and preserve their placidity of demeanor while they are being robbed of their rights by the bully government which holds them by the throat.[14]

In spite of the storm of protest and excitement sweeping Cuba, Wood kept assuring Washington that there was no need to worry. "The people of Cuba lend themselves readily to all sorts of demonstrations and parades, and little significance should be attached to them," he cabled Root on March 4th. Two days later, he reported: "Nothing to cause anxiety." On March 8th, he reported "everything quiet throughout the island," and by the 20th, he was cabling: "TRANQUILLITY ISLAND COMPLETE." Three days later, he wired: "One thing you can be sure—there will be no serious disturbance in Cuba." He kept repeating, in his dispatches, that the people who mattered, the conservative element—business men and wealthy Spaniards—favored adoption of the Platt Amendment.[15]

Washington received other evidence on this last point. One Congressman wrote after a trip to Cuba in March: "I found by careful inquiry that the business element of Cuba, the shrewd, calculating fellows who see fortunes ahead in sugar and tobacco, do not really want a free and independent Cuba, and while they would prefer annexation, feel that the Platt Amendment is absolutely necessary if the island is to have its own government."[16] Likewise, Representative John Dalzell of Pennsylvania, who had also just returned from Cuba, reported that the "men who have property interests at stake, the business men of the island, the bankers and planters . . . without exception favor adopting the Platt Amendment."[17]

Yet there were different reports. The *New York Times* correspondent reported that many Cuban conservatives, especially the Spanish element, favored rejection of the Amendment, feeling that this would lead to annexation.[18] Wood wrote to Root that "commercial interests and great agricultural concerns" also were urging defeat for the same reason.[19] Moreover, Edwin T. Atkins informed Platt that the conservatives in Cuba were alarmed because acceptance of the Amendment would be followed by withdrawal of American troops, "and I think that because of this, much quiet influence has indirectly been thrown against its acceptance." [20]

While these reports of conservative opposition to the Amendment had substance, the fact remains that the majority of Cuban landowners, planters and merchants supported it. For one thing, they were convinced that American capitalists would not invest in the island on a very large scale unless they were guaranteed against protection from radical legislation, and this, they knew, was one of the chief aims of the Platt Amendment. These Cubans were quite ready to welcome complete American economic domination of their country so long as they could obtain a share of the profits.* They were impressed by the report of Luis Abad, Secretary of the Commission of Economic Corporations, who wrote in *La Discusión* of March 21, 1901, shortly after a long stay in the United States, that American business men had told him "that since Congress voted the Platt law, the value of property in Cuba has gone up fifty percent."

Actually, the Cuban conservatives feared the Cuban people more than they feared American imperialism. Indeed, they looked upon the power of the United States as a safeguard against the militancy of the Cuban masses—the workers who, as we have seen, were beginning to revive their trade unions and conduct militant strikes, and the peasants, many of them Negroes, who looked forward to obtaining more from the victory over Spain than political sovereignty. Had the Cuban Constitution restricted suffrage to property owners and the literate, the fears of the conservatives of a truly independent Republic might have been considerably reduced. But when the radicals in the Constitutional Convention beat back all attempts to restrict the vote, and the Constitu-

---

\* Two years later, in analyzing the steps leading to adoption of the Platt Amendment by the Cuban Convention, *Appeal to Reason* noted that while American capitalists had taken over much that was "worth owning in Cuba" during the military occupation, they had left "enough in the hands of the aristocracy of Cuba to have them on the side of property against the people, allies who would sell their country into any kind of servitude for the privilege of having part of the loot." (Aug. 22, 1903.)

As William J. Pomeroy points out, the wealthy Filipinos also favored a policy of "accommodation with the Americans," hoping thereby to share in the economic exploitation of the islands. (*American Neo-Colonialism: Its Emergence in the Philippines and Asia*, New York, 1970, p 83.)

tion embodied universal suffrage, many landowners and businessmen began to look with favor on the idea of having the United States rescue them from successful attempts of the Cuban masses to gain the benefits of independence for themselves. In an interview with American reporters, J. A. Hanial, manager of the investment department of J. M. Ceballos & Co. and of the Development Company of Cuba, made the following significant observation:

> In a recent speech before the Constitutional Convention at Havana, Senor Calixto Gomez,* the colored leader, warned his race that to give any control whatsoever to the United States meant forcing the Cuban colored people to accept the same low social and political status which the negroes of the South labored under, and hence the colored Cubans, being in the majority, should stand against the Platt amendment.† Since then it has been easy to discern a change of sentiment among the "intelligent" in favor of the Platt amendment, and I am sure that it will be adopted.[21]

The majority of Cuban planters and merchants favored adoption of the Platt Amendment, but urged the Convention to negotiate for a reciprocity agreement with the United States as a reward for acceptance—both Círculo de Hacendados y Agricultureros de la Isla de Cuba (Club of Planters and Agriculturists of the island of Cuba) and the Republican Party of Oriente took this position in late March, 1901[22] —but accept the Amendment with or without reciprocity. Little wonder Senator Platt boasted, "Among the more conservative and responsible people of Cuba there has been no objection." [23]

This was all very reassuring to the Administration. But what Washington really wanted to know was what was the Convention going to do about the Platt Amendment. On this point, Senator Rayfield Proctor, also a visitor to Cuba, was not reassuring. He had tried to convince the delegates that their fears that the Amendment would "limit Cuban independence" were unjustified, but he could not report much success.[24] Nor was Wood more reassuring. On March 6th he had been confident that "it will be accepted." On the 20th, he wired that Máximo Gómez and Diego Tamayo favored a proposition "which embodies

---

\* The reference was to Juan Gualberto Gómez.

† It is strange that Gómez did not quote the Supreme Court decision in the Neely case to buttress his argument. The decision seems hardly to have been known in Cuba.

many features of Platt Amendment," that Gómez was "willing to grant coaling station," and, in any case, "promises no disturbance." But he was not so sure that the Convention would adopt the Amendment. He then asked Root: "Can you indicate our action in case Convention should refuse to accept Platt Amendment."[25] Root immediately shot back: "The Platt Amendment is, of course, final and the members of the Convention who may be responsible for refusing to establish relations on that basis will injure only themselves and their country. If the Convention takes such a course it will have failed to perform the duty for which it was elected and the duty must be performed by others."[26]

But soon Root decided on a different tact. Washington was learning that despite Wood's "optimistic dreams,"[27] the Cubans found most of the articles of the Amendment objectionable, but the most resented of all was Article Three, which provided for the right of intervention by the United States. This clause, all but the most conservative Cubans insisted, destroyed Cuba's independence in advance by making it possible for the United States to interfere in Cuba's internal affairs whenever it suited her interests. On March 28, *The State* published a letter from General Emilio Núñez in Havana which gave Root an opportunity to try to win over the Convention. Núñez urged clarification of Article Three. "I am willing to consent that the United States will retain the right to intervene in Cuba, but only with the authorization of the United States Congress, when the Cuban government, is unable to protect property and life as a consequence of a permanent state of disorder." The next day, Root wrote to Wood that Article Three gave the United States "no right which she does not already possess and which she would not exercise." However, it did not imply ordinary and habitual meddling in Cuban affairs; the contemplated intervention would be exercised only if absolutely necessary and for such major causes as "actual failure or imminent danger."[28] Wood immediately requested that Root embody such an assurance in a formal statement which he could show to the Cubans. The Secretary of War cabled Wood on April 2: "You are authorized to state officially that in the view of the President the intervention described in the third clause . . . is not synonymous with intermeddling or interference with the affairs fo the Cuban Government." The United States would also intervene, "based upon just and substantial grounds," to preserve Cuban independence or to maintain the protection of life, liberty and property.[29]

The Cubans were not impressed, *La Patria* insisted that the Amendment was still "a blow aimed at Cuba's independence and sovereignty," and that Root had done nothing to soften the blow. "A letter from the Secretary of War cannot modify or change a law of Congress. . . . We believe that Mr. Root's letter will not produce any effect whatever upon the Convention." This was an accurate prediction. On April 4, Wood still could not assure Root that the Convention would do the desired thing. Manuel Sanguily was an "ardent champion" of the Amendment, but the "radical element" was making "desperate efforts" to prevent adoption.[30]

Wood distorted Sanguily's position. It is true that Sanguily favored accepting the Platt Amendment, but the Cuban patriot was anything but an "ardent champion" of it. He made his position clear in *La Discusión* of March 21 with the statement: "Independence with some restrictions is preferable to a continuance of military rule which would surely follow a rejection of the Platt Amendment." It was realistic to understand, Sanguily continued, that the Cubans had already been forced into submission "by the power of the new Conquistadores" and should make the best of a bad situation. He was not greatly disturbed by Article 3 since "nobody can deny that the Americans can exercise the right to intervene whenever they wished to do so even without that article." Sanguily rejected the position of a number of delegates who argued that resistance should continue in the hope that the American Congress would soon repeal the Platt Amendment. Powerful interests in the United States, unfortunately supported by a majority of the American people, had decided that "Cuba must remain the prize of their commercial ambitions." He could see only two roads the Convention could follow: "Either reject the Amendment in its entirety or accept it in its entirety. In the former case, we will say farewell to our desire to see Cuba independent. In the latter case, we will at least see the end of military occupation and the establishment of a Republic dedicated to the practice of law within constitutional limits."[31]

But at this time Sanguily stood more or less alone. More typical of the Cuban point of view was Salvador Cisneros y Betancourt's *Voto Particular Contra La Enmienda Platt* delivered in the Convention on March 15, 1901. Cisneros urged rejection of the Platt Amendment and charged the United States with exercising "the power of the strong against the weak." The United States had already departed from "the principles of justice" in its "arbitrary occupation of the Philippines and Puerto Rico," and was seeking, through the Platt Amendment, to achieve the same objective indirectly in Cuba.[32]

The viewpoint of the majority of the delegates to the Convention, indeed the viewpoint of the vast majority of the Cuban people, was set forth in the brilliant *Ponencia a la Convención* (Report to the Convention) of the committee appointed, shortly after the body received the Platt Amendment, to prepare the answer to the United States. It was presented to the Convention on March 26, 1901 and shortly thereafter adopted by the body. Written by Juan Gualberto Gómez, the Negro delegate from Santiago and secretary of the committee,* it is the best expression of Cuban feeling throughout the entire period following the receipt of the American proposals. Never published in English to any extent and rarely even mentioned in most American historical works dealing with the Platt Amendment,† it is truly one of the great documents in the history of Cuba and its relations with the United States. It merits analysis both as the authentic voice of Cuba during this critical period in its history, and as one of the finest expression in the literature of anti-imperialism.

In the introduction reference is made to three documents—the Platt Amendment, the Joint Resolution of Congress of April, 1898, and the Treaty of Paris—in order to demonstrate that the first violated the letter and spirit of the other two. In essence, the Platt Amendment "tends through the terms of its principal clauses, to put the island of Cuba under the dominion, jurisdiction, and sovereignty of the United States," and this "without fulfilling the promise which they contracted to leave the government and authority of the island to its own people." Although the Congress of the United States could legislate only for that nation,‡ it took upon itself "to dictate" to the Cuban people and gave them only the choice between accepting the sovereignty of the United States or "the continuation of its military intervention, already unbear-

---

* The fact that Gómez was a Negro was played up in the American press. In one dispatch from Havana, Gómez was reported to have declared "that the black blood in his veins made him opposed to the Americans, intimating that their treatment of his race stamped them as unfriendly to the negro. 'I would rather be under the sovereignty of Spain than that of the United States.'" (*The State*, April 11, 1901.)

† Jenks (*op. cit.*, pp. 80-81) mentions the *Ponencia* in passing, but nearly all other historians dealing with this period ignore it.

able because unjustified, for such a long time, and distasteful for an infinity of reasons." The introduction concludes with the explanation that out of deference to the government of the United States and the American people and for the information of the civilized world, the Report would analyze one by one the clauses of the Platt Amendment, "so that there is no doubt in any impartial mind that the Convention cannot enter, by proceeding correctly and patriotically, the road that the indicated resolution of Congress and the government of the United States is trying to lead them on."

The Report then expressed no objection to Articles 1, 2, 4 and 5 of the Platt Amendment, pointing out that their essence had already been set forth in the Report of the Committee on Relations adopted by the Convention on February 27. While it was necessary to point out that the United States, in these articles, asked for guarantees it did not demand of "other independent and sovereign people" with which it maintained relations, nevertheless, since these four articles did not really "destroy the fundamental principle of independence and sovereignty," and, "in deference" to the friendship between the United States and Cuba, the Convention could accept these provisions and even recommend them "as something good for the Cuban government which is being constituted."

But the same could not be said for Articles 3, 6, 7, and 8. On the contrary, these provisions had to be rejected, for "they tend to destroy the independence and sovereignty of the people of Cuba, mutilate the territory of the fatherland, and retreat completely from the Joint Resolution of Congress, the Treaty of Paris, and from all the agreements and declarations made previously by the government of the United States." One had but to undertake a "simple examination" of these articles to see the "correctness" of this characterization, and this the Report proceeded to do.

Gómez's main attention was directed toward Article 3, the intervention clause. He listed three reasons why the United States wanted the Cuban government to recognize the right of intervention, and analyzed each one.

1. "For the preservation of Cuban independence." It was to be assumed that this was to preserve Cuba from foreign aggression. But this was unnecessary since the Cuban government would be even more concerned than the United States to resist such aggression, and would

take the initiative in calling for assistance from friendly nation, especially the United States. But it had to be the Cuban government which must determine when its independence was threatened:

> For the United States to reserve to itself the power to determine when this independence was threatened, and when, therefore, it should intervene to preserve it, is equivalent to handing over the keys to our house so that they can enter it at any time, whenever the desire seizes them, day or night, whether with good or evil design.

2. "For the maintenance of a government adequate for the protection of life, property, and individual liberty." There was simply no way, no matter, what new verbiage was added, of reconciling this provision with the sovereignty of Cuba so long as it was left to the United States to determine which Cuban government merited the qualification of "orderly" and which did not. Indeed, if this were accepted, the public power of Cuba would not be the product of the will of the Cuban people but of that of the government of the United States. To the United States, in theory and in fact, would belong the power to direct Cuba's internal life. Then followed a prophecy which was frequently to be fulfilled in the history of Cuba after 1902:

> The only Cuban governments that would live would be those which count on the support and benevolence of the United States, and the clearest result of this situation would be that we would only have feeble and miserable governments, conceived as incapable from the time they were formed, condemned to live more attentive to obtaining the blessings of the United States than to serving defending the interests of Cuba—in a word, we would have a fiction of government and soon we would be convinced that it would be better that we had none, and that it would be better to be officially and openly administered from Washington than by discredited Cuban functionaries, pliable instruments of a foreign and irresponsible power. . . .
> To put into a treaty the power that the United States may intervene in this island to protect life, property and liberty, is the same as disauthorizing all Cuban governments before they are born, condemning them to a state of inferiority so shameful, so humiliating, that no worthy and meritorious Cuban would lend himself to participate in it, and so stultifying that no government of Cuba would be able to fulfill the most elementary duties of government,

since no one would take it seriously, knowing that the last word with respect to its acts would be said by the government in Washington. During the periods when no intervention took place, Cuba would really be without a government.

How, after all, would it be decided that property and liberty were not sufficiently protected? The United States had already fully intervened in Cuba, and there were murders, robberies, arson, and kidnappings occurring. The intervening government had not been able to prevent them, nor could any other government. In fact, in the states of the American Union such crimes occurred daily. But suppose such crimes, as was inevitable, occurred once a "pseudo-independent Cuban government" was constituted. Would it not give the United States the opportunity to intervene? It might be argued that intervention would not occur for such frivolous reasons. But who, in the last analysis, determined when the right of intervention under the Platt Amendment, "of which there is no other example in history," would occur? "The vagueness and elasticity of the concept augments the gravity of its scope; and no matter from what point of view one looks at it, its end would be nothing less than the extinction of the power of the future governments of Cuba and the sovereignty of our Republic."

3. "For discharging the obligations with respect to Cuba imposed by the Treaty of Paris on the United States now to be assumed and undertaken by the Government of Cuba." The obligations imposed on the United States by the Treaty of Paris applied only during its period of occupation of Cuba. "The day on which the occupation ceases, its responsibility also ceases." It was true that the United States had insisted on the insertion in the Treaty of a provision that it would advise the Cuban government to accept the same obligation. But this had been taken care of by the Constitutional Convention which had provided that the Republic of Cuba should assume all obligations imposed on the United States. To permit the United States, once the military occupation ceased to have the right to intervene in order to force the Cuban government to fulfill this provision, would "impair the law, the prestige and the authority of this government."

In its separate parts and in its totality, then, Article Three could not be reconciled with the principle of Cuban independence. All authorities in the field of political science agreed that whoever had the right to impose mandates was the government. Sovereignty, according to these authorities, implied independence of all other states. As Professor John W. Burgess of the Department of Political Science, Columbia University, put it: "Power cannot be sovereign if it is limited. The sovereign is the one that imposes the limitation, and if it does not achieve power which is unlimited or limited solely by himself, it is not sovereign." Clearly then, whoever had the right of intervention in a country to exercise acts of government would be the one to exercise supreme power, the one who would be the true sovereign.

> All this leads us to declare that Article III of the Amendment, if put into practice, would annul the contract the United States made with the people of Cuba not to exercise in the island jurisdiction and domination as soon as a government, elected by the people after pacification, was constituted. The United States would be the superior legal power of the island of Cuba. In a word, Article III would transfer to the United States the sovereignty of what could only be improperly be called the Republic of Cuba.... The committee must, therefore, consider this Article as absolutely unacceptable, and conveys to the Convention its judgment that if it wishes to preserve the independence of Cuba, it must reach the same conclusion.

The searching analysis of Article Three completed, the Report turned to the Sixth Article dealing with the Isle of Pines. The discussion here was brief. The Isle of Pines belonged within the limits of Cuba "geographically, historically, politically, judicially, and administratively," and it could not for that reason belong to the United States. Hence there was absolutely no need to leave the question of ownership to future adjustment by treaty. It was part of the "constitutional boundaries of Cuba," and there it must remain.

Article Seven, the Report continued, was really an organic outgrowth of the third article and hence likewise unacceptable. If the United States was conceded the right of intervening in the life of Cuba and the island thereby reduced to the category of a dependency, more or less autonomous of the American government, then it would be quite logical to continue the subordination of Cuba by granting coaling naval stations to the foreign dominating power. But once Cuba took a stand in favor of its independence and sovereignty by rejecting Article Three, it had no alternative but to turn down the seventh Article. But there were other reasons too. What about the possibilities of clashes between the Americans established on Cuba's coast and the inhabitants of the island? What about the moral consequences of installing within the country a series of foreign fortifications? And what if the United States became involved in a war with another power and made use of the American naval station on the island of Cuba? Cuba would then be drawn "forcefully into a conflict in the preparation of which we would have no voice, whose justice we would have no knowledge of beforehand, whose direct cause perhaps does not interest us in the least."

What real interest could we have then to expose ourselves to foreigners? Our supreme longing is for peace, internal and external peace. Within the formula of the Joint Resolution of April, 1898, applied with integrity, with honesty and good-faith, we would be sure to live in peace, inside and outside of our house. In any other way, there is for our country only somber horizons and very sad perspectives.

One thing was certain: the Cuban people were most dismayed by the demand that part of their national territory be traded away for coaling or naval stations. Of all the Articles in the Platt Amendment this had aroused the greatest indignation, and the cry of *"Nada de Carboneras"* had dominated all popular protest demonstrations. "It is impossible for the committee not to realize the depth and justice of this public indignation. It is impossible, therefore, to recommend the Seventh Article which involves along with a mutilation of the fatherland, a constant menace to our internal and external peace, and causes a deep wound to the feelings of our people."

Article Eight, requiring the Government of Cuba to embody the provisions of the Amendment into a permanent treaty with the United States, would convert the island into a never-ending dependency of the United States, for its effect "would be to subjugate us forever." Certainly in view of the obnoxious nature of Articles 3, 6, and 7, it was impossible for the Convention to accept this Article.

Having examined the objectionable article, the Report presented its conclusions. The first thing it noted was that a lamentable change had occurred in the concept that the United States had now, regarding its rights and obligations with respect to Cuba, and that which was manifested three years before. Then, it had declared that Cuba was and should by right be independent. Now it regarded Cuba as a conquered country in which the United States, the victor, as a condition of evacuating it, imposed conditions which were "hard, harsh, humiliating: limitation of independence and sovereignty, power of intervention, and territorial concessions."

Instead of having made war with Spain to insure the independence of Cuba, the United States has declared war on Cuba itself. Did this policy agree with the principle established nobly and generously in Article IV of the Joint Resolution of April, 1898, which the Amendment says it is complimenting? The Committee does not think so.

Even worse than some of the articles of the Amendment was the method followed by the United States in its plan to end its military occupation of Cuba. Originally, in keeping with the spirit of the Joint Resolution, the Cubans had been told that the following procedure to end the occupation would be pursued: creation of the Cuban government; transfer to this government of the power now exercised by the United States; and leaving this government in possession of all the attributes of sovereignty. This was just and reasonable. But now there was a new procedure.

A people occupied militarily, although by a force which should be considered an ally not an enemy, is being told that before constituting their own government, before being free in their own territory, they should grant the military occupants who came as friends and allies, rights and powers which would annul the sovereignty of these very people. That is the situation created for us by the method which the United States has just adopted. It could not be more obnoxious and inadmissible.

Apart from all this, there was the real question whether the Convention had the power to accept the American ultimatum and adopt the Amendment. The original order calling the Convention into being (No. 301) had provided that it adopt the Constitution of Cuba, and as part of it, provide and agree with the government of the United States with respect to the relations that should exist between that government and Cuba. But Order No. 445 had modified the original order, and established that, instead of agreeing with the government of the United States, the Convention should only express an opinion of what the relations could or should be. Even if it was argued that the original order had never been superceded, this did not change the fact that the Convention only had the power to establish in Cuba an independent and sovereign state.

This is why it was convoked. For everything which is conducive to constituting a nation in this form it has ample power. But it does not have the power to reduce its independence or sovereignty. The nation—though there are treaty makers who think otherwise—can renounce its rights, but it has to do so in an express form. But this Convention has no power to turn Cuba into a vassal state of the United States. It is necessary for this purpose to convoke another Convention, to which would be given the mission of resolving that problem. But this Convention has been called into being only to establish a national state with all the essential attributes of independence and sovereignty.

Since the United States indicated in the Amendment that it wished to fulfill the declaration of the Joint Resolution, it should, in the judgment of the committee, pursue the following course. First, it should allow the government of the Republic of Cuba to be set up as provided for by the Constitution written and adopted by the legitimate representatives of the people of Cuba at a Convention called by the government of the United States. Then when this government was formed, the powers now exercised by the government of the United States should be turned over to it. Finally, the American troops should retire from the island. "Then and only then will the Joint Resolution and Treaty of Paris have been fulfilled. Independent and sovereign Cuba will exist and be a reality capable of doing everything which independent and sovereign people can do." Nor would the United States suffer by pursuing such a just policy. For if, after an independent and sovereign Republic of Cuba were established, the government of the United States still believed it necessary for its interests to achieve what Cuba could not now grant, and if this was "compatible with the laws and interests of Cuba," the issue could be resolved by a treaty between the two countries.

What is probable is that at that moment, grateful Cuba, having been left entirely free and independent, and with its confidence not having been abused or tricked, would grant the maximum of concessions in favor of the United States. Then, in effect, our government would not be embarrassed by the presence of any foreign power on the island. Then there could not be doubts and resentments in the Cuban soul. For then there would have been converted into positive reality what are still for Cuba overwhelming anxieties and infinite hopes—the reality of liberty and independence.[33]

We have dealt at length with the *Ponencia* of Juan Gualberto Gómez partly because Americans are entitled to know specifically what the Cuban people thought of the policy of the government of the United States as set forth in the Platt Amendment, and also because it is a masterful document which shows that the Cubans did not lack for men who could stand up against American imperialism. The brilliant analysis shows up the Platt Amendment for what it was—a cynical violation of the American pledge to Cuba, a design to rob the Cubans of real independence, to deprive them of the rewards of victory, a victory for which they themselves were largely responsible, and a plot to cripple the Republic of Cuba before it was even born. Like the Ostend Manifesto of 1854, it was a brigand's document.

Early in April, 1901, *La Patria* reported that "the Platt Amendment is already practically rejected."[34] On April 3, by the overwhelming majority of 23 to 3, the Convention voted down a set of proposals by Gonzalo de Quesada which he called "a lesser evil" than the American plan as it stood, and which he believed would make the Amendment "compatible with Cuban dignity."[35]* On April 6, a motion to accept the Platt Amendment was defeated—24 to 2—with only the sole Conservative Party representative and Joaquín Quílez, characterized by A.

---

* Quesada substituted for the hated Article Three one which granted the United States the right to intervene only in accordance with the Monroe Doctrine "which guaranteed the independence of the Republics of the Americas". He added to the Article dealing with sanitary plans the provision that their execution and direction "shall be exclusively by the Cuban government." On the question of the Isle of Pines, he added the provision that while its final disposition should be settled by a future treaty, until that was achieved, it would be considered "as part of Cuban territory." On the question of the coaling and naval stations, he specified that they would always be installed outside the radius of established cities and that the American authorities at these stations would have absolutely no power to intervene in Cuban governmental or other affairs. Finally, he added an article favoring a reciprocity treaty between the United States and Cuba. (Enrique H. Moreno Pla, *Gonzalo de Quesada, Estadista,* La Habana, 1962, pp. 30-32.)

R. Robinson as "an instrument" of Wood because of a previous appointment, voting in its favor.[36] Six days later, on April 12, a vote on non-acceptance of the Platt Amendment was carried 18 to 10.[37]

As was to be expected, the imperialist press in the United States viewed the vote as "a humiliation inflicted on the American people," and as complete proof that "the Teller Amendment was ill-considered, untimely and foolish."[38] Some papers interpreted the vote as reflecting the views of only the Cuban politicians and not of the people. But the New York *World* put the record straight: "If the members of the Convention, elected as they were under American supervision and acting as they were with Gen. Wood in direct contact with them day by day, voted thus overwhelmingly, what must be the feeling of the Cuban people?"[39] Representative James L. Slayden, a Spanish-speaking Congressman from San Antonio, Texas, just returned from a fifteen-day trip to Cuba, answered this question two days after the Convention had voted:

> I do not believe that 10 percent of the Cubans cheerfully accept the Platt Amendment. . . . If it is accepted, it will be done, as one distinguished gentleman, a delegate to the Constitutional Convention, said to me, in the same spirit and in circumstances very similar to those in which the citizen yields his purse to the robber who has him covered with a pistol.[40]

# CHAPTER XXVIII
# Cuba Yields to Force

ON APRIL 13, the Cuban Convention suspended further business "while a committee of five members shall be sent to Washington" to discuss "political and commercial relations." (The committee consisted of Domingo Méndez Capote, President; Pedro Betancourt, Rafael M. Portuondo, Diego Tamayo, and Pedro Gonzales Llorento.) Two days later, Wood informed Root that Méndez Capote wanted advance assurance that the commission would be received by the Administration. He urged the Secretary of War to receive the group, for while the "apparent purpose" of the trip would be to seek information on the disputed Articles in the Platt Amendment, this was only for the public consumption. "Purpose of this visit is in reality to accept Platt Amendment," he cabled, adding that he had been told this by the members of the commission. Nevertheless, "everything depends upon this being unknown." Everything, too, looked good for the United States. A "gradual reaction" was taking place "throughout the country in favor of the Platt Amendment." The commission's visit would complete the trend for adoption. "Information received will remove doubts and amendment will be accepted." Wood concluded that "this is the Latin method but we are after results."[1]

How much truth there was in Wood's evaluation of the purpose of the commission's visit to Washington is difficult to say. As we have pointed out previously, he seems to have had an insatiable yearning to assure Washington that everything was going smoothly in Cuba, and he always had a tendency to underestimate Cuban opposition to American politics. Then too, he might have felt that only by depicting the real purpose of the visit as a paving of the way for adoption of the Amendment, could he make sure the commission would be received at the White House. At any rate, accurate or not, Wood's cable must have had the effect of stiffening Washington's determination to make no concessions to Cuba. Why concede anything when the Convention could be counted on to swallow the Amendment as it stood?

Despite Wood's assurances, the Administration was taking no chances. Three days before the commission arrived in the United States, the press published a warning by Senator Platt to the Cubans that America's patience was nearing its end, and that they should not expect any modifications in the Amendment bearing his name. "Our overtures are entirely friendly and it does not seem to me that they will not be accepted. But if they are not at once, we shall occupy until they are."[2] Either the Cuban commissioners were unaware of this threat or, if they were, they ignored it. A newspaper man who met the Cubans at Jacksonville, where they arrived on April 23, reported that "while somewhat reticent as to their mission, [they] showed plainly today their hostility to America and the Platt Amendment." General Rafael M. Portuondo told the reporter that "Ninety-nine per cent of the Cuban people desire absolute independence," and that the United States would be wise to adopt a policy which would fulfill this wish. "I do not mean that in the event that independence is not granted war or revolution would follow, but there would be no sympathy, no friendliness between the peoples."[3] But such predictions meant little to the Administration, which was determined to limit Cuba's independence regardless of the consequences to friendly relations "between the peoples" of Cuba and the United States.

On the morning of April 25, the commission met with President McKinley, Secretary Root being present. Pleasantries were exchanged. Speaking for the commission, Méndez Capote politely informed the President that "United States soldiers and Cubans had fought side by side and had driven Spain from the island, and that the ties between the two countries were bound in blood." He invited McKinley to come to Cuba to see for himself the affection in the island for the United States, and then asked the President to do something for Cuba in the way of a commercial treaty mutually beneficial to both countries. McKinley replied that it was impossible to settle economic questions until the political issues were disposed of. He told the delegates to first form their government and then they would be in a position to enter into negotiations with the United States as to trade relations. Méndez Capote answered that he thought that something should be done while the

Cuban government was forming. But McKinley said that this was impossible, thanked the delegation for the invitation to visit Cuba, and told them to assure the Cuban people of his friendly interest in them and his desire to see them contented and prosperous. With this, the interview ended.[4]

It was at two afternoon conferences with Root on the 25th and 26th that the commission got down to the basic issues. According to the notes taken by the Cubans, Root began the talks by presenting a long analysis of Cuban-American relations in which, to put it mildly, he turned history upside down. Flying in the face of evidence in the records of the American government, Root claimed that the United States had always been a champion of Cuban independence and had never imposed obstacles in her path when Cuba sought to achieve liberation from Spain. The United States had always had but one wish for Cuba—to see it independent.

Following this historical lecture, Root presented a lengthy defense of the Platt Amendment which he characterized as representing only the desire of the United States "to protect the small Republic of Cuba, situated in our vicinity and consequently under the influence of the United States." Recognizing the bitter opposition in Cuba to Article 3, Root assured the commission that the United States had no intention to intervene in Cuban affairs and could gain no benefit from such intervention. All it wanted was solely for Cuba's good, for instead of weakening her independence, Article 3 "fortifies and perpetuates it." In any case, the article was simply "an extension of the Monroe Doctrine. It is the Doctrine itself as international principle." While the Monroe Doctrine was not recognized in international law, the Platt Amendment would be, and thus European nations would have to recognize the American right of intervention in Cuba, and thus none of the powers could threaten the independence of Cuba "without undertaking first to fight the United States."

Elaborating his opinion as expressed in the dispatch of April 3, Root assured the Commission that the United States would "intervene only in case of great disturbances, similar to those which occurred in 1888, and with the sole and exclusive purpose of preserving unharmed the independence of Cuba." Since the third Article was designed solely for Cuba's own protection, intervention would occur "only for the sake of preventing foreign attacks . . . or where there exist[ed] a state of real anarchy in the Republic." Hence there was no need for the Cubans to fear the Article would destroy their Republic's independence and sovereignty. Nor was there any reason to fear Article Seven. The naval bases were to be used only for military defense of both countries, and would never be used to interfere in Cuba's internal affairs.

When Root had finished, Méndez Capote turned the discussion immediately to the question of commercial relations. He insisted on the need for tariff reciprocity between Cuba and the United States. Root explained that reciprocity would have to await the establishment of a Cuban government competent to enter into a reciprocity treaty. But he did make one concession: he explained that, speaking only for himself and in the name of the President, he could give assurances that once the government of Cuba was established, representatives would immediately be appointed to study and propose a mutually beneficial commercial treaty. With this promise, the first afternoon's discussion closed.

Meeting after the session, the commissioners evaluated the meaning of Root's long discourse. It all added up, according to Marquez Sterling, who accompanied the commission as secretary, to "words, words." The Monroe Doctrine, which was supposed to serve as barrier against infringement upon the independence of governments in the Western hemisphere, was being used to destroy the independence of the Cuban Republic.

The next afternoon Root was told that the commission was still not satisfied with his assurances on Article 3. The Secretary of War then launched into another lengthy discussion of the Article, again giving assurances that the right of intervention would not be used casually. To his own interpretation that the Amendment would not destroy or even weaken Cuba's independence, he added that of Orville H. Platt. The Senator, in response to Root's information that "the members of the Cuban Constitutional Convention committee are apprehensive that the provisions regarding intervention in the third clause . . . will have the effect of preventing the independence of Cuba, and will in effect establish a protectorate or sovereignty on the part of the United States," sent a letter which the Secretary of War showed the commission. Platt wrote that the Amendment "was carefully drafted with a view to avoid any possible claim that its acceptance by the Cuban Constitutional Convention would result in the establishment of sovereignty or in any way interfere with the independence or sovereignty of Cuba." Speaking for himself, he found it "impossible that any such construction can be placed upon the clause." The Amendment had to be considered "as a whole," and anyone reading it as such could only conclude that "its well defined purpose is to secure and safeguard Cuban independence and to establish at the outset a definite understanding of the friendly disposition of the United States towards the Cuban people, and its expressed intention to assist them, if necessary, in the maintenance of such independence." While he could not speak for the entire Congress, he believed that his views represented those of his colleagues and "that such purpose was well understood by that body." Naturally, Platt did not mention the fact that a substantial number of his colleagues had interpreted the Platt Amendment as infringing on the sovereignty of Cuba and establishing a United States protectorate in the island.

Again, as in the previous afternoon, the commission spent little time defending Cuba's case against the Amendment, and concentrated on tariff concessions. Having met with the President and the Cabinet since the last session, Root made another slight concession. He conceded the possibility that the Cuban tariff might be modified at once, by authority of the Military Government, and he promised to see what could be done. The question of the United States tariff, however, would still have to await the establishment of a Cuban government. But he confirmed the declaration that immediately thereafter the issue would be taken up. Finally, McKinley himself corroborated the Secretary's statement, as the commission, escorted by Root, took formal leave of the President on April 27.[5]

After the commission had left for Cuba, Root wrote Platt that in his view, the visit had been worthwhile, and had accomplished three things: (1) dissipation of "real misunderstandings" about the Platt Amendment; (2) furnishing arguments for those who were in favor of acceptance, to be used in Cuba; (3) creation of "a feeling of kindness toward the United States."[6] If the main objective of the visit had been to secure the promise of tariff concessions in return for the Cuban Convention's approval of the Platt Amendment, the commissioners had reason to be satisfied. For the Cubans had secured commitments from both the President and the Secretary of War. But if the purpose of the visit was to secure some modifications in the obnoxious Articles of the Amendment, it was a failure. All the Cubans got was a lengthy and wordy interpretation of the Amendment by Root; the information that the Administration regarded the right of intervention under Article 3 as "simply an extension" of the Monroe Doctrine and thus gave the United States no new right which she did not have before; and the assurance, verbal in the case of the Secretary and written in the case of Platt, that the United States would never take unfair advantage of the right to intervene. Beyond that, there were of course the usual receptions, luncheons, dinners, much flattery of the American and Cuban people, and endless expressions of friendship and good will. But on the issue of abandoning or even modifying the Articles in the Amendment to which the Cubans objected, the Administration did not budge an inch. All the Cubans could do now, in the judgment of most American papers, was to accept the Platt Amendment, and hope that the United States would not exercise the power bestowed upon it. Otherwise they would never have a government of their own, and even "limited independence" was better than no independence at all.[7]

However, the Cubans were advised not to take the promise of economic concessions seriously. *The State,* of course, warned them not to believe a word on this subject uttered by anyone associated with the Administration. "The bad faith of the Administration has been so plainly shown in its prosecution of the policy of imperialism that we would hesitate to accept the written and definite pledge of Wm. McKinley in regard to our insular affairs."[8] But even Republican organs warned that if they accepted the Platt Amendment on the basis of a promise of tariff concessions, the delegates would be guilty of leading their people down a false road, and that there would be "a bitter awakening for the Cuban people . . . when the news became known at the next Congress that no reciprocity will be granted." Cuban planters, in particular, were advised not to put everything they had or could borrow into raising sugar on the basis of the promises of McKinley and Root. The beet sugar planters in California, Nebraska, Michigan, and Colorado would not sit idly by and see themselves ruined by an influx of Cuban sugar.[9] In the last analysis, the decision on reciprocity, declared the Providence (Rhode Island) *Journal,* depended "not upon the character of the government in Havana, but upon the will of Congress as influenced by the demands and power of the protected interests in this country." If the Cubans really wanted favorable conditions for the growth of the sugar industry, they would not achieve it even by "the speedy acceptance of the Platt Amendment." Only one condition would produce the desired results: "the annexation of Cuba." [10]

But the Springfield *Republican* held out a major reason for the Cubans to continue to hope for tariff concessions. They would not be fighting alone. "American capital is being heavily invested in the island and will be able to start a warm backfire for free trade here at home. It will be represented more and more strongly in the lobby at Washington as time passes, and if the Cubans are willing to yield full independence at a price reckoned in terms of tariff reduction, they will not want strong money influence to help them even now." The real question, as the anti-imperialist *Republican* saw it, was whether the promise of tariff reduction, even though likely to be fulfilled was "a price glittering enough to tempt Cuba to barter away its independence." [11]

There is no doubt that Washington was now using the carrot and stick technique. This tactic was clearly exemplified by Senator Platt's statements. Before the commission had arrived in Washington, Platt, it will be recalled, had publicly warned the Cubans that if they did not accept all of the Articles of his Amendment "at once, we shall occupy until they are." He continued to brandish the stick of permanent occupation over the head of the Cubans, warning them, a magazine article published early in May, that the United States would never leave Cuba until the Amendment guaranteeing "stability" under the new Republic was adopted.[12] At the same time, in a letter to Dr. Joaquín Quilez, a delegate to the Cuban Convention who had already voted to accept the Platt Amendment, Platt held out the carrot of reciprocity. After repeating most of the same reassurances and explanations which he had given to the Cubans in his letter to Root, he went on:

> Of course we can only determine treaty relations with an independent and fully established government. The very first steps toward reciprocal treaty relations is the establishment of a Cuban government. No one man can speak for the future action of his nation, but I can say this, that I find in the United States but one sentiment, and that is that as soon as Cuba shall have put herself in a proper position to make a commercial treaty, there will be every disposition to agree to treaty relations which shall be for the benefit of both countries. . . .[13]

Platt must have known that he was lying when he wrote that there was "only one sentiment" in the United States on the question of granting Cuba reciprocity if she adopted the Amendment bearing his name.* (The Cubans, as we shall see, were soon to discover exactly how fully Platt distorted the truth in this connection.) But so long as men like Quilez could make use of this assurance in order to weaken opposition in the Convention against the Amendment, what did it matter if the truth was stretched.

On May 6, the commission made its report to the Convention, and the delegates plunged immediately into secret sessions. Throughout the next weeks, the debates were mainly over Articles Three, Six, and Seven, and Root's interpretation of them. But several factors were weakening the opposition to accepting the Platt Amendment. One was the point Manuel Sanguily had emphasized almost from the beginning: acceptance was the better alternative to continued occupation. Even some of the most radical, most nationalistic delegates were concluding that the Republic with the Platt Amendment was better than Cuba forever under American military rule. The second factor was the promise by the Administration of a reciprocity tariff on sugar and tobacco with Cuba once the Republic was established. This was seized upon as sweetening the bitter pill sufficiently to enable Cuba to swallow it, and the planters and commercial interests put pressure on the Convention to hasten the day when they could begin enjoying the anticipated rewards. A third factor was the support of the Amendment by Máximo Gómez and Tomás Estrada Palma. Gómez had already made his position clear in late February, and he continued to use his influence to obtain acceptance after the Cuban Commission returned from Washington. Now he received support from Estrada Palma. In a letter from the United States to Gonzalo de Quesada, which was meant to be shown to all the delegates, Estrada Palma announced his position. While he deplored "the brusque, dictatorial manner" with which the Amendment was being imposed on Cuba, and insisted that this "wounded my dignity as a Cuban," he advised Quesada against rejecting it. The Cubans

---

* The editorial from the Providence (R.I.) *Journal* cited above, warning the Cubans to bear in mind that there was considerable opposition in the United States to tariff reduction on Cuban sugar, is in the Orville H. Platt Papers, Connecticut State Library, so the Senator knew that he was telling an untruth when he wrote that there was "only one sentiment" on this issue.

really had no right to reject the Amendment since the United States was entitled to some guarantee of order in Cuba. He himself had told American political leaders before the passage of the Joint Resolution in April, 1898 that United States intervention in the Cuban Revolution would give it a base from which to insure future internal peace there. In his opinion, the Platt Amendment was a fair compromise of United States and Cuban interests.[14]

The effect of the pressure of these various forces for acceptance was evident by mid-May, when Méndez Capote brought Wood a proposition to relay to Washington. The Cuban delegate assured Wood that the Convention would adopt the Platt Amendment by a large majority if Articles Three and Seven were slightly re-worded. In the Cuban wording, Article Three would grant the United States the right to intervene to avert a threat from without, or, in case of internal anarchy, to re-establish government "in accordance with the Constitution of Cuba." The obvious purpose was to prevent intervention as the first step toward annexation or permanent occupation. Article Seven would grant the United States naval stations in Cuba "on such conditions that they will only serve the military or naval purposes to which they should be applied."[15]

Wood thought these propositions acceptable, and forwarded them to Root on May 17, asking for instructions. The Secretary of War replied the same day. He did not reject the propositions outright, but informed Wood that "it would be better for the convention to use the exact words of the Platt Amendment and add their construction rather than to substitute their construction for the words of the law."[16] Wood conveyed this information to the Convention.

Then on May 19, the Committee on Relations submitted majority and minority reports to the Convention which went far beyond Méndez Capote's propositions. The majority report proposed an appendix to the Constitution which would contain not only "the exact words of the Platt Amendment" as Root demanded, but the text of the Joint Resolution of Congress and Article I of the Treaty of Paris, as well as long extracts from Root's various explanations and assurances that "the Platt law has for its object the guaranteeing of the independence of Cuba, and does not mean interference with its government or the exercise of a protectorate or of sovereignty, and also that intervention will take place only when independence is endangered by outside powers or grave internal disturbances, creating anarchy, and . . . that the naval stations will not be used for vantage points of intervention, but only to protect Cuba from foreign powers. . . ." Stating that these quoted "declarations and assertions made by the Secretary of War of the United States constitute an authoritative interpretation of the so-called Platt Amendment," the committee also proposed certain additions to Articles Three, Six, Seven, and Eight. Added to the third Article was an assurance that intervention should be only "to prevent the action of a foreign power or disturbances causing a state of anarchy," that it should always be "the act of the United States and not of isolated agents," that it "shall suppose neither sovereignty nor a protectorate, and shall only last sufficiently long to establish normal relations," and finally, that the United States should "not have the right to interfere in the government, but only the right to preserve independence." The seventh Article had added to it an assurance that the naval stations "do not give the United States the right to interfere in the interior government, but are established with the sole purpose of protecting American waters from foreign invasion, directed against Cuba or the United States." An addition to the sixth Article stated that the ownership of the Isle of Pines should be settled by a future treaty, and appended to the eighth was a suggestion for a treaty of commerce based on reciprocity. The report also included the text of the letter addressed to Root by Platt which had been shown to the commission in Washington, and in which the Senator had disavowed any intention of establishing a portectorate over Cuba.

The minority report boldly substituted for the third Article: "That the government of Cuba subscribes to the Monroe Doctrine and will help the United States to enforce it against other nations trying to vindicate it." It replaced the seventh Article with one providing for Cuban maintenance of naval stations to be handed over to the United States in time of war. But the minority also commented bluntly that if what had been told the Cuban Commission in Washington was true, the Platt Amendment as adopted by Congress did not really "express the wishes of the United States. It was intended to protect the independence of Cuba, but the wording gives it other interpretations." It charged the United States with being "inconsistent in asking naval stations, when the Amendment provides that no concessions shall be given to foreign powers. Such a demand raises the question whether the United States do not consider Cuba part of their possessions." [17]

On May 28 the report of the majority, embodying the Platt Amendment and the additions, was adopted by the Convention 15 to 14, with the deciding vote being cast by the President, Méndez Capote.[18] *El Mundo* of Havana commented sadly that the acceptance of the majority report was a dark day for Cuba. "By the vote . . . Cuba's independence and nationality were made subjects of the United States. In the future we shall be only a name on the map of the world." [19] However, the imperialist press in the United States heaved a sigh of relief. The *New York Times* hailed the fact that even though it was not done "with the best grace in the world," at any rate, "finally and fully, the Cuban Constitutional Convention has assented." [20] The anti-imperialist press felt that the Cubans had done better than might have been expected. "They have parried with supreme skill the blow treacherously aimed at them by their great neighbor and vaunted 'benefactor,'" observed *The State*.[21] The New York *Evening Post* believed that the Cubans had outsmarted the United States and "left Secretary Root looking uncommonly foolish." [22] But the *Daily People* disagreed. The attempt to compromise with the imperialists was a fatal mistake. It rarely succeeded, for one thing, and even when it did, it was only temporary. "There is no permanent compromise possible when Principle is at stake," declared the Socialist Labor Party organ. "By rejecting the Platt Amendment outright, the Cubans would have gone down with colors flying and with principle on their side to assist them in future struggles. This principle will survive and be taken up again at a more propitious season by others. It is bound to prevail." [23]

Wood relayed the majority report to Washington, together with the information that eevrything was quiet in Cuba, and that "the acceptance of the Platt Amendment has produced a general feeling of relief." Obviously, Wood interpreted the vote as adoption of the Amendment. But Root quickly let him know that the Cubans were not to be let off so easily, and that they could not yet look forward to the withdrawal of the American army since they had not adopted the Amendment in the form that would justify it.[24] A conference at the White House was held immediately, attended by McKinley, Root, Platt, and Spooner, and it was decided that the Platt Amendment had not been adopted "substantially" as required in its preamble. The *New*

*York Times* reported that the Cubans' action was "so unsatisfactory that it has inspired anger among the President's advisors. . . . The patience of the administration is exhausted." [25]

In a lengthy letter to Wood, written with characteristic coldness, Root laid down the law to the Cubans, informing them that the Platt Amendment had to be accepted without change. He charged that the Cuban Commission's recollection of their conferences in Washington was in many respects inaccurate; he objected to the publication of Platt's letter which he had marked "confidential"; he accused the Cubans of impropriety in making use of statements made by him in private conversation; and he insisted that some of the "explanations," particularly the mention of reciprocity negotiations, actually changed the meaning of the Amendment. He concluded that in general, "the acceptance of the Platt amendment is surrounded by such a cloud of words, by way of recitals and explanations, that it is difficult to tell what the real meaning is." [26] Since many of the words had come from the Secretary himself, it is obvious that they had been employed solely to soft-soap the Cubans.

The imperialist press, though somewhat embarrassed that the Administration's own explanations of the Amendment had been repudiated when the Cubans used it, justified Root's ultimatum. The New York *Tribune* informed the Cubans that the Platt Amendment was as mandatory as a court injunction and had to be respected and obeyed as it stood. "It is not to be amplified by him to whom it is addressed with his own interpretations of its meaning and his own limitations of its scope." The *New York Times*, forgetting that only a few days before it had accepted the Convention's action, now declared that the Amendment was a contract, and that "a contract cannot be altered or vitiated by footnotes and marginal additions by one of the parties." [27]

"Now the whole issue is brought down to a question of pure force," declared the Philadelphia *North American* on June 5, 1901, in summing up the situation facing the Cubans. Actually, it had always been a question of "pure force." On March 25, 1901, Dr. M. F. Coomes, a Louisville, Kentucky doctor who was a friend of Cuban independence,*

---

* On March 24, 1901, the Louisville *Courier-Journal* published a letter Dr. Coomes had received from Emilio Núñez in which the Cuban General noted that while he was willing to make many concessions to the United States in order to achieve a Republic, "I can not be willing to consent to those things disguised as

put the whole issue in proper perspective in a letter to William Jennings Bryan: "The *Courier Journal* of today says that the Cubans are falling into line. Well most of us us would fall into line if we were surrounded by Bayonets and Mausers." [28]

The Cubans had no more room to maneuver. The Convention could refuse to accept Root's ultimatum, dissolve, and throw upon Washington the responsibility for the next step, or it could accept the Platt Amendment. It took nine weeks of debate before the decision was reached. Wood was irritated that the Cubans did not immediately throw in the sponge. "Whether it is absolute bad faith or inability to appreciate that no one can interpret the scope of the Platt amendment except congress I do not know," he wrote to Root.[29]

On June 12, 1901, the Convention bowed to force and accepted the Platt Amendment as passed by Congress, by a vote of 16 to 11. Explaining his vote in favor, Manuel Sanguily noted that the main reason was "because while it is an imposition of the United States, all resistance would be definitely unfavorable for the aspirations of the Cubans." José N. Ferer, who switched from opposition to acceptance, explained his change: "I believe it has already been resisted sufficiently, and now can no longer be resisted. I considered opposition to the Platt law advantageous and necessary as long as there was a hope that it would be modified or withdrawn by the American Congress, and because of this I voted against the the motion to accept even with modification. Today I consider such opposition useless, dangerous and unproductive, if one keeps in mind the great opening that the Supreme Court has given to the imperialism of the United States,* and furthermore the hope is lost that the Congress of that nation will reconsider its action on the Platt Amendment.† This is why I took this stand, and because it is the only way to establish the government of the Republic."

---

big benefits for the Cuban people when in the end they are inspired by selfish motives."

* Ferer was probably referring to the Supreme Court decision in the case of Puerto Rico upholding the annexation of the island.

† Louis Abad, Secretary of the Commission of Economic Corporations, had much to do with influencing members of the Convention, saying that they could expect no better treatment from the next session of Congress so far as the Platt Amendment was concerned. Upon his return from the United States, Abad wrote in *La Discusión* that if the Convention rejected the Amendment, the chances were that the next session of Congress would act even more severely. "If

Four members opposed to the Amendment absented themselves. The Platt Amendment was incorporated into the Cuban Constitution as an addition to the document. The honor roll, made up of the eleven who voted against bowing to American imperialism's mailed first, consisted of: Juan Gualberto Gómez (Santiago), Salvador Cisneros Betancourt (Puerto Príncipe), José S. Alemán (Santa Clara), Manuel R. Silva (Puerto Príncipe), Rafael Portuondo (Santiago), Edualdo Tamayo (Santiago), Rafael Manduley (Santiago), Alfredo Zayas (Havana), José Lacret Morlot (Havana), Luis Fortún (Matanzas), and José Fernández de Castro (Santiago).[36] Nine of the eleven came from Oriente, the seat of the most revolutionary fervor during the first and second wars for independence.

The news that the Cubans had finally ratified the Platt Amendment was greeted with "gratification" in Washington. The imperialists had good reason to be gratified. Not only had they crushed Cuban resistance, but they had just won a victory over the people of the Philippines. On March 6, 1901, General Funston had captured Aguinaldo at his secret hideaway, and while the Filipinos continued to fight on in guerrilla warfare until April 16, 1902, when the last of the independence fighters surrendered, the back of the insurrection had been broken.*

---

the Republicans who have offered the Platt law found themselves slighted by the Cuban Convention, it is very possible that they would authorize another Cuban Convention . . . and would give Cuba another law and perhaps a worse one for the Cubans. Meanwhile, it would turn a deaf ear to the appeals for reciprocity so that Cuba would gain nothing but even stand to lose. Then many Americans would be able to realize their dreams of buying the rich vegas of Vuelta Abajo and the great mills of Havana, Matanzas and Las Villas at fire sale prices." (*La Discusión*, March 21, 1901.)

* The war of aggression against the Filipinos was officially terminated by edict of President Theodore Roosevelt on July 4, 1902. It had lasted three years and had required the services of 126,468 American soldiers of whom 4,234 were killed and 2,818 wounded. The Filipinos were the ones who suffered most. In addition to losing their independence, 16,000 Filipino soldiers were killed, and over 200,000 civilians died because of famine and pestilence. Property damage in the Philippines amounted to many millions of dollars. (Leon Wolff, *Little Brown Brother; How the United States Purchased and Pacified the Philippine Islands at the Century's Turn*, New York, 1961, pp. 356-58.) However, guerrilla resistance continued in the Philippines for many years; indeed, the last Filipino guerrilla leader on the island of Luzon was not captured and executed until October, 1911.

Sergio Aguirre, the Cuban historian, believes that events in the Philippines influenced the decision of quite a few of the delegates to the Constitutional Con-

Defending the Cuban Convention for having finally adopted the Platt Amendment, *The State* asked on June 14, 1901: "What was left to them but to yield? The future gave no hope and the conditions of the present were not only humiliating but prejudicial to the recuperation of the island and the development of its rich resources for the benefit of a people long stricken with the extremist poverty." Undoubtedly this explains the major reason for the final vote. The majority of the delegates voted to ratify because they were now completely convinced that only thereby could American military occupation be ended, a Republic established, and the economic recuperation of the island be advanced.

There were many words of condemnation of the Administration in anti-imperialist circles for having forced the Cubans to swallow the bitter pill. But they were all summed up eloquently by Daniel H. Chamberlain, former governor of South Carolina, who wrote in the Springfield *Republican*: "A great act of national perfidy and oppression, done in the sight of the world and to a helpless people, is not to be trammeled up by the forced acquiescence of the object and victim. It remains open to question, it will ever remain open." [31]

"You can not understand the Platt Amendment," Elihu Root wrote years after its adoption, "unless you know something about the character of Kaiser Wilhelm the Second." [32] Following this lead a number of scholars have argued that the fear that Cuba might be dominated by a foreign power was the important factor behind the ultimatum to her in the form of the Platt Amendment. Root looked upon Germany as a "predatory nation," and feared it might have designs on the Caribbean. There had already been German interference in Haiti, and with plans progressing for an Isthmian Canal, the United States could not tolerate a hostile foreign power dominating Cuba, the sentinel of the Caribbean. Hence the need for the United States to limit Cuba's public debt, reserve the right of intervention, and demand naval stations on Cuban soil. [33]

It is not difficult to grasp the superficiality of this interpretation. Apart from the fact that, as Philip C. Jessup, Root's biographer, points

---

vention to vote for the Platt Amendment since they were anxious to avoid a military clash with the United States which could be as ruinous to Cuba as it turned out to be for the Philippines. (Interview with Sergio Aguirre, University of Havana, Department of History, July 27, 1966.)

out, the Secretary of War was needlessly alarmed since Germany had no intention of dominating Cuba or the Caribbean, the proposals of the Committee on Relations of February 26, 1901, forbade any military or territorial concessions to a foreign power, and the Cuban Constitution included provisions limiting the Cuban debt substantially, as did Article Two of the Platt Amendment. Finally, the Cubans, as Juan Gualberto Gómez made clear in the famous *Ponencia*, were ready to incorporate the Articles in their Constitution which forbade Cuba's ceding any part of the island to another government, and preventing any foreign power from attaining "mortgage rights" over the island.

We must look elsewhere, therefore, to understand the significance of the Platt Amendment. By 1901, American investments in Cuba had grown apace. But, as Philip C. Wright points out, "considerable as were these, they were insignificant as compared with the investment correctly foreseen as easily possible under more favorable conditions."[34] Cuba was an island rich in resources, and extremely inviting to American investment and trade. "Of all the territories involved in the Spanish War," Wood pointed out to Theodore Roosevelt, "the Island of Cuba is infinitely the most valuable."[35] But secure investment demanded protection from the danger of radical legislation. An American capitalist exploring the economic resources of Cuba wrote to McKinley from Santiago de Cuba in March, 1901, that he and other capitalists were preparing to invest heavily in the island "on their confidence that the United States will either stay in control or will insist that the succeeding government shall afford adequate protection."[36] Another capitalist declared publicly in the same month that no considerable amount of capital would be invested in Cuba "until it was established beyond reasonable doubt that law and order and a substantial government are to be a fixture."[37] Root, a member of the dominant monopoly capitalist class of the United States, was convinced that the Cuban masses would turn on the business community as soon as American troops were withdrawn and could only be held in check by the threat of intervention.[38]

Of course, many American capitalists felt that the only way to guarantee "adequate protection" for their investments was by annexation of Cuba.* But, as we have seen, annexation was at this time

---

\* Edwin F. Atkins, an important figure in the Sugar Trust and a leading annexationist, felt, as he explained to Platt, that the Platt Amendment did not go far enough in protecting "property owners . . . against vicious legislation or

impossible. There was that "foolish Teller Resolution," as Platt had phrased it, and there were those Cubans who had fought for thirty years against Spain for independence, and would not tolerate annexation. Hence, although a number of American, Cuban and Spanish business interests in the island implored the Administration to have Cuba annexed, their wishes could not be fulfilled.[39]

Important American business interests, especially the Sugar Trust, sought assurance that Cuba would have a government that would provide "adequate protection" for investment, and that the United States would retain the right of intervention in Cuban affairs.[40] Sugar, the chief Cuban product, Professor Edwin M. Borchard of Yale Univesrity notes, could be "profitably exploited only by vast corporations, who control by concession or otherwise, large areas of land . . , and an immense supply of cheap labor."[41] Immediately after the adoption of the Platt Amendment, *The Nation* reported the enlargement of the capital stock of the American Sugar Refining Company, "commonly known as the Sugar Trust," and noted that this foreshadowed "the acquisition of properties in Cuba for the production of sugar." At the same time, the Sugar Trust took up the call for the free importation of Cuban sugar into the United States.[42]

"Are you in favor of annexation?" Harry O. Havemeyer, President of the American Sugar Refining Company, was asked in late July, 1901. "I don't believe in managing Cuba. We can get all we want by tariff changes." "Is the American Sugar Refining Company preparing with its $115,000,000 new capital to buy up extensive plantations in Cuba?" "The entire atmosphere in Cuba is now suitable for such investments," replied the head of the Sugar Trust.[43] One American paper summed up the whole issue immediately after the adoption of the Platt Amendment. "Cuba is now in a position to attract the investment of American capital." [44] The right of intervention was a form of insurance for such investment.

---

administration upon the part of a Cuban Government." But Platt, conceding that he had originally been in favor of "very much more stringent measures," assured Atkins that to have included them in the Amendment would have increased opposition to it in Cuba, and "we should not only have had that difficulty [of getting it adopted in Cuba] increased, but we should have had a party in the United States giving aid and comfort to the Cuban radicals." (Atkins to Platt, June 3, 1901; Platt to Atkins, June 11, 1901, Orville H. Platt Papers, Connecticut State Library.)

Perhaps the most sickening aspect of the move to get the Cuban and the American people to accept the Platt Amendment was the Administration's propaganda campaign to convince them that it was designed not to destroy but to strengthen Cuba's independence. Root kept harping on this theme in his interviews with the Cuban Commission, emphasizing that Article Three merely gave the United States international sanction for what she had pledged herself to do under the Monroe Doctrine: protect the sovereignty of the countries of the Americas from outside aggression, and Cuba should even be grateful that her independence would be strengthened thereby. But as M. Marquez Sterling correctly pointed out: "It is neither legal nor just that the Monroe Doctrine, aimed against overseas invaders of America, should be used to invalidate the political independence of Cuba."[45] Platt even wrote publicly that his Amendment was not only an extension of the Monroe Doctrine but even a logical extension of the Teller Resolution. To be sure, the United States in this document had disclaimed control of Cuba "except for the pacification thereof." But "pacification," wrote Platt with a straight face, was a long-term process, and must be considered very broadly. In this sense, the Platt Amendment was a *part* of the pacification of Cuba, and thus in perfect harmony with the Teller Resolution. The Amendment also carried out the full intention of the Joint Resolution of Congress since it made Cuba not only independent but more independent that she would be without it. Under it Cuban independence was guaranteed by the United States. "Cuba needs a real not a paper independence, and this the United States alone can assure her," Platt concluded, still with a straight face.[46]

Such hypocrisy annoyed even some of the newspaper supporters of the Platt Amendment. During the Congressional debate, the Washington *Post,* a leading pro-Administration, Republican newspaper, ran an editorial, "Let us be Honest." The *Post* declared:

> Foolishly or wisely, we want these newly acquired territories, not for any missionary or altruistic purpose, but for the trade, the commerce, the power, and the money that are in them. Why beat about the bush and promise and protest all sorts of things? Why not be honest. It will pay.
>
> Why not tell the truth and say what is the fact—that we want Cuba, Porto Rico, Hawaii and Luzon, . . . because we believe they

will add to our national strength and because they will some day become purchasers at our bargain counters?[47]

Since the United States could not have Cuba directly, the Platt Amendment was devised to achieve the objective indirectly. As Ralph H. Parker puts it in his study, "Imperialism and the Liberation of Cuba":

> By this Amendment, especially the right of intervention, conceived in an imperialist group, Cuba became, not a sovereign state, but a part of the new American empire. Veiled in conciliatory language, this Amendment became the vehicle of American imperialism and the foundation of much of Cuba's subsequent troubles. . . .
> Instead of being a colony, Cuba now became a protectorate, distinctly in the "sphere of influence" of the United States. A new imperialism had displaced the old. Spain, clinging to the old colonial imperialism of the seventeenth century, gave way to a new country whose imperial dreams were economic and financial.[48]

That the Platt Amendment would become, as Parker phrases it, "the vehicle of American imperialism," was foreseen, it will be recalled, by the *National Labor Standard* shortly after it was adopted by Congress. The Amendment established a precedent for intervention by American imperialism throughout Latin America, especially the Caribbean. Indeed, a study of Root's colonial policy points out that this is precisely what the Secretary had in mind: "Mr. Root's policy in regard to Cuba was intended by him not merely to apply to the island of Cuba but to form a basis of a future Caribbean policy of the United States." [49] Not for nothing had José Martí warned on the eve of his death that a free and independent Cuba must not serve as an auxiliary for the penetration of United States imperialism in Latin America! [50]

Many historians have exonerated Root of the disastrous effects of the Platt Amendment on Cuba's subsequent history, arguing that it was only because his interpretations were later abandoned that the measure was injurious to the Cuban Republic.[51] Even so ardent an anti-imperialist as Leland H. Jenks wrote that Root was a statesman "who in an age of imperialism encouraged self-government." [52] But Leonard Wood gave the answer to these defenders of the imperialist Secretary of War of an imperialist government. On October 28, 1901, in a letter to Theodore Roosevelt, the annexationist Military Governor of Cuba who had played so large a part, as Root's agent, in forcing the Amendment on the island, wrote: "There is, of course, little or no independence left Cuba under the Platt Amendment." [53]*

---

* In the light of this and other similar comments by Wood on the true nature of the Platt Amendment, one can see how absurd is James Harold Hitchman's conclusion that the Amendment was intended to prevent Cubans and foreign nations from weakening Cuban sovereignty, and not to make Cuba a protectorate of the United States. "While the Platt Amendment," he writes, "wounded the Cuban spirit necessary for republic building, at the same time it guaranteed *Cuba Libre* and prevented no single sovereign act except self-destruction." Dr. Hitchman's sole regret is that the United States did not continue the Occupation, and he blames the problems that plagued the Cuban Republic on "the premature termination of the intervention." (James Harold Hitchman, "Leonard Wood and the Cuban Question, 1898-1902," unpublished Ph.D. thesis, University of California, Berkeley, 1965, pp. 3, 434.)

## CHAPTER XXIX
# The Battle Over Reciprocity

AS EARLY AS 1899, General James H. Wilson had reported to Washington that the establishment of proper trade relations with Cuba was even more important than the settlement of political relations. He proposed that by tying Cuba's principal export—sugar—to the American market, and by keeping the marketing conditions subject to its control, the United States could gain an influence over Cuba that could never be destroyed. The instrument to achieve this goal was a reciprocity treaty. "I have not felt it necessary to explain to you," Wilson wrote to Root on November 3, 1899, "or anybody else that such a treaty as I have proposed would practically bind Cuba, hand and foot, and put her destinies absolutely within our control." [1]*

Political and economic relations with Cuba were, of course, closely intertwined. Since the major purpose of the Platt Amendment was to protect American investments and other economic interests in the island, it was logical to follow this up with a program by which both would increase. Like Wilson, American business interests felt that a reciprocity agreement was the best means of attaining these objectives. By admitting Cuban sugar free or at considerably reduced rates, the profits for American investors in sugar production would grow and the extent would rise. So, too, would the profits of the sugar refiners in the United States, already dominated by the American Sugar Refinery Company, the Sugar Trust. A corresponding reduction of Cuban tariffs on American imports would give U.S. business a monopoly of the island's market. In his first annual report in 1900, Leonard Wood had stressed the need for reciprocity in order to increase American investment in and exports

---

\* "If my views are carried into effect," Wilson wrote to Roosevelt, "Cuba will be in the Union within ten years." (Wilson to Roosevelt, July 5, 1899, Theodore Roosevelt Papers, Library of Congress.)

to Cuba.[2] In his annual report for 1901, Secretary of War Elihu Root had strongly urged a reduction in duties upon Cuban sugar and tobacco, and pictured a vast market potential for American goods which "would contribute far more to our prosperity than the portion of our present duties which we would be required to concede."[3] President McKinley had stressed the same point in his annual messages of 1899 and 1900, where he had stated the need for Cuban reciprocity, and in his last speech, made at the Pan-American Exposition at Buffalo, New York on September 5, 1901, just before his assassination, he had concluded with a strong plea for reciprocity.[4]

Theodore Roosevelt, who took the oath of office on September 14, 1901, was a leader of the imperialist forces in the United States, and while cool toward reciprocity in principle, he was eager to see Cuba dominated economically as well as politically by the United States. On May 4, 1901, while still vice-president, Roosevelt had been appealed to by Wood to do what he could to help obtain a reduction on duties on Cuban sugar and tobacco as the best way of controlling "the whole future of Cuba." The future President heartily concurred: "I exactly agree with the policy you indicate. A *differential rate in favor of Cuba would tie her to us, and we must consistently give as well as get if we expect to make our new policies a success.*"[5]

Wood, as we know, was at heart an annexationist, and even after the Platt Amendment was adopted and accepted by Cuba, he still believed that it was manifest destiny that the island should some day belong to the United States. For the present this might be impossible, but since it was inevitable that it would be ultimately achieved, it was incumbent upon the United States to develop a prosperous Cuba by a reciprocity agreement so that she would be an asset to the American Union. Wood touched on this briefly in a letter to Root on October 25, 1901, in which he wrote that "as we shall sometimes own or at least must always control the destinies of Cuba . . . it really behooves us to do something for her. . . ."[6] But he developed this theme fully in a long, confidential letter to President Roosevelt on October 28, 1901, calling vigorously for Congressional action to relieve the stagnated sugar industry of the island. This letter is so revealing of the imperialist design behind reciprocity that it deserves rather extensive quotation:

> This is a natural sugar and tobacco country and as we must, in any case, control its destinies, and will probably soon own it, I

believe it sound policy to do what we can to develop it and make it prosperous. . . .

With the control which we have over Cuba [by the Platt Amendment], a control which will soon undoubtedly become possession, combined with other sugar producing lands which we now own, we shall soon practically control the sugar trade of the world, or at least a very large portion of it. . . . *I believe Cuba to be a most desirable acquisition for the United States. She is easily worth any two of the Southern States, probably any three, with the exclusion of Texas.* . . . *It is probable that as soon as our home sugar producers realize our policy is to give Cuba a chance they will undoubtedly transfer their industries to Cuba and the Island will, under the impetus of new capital and energy, not only be developed, but gradually become Americanized, and we shall have in time one of the richest and most desirable possessions in the world.* . . .[7]

Roosevelt quickly informed Wood that he was "delighted" to receive such a precise description of the benefits to United States interests of reciprocity. "It gives me the clearest view I have yet had of conditions in Cuba. Root feels as strongly as you do as to what our action should be on the tariff, and it is of course unnecessary to say that I shall back you up most heartily."[8] In his first annual message to Congress on December 3, 1901, the President, while skeptical as to the general applicability of reciprocity as a principle of national policy, uniquivocally advocated the measure with respect to Cuba. Here Roosevelt spoke in generalities like "weighty reasons of morality and national interest," and stressed that in view of Cuba's acceptance of the Platt Amendment, "we are bound by every consideration of honor and expediency to pass commercial measures in the interest of her well-being."[9] But in his private correspondence, Roosevelt made it quite clear that he believed reciprocity "would tie Cuba to us," and lead to control of the Cuban market with incorporation of the island as the ultimate outcome.[10]

Not all who favored reciprocity did so because they wished to see Cuba dominated economically by the United States and eventually annexed. There were individuals who had fought against the Platt Amendment, and felt that having promised Cuba tariff concessions in order to get her acceptance, the United States had to honor its pledge. They argued further that on the basis of this pledge, Cuban planters had made strenuous efforts to increase sugar production, and had raised their output from 308,000 tons in 1899 to 613,000 tons in 1900, while the output for 1901 was estimated at something over 800,000 tons. Unfortunately, the world price on sugar had been driven down due to the tremendous increase in production of European beet sugar.* Cuban planters were finding increasing difficulty in marketing their sugar profitably against the heavy competition of the European beet sugar producers heavily subsidized by government bounties, especially for the export trade.† Cuba thus faced an economic crisis unless the United States stepped in and reduced tariffs on sugar from the island. "The situation," wrote Albert G. Robinson in December, 1901, after his return from Cuba, "demands Congressional action by February 1 at the latest. . . . The island should not be turned over to the new Cuban government in as bad an economic status as it was when they received it. This can only be averted by immediate action providing an ample concession in the United States custom-house which is now ready for the cutting. Future arrangements may be left for adjustment by treaty between the two governments." [11]

But the driving force behind the reciprocity came not from those who were mainly concerned with helping the Cubans and felt that it was a necessity of the utmost urgency if the people of the island were to avoid economic disaster. It came rather from Wood, Roosevelt, Edwin F. Atkins, Henry O. Havemeyer and others who wished to use reciprocity as a method of Americanizing Cuba's economic life, monopolizing its resources and trade preparatory to annexation. Still, the imperialists made effective use of the arguments of the pro-Cuban sympathizers and turned them to their own purpose.

---

* Early in January, 1902, Wood reported that sugar brought nearly two cents per pound less than at the same time the preceding year: "The prices are now 3 2/5 to 3 1/2 cents as compared with 5 1/4 to 5 1/3 cents last year at this time." (Wood to Elihu Root, Jan. 6, 1902, Elihu Root Papers, Library of Congress.) "This year's crop of sugar," Wood wrote to Roosevelt, "will be over 800,000 tons, most of which under present prices, must be sold at little or no profit. . . ." (Wood to Roosevelt, Oct. 28, 1901, Theodore Roosevelt Papers, ibid.) On February 11, 1902, James H. Wilson wrote to Senator Foraker: "I learn from my private correspondence that the planters are piling up suger in the hope of better prices, but that many of them are on the verge of failure because they cannot obtain enough money for their sugar to pay for making it." (James H. Wilson Papers, ibid.)

† Under this system, an artificially low price was created on exported sugar, which was maintained by taxing home consumption heavily. The purpose was to foster production by guaranteeing a market for the surplus not required for domestic consumption.

With Congress dominated by Republican protectionists, and the beet-sugar lobby exerting its influence, it would be no easy task to get a reciprocity arrangement. The beet-sugar industry was a powerful force in a number of states. Its real growth had begun in 1897 with the enactment of the highly protective Dingley Tariff, which imposed a duty of $1.95 per hundredweight on refined sugar. In addition there was provision for countervailing duties against direct and indirect bounties upon European sugar, thus further guaranteeing an advantage for domestic sugar. State legislatures gave further encouragement in the form of bounty measures, usually providing for the payment to the manufacturer of one cent per pound on the finished product. With this assistance, beet sugar production rose from 2,203 tons in 1890 to 76,859 tons in 1900-1901, and had rapidly overtaken the cane sugar industry of Louisiana. Sales were expanded throughout the middle West, especially by the American Beet Sugar Company, incorporated by Henry T. Oxnard in 1899 with a capitalization of $20,000,000, and by the Standard Beet Sugar Company organized in 1899 with a capital stock of $1,000,000. By the turn of the century, the American beet-sugar industry was Big Business, and its influence would be employed in opposing lowering of duties on Cuban sugar.[12]

To overcome this formidable opposition, a vast propaganda campaign was launched in favor of reciprocity before Congress opened its session on December 3, 1901. Wood, who had determined "to bring every proper influence to bear to stir up public opinion in favor of reciprocity,"[13] began his part in the campaign as early as September, when he circulated letters to the Mayors of all Cuban municipalities and to the entire membership of the Cuban judiciary, asking them to determine and forward the views of the people or their municipalities or districts on the reduction of U.S. import duties on sugar and tobacco.[14] The result, as Wood had anticipated, was a deluge of messages* to the Military Governor, not only from Mayors and judges, but from planters' and merchants' organizations, political parties, and private citizens, all urging a reduction of United States tariffs on Cuban products.* The letters and petitions emphasized that in view of the steady

---

* Most of the messages endorsed the Petition of the General Society of Merchants and Business Men of the Island of Cuba to President Theodore Roosevelt. The Petition opened: "Each day that elapses in the life of the people of Cuba, shows a new phase of increasing decadence in her economic situation." It went on

decline of the world price of sugar, an economic disaster for Cuba, with bankruptcy for the planters and unemployment for the workers, was inevitable unless she immediately secured a preferential position in the American market through tariff concessions. A number of correspondents pointed out that, having made a dependency of Cuba through the Platt Amendment, the United States had thereby assumed the duty of seeing that she maintained a civilized standard of living.[15]

During September and October, Wood forwarded all these appeals to Washington, accompanying them with the assurance that the economic crisis was strengthening the feeling among the propertied classes, Spanish and Cuban alike, for annexation.[16] While Wood accurately reflected the thinking of significant elements of Cuban propertied interests, it must be noted that many who responded to his circular letter did so simply to achieve immediate economic relief and had no conception that they were being used to advance imperialist designs on their country.

Beginning in October, Wood also mailed from Havana each week six hundred copies of the Sunday edition of the Habana *Post* containing reports of demonstrations in the capital in favor of reciprocity and editorials supporting the demand. These were distributed among American newspapers which reprinted the material.[17] For the *Outlook*, Wood wrote an article entitled, "Reasons for Reciprocity between the United States and Cuba," in which he urged tariff concessions as a moral obligation of the United States, and as a vital necessity to Cuba.[18] To win the support of the anti-imperialists, he even omitted his usual reference

---

to emphasize that the "production of Cuban sugar and tobacco, together with all the industries derived therefrom or related thereto, will decrease rapidly until they totally disappear, if the government of the United States . . . does not open the markets of the Great Republic to the products of this country; and does not grant, in the proper degree, according to the respective market-condition of each product, either the total suppression or an adequate reduction of the duty that they now pay on being imported into the Union." It noted, too, that such action would "promote a larger exportation to this island, of American manufactures and American products in general," observing that an increase had already been achieved "through the modifications introduced in the Cuban tariffs, by the Government of intervention." The Petition urged speedy action on reciprocity, warning that otherwise "the difficulties created by the acute economic crisis from which we are suffering would, *ipso facto,* encumber the road of the new [Cuban] government." (Records of the United States Military Government of Cuba, Box 20, 1901, 3759, National Archives.)

to the value of reciprocity in dominating Cuba's economic life in the interest of the United States. Wood ordered four hundred copies of the magazine and circulated them to newspapers throughout the country.

In November, Wood sent to Washington a delegation of nine prominent Cubans, whose mission was to urge reciprocity on Congress and the public. The group addressed a series of petitions to President Roosevelt and the President of the Senate, asking for a mutual reduction in import duties of 50 percent on all Cuban-American trade.[19] In his own report for 1901, published early in December, Wood called for a 50 percent reduction in the duties on Cuban sugar.[20]

While in New York in December, Wood made arrangements with Francis B. Thurber, President of the United States Export Association, a propaganda organization promoting American manufacturers, to circulate pro-Cuban reciprocity material throughout the country.* Thurber, who had extensive acquaintance with American manufacturers, had, of course, his own axe to grind in favor of reciprocity as a stimulant to American exports to Cuba. It was therefore natural that Wood should turn to Thurber for assistance in putting the case for reciprocity before the American people. On December 12, 1901, Wood authorized Thurber "to send two issues of 80,000 circulars in accordance with the sample enclosed, together with additional information which will be forwarded to you on my return." In all, four such editions were mailed, two what Thurber termed, "a list of 80,000 leaders of thought" in the United States—editors, businessmen, ministers, teachers, etc.† The total cost of $11,520 was borne by the Cuban treasury. In addition, the United States Export Association mailed out for General Wood from 250 to 1,000 copies of American newspapers containing editorials and other items in favor of reciprocity. These went principally to Congressmen. In February, 1902, Wood also authorized the mailing

---

\* Thurber had been employed by Secretary of War Root in May, 1901 to gather preliminary material that might be useful from the standpoint of American exports as a basis for future reciprocity negotiations once Cuba had established her own government. (Root to Wood, May 16, 1901, enclosing Thurber to Root, May 11, 14, 1901, and Root to Thurber, May 13, 1901, Elihu Root Papers, Library of Congress.)

† Thurber, in his own right as president of the United States Export Association, also distributed broadsides and articles to the same "leaders of thought" in the United States. (*See* Thurber's testimony before the House Committee on Ways and Means, in *Cuban Sugar Sales,* Washington, 1902, pp. 420, 428-36.)

of 10,000 copies of the pamphlet, *Industrial Cuba,* to the President, members of the Cabinet, all Senators and Representatives, and 9,500 leading newspaper editors.

Wood later testified that he had authorized expenditures totalling $15,626.82 from the treasury of Cuba for propaganda in behalf of reciprocity, and that Congress was the major objective of his drive.[21] It is indeed an ironic fact of history that the American Military Governor was using the Cubans' own money to accelerate the economic domination of their country by United States interests.

Americans who had a large financial interest in the Cuban sugar industry were also active in the propaganda campaign for reciprocity. Edwin F. Atkins, the champion of annexationism, a leading figure in the Sugar Trust, probably the largest single owner of Cuban sugar properties, and chairman of the Associated American Interests in Cuba, was the spokesman for this group. His article, "Cuba's Imminent Bankruptcy," in the December, 1901, issue fo the *North American Review* called for prompt and decisive action from Congress as the only way to save Cuba from the direst disaster. Bankruptcy, he warned, threatened the island, and its consequences would be disastrous for American investment prospects, since "its population, deprived of employment, will again be in a fit state of rebellion against any established government."[22]* Atkins' article was sent to hundreds of American newspapers for reprinting.[23]

The most powerful propagandist for Cuban reciprocity was the American Sugar Refining Company. The Sugar Trust stood to reap the greatest rewards from the enactment of Cuban reciprocity. For one thing, apart from the gains accruing to it from ownership of Cuban sugar properties, it would obtain cheap raw sugar, the benefits from which would go mainly to the near monopolistic Sugar Trust in increased profits rather than to the American consumer through reduced prices. For another, since Cuban planters were already utterly dependent upon the great combine for disposing of their large crop, and were unable to afford to hold out for better prices, they would be forced to give the Trust rebates from the New York market price.[24] Then again,

---

* Albert G. Robinson stressed the same point, warning the United States "that all of Cuba's revolts and insurrections for the last hundred years have grown out of conditions of economic distress to which the mother country was blind, and which she steadily refused to relieve." (*The State,* Dec. 21, 1901.)

free Cuban sugar or drastically reduced tariffs would enable the Trust to weaken and ultimately destroy its competitor, the beet-sugar industry. Already engaged in a bitter price war with the American Beet Sugar Company and the Standard Beet Company in the Missouri River Valley, Henry O. Havemeyer, President of the American Sugar Refining Company, viewed Cuban reciprocity as a powerful weapon in the campaign against the Trust's rival.[25]

It is not surprising therefore that the Sugar Trust paid to have articles attacking the beet-sugar interests and advocating Cuban reciprocity inserted in newspapers and magazines. Excerpts from these articles were then distributed to scores of newspapers, particularly in the mid-West where the beet-sugar interests were powerful, and to educators and business people. The Trust also printed and distributed 250,000 copies of *Facts About Sugar,* a pamphlet outlining arguments in favor of Cuban reciprocity. In none of the articles, editorials and pamphlets, whose publication and distribution was financed by the Sugar Trust, did the name of the monopoly combine appear. Had the Trust's identity been disclosed, the major purpose of reciprocity would have been brought out into the open and the effect of the propaganda nullified.[26] Although he spoke out only because his company's profits were at stake, Henry T. Oxnard, President of the multi-million dollar American Beet Sugar Company, voiced the truth in his indictment of the Sugar Trust:

> Its methods are vicious and corrupt. It never comes out into the open, even when interested in a tariff rate, but its agents are always in evidence, secreting themselves behind the frailest of fortifications under high-sounding commercial names. It never hesitates in subsidizing whatever stands in its path, and uses the press freely for that purpose, spending vast sums of money in its efforts to destroy American beet sugar. It has made a hot and extensive campaign for free sugar from Cuba for the past six months on several lines. It has paid liberally for space in "patent inside" papers, and it has caught some of our protectionist friends.[27]

Thus a combination of forces worked together to flood the nation with pro-Cuban reciprocity propaganda in the fall of 1901 and the winter of 1901-1902. The Sugar Trust, other American owners of sugar properties in Cuba, the annexationist, pro-imperialist Military Governor of the island, and the publicity organization for the advancement of

American manufacturers were leagued in this campaign. This campaign undoubtedly created widespread public sympathy for Cuban reciprocity, except in Louisiana and the beet sugar states of the middle and far West. The *Literary Digest* reported on December 21, 1901 that sentiment as reflected in the American press, except for the press in the beet-sugar areas, were nearly unanimous for the admission of Cuban sugar at half the prevailing tariff rates.[28] Most newspapers, of course, put the case for this reduction on the grounds of humanitarian interest in Cuba's economic welfare, the necessity of keeping the pledge that had induced the Cubans to accept the Platt Amendment, and the danger of a rebellion in the island if Congress did not act. But the New York *Journal of Commerce* said quite frankly that even if tariff reduction inured mainly "to the profit of the Sugar Trust," this did not matter. "That this corporation happens to be on the right side of the discussion is certainly no reason for obscuring its real merits." [29]

It soon turned out, however, that it did matter. The President's recommendation in his message to Congress on Cuban reciprocity had been referred by the House to the Committee on Ways and Means, which did not open hearings until January 15, 1902. But on January 10, Elihu Root wrote to Wood that the beet-sugar forces "are endeavoring to create the impression, with some success, that the sugar trust controls the output of Cuba, and that a reduction of duties on raw sugar would enure [sic] not to the benefit of the Cuban planter but to the trust." Root therefore instructed Wood to secure "authentic and definite information" on the subject "as speedily as possible," and recommend the dispatch to Washington of Luis V. Placé, whose vigorous personality "and thorough knowledge of the subject would prove invaluable in the forthcoming battle." [30]\*

When the hearings began before the Committee on Ways and Means, the case for reciprocity was opened by Edwin F. Atkins. He urged the adoption of a measure removing the duty on Cuban sugar

---

\* Although he did not appear at the hearings, Tomás Estrada Palma issued a number of statements to the press pleading for "reasonable reductions of the import duties" on Cuban sugar and tobacco. He emphasized that "this is the only way for Cuba to escape the absolute ruin of these two industries [sugar and tobacco] which are the only bases of Cuba's wealth," and went so far as to insist that "without this benefit all the sacrifices of the Cubans for their freedom will be as naught, for in a starving condition they cannot enjoy their independence." (*The State*, Jan. 4, 1902.)

and establishing mutual reduction of 50 percent on all other schedules in the Cuban-American trade. But the opponents of reciprocity weakened the effect of Atkins' testimony by compelling him to admit that he held stock in the American Sugar Refining Company and that he was interested with Havemeyer in the Trinidad estate in Cuba.[31] The general impression left by Atkins' testimony was that the Sugar Trust, in which he held a substantial interest, would be the chief beneficiary of reciprocity.

Neither Placé nor a Cuban planter by the name of Mendoza, who followed Atkins, made the good impression Secretary Root had hoped for.* They failed to make clear that the Cuban people and not merely the Cuban and American planters and the Sugar Trust would benefit from reciprocity. At one point, Representative Robertson of Louisiana asked, "Is there any representative of the Cuban people here who is regularly accredited?" One might ask if the Congressman from a state many of whose people were disenfranchised simply because they were Negroes was "regularly accredited." But he had made an effective point. Perhaps *The Public* put it best when it commented: " 'When thieves fall out, honest men get their dues'—sometimes." [32]

Among others who appeared during the first two days were Hugh Kelly, joint owner of the Central Teresa and director of the Chaparra Sugar Company. Since Kelly placed major emphasis on the advantages the United States would gain from monopoly of the Cuban trade through reciprocity, his testimony did not convince anyone that Cuba's needs were paramount with those who favored tariff reduction.[33] The same effect was created by testimony offered by representatives from the New York Merchants' Association and the New York Produce Exchange— the latter made up of 3,000 businessmen, who among them handled 75 percent of the commerce with Cuba—since they also stressed that the result would be a complete monopoly of Cuban trade by American producers and businessmen.[34]

The outlook, after the first two days, was so discouraging to the advocates of reciprocity that on January 16, Wood wrote to both Roosevelt and Root that he was sending to Washington "four prominent planters, men actually engaged in the business of raising sugar,"

---

* Placé antagonized the anti-imperialists when, upon arriving in the United States, he declared: "I came here to offer your people the trade of Cuba." (*The State*, Feb. 12, 1902.)

who would testify. He was convinced that "if we do not get a reasonable reduction of sugar, we shall find it embarrassing to get out of here, as the chaotic business condition, accompanied by a lack of employment, might result in such a condition of affairs as to render our presence here desirable." A tariff cut of at least 25 percent was absolutely essential.[35]

The new delegation, accompanied by George R. Fowler, a native Cuban and principal owner of the North American Sugar Company— he owned 930 out of 1,000 shares of stock—testified toward the end of the hearing. They also stressed the importance of the Cuban trade awaiting American exploitation, and gave assurance that reciprocity would not lead to mushroom growth of the sugar industry, pointing to the scarcity of labor in the island.[36] This did not do much to buttress the argument that unemployment would be a serious problem in Cuba if Congress did not act.

In all, fifteen witnesses appeared in behalf of reciprocity, of whom three were American planters in Cuba. But Wood decided that testimony was not enough, and during January, he had written "a great many letters to Congressmen and Senators urging all possible speed on the Cuban question."[37] Several Congressmen voiced their resentment against such outside pressure, and Root cautioned Wood not to continue sending "circular letters" to members of Congress. The Military Governor replied: "I fear that possibly I may have carried the war a little too actively into the enemies' country in writing to various Senators and Representatives."[38]

The opponents of reciprocity, led by Henry T. Oxnard and a large group of beet-sugar producers from all over the country, protested that their industry would be ruined should the tariff on Cuban sugar be reduced;* they ridiculed the idea of distress in Cuba, and stoutly maintained that the sugar refining trust was behind the agitation for relief to Cuba. The Trust, they charged, had already bought up existing Cuban sugar supplies and reciprocity was both a scheme to bring the monopoly

---

* Hawaiian sugar planters also testified against reciprocity, and argued that the island had expected a protected market for her sugar on annexation to the United States, and certainly had not anticipated being "plunged into bankruptcy that Cuba's absentee sugar planters may be put on a more favorable footing than she." Testimony against concessions to Cuba also came from the resident commissioner of Puerto Rico. (*House Document No. 535*, 37th Cong., 1st Sess., pp. 322-56.)

cheap raw materials and huge profits, without really improving the position of the Cuban planter who had lost control of his product, and at the same time, a weapon to be used in the Trust's war against beet sugar. Should aid really be needed for Cuba, it ought to be given in the form of a governmental relief program for the island to be financed out of general taxation and not by destroying a few selected industries.[39]

When the Committee on Ways and Means failed to take prompt action after the hearings ended on January 29, it was clear that reciprocity was getting nowhere. President Roosevelt, obviously annoyed, wrote that he would "stand absolutely firm," [40] but Senator Platt informed the President that it was not going to be easy to get his wish. Fear of opening a wedge into the protective tariff was behind the reluctance to take "any action in behalf of Cuba," the Connecticut Senator noted.[41] However, Root, predicting that the reciprocity bill might be rejected by Congress, laid the blame on the success of the beet-sugar lobby "in creating the impression" that the American farmer was being punished "for the real benefit of the sugar trust, which would simply pocket the amount of the duty without giving any increase in price to the Cuban producer." [42] Shortly after Root expressed this opinion, Representative Thayer of Massachusetts introduced a resolution in the House providing that a committee be appointed to investigate the benefit to the Trust from reduced duties and to probe its activity in influencing public sentiment.[43]

In spite of strong opposition, Administration pressure produced some results. On March 18, 1902, the Republican Caucus agreed to support reciprocity by a vote of three to one. The following day, Sereno E. Payne, Congressman from New York and Chairman of the House Committee on Ways and Means, offered a bill in the House authorizing the President to negotiate a commercial treaty with Cuba, after the island had established its Republic, providing for a 20 percent reduction of import duties on Cuban products, providing the Cubans agreed to grant a similar concession to the United States. (The life of the proposed reciprocity treaty was limited to last only to December 1, 1903.) Although the friends of reciprocity condemned the bill as "mean and niggardly," it was as far as the Committee on Ways and Means would go. The opponents of a larger reduction cited the action of the International Sugar Conference at Antwerp, representing the European countries which had been paying bounties to their beet sugar growers, in voting to end direct and indirect bounties, "to be enforced under international control, from the month of September, 1903." The foes of reciprocity argued that with European bounties on beet sugar abolished, the artificial stimulation ended, European beet-sugar production would decline drastically, world oversupply of sugar would soon be eased, and Cuba would be able to compete profitably in the world market. They were deaf to the question asked by the friends of Cuba: "What is Cuba to do until September, 1903?" [44]

Payne's bill was referred to the Committee on Ways and Means which reported it out favorably on March 3. In urging defeat of the bill, two of the majority reports charged that it would not aid Cuba materially but would only benefit the Sugar Trust. Representative Cooper of Texas offered to vote for the bill if guarantees could be included against the Trust reaping the major benefit.[45] On April 8, the House voted to consider the bill, and nine days of vigorous debate followed. On April 18, the last day of debate, after the Administration's spokesman had delivered a final plea for the bill, Representative Morris of Minnesota offered an amendment which abolished the high tariff on refined sugar entering the United States. (The duty on refined sugar varied from 1.95 to 1.825 cents per pound.) This amendment, aimed at the Sugar Trust, was the work of a coalition of Republican and Democratic beet-sugar Congressmen and anti-trust Democrats and Populists. The real purpose of the first two groups was to kill the reciprocity bill in the Senate, for if the amendment were left in the bill as passed by the House, the Republican protectionists and the Sugar Trust, faced with foreign competition, would defeat it. If it were eliminated by the Senate, it would prove that reciprocity was designed to benefit primarily the Sugar Trust.[46]

The Payne bill, with the Morris amendment, passed the House by a vote of 246 to 54. In the Senate, the amended bill was consigned on April 19 to the Committee on Relations with Cuba. But the atmosphere in the Senate was clearly revealed a week later when that body unanimously passed the following resolution introduced by Teller of Colorado, a beet-sugar state:

> Whereas it has been currently reported that nearly the entire crop of Cuban sugar has been purchased and is now held by what is generally known as the Sugar Trust, which is the principal consumer of raw sugar in the United States, and that any concessions

given to the raisers of cane sugar in the island of Cuba or any measures intended for their relief by admitting their sugar at reduced rates of duty into the United States will only benefit the said Sugar Trust, and that the Cubans will receive no real benefit from such concessions; and

Whereas, it is alleged that a large number of citizens of the United States have acquired large holdings of cane-producing lands in Cuba and are now especially urging the reduction of duty on sugar under the claim that such reduction will benefit the people of Cuba; Therefore, be it

*Resolved,* That the Committee on Relations with Cuba be, and is hereby, directed to make an investigation as to the truth of such charges and report to the Senate.[47]

Teller was a member of the sub-committee of the Committee on Relations with Cuba appointed to conduct the hearings, along with Platt of Connecticut and Burnham of New Hampshire. Platt, a champion of the Sugar Trust, clashed frequently with Teller, spokesman for the beet-sugar interests. In these clashes, the real interests of Cuba were completely overshadowed. But the six weeks hearings from May 1 to June 16, 1902, did reveal that Americans held substantial sugar properties in Cuba,* and that many Cuban planters were dependent on the Sugar Trust for advances of capital and as chief purchaser of their sugar. While Henry O. Havemeyer admitted that the American Sugar Refining Company purchased about 65 percent of the raw sugar imported from Cuba, the independent refineries taking the balance, he failed to point out, as was disclosed later, that the Sugar Trust held more than half of the $100,000,000 of preferred stock in the National Sugar Refining Company, the chief independent refinery, while Havemeyer himself owned all but a small block of the $10,000,000 of com-

---

* Conflicting testimony on the extent of American investments in sugar properties in Cuba made it impossible for the sub-committee to reach a definite conclusion on this question. Governor Wood, for example, listed only seven American plantations; Herbert J. Browne, a student of Cuban affairs, enumerated fifty-four plantations owned by American syndicates, firms, or individuals, while Truman G. Palmer of the Spanish Treaty Claims Commission offered statistics showing ninety-three centrals and seventy-three sugar-producing estates as American owned. (See *Cuban Sugar Sales,* pp. 173-74, 339-40, 361-97.) One difficulty was to determine whether the plantations belonged to native Americans or to Cubans and Spaniards who were Americans by naturalization. Palmer estimated that the inflated war claims of the various American owners, native and naturalized, totaled some forty-one million dollars. (*Ibid.,* pp. 394-95.)

mon stock. Furthermore, the National had secured a 25 percent interest in the supposedly independent McCaham Refinery in Philadelphia. In short, by 1902, Cuban sugar planters were at the mercy of the American Sugar Trust.[48]

A sensation was created on June 11, 1902, during the cross-examination of Francis B. Thurber by Senator Teller. Two startling facts emerged: first, that Governor Wood had appropriated monies from the Cuban treasury to conduct a campaign in the United States under Thurber's direction; and second, that Thurber had received $2,500 from Henry O. Havemeyer for propaganda work in behalf of reciprocity. Immediately, the anti-imperialist and anti-trust press charged that the annexationist Military Governor of Cuba and the Sugar Trust were closely linked. The beet-sugar forces, of course, were jubilant, convinced that "the Reciprocity bill had suffered a stunning blow."[49] Root promptly announced his approval of Wood's actions, and the Governor defended himself by stating that he would have been derelict in his duty "had I not made every proper effort to obtain for Cuba those commercial relations on which her stability and prosperity as a nation depend." He dismissed the use of Thurber as unimportant since he had simply used him as he "would have used a directory" to distribute information to the American people.[50]

Wood, however, failed to explain why he felt it proper to use Cuban funds to pay a lobbyist who was working simultaneously for the Sugar Trust. Even the pro-reciprocity *New York Times* called the whole affair a "sad blunder" on the part of Secretary Root and General Wood, and criticized Thurber for using money from the Cuban treasury to advance the reciprocity cause and then going to Havemeyer for additional funds to promote the campaign.[51] The pro-Administration magazine, the *Outlook*, insisted that Wood's character was above reproach, but conceded that "he had made a serious mistake in secretly using public funds to promote the agitation of the Export Association in behalf of his policy."[52] It said nothing, however, about the Sugar Trust, but the Boston *Evening Transcript* felt that both Wood and Thurber had "acted indiscreetly in view of the focusing of the legislative conflict around the Sugar Trust."[53]

By the time the subcommittee held its last session five days after Thurber's disclosure, the cause of Cuban reciprocity appeared to be a lost one for this session of Congress. The majority of the American people were now convinced that a conspiracy existed between the Sugar Trust and the Administration to use reciprocity for the benefit of the monopolistic, imperialist forces in the United States rather than to assist the Cuban people in their need. Things looked so bleak for reciprocity that it was decided at a White House conference that only a special appeal from President Roosevelt could keep it from being buried.[54] On June 13, Roosevelt sent a message to Congress pleading for favorable action on Cuban reciprocity. While repeating the familiar arguments, the President emphasized that reciprocity was a step in line with the great new American imperialist policy:

> The events following the war with Spain and the prospective building of the Isthmian Canal render it certain that we must take in the future a far greater interest than hitherto in what happens through the West Indies, Central America, and the adjacent coasts and waters. We expect Cuba to treat us on exceptional foot politically, and we should put her on the same position economically.[55]

Not a word, however, about the role of the Sugar Trust in the drive for reciprocity! Not a word of encouragement, either, to those who were trying to deprive the Sugar Trust of its special benefits and thus enable reciprocity to get new support! No wonder the President's message failed to win any new adherents for reciprocity.

In an effort to rescue the dying cause, the Administration-dominated Senate Committee on Relations with Cuba finally agreed upon the so-called Platt bill. This measure called for a straight 20 percent reduction on duties for a two-year period. To this was added an amendment offered by Senator Spooner which authorized the President to end the arrangement whenever he was satisfied that the benefits of the concession were going to the purchaser in the United States (the Sugar Trust) rather than to the Cuban producers. Nothing, however, was said about removing the tariff differential in favor of domestically refined sugar.[56] Even then, the bill was never reported out of committee, for a Republican caucus showed that it would never pass the Senate.[57] As was expected, the Payne bill, with the Morris amendment was so obnoxious to the Sugar Trust and protectionists in general, was also never reported by the Committee on Relations with Cuba.[58] Even Roosevelt abandoned hope of legislative action, and decided upon the alternative of negotiating a treaty with Cuba after Congress adjourned.*

On July 1, 1902, the first session of the Fifty-seventh Congress adjourned without having taken any action on reciprocity with Cuba. The Democrats in the House immediately drafted as the first plank in the fall Congressional campaign a denunciation of the President and the dominant faction of the Republican Party in Congress "for having, at the behest of the Sugar Trust, refused relief to Cuba." The plank pointed out that the Democrats and a minority of the Republicans had succeeded in passing a Cuban reciprocity bill in the House that gave no benefit to the Sugar Trust, but that the bill was strangled in the Senate because it did not protect the monopolistic refining company. Representative Ball of Texas made the point quite clearly when he said on the floor of the House:

> All this talk about the bravery and fidelity of the President in discharging a duty to Cuba is pure, unadulterated Pecksniffian buncomb.† Why? Because every member of this House and every Senator knows that if the President of the United States desired Cuban reciprocity above protecting the sugar trust, all that he has to do is to dissolve the firm of Havemeyer, Roosevelt, Wood, Root Thurber and Company and go into partnership with the American people, and a majority of Congress will give Cuba reciprocity and strike down the sugar trust.
>
> A single message from the President of the United States, instead of rejecting the rebate plan, would give the votes necessary to give reciprocity to Cuba before Congress adjourned, reciprocity —not with the sugar trust, but with the Cuban people. No, they prefer to let reciprocity fail before the sugar trust shall be touched. ... We find that Governor-General Wood, our military officer in command of Cuba, with the approval of that great warrior, Secretary Root, and with the full knowledge of the President of the United States has gone into the Cuban treasury and looted it for the purpose of carrying on a propaganda among the "leaders of public thought." We found more—that he not only did that, but there comes to the front one of the most notorious lobbyists that

---

* Roosevelt submitted the treaty he negotiated with Cuba to the Senate in December, 1902. The treaty was approved several months later, and became effective in December, 1903. As a result, Cuban sugar received a 20 percent preferential reduction in the American tariff, and various American products received from 20 to 40 percent reductions in the Cuban tariff.

† Pecksniff was the canting hypocrite in Charles Dickens' *Martin Chuzzlewit*.

ever infested the halls of this capitol as the joint agent of our highest officials and Mr. Havemeyer, the sugar trust's president, in order to carry out this propaganda.[59]

Whether the beet-sugar forces in the end would have accepted reciprocity even with the Morris amendment aimed at the Sugar Trust, is, of course, open to question. But there is no doubt that the refusal of the Administration and its forces in the Senate even to consider the Cuban reciprocity bill passed by the House,* convinced public opinion that the motivating force behind the drive for reciprocity was not concern for Cuba's welfare but for the profits of leading monopolists in the United States. With the popular hatred of the trusts so widespread in the United States at this time, and the work done by the anti-imperialists in showing the relationship between the rise of monopoly and imperialism, the early public support for reciprocity in order to assist Cuba speedily vanished.

The Cubans did not lack for advice on what course they should pursue in order to get the benefits of the American market for their sugar. Representative Francis G. Newlands of Nevada, author of the resolution annexing Hawaii, advised the Cubans that they should follow the Hawaiian example and let themselves be annexed to the United States. On February 4, 1902, he introduced a joint resolution in Congress inviting Cuba to become a part of the United States, first as a territory and then as a State of the Union to be called the state of Cuba. (His resolution also authorized a 5 percent reduction on the present crop of Cuban sugar, in consideration of Cuba's granting preferential rates to the United States.) Only by accepting this invitation could Cuba really begin to enjoy the benefits of the American market.[60]† Although Newland's advice to the Cubans brought no response from the island, the annexationists were not discouraged. Representative Payne

---

\* The Administration also found unacceptable a rebate plan proposed by the Republican opposition, providing that the remitted duties should be used by the Governor of Cuba for public works instead of being distributed among the planters. (Roosevelt to Charles R. Miller, June 14, 1902, Theodore Roosevelt Papers, Library of Congress.)

† Asked why he did not want Cuba immediately admitted to statehood, Newlands answered, "Because I do not think Cuba is as yet prepared for statehood." Pressed to explain why, he declared: "I do not think its people have become sufficiently familiar with American ideas and American institutions to entitle her at present to become a State of the Union." (*The State*, Feb. 6, 13, 1902.)

felt that annexation was out of the question for the time being, but he advocated reciprocity because "I am in favor of preparing her as best we can for the day of her incorporation within our limits." [61] Then on the day before Congress adjourned, Senator Stephen B. Elkins of West Virginia called up a resolution which he had introduced earlier, authorizing the admission of Cuba as a State of the Union upon her own voluntary application. Although he denied the connection, Elkins made it clear that he believed that the defeat of reciprocity would force Cuba to seek annexation to the United States in order to avoid economic ruin, and he had opposed reciprocity with that object in mind.* The Cubans really had no alternative, he argued, but to favor annexation. "Under the Platt Amendment she can never be a free and independent nation." Was it not wiser to become fully part of the United States and enjoy the advantages this would bring rather than remain seemingly indepent and actually dominated by her powerful neighbor to the North? "The people of Cuba will soon learn that it is far better to be a State in the American Union, with Senators and Representatives in Congress, than to be a dependent nation. This furnishes one of the reasons why I think her people will prefer giving up her national existence and becoming part of the great Republic." [62]

But there were those in the United States who had different advice for the Cubans. Writing in the *Appeal to Reason,* Ernest Untermann, a leading Socialist journalist, urged the Cuban people to beware of reciprocity with the United States. The battle in Congress had revealed clearly that the benefits of reciprocity would go primarily to the Sugar Trust. "Neither the American people nor the Cuban people would benefit thereby." For the immediate future, the Cubans would be wise to pull in their belts and ride out the economic storm. There were brighter prospects on the horizon. The agreement ending the payment of govern-

---

* The Cubans were evidently aware of this brazen attempt to use the reciprocity issue to force them to accept annexation as the alternative to economic ruin. On June 23, 1902, Herbert G. Squiers, the American Minister to the new Republic of Cuba, wrote to Secretary of State John Hay: "The Cubans who are opposed to annexation, and there are more of them than is generally believed, feel that they have been badly and unfairly treated; that while independence has been given them, it is in form only; that they are being forced into annexation or starvation as their only alternative." (Squiers to Hay, June 23, 1902, State Department, Cuba, Dispatches, vol. I, No. 33, NA.)

ment export bounties to European beet-sugar producers was due to end in September, 1903, and if Cuba could hold out until then without capitulating to the mirage of reciprocity with the United States, she need not be, as she was now, almost entirely dependent on the American Sugar Trust. Other buyers would be anxious to get her sugar, and she would develop close economic ties with many nations and not be subject only to the influence and domination of the United States.*

In the long run, however, Untermann insisted, only Socialism could solve Cuba's economic problems, for only thereby could the great resources of the island be used for the benefit of the Cuban workers and peasants and not for the profits of the capitalists and planters and the foreign imperialists. He predicted that the time would come, in the not too distant future, when the farmers and workers in the United States would take over ownership of the sugar industry in their country, and would unite "with their comrades in Cuba, for the purpose of owning and controlling not alone all their industries, but their government as well." [65]†

It was in this atmosphere seething with charges and counter-charges

---

* Almost a year later, on March 28, 1903, Manuel Sanguily in his famous address in the Cuban Senate opposing a reciprocity treaty with the United States, made precisely the same arguments. "Reciprocity," he noted, "is not a benefit for the Cuban producer, nor is it even one for the American consumer. It is doubtless a calculated and positive advantage for the American Sugar Trust, and this can be understood when it is realized that the Trust is the only purchaser of sugar in Cuba. In Havana, four houses, all agents of the Sugar Trust, are the only purchasers of sugar. Certainly, it must be conceded that when the seller has only one purchaser for his merchandise, the price will be determined by the will and even the caprice of the purchaser, and this, because of the position of the American Sugar Trust, is exactly what occurs with the sale of our sugar." Sanguily urged Cuba to establish economic relations with European and other countries for the sale of sugar so as not to be dependent solely on the United States. (Manuel Sanguily, *Discursos y Conferencia*, La Habana, 1919, vol. II, pp. 351-92, and reprinted in *La Lucha Anti-Imperialista en Cuba*, La Habana, 1960, vol. II, pp. 47-107).

† At its founding convention at Indianapolis in July, 1901, the Socialist Party of the United States called upon "the wage workers of Cuba . . . to organize for self-protection against the encroachments of capitalism into trade unions, and to affiliate with the International Socialist movement in order to bring about the emancipation of the working class from wage slavery, as capitalist expansion will not fall until the capitalist system is abolished." (*Proceedings*, p. 23.)

of corruption, lobbies for the Sugar Trust, imperialist plots and counter-plots, and, at the same time, marked by the presentation of a vision of the eventual establishment of a Socialist Cuba, that the Cuban Republic was born.*

---

* As far back as 1888, the Workmen's Advocate, official organ of the Socialist Labor Party of the United States, published in New Haven, Connecticut, predicted that without an effective Socialist movement, the Republic of Cuba growing out of a new Revolution would be "a sham republic." Its comment went:

"It is true the Cuban revolutionaries, as a whole, are not Socialists, nor have they any greater ambition than the political independence of their fertile land. Perhaps they may learn something by their defeat [in the Ten Years' War] and subsequent, suffering, but it is hardly probable that they will ascribe their condition to anything but Spanish domination. Among the revolutionists there is, however, a sprinkling of Social-Democrats, and to them belongs the honorable duty of economizing their force, so that when the next Cuban revolution is fought, it will be to establish something more than a sham republic which will need soon to be overthrown, and perhaps entail a civil war. Cuba needs a socialist agitation until she enters into another conflict with Spain." (Workmen's Advocate, May 19, 1888.)

## CHAPTER XXX
# The Republic of Cuba

IN HIS ANNUAL REPORT in November, 1901, Secretary of War Elihu Root announced that with the adoption of the Platt Amendment by the Cuban Constitutional Convention, the Constitution could be considered "as an adequate basis for the formation of the new government to which when organized and installed, the control of the island is to be transferred. . . ." No specific date was set for this event, but Root expressed confidence that it would occur "before the close of the approaching session of Congress."[1] While Root gave the impression that all had now worked out in Cuba as the United States had hoped for, the truth is that there was one further problem to be solved before the Administration felt satisfied to turn over their country to the Cubans. This revolved about the man to be the first President of the Republic of Cuba. Obviously if the person elected were a radical nationalist Cuban, opposed to the Platt Amendment, all the work thus far achieved, all the energy expended in forcing the Cubans to swallow the Amendment, might be undone. For the Amendment still had to be incorporated into a permanent treaty between the United States and Cuba, and with an *antiplattista* (as the foes of the Platt Amendment were called in the island) as President, this would certainly create new difficulties.

From the moment that the question of the presidency first emerged during the meetings of the Constitutional Convention, Washington's choice was clear. "Cuba's President. [Estrada] Palma's Selection Would Please Washington," read a headline in an American paper as early as April, 1901. The article explained that the Administration was willing to settle for Máximo Gómez if the General decided to seek the office, but preferred Estrada Palma. Both Gómez and Estrada Palma had revealed, since the Occupation began, a willingness to cooperate with the United States, had been influential in keeping radical elements in check, and had contributed considerably to the trend favorable to the Platt Amendment. But since Estrada Palma was, on top of all this, known to favor eventual annexation of Cuba to the United States, while Gómez remained a firm advocate of independence, the former was Washington's favorite candidate.[2]

Actually, the Administration knew by the time this article was published that Gómez was not going to seek the presidency. On February 24, 1901, Wood informed Root, following a long conversation with the General, that Gómez had told him "that he does not want to be President, but that he wants Estrada Palma to be president and that he, Gómez, with the political and moral support of the army element will support Palma's government and make it stable and enduring. . . . Gómez leaves for the United States in a few days to see Palma."[3] Events were to prove that this was a correct report except for the time Gómez left for the United States. In late June, 1901, soon after the adoption of the Platt Amendment by the Convention, Gómez announced that he would not seek the Presidency for himself, but that he would do his utmost to elect Estrada Palma, and that he was leaving for the United States to see his old friend and companion, and discuss the presidential campaign with him.[4]*

---

* In June, 1902, American newspapers featured the sensational news that General Wood had paid Máximo Gómez $25,000 from the Cuban treasury not to run for President but instead to campaign actively for Estrada Palma. Wood refused to acknowledge the payment, but Elihu Root asserted that the money was paid with his and President Roosevelt's consent. It was justified on the ground that if the "radical element" had triumphed in the presidential election, "the conditions in Cuba might have paralleled those in the Philippines, and the United States government, after fighting Spain to secure freedom for the Cubans, would have been obliged to turn upon them the force of her arms." In Havana, Estrada Palma called a press conference, and with Gómez at his side, denied that any payment had been made to get the General to withdraw from the campaign. (*New York Times*, June 15, 16, 17, 1902; *The State*, June 16, 1902; *Daily People*, June 16, 1902.)

There is no evidence in the papers of Leonard Wood, Elihu Root and Theodore Roosevelt to substantiate this charge against Gómez nor is the incident mentioned in any Cuban historical work. Cuban historians whom I have questioned doubt that there is any truth to the charge. While they are critical of Gómez for having endorsed Estrada Palma for President, regarding it as the third mistake he made during the period of the Occupation, they feel strongly that he was not the type of person who could be bought by the United States. He acted as he did because of lack of political understanding and not because he was bribed. (Letters of Sergio Aguirre and Julio Le Riverend in possession of the author.)

Gómez arrived in the United States during the first week of July, and received a warm welcome in Washington and New York. At a dinner in the latter city, he referred to Estrada Palma as the hold-over President of Cuba, since he had been elected to that office during the first War for Independence, and voiced the hope that he would occupy the position of President of the Republic of Cuba when it was set up upon the withdrawal of American troops.[5] Gómez was also widely quoted in the American press as favoring the closest relations between Cuba and the United States, leading eventually to annexation. "Cuba and the United States belong together," he was reported to have said in a speech before the Union League Club in New York. "It is only a question of gravitation when they will be together. Cuba cannot get along without the United States."[6] This use of an expression which originated with the annexationists as early as the time of John Quincy Adams in the 1820's was widely reported in Cuba, and upon Gómez's return to the island, a disturbed reporter for *La Lucha* asked the General, "It appears that you have become an annexationist." Gómez replied harshly, "Yes, but none of those who say so, smell of powder as much as I do."[7]

To put at rest the rumors spreading through Cuba as to what he had actually said in the United States, Gómez published a public letter in which he declared that he had made it clear to the American government and people that "there is not a single man in Cuba who does not urgently desire to see his free flag waving, a flag which covers so many sorrows and sacrifices for liberty." He saw "in each American a brother who by shedding his blood together with ours for the emancipation of the Cuban people, has incurred our gratitude as an obligation." This could be best fulfilled by the people of both countries jointly cooperating "to maintain the peace and independence of Cuba." He assured the Americans that the Platt Amendment was no longer a controversial issue in Cuba, and would not be an issue in the presidential campaign.[8]

While Gómez had clearly refuted the charge that he had turned annexationist, his assurance to the United States that the Platt Amendment had ceased to be an issue in Cuba and would not figure as one in the presidential campaign was without foundation. Bartolomé Masó, reflecting a widespread feeling in the island, launched his candidacy for the presidency with a letter to *El Mundo* in which he clearly made the Platt Amendment the major issue. While hailing *La Marina Cubana*, organ of the Association of Industrial Mariners, he observed that the Association, like the Cuban people, could only prosper if it enjoyed the rights of full freedom under the law. Yet there was one law which if it remained unaltered, could smash the freedom of the Association and of the Cuban people, "as powerful boats are smashed against the rocks."

> "The law," Masó concluded, "is the law of force, which has been born in the Platt law, this vicious law which has made us suffer much horrifying disappointment, making us accept, among other humiliations, intervention which, as the Italian Professor Camazza Amari says: 'Intervention is a result of a tendency which the strong have to dominate the weak and impose their law upon them and attack and destroy in their turn the autonomy of the State.' " [9]

As might be expected, this statement convinced Washington that Masó was not the man to whom Cuba's future as a Republic should be entrusted. But the Administration was not the only one alarmed by Masó's letter. As Rafael Martínez Ortiz points out, Masó, by his letter, lost the support of "the better elements of the country." Those in Cuba who had endorsed the Platt Amendment, and those who had opposed it but had finally voted approval, longed for peace and the end of American Occupation, and of course the planters and merchants looked forward to reciprocity with the United States. Masó's election, they were convinced, would doom the chances of securing a reciprocity agreement, and would postpone indefinitely the day when American troops would evacuate the island.[10]

Masó's letter catapulted the "better elements" into immediate action on behalf of Estrada Palma. On August 18, a group of prominent Cubans, led by José Miguel Gómez, Domingo Méndez Capote, General Ruiz Rivera, Pedro Betancourt, and Diego Tamayo, sent Estrada Palma a letter urging him to seek the presidency, and asking his views on the major issues confronting Cuba and how he proposed to deal with them if elected President.[11] Estrada Palma's lengthy reply, sent from the United States on September 7, 1901, was read to a distinguished gathering on September 27 at the home of General Emilio Núñez, Governor of the province of Havana. The main question of concern to the men at the meeting was Estrada Palma's views on what the President of the

Republic should do about the Platt Amendment. On this issue, Estrada Palma wrote:

> The Cuban government in making a treaty should try to interpret the Platt Amendment so as to give the meaning most favorable to the interests of Cuba and to her sovereignty and independence. She will fulfill the treaty but expects the United States to do likewise and to respect her independence which is recognized in one of the clauses of the Platt Amendment in the most solemn manner.[12]

This position satisfied the majority of those at the meeting. But not Juan Gualberto Gómez. The Negro leader had urged Estrada Palma to take the position that as President he would accept the Platt Amendment, "but that if the opportunity to repeal it should pass through your door, you will not let it pass by but will seize upon it." But Estrada Palma refused to accept this position even though, for Juan Gualberto Gómez, it represented a compromise.[13] During the extensive debate following the reading of Estrada Palma's letter, Gómez urged the meeting not to accept his stand and to refuse to endorse him for President. But the majority rejected his demand, and Estrada Palma was endorsed by a vote of 23 to 2, with Juan Gualberto Gómez and Ezequel García voting in the negative. The group then decided to publish a manifesto to the people of Cuba urging the election of Estrada Palma as the first President of the Republic. This manifesto, written by Domingo Méndez Capote and Alfredo Zayas, hailed Estrada Palma as "the most suitable candidate" for President, a man who was entitled to the votes of all Cubans since he displayed "the qualities of prudence, integrity and civil mindedness which in a government gives promise of morality, order and peace." This manifesto, dated September 28, 1901, was signed by 32 distinguished Cubans, led by General Máximo Gómez, and including among them Manuel Sanguily, Domingo Méndez Capote, and Gonzalo de Quesada. It was widely distributed throughout the island.[14]

The news of the manifesto evoked enthusiasm in pro-Administration circles in the United States. The Philadelphia *Public Ledger,* an Administration organ, observed: "Señor Tomas Estrada Palma, whose name is just now prominently mentioned for the presidency of the new Cuban republic, should make an ideal executive. He seems to have all the necessary qualifications for the position, and possesses the confidence alike of Cubans and Americans. A wise and conservative man is needed to pilot the Republic safely through many dangers which are reasonably sure to arise in its early days. It is, therefore, very gratifying that many signs point to the choice falling on Estrada Palma. His love for Cuba is unquestioned and his friendship for the United States amply demonstrated." [15]

Although they lacked the influence of the personalities backing Estrada Palma, the followers of Masó were not inactive. They had an important and popular issue—repeal of the Platt Amendment—and they acquired the support of a tireless fighter for Cuban sovereignty, Juan Gualberto Gómez. After the endorsement of Estrada Palma by the National and Republican party leaders despite his refusal to support repeal of the Platt Amendment, Juan Gualberto decided to back Bartolomé Masó. For this purpose, he helped form the *Partido Republicano Independiente* (Independent Republican Party) of which he became President. Together with Rafael Fernández de Castro, Juan Gualberto Gómez rallied behind the new party the Republicans of Oriente, led by Castillo Duany, liberal Camagüeyans, and the progressive elements in Matanzas, all of them known as *antiplattistas*. The Party's platform stood firmly "for the principles of the Revolution and the absolute independence of Cuba," meaning, of course, repeal of the Platt Amendment. To further Masó's cause, Juan Gualberto founded the newspaper *La República Cubana*, through which he appealed especially for workingclass endorsement of the *antiplattista* candidate,* and the response was such as to indicate wide support for Masó in Cuban labor circles.[16]

The growing support for Masó was not ignored by General Wood. He reported in alarm to President Roosevelt on October 28, 1901 that Masó had gained the enthusiastic backing of "the radical and discontented element," especially the Negroes, and that this created a highly dangerous situation.[17] But Wood was determined to prevent this situation from getting out of hand, and he hit upon a simple device. In appointing members of the *Junta Central* (Electoral Commission) to supervise the election, watch the voting, and count the ballots, Wood

---

* Juan Gualberto Gómez had a wide following in Cuban working-class circles; indeed, he was urged by many workers to found a Workers' Party. He was a champion of labor, and condemned those who were concerned with protecting animals but showed "a lack of consideration of the needs of the working class, who with their personal labor contribute to the personal wealth of the country." (*Horrego, op. cit.*, p. 174.)

named only men favorable to Estrada Palma. This technique was commonly used by political machines in the United States to steal elections. Naturally, Masó and his followers insisted that at least one member of the Electoral Commission be a man whom the *antiplattista* candidate would suggest. But Wood rejected the appeal, whereupon the Masoites turned to Washington for justice. Here, too, as might be expected, the answer was a rejection. Masó was informed that Wood had complete authority to administer the presidential election as he saw fit. Rafael Martínez Ortiz, though decidedly pro-Estrada Palma in his account, concedes: "Masó's cause was obviously not looked upon with favor in Washington. The possibility, no matter how remote, of having a candidate elected who was on record as an opponent of the Platt Amendment . . . was enough to cause his appeal to be rejected." [18]

Charging that the election was rigged by Washington, the Masoites refused to participate further in the campaign, and Masó formally withdrew his candidacy. As Juan Gualberto Gómez put it: "There will be electoral meetings but no elections; there will be a victory but without a fight. From the ballot boxes will come out the representatives of a people as officeholders come out of a pen of a minister. Estrada Palma will be the President through the decision of a government, but not through the wish of a people. . . . We prefer bitter isolation to participation in the shameful victory of his guaranteed triumph." [19]

While Wood in Havana and Roosevelt and Root in Washington heaved a sigh of relief at Masó's withdrawal, there was widespread indignation among many Cubans over the open favoritism shown by Washington for the candidacy of Estrada Palma. Not all that who protested would have voted for Masó, but there was a strong feeling that a Republic which began with a President whose election was promoted unfairly by the authorities of the United States was not beginning its career in a way that augured well for Cuba's future. For the first time, even Máximo Gómez came under severe attack, and he was criticized for remaining silent while the United States arbitrarily deprived Masó of his equal rights.[20]

On December 31, 1902, the uncontested election was held, the people voting for presidential electors. Inevitably, Estrada Palma, the joint candidate of the National and Republican parties, was elected. Those who opposed Estrada Palma could only show it by staying away from the polls, and this they did in droves. "The elections were very quiet," went a typical report, "and as was natural in view of the fact that there was but one ticket in the field, the vote was light." [21] The imperialist press in the United States praised the Cubans for their wisdom in electing "a conservative man like Estrada Palma." [22] But the New York *Evening Post* expressed concern that "only a quasi-election of the first president of the quasi-republic of Cuba" should have occurred.

> A vigorous opposition is as much needed in Cuban politics as in America or England, but there is to be apparently only a kind of sullen discontent, expressed by abstention from voting. . . . General Maso and his supporters . . . are undoubtedly right in assuming that the candidacy of Senor Palma was quietly favored by the American military government. This in itself made a bad impression in the island and tended to give the election a farcical character . . . . A presidential election, with only one candidate, general indifference, and the lightest of light votes—that cannot appear normal to us.[23]

The Havana correspondent of a leading London newspaper sent the following dispatch:

> Palma is regarded in Cuba as a friend of the Americans, and not altogether sound on the question of Cuban independence. He was certainly the American candidate at the Presidential election, and had he not been placed at the head of the poll it is probable that "Free Cuba" would have been adjourned for a short time. This consideration seems to have secured him his majority.[24]

On February 24, 1902, the seventh anniversary of Cuba's final revolt against the rule of Spain, the electoral college met and elected Estrada Palma, without opposition, as the first President of the Republic. A month later, on March 27, in a message to Congress, President Roosevelt announced that "the time is near for the fulfillment of the pledge of the United States to leave the government and the control of the Island of Cuba to its people." The long-awaited event would take place on May 20, 1902.[25]

Estrada Palma left the United States for Cuba in mid-April. As he departed from Point Comfort, Virginia, he told reporters: "This country has been my home for twenty years, and I regret to leave. But my people have called me and my duty is there." The *Daily People* felt that neither Estrada Palma nor the Cuban people could be congratulated on his return to the island.

> When he fled from his native country he was an insurgent. He fought for the freedom of his country, and thought that fight was lost, it was one in which he won fame and honor, not for victory, but for his courage and tenacity. Twenty-five years have wrought many changes in the country. The people, the customs, the needs, and the hopes are not the ones that Palma knew. Cuba has forged ahead, and the driving forth of the Spaniards has given her hopes and tasks that force still newer considerations upon her. Palma, sentimentally, is ideal. Practically he is the most impossible of all men, and it is an outrage to take him from the retirement of his old age and plunge him into the fight and the struggle of a nation that he never knew, because it is not his nation, no matter what it was when he left it.

Estrada Palma arrived in Cuba on April 20, landing at Gibara where he issued a call for cheers for Cuba Libre and for the United States.[26] Then he visited the city of Bayamo, his birthplace, Manzanillo, and Santiago de Cuba, and began his trip to Havana for his inauguration, crossing the island by the route followed by Gómez and Maceo in the great western invasion.

While Estrada Palma moved slowly toward Havana, the Cuban people were receiving a sharp reminder of their sufferings during the late War for Independence. This time the practices which had shocked the world were not those of Spain but of the government which had protested Spanish atrocities against the Cubans, and had even justified going to war in order to end them. It was revealed in April-May, 1902 that in order to end the Philippine war as quickly as possible, the United States Army had employed methods against the Filipinos which reminded the world of Valeriano Weyler. To carry out the war of aggression against the Filipinos more effectively, General "Jake" Smith took over the job of pacifying Samar. His first move was to order all civilians out of the interior. When they came straggling into the coastal towns they were all thrown into stockades—concentration camps—and, like the *reconcentrados* in Cuba, they died like flies. "I want no prisoners. I wish you to kill and burn; the more you burn and kill the better it will please me." All persons who had not surrendered and were capable of carrying arms were to be shot, and this included Filipino boys of ten years of age! Finally, Smith gave his infamous order that Samar be converted into a "howling wilderness." The order was carried out to the letter by his subordinate, Major Waller of the United States Marines, and within six months Samar "was quiet as a cemetery." [27]

When the news of these brutal outrages reached the United States, there was a wave of protest.* *The State,* a longtime foe of Spanish despotism in Cuba, declared bitterly on April 29, 1902:

> In the Philippines we have Spanish concentration, Spanish killing of prisoners without quarter, Spanish destruction of towns and habituation giving shelter to "rebels." . . . We find the United States in the position of Spain—indeed a far worse position. . . . In the name of humanity, in the name of civilization, in behalf of endangered American interests which give us the right and the duty to speak and to act, *The War in the Philippines Must Stop.*

Stephen Bonsal, who had been in both Cuba and the Philippines, wrote in *Collier's Weekly* that Weyler's policy and that of the United States in the Philippines was identical, and if anything, the latter was worse. He charged, too, that the Administration was as guilty as General Smith and Major Waller for "what has been done in Samar. . . . When the facts are known it will be clear as day that Gen. Smith and Maj. Waller were sent to the island to carry out a campaign the nature of which had been fully decided in Washington." [28] Since Elihu Root, Secretary of War, publicly justified the methods used by Smith and Waller as "the most humane possible," it is clear that Bonsal knew whereof he spoke, even though as a result of the nationwide protests, both Waller and Smith were court-martialed and retired from the service.[29]

In Havana the *Diario de la Marina,* long-time defender of Spanish rule in Cuba, seized upon the reports from the Philippines to suggest that Anglo-Saxons wire an apology to General Weyler. "How scandalized were the Americans and the English over all that happened in

---

* Earlier there had also been an outburst of indignation when the Atlanta *Constitution's* special correspondent in Manila wrote in the December 27, 1901 issue that, when the American Declaration of Independence was circulated among the Filipinos in English and Spanish, it was suppressed by the United States Army because it was "A Damned Incendiary Document." The *Appeal to Reason,* a Socialist weekly, published the full text of the Declaration of Independence on March 8, 1902, under the heading: "The Document Suppressed by the United States."

Cuba, and particularly over the reconcentration system under Weyler," it editorialized on January 25, 1902. "How humane, how charitable, how sensitive were the Anglo-Saxons! And what savages, what barbarians, what cruel beasts we Latins were! O you hypocrites!"

It is a sad fact that Estrada Palma who had been so eloquent in denouncing Weyler's policies in Cuba remained silent about the practices of the United States in the Philippines which equaled those of the hated Spanish "Butcher." During his tour enroute to Havana, he had only words of praise for the United States and its role in Cuba, and ended each speech with a toast to the Americans. To Estrada Palma, May 20th, the day when the Republic of Cuba would be established, would not symbolize for the Cubans a day to remember all the sacrifices made by themselves and by so many of their fellow-countrymen who had not lived to see the great event. Rather, as he told audience after audience on his tour:

> This day [May 20] will forever mean to us of Cuba that one of the greatest and most powerful nations of modern times, not content with helping us to win our liberty, not satisfied with having spent the blood of her loyal sons in torrents in our behalf, has justly and wisely stood between us and the rest of the world, has shown us how to govern our young Republic, has continued to extend to us her guiding hand and her councils, and now, having done so, she fulfills her pledge to us and to the world and generously turns over to our government the island she has helped us to wrest from our enemies.[30]

The most pro-imperialist spokesman in the United States could not have painted the role of his country in Cuba in more glowing colors. It is not difficult to imagine the feelings of the former *mambises* in the audience as they listened to such remarks by their first President. Fortunately, not all Cubans were so indifferent to the contributions of their own revolutionary patriots. On May 18, 1902, the anniversary of José Martí's death, Cuban flags were flown at half-mast all over the island, and special services were held in churches.[31]

The great day finally arrived. On May 20, 1902, the streets of Havana were decorated with Cuban flags. On many streets and in all the parks there were triumphal arches, bearing slogans alluding to the struggle for independence, with the names of José Martí and Antonio Maceo featured. Bands of musicians roamed through the streets playing the "Hymn of Bayamo" and the "Hymn of the Invasion." From the early morning, thousands gathered near the Governor's palace waiting for the moment when the Stars and Stripes would be lowered and the flag with the lone star would fly over the building and over the old fort of El Morro, the flag in which, as Martí had written, it is not easy to tell

> si en ella se prolongaba el cielo
> o si el cielo surgió de ella.
>
> (whether the flag was an extension of the sky, or whether the sky flowed out the flag.)

Exactly at noon, at the Governor's palace, in a ceremony attended by distinguished Cubans and Americans, including among the latter William Jennings Bryan, General Leonard Wood delivered a letter from Theodore Roosevelt to the President and Congress of the Republic of Cuba. The President of the United States wrote that the Military Governor was authorized to "declare the occupation of Cuba by the United States be at an end," and expressed the best wishes and earnest hopes of his government "for the stability and success of your government, for the blessings of peace, justice, prosperity and ordered freedom among your people, and for enduring friendship between the Republic of the United States and the Republic of Cuba." After reading the document, Wood undid the halyard from the flagstaff on the Governor's palace, and lowered the American flag. At the same time, the American flags on the Morro Castle and on the Santa Clara and Punta fortresses were lowered. The jurisdiction of the United States had ended. In the meantime, a Cuban flag had been bent on the halyard of the Palace flagstaff, and Wood and Máximo Gómez raised it, the latter with tears trickling down his cheeks. "It was the crowning moment of Maximo Gomez's life when he raised the flag of his long devotion over the palace, the nerve center of Spain's power in the island," wrote a reporter at the scene. At the Morro castle, General Emilio Núñez raised the Cuban flag.

As the Cuban flags flew free, from the streets of the city a tremendous cheer arose. The cheer was caught up by the people on the roofs and resounded throughout the entire city.

Wood then formally put the government of the island in Cuban hands with the statement: "Under the direction of the President of the United States, I now transfer to you as the duly elected representative of the people of Cuba, the government and control of the island, to be held and exercised by you. . . . This transfer of government and control is upon the express condition, and the Government of the United States will understand by the acceptance thereof you do now assume and undertake all and several, the obligations assumed by the United States with respect to Cuba. . . ." President Estrada Palma* accepted the government with the following statement:

> As President of the Republic of Cuba, I hereby receive the government of the island of Cuba which you transfer to me, and take note that by this act the military occupation of Cuba ceases. . . . I declare that the Government of the Republic assumes as provided for in the Constitution, each and every one of the obligations concerning Cuba imposed upon the United States by virtue of the treaty entered into on the 10th of December, 1898, between the United States and her Majesty the Queen of Spain.

With the completion of this act, General Wood and his staff were driven to the pier where they entered a launch and were taken to the *Brooklyn*. The naval vessel got under way at once, sailing towards the United States.

While this was occurring at Havana, a similar scene was being enacted at Santiago de Cuba. Here, at noon, General Whiteside turned over the authority to his Cuban successor, and sailed away with two troops of the Eighth Cavalry.[32]

Although eight batteries of American artillery remained on Cuban soil,* the American military occupation of Cuba was technically at an end. The Republic of Cuba had at long last been born, "the Republic," as René E. Reyna Cassio writes, "which owes its existence to the *chaveta* of the tobacco workers and the *machete* of the *guajiro*."[33]

---

* On September 12, 1902, President Estrada Palma wrote to President Theodore Roosevelt complaining that not only were American troops still in Cuba, but additional troops were being sent to reinforce them. While he understood why the United States felt it necessary to keep troops, he noted that "the continued occupation by American troops after the establishment of the Republic of Cuba, and the apparent increase of the American forces, is apt to impress the popular mind with the idea that Cuba is not entirely free, that some control is still being exercised by the United States and that the Cuban government may not be an entirely free agent." (Theodore Roosevelt Papers, Library of Congress.)

Comments in the American press on the stirring events in Cuba were mixed. *Harper's Weekly,* a leading imperialist journal, showed its contempt for the Cuban people and their government by featuring a cartoon of Estrada Palma as a barefoot peasant sitting by a tree in a jungle, a bowl of soap suds in his lap, and at his lips a clay pipe from which he was blowing a big bubble inscribed, "The Cuban Republic." [34] Generally, however, the press wished the new Republic well, but the imperialist press reminded the Cubans of all that the United States had done for them. It had rescued the island from Spanish despotism when the hope of the Cubans for independence had all but disappeared; it had rebuilt the devastated country, and, unlike other nations, had voluntarily resigned its power over Cuba after only three years of occupation. The Cubans should at least be grateful.[35] But the anti-imperialist newspapers were quick to note that the United States had refused to assist the Cubans in their struggle until it became evident that they might win their independence all by themselves. "The truth is that the liberation of the island was nine-tenths gained by their own exertions and sacrifices. In a three years' war they had so weakened and undermined Spain's empire in Cuba that the fabric collapsed at one slight blow from the United States." Furthermore, "what has been done in the island has been done with the money of its own people, collected and disbursed by the Americans." Finally, while the United States had allowed the Cubans to celebrate "Independence Day," it was an independence "with a string attached to it." [36]

"The Platt Amendment is the string," declared *The State.* "The Cubans may range up to the length of the string. They will exercise a limited freedom under the shadow of a mighty arm, as capable of vengeance as of defense." [37]

"Of what use, the Cubans will ask," observed the New York *Evening Post,* "is it for us to attempt to run a government if it is a government with a string attached to it, which Congress may pull at any moment. The United States can do its best for the new Republic by repealing the Platt Amendment, for thereby one of the greatest stumbling blocks in the way of the Cuban Republic will be removed." [38]

The Socialist *Daily People* was blunter in its editorial noting Cuba's "Independence Day":

Cuba was proclaimed a republic to-day, but to her independence there is a string, and the end of the string is held by the United States. The departure of the Americans did not end their control. It is customary to speak of Cuba as a free and independent republic, but as a matter of fact, she is not so. . . . Cuba is bound to and is dependent on the United States.[39]

On the European continent, press opinion invariably emphasized that the new Republic was in reality a "sham" government. *Journal des Débats* of Paris observed: "So far as Cuba is concerned, it is known that her independence is only relative, if even that. The Platt Amendment, adopted by the American Congress, placed Spain's former colony under the disguised protectorate of the United States." The Liberal *Indépendence Belge* pointed to the Cubans' experience with American "liberation" as a warning to other colonies of European powers not to look to Uncle Sam for unselfish assistance in their independence struggles since "selfish and material imperialism alone actuates the United States Government."

In London, the *Saturday Review* noted that those who were taken in by appearances alone might conclude that "something very fine and generous has actually happened with the end of American occupation of Cuba." It went on: "The facts are much less one-sided. It is true that the American troops and officials have been withdrawn, the American flag hauled down, and a republic of sorts inaugurated. But it is not true that the republic is independent even in the management of its internal affairs, while so far as foreign relations go, it is undisguisedly under the thumb of Washington. The republic has been obliged to cede naval and coaling-stations to the United States; it has no power to declare war without American consent; it may not add to the Cuban debt without permission; even its control over the island treasury is subject to supervision. Moreover, the United States retains a most elastic right of intervention." [40]

While hailing the establishment of the Republic, the Havana *Post* noted that the new government began its career limited in such a way by American imperialism as to practically guarantee its inability to function effectively:

> It is idle to think or speak of Cuba as a free national entity. Cuba will no more be allowed to make a contract or a treaty with another nation, excepting the United States, than Florida or New

York. She will no more have the right to declare war than Massachusetts. Cuba is a quasi-military department of the United States.

But this is not all. The remaining wealth of the island, both public and private, will fall into the grasping hands of American capitalists. Corrupting foreign influences will have free play, and in a short time the country may find itself with its whole substance consumed and its future heavily mortgaged. Will peace be preserved under these conditions? Will anything in the shape of a decent government be able to exist?[41]

In an editorial entitled, "Cuba as a Republic," a leading London paper congratulated the United States on having overcome all opposition in Cuba to the Platt Amendment, having succeeded in getting its favored choice selected as President of the new Republic, and having put the island in shape for future economic penetration by American capitalists. But it warned Washington not to conclude that its troubles in Cuba were over. "There are not wanting those who foresee trouble even under these circumstances, since the desire to be entirely free from control may spring up in Cuban breasts, and lead to a revolt as it has so often done before." [42]

The history of Cuba after May 20, 1902 bears out the accuracy of this prediction.

"Cuba supplies us with the formula of American expansion in the West Indies and South America," the *Saturday Review* of London commented following Estrada Palma's inauguration.[43] The imperialist forces in the United States agreed with this estimate, and they went even further. The Cuban model must "also be applied to the Philippines." [44] Indeed, even many anti-imperialists applauded this approach. "We can do for the Philippine Islands even at this late hour what has been done for Cuba," *The Public,* a leading anti-imperialist weekly declared hopefully. "We can revive the Filipino republic as we revived the Cuban republic. And as with Cuba this is our pledged duty." [45]

On May 18, 1899, the anti-imperialist Springfield *Republican* conceded that the disbanding of the Cuban Liberating Army deprived the Cuban people of their main protection against the plans of imperialist forces in the United States. Hence it was not "difficult to understand the hesitation of the patriots of the war for independence against Spain to give up their arms, since in doing that, they place their aspirations for independence at the mercy of the United States." But there really was no reason for the Cuban patriots to be unduly alarmed. The American people had given Cuba an "indelible pledge" that she would be an independent nation, and the anti-imperialists were determined to make certain that this would be fulfilled.

But the anti-imperialist movement proved to be a frail reed for Cuban independence to lean on. Apart from the fact that the anti-imperialists were primarily absorbed by the Philippines, they were actually more concerned with form than reality. To many of them the departure of American military forces from Cuba and the existence of the Republic was evidence enough that the "indelible pledge" had been fulfilled. Indeed, all along, many anti-imperialists frankly proclaimed that their objective was to secure for the Filipinos what we were giving the Cubans—"What is due to the people of Cuba is due to the people of the Philippines," was the way Andrew Carnegie put it—and when the Republic of Cuba was established, anti-imperialists not only insisted that their campaigns in behalf of the Cubans had been a total success, but now began to call for a similar form of independence for the Philippines.

This position was especially attractive to those who had difficulty swallowing the brutal methods employed by the United States in achieving domination over the Philippines, but who believed that American rule over the islands in some form was justified. On December 10, 1903, Jacob Schurman, President of Cornell University and a member of the Philippine Commission in 1899, wrote to Josephine Shaw Lowell, a wealthy social worker: ". . . I believe there is no practical difference between Professor James's view and mine in regard to the future of the Philippines. At any rate I keep hammering away at the phrases *Philippine Independence* and *treat the Philippines like Cuba.*" [46] Schurman wrote to the New York *Tribune* a week later, pointing out: "We may give the Philippines independence like that of Cuba under American protection." [47] In February, 1905, Schurman, Mrs. Lowell and a group of academicians joined together to form the Filipino Progress League with a program "to promote the fulfillment of the hope expressed by President Roosevelt that the Philippine Islands shall stand 'in some such relation to the United States as Cuba now stands.'" [48]

Thus Cuba became the prototype for American imperialism. While the exact form of intervention and control over overseas areas varied from a compulsory customs receivership, frequently guaranteed by a treaty arrangement, to a "financial protectorate" imposed upon a country, to forcing an "undesirable" political leader out of office by withdrawing or withholding diplomatic recognition, to promoting revolutions favorable to American interest, to the transformation of a nation into a "client state" run by American appointed officials, to armed intervention to protect American propertied interests—the purpose was always the same, American economic and political domination without outright seizure of colonies by the United States. U.S. capital and enterprise having replaced the British as the dominant factor in Latin America, and the United States having become a capital surplus nation, it sought outlets for this surplus, generally abroad and particularly in Latin America. The instrument through which American domination was established in this part of the world and steadily reinforced was neocolonialism, and Cuba was the model. Cuba illustrated how American monopolies could gain a protected sphere of influence with a form of independence masked by U.S. intervention and control. The Western Hemisphere was converted into a preserve for North American imperialism while the United States could continue to boast of her anticolonial traditions and philosophy.*

American imperialism could look back with satisfaction on the course of events since 1898. Senator Chauncey M. Depew, a Wall Street banker, rang down the curtain on the birth of American imperialism with words of praise for a "job well done": "The American people now produce $2,000,000,000 worth more than they consume, and we have met the emergency and by the providence of God, by the statesmanship of William McKinley, and the valor of Roosevelt and his associates, we have our markets in Cuba, in Porto Rico, in the Philippines, and we stand in the presence of 800,000,000 people, with the Pacific an American lake. . . . The world is ours. . . ." [49]

---

\* Frank Freidel notes that after 1902 the "thirst for additional colonies had suddenly and permanently been slaked," and that there "was not to be the grandiose building of empire that some jingoes had hoped would be America's future." ("Dissent in the Spanish-American War and the Philippine Insurrection," in Samuel Eliot Morison, Frederick Merk, Frank Freidel, *Dissent in Three American Wars*, Cambridge, Mass., 1970, p. 93.) But he fails to see that a different form of empire building emerged, largely modeled after the Cuban experience.

# Reference Notes

## CHAPTER XV
## Cuban-American Relations During the War

1. Finley Peter Dunne, *Mr. Dooley's Philosophy*, New York, 1900, pp. 13-18.
2. John F. Kendrick, "The Cuban Army of Liberation," speech of 1951, published in *William McKinley Camp Bulletin*, vol. XXVIII, March-April, 1955. Copy in Chicago Historical Society.
3. Calixto García to Estrada Palma, May 1, 1898, Archivo Nacional. Hereinafter cited as AN.
4. Arthur Hobson Quinn, editor, *The Literature of the American People*, New York, 1951, pp. 573-74.
5. Escalante, *op. cit.*, pp. 386-96; Portell Vilá, *op. cit.*, pp. 181-83; Rubens, *op. cit.*, pp. 394-95.
6. Escalante, *op. cit.*, p. 405.
7. Enrique Collazo, *Los Americanos en Cuba*, La Habana, 1910, pp. 39-41; Portell Vilá, *op. cit.*, p. 185.
8. Escalante, *op. cit.*, pp. 413-14; *The State*, May 27, 1898.
9. Calixto García to Máximo Gómez, Bayamo, 11 de Mayo, in Escalante, *op. cit.*, pp. 413-14.
10. Gómez to Major General J. Rabí and M. Capote, undated, but probably around May, 1898, in Rodríguez, *Gómez*, pp. 22-23; Gómez, *Mi Diario*, pp. 410, 413-14; *The State*, Oct. 2, 1898.
11. Portell Vilá, *op. cit.*, p. 199.
12. *The State*, Feb. 16, 1899.
13. N. G. Gonzalez, *In Darkest Cuba*, pp. 42-43; *The State*, May 2, July 19, 20, 1898.
14. *The State*, July 5, 8, 20, Oct. 2, 1898.
15. Gonzalez, *op. cit.*, p. 89.
16. *Ibid.*, pp. 95-96.
17. *The State*, June 14, 1898.
18. *Ibid.*
19. Escalante, *op. cit.*, pp. 427-30; Admiral William T. Sampson to Secretary of War, June 12, 1898, *Adjutant-General of the Army, Correspondence Relating to the War with Spain*, Washington, 1902, vol. I, p. 40.
20. García a los Jefes de Oriente, Mejía, Holguín, June 10, 1898, AN.

21. Portell Vilá, op. cit., p. 236.
22. Escalante, op. cit., pp. 439-50.
23. Sampson to Secretary of Navy, June 18, 1898, copy in William McKinley Papers, Library of Congress; French E. Chadwick, *The Relations of the United States and Spain: The Spanish American War*, New York, 1911, vol. I, p. 385; Portell Vilá, op. cit., p. 237; Escalante, op. cit., pp. 450-51.
24. Associated Press dispatch, *The State*, June 15, 1898.
25. *Ibid.*, June 17, 1898.
26. Chadwick, op. cit., vol. I, pp. 387-88; R. H. Titherington, *A History of the Spanish-American War*, New York, 1900, p. 217.
27. Portell Vilá, op. cit., p. 238.
28. Associated Press dispatch, *The State*, June 21, 1898.
29. Associated Press dispatch, *ibid.*, June 22, 1898.
30. García to Gómez, Siboney, July 15, 1898, AN; Juan Jerez Villarreal, *Oriente: Biografía de una provincia*, La Habana, 1960, pp. 293-94.
31. Escalante, op. cit., pp. 494-95.
32. *Ibid.*, pp. 453-54.
33. A. J. Gardner to S. E. Barton, Key West, Florida, May 17, 1898, Clara Barton Papers, Box 51, Library of Congress.
34. R. A. Alger, *The Spanish-American War*, New York, 1900, pp. 7-22.
35. Millis, op. cit., pp. 238-42.
36. Portell Vilá, op. cit., p. 236.
37. Quoted in Millis, op. cit., p. 245.
38. Sampson to Secretary of Navy, June 18, 1898, William McKinley Papers, Library of Congress.
39. Wm. H. Shafter to Henry C. Corbin, June 7, 1898, Henry C. Corbin Papers, Library of Congress.
40. Millis, op. cit., pp. 246-47.
41. H. H. Sargent, *The Campaign of Santiago de Cuba*, Chicago, 1914, vol. II, pp. 30-35; Alger, op. cit., pp. 72-73.
42. Sargent, op. cit., vol. II, p. 35.
43. *Ibid.*, pp. 36-38.
44. Associated Press dispatch, *The State*, June 24, 1898.
45. Joseph Wheeler, *The Santiago Campaign*, Philadelphia, 1899, pp. 10-14; Chadwick, op. cit., vol. II, pp. 23-26; Jerez, op. cit., pp. 293-94.
46. *Heraldo de Madrid*, Sept. 9, 1898, reprinted in Portell Vilá, op. cit., p. 240.
47. García to Estrada Palma, June 27, 1898, original in AN; reprinted in *Boletín del Archivo Nacional*, 1936, pp. 108-12.
48. General W. Ludlow to García, near Santiago, July 15, 1898, AN; Escalante, op. cit., pp. 495-96.
49. General Shafter to Henry C. Corbin, June 25, 1898, in *Correspondence Relating to the War with Spain*, vol. I, pp. 53-54; John Black Atkins, *The War in Cuba*, London, 1899, p. 108.
50. *New York Tribune*, May 23, 1898.
51. *The State*, June 28, 1898.
52. *Ibid.*, July 8, 1898.
53. Atkins, op. cit., pp. 288-89; General Shafter to Henry C. Corbin, June 25, 1898, *Correspondence Relating to the War with Spain*, pp. 54-55; Richard Harding Davis, *The Cuban and Porto Rican Campaign*, New York,

1898, pp. 17-72; Richard Harding Davis, *Notes of a War Correspondent*, New York, 1910, pp. 45-51; Edward Marshall, *The Story of the Rough Riders*, New York, 1900, pp. 54-96; Portell Vilá, *op. cit.*, pp. 242-44; *New York Tribune*, June 29, 1898; Testimony of General Lawton, Dodge Commission, *Senate Document* 221, 56th Congress, vol. IV, pp. 944-53.
54. Chadwick, *op. cit.*, vol. II, p. 69.
55. Chadwick, *op. cit.*, vol. II, pp. 69, 75; Atkins, *op. cit.*, p. 108; Felipe Martínez Arango, *Cronología Crítica de la Guerra Hispano-Cubana-Norte-Americana*, La Habana, 1958, pp. 56-60; Portell Vilá, *op. cit.*, pp. 247-48; Jerez, *op. cit.*, pp. 294-95.
56. Chadwick, *op. cit.*, vol. II, pp. 84-85. See also *New York Tribune*, July 10, 1898.
57. *New York World*, July 14, 1898.
58. *The State*, July 20, 1898.
59. Nicolás de Cárdenas, *Recuerdos de la guerra*, La Habana, 1923, p. 164.
60. Associated Press dispatch, *The State*, July 7, 1898.
61. *Ibid.*, Nov. 21, 1898.
62. General Shafter to A.G., U.S.A., In Camp near Santiago, July 4th, 1898, B. F. Montgomery Papers, Rutherford B. Hayes Memorial Library, Fremont, Ohio.
63. *The State*, July 16, 25, 1898.
64. Varona Guerrero, *La Guerra de Independencia*, vol. III, pp. 1600-03; Martínez, *op. cit.*, pp. 72-75; Collazo, *op. cit.*, p. 78; José Müller y Tejeiro, *Battles and Capitulation of Santiago de Cuba*, Washington, 1899, pp. 95-97; Escalante, *op. cit.*, pp. 494-96; Portell Vilá, *op. cit.*, pp. 249-50; Kendrick, "The Cuban Army of Liberation," *op. cit.*
65. General Shafter to Adjutant General of the Army, July 10, 1898, *Corresondence Relating to the War with Spain*, vol. I, p. 122.
66. *The State*, Nov. 21, 1898.
67. Alger, *op. cit.*, p. 192; H. C. Corbin to Major General Shafter, July 9, 1898, B. F. Montgomery Papers, Hayes Memorial Library.
68. Alger, *op. cit.*, p. 210.
69. R. W. Alger to Maj. Gen. Shafter, July 15, 1898, B. F. Montgomery Papers, Hayes Memorial Library.
70. War Department, *Annual Report*, 1898, p. 122.
71. "Annual Reports of the War Department, 1898," 55th Congress, 3rd Session, *House Document No. 2*, vol. III, p. 159.
72. Willis Fletcher Johnson, *The History of Cuba*, New York, 1920, vol. IV, p. 139; *The State*, July 19, 1898.
73. Col. Curtis V. Hard to McKinley, July 25, 1898, William McKinley Papers, Library of Congress.
74. Collazo, *op. cit.*, p. 88; Víctor Concas, *La Escuadra del Almirante Cervera*, La Habana, 1916, p. 127.
75. Shafter to A.G., U.S.A., July 15, 1898, B. F. Montgomery Papers, Hayes Memorial Library. Emphasis mine. P.S.F.
76. Collazo, *op. cit.*, p. 151.
77. *The State*, July 20, 1898.
78. Shafter to Adj. Gen'l, July 4, 1898, B. F. Montgomery Papers, Hayes Memorial Library.
79. Copy in Henry C. Corbin Papers, Library of Congress.

80. Escalante, op. cit., p. 543. Also reprinted in "Ideario de la Independencia," Revolución, La Habana, Oct. 27, 1961.
81. Escalante, op. cit., pp. 536-37; The State, July 23, 1898.
82. The State, July 20, 1898.
83. Ibid., July 23, 1898.
84. Reprinted in ibid., July 28, 1898.
85. Reprinted in ibid.
86. General Shafter to the Adjutant General of the Army, July 23, 1898; Shafter to Secretary of War, July 29, 1898, Correspondence Relating to the War with Spain, vol. I, pp. 174-75; Chadwick, op. cit., vol. II, p. 254; The State, July 31, 1898.
87. The State, Aug. 3, 1898.
88. Ibid., July 23, Aug. 11, 13, 1898.
89. Ibid., July 23, 25, 1898.
90. New York World, July 12, 1898.
91. New York Times, Aug. 13, 1898; Foreign Relations, 1898, pp. 819-21.
92. The State, Aug. 13, 1898.
93. Rubens, op. cit., pp. 380-81; Portell Vilá, op. cit., p. 265; The State, Aug. 14, 1898.
94. Gonzales, op. cit., p. 314.
95. Ibid., pp. 333-34.
96. New York Tribune, Aug. 14, 1898.
97. A. J. Gardner to S. E. Barton, Aug. 17, 1898, Clara Barton Papers, Box 51, Library of Congress.

## CHAPTER XVI

## The Devastated Island

1. Gonzalez, op. cit., p. 178.
2. Robert P. Porter, Report on the Commercial and Industrial Condition of the Island of Cuba, November 15, 1898, Treasury Department, Document No. 2072, 55th Cong., 2nd Sess.; Robert P. Porter, Industrial Cuba, New York, 1899, pp. 4-8; Leonard Wood to McKinley, Nov. 27, 1898, William McKinley Papers, Library of Congress; The State, Aug. 23, 1898.
3. N. G. Gonzalez in The State, Sept. 8, 1898.
4. The State, Nov. 5, 1898.
5. New York Evening Post, Oct. 15, 1898.
6. Leonard Wood, "Santiago Since the Surrender," Scribner's Magazine, vol. XXV, May, 1899, pp. 515-18; Franklin Matthews, The New-Born Cuba, New York, 1920, p. 300; Johnson, op. cit., vol. IV, pp. 142-43.
7. "Report of the War Department," House Document 2, 56th Cong., 1st Sess., vol. IV, p. 218.
8. Civil Report of Major General John R. Brooke, Washington, D. C., 1900, pp. 366-67.
9. Clara Barton to President, Austrian Association, Red Cross, May 20, 1898, Clara Barton Papers, Box 42, Library of Congress.
10. Final Report of the Central Cuban Relief Committee to Secretary of State, Feb. 15, 1899; J. Gardner to S. E. Barton, Aug. 24, 1898, ibid., Boxes 42, 51.

NOTES 677

11. New York *Tribune*, July 21, 1898.
12. Clara Barton to Stephen E. Barton, Aug. 31, 1898, Clara Barton Papers, Box 36, Library of Congress.
13. Wood, *op. cit.*, p. 520; Leonard Wood, "The Military Government of Cuba," *Annals of the American Academy of Political and Social Science*, vol. XXI, p. 154; Johnson, *op. cit.*, vol. IV, pp. 143-46.
14. Porter, *Industrial Cuba*, *op. cit.*, p. 63; Hermann Hagedorn, *That Human Being, Leonard Wood*, New York, 1920, p. 41; William E. Hobbs, *Leonard Wood, Administrator, Soldier and Citizen*, New York, 1920, p. 56.
15. Wood to Elihu Root, Feb. 23, 1900, marked "confidential," Elihu Root Papers, Library of Congress.
16. M. Marquez Sterling, *Proceso Histórico de la Enmienda Platt, 1897-1934*, La Habana, 1941, p. 66.
17. Clara Barton to S. E. Barton, Santiago de Cuba, Aug. 3, 1898; W. E. Cramer to S. E. Barton, Gibara, Oct. 24, 1898; Final Report of the Central Cuban Relief Committee to Secretary of State, Feb. 15, 1899, Clara Barton Papers, Boxes 35, 52, Library of Congress.
18. S. E. Barton to Brigadier-General Leonard Wood, Nov. 13, 1898, *ibid.*, Box 52.
19. Clara Barton to Fred M. Page, Oct. 25, 1898; Clara Barton to President William McKinley, Oct. 28, 1898, *ibid.*, Boxes 37, 57.
20. Rafael Martínez Ortiz, *Cuba: Los Primeros Años de Independencia*, Paris, 1919, vol. I, p. 19.
21. S. E. Barton to Major-General Leonard E. Wood, March 24, 1900, Clara Barton Papers, Box 52, Library of Congress.
22. Clara Barton to Fred M. Page, Oct. 25, 1898, *ibid.*, Box 41.
23. *Cf.* Wood, "The Military Government of Cuba," *op. cit.*, pp. 154-55.
24. C. A. Schieren to S. E. Barton, Sept. 28, 1898, Clara Barton Papers, Box 35, Library of Congress.
25. W. E. Warner to S. E. Barton, Oct. 24, 1898, *ibid.*, Box 52.
26. W. E. Warner to S. E. Barton, Oct. 2, 1898, *ibid.*, Box 52.
27. G. W. Hyatt to S. E. Barton, Oct. 17, 1898, *ibid.*, Box 37.
28. G. W. Hyatt to S. E. Barton, Nov. 3, 1898, *ibid.*, Box 52.
29. Joseph P. Sanger to Clara Barton, Jan. 29th, 1899, *ibid.*, Box 51.
30. Fred M. Page to Clara Barton, Vedado, Havana, Oct. 20, 1898, *ibid.*, Box 37.
31. W. E. Warner to S. E. Barton, Oct. 24, 1898, *ibid.*, Box 52.
32. J. K. Elwell to Clara Barton, Sancti Spiritus, Nov. 18, 1898, *ibid.*, Box 51.
33. W. E. Warner to S. E. Barton, Holguín, Oct. 24, 1898; Joseph P. Sanger to Clara Barton, Matanzas, Jan. 29th, 1899, *ibid.*, Boxes 51, 52.
34. G. W. Hyatt to S. E. Barton, Nov. 3, 1898, *ibid.*, Box 52; Johnson, *op. cit.*, vol. IV, p. 147.
35. Charles T. Andrews in Seneca County (N. Y.) *County Courier*, in Charles T. Andrews Paper, Cornell University Library.
36. Report of Miss Adams, 1898, Clara Barton Papers, Box 51, Library of Congress.
37. Julio Carbonell, "Labors of the Red Cross in Cuba," unpublished manuscript, Nov. 27, 1899, Copy in Clara Barton Papers, Box 51, Library of Congress.
38. *Ibid.*

39. A. Garden, *Clara Barton protectora de los reconcentrados Cubanos*, La Habana, 1954, p. 19.
40. Elvin Laverne Valentine, "Military Government of Cuba, 1898-1902," unpublished M.A. thesis, University of Wisconsin, 1924, p. 18.
41. Robert P. Porter, *Special Report, The Province of Santiago, etc.*, Washington, 1898, p. 4.

## CHAPTER XVII

## Prologue to Military Occupation

1. *Journal of the Knights of Labor*, April, 1899, p. 5.
2. *The State*, June 15, 1898; Gonzalez, *op. cit.*, p. 54.
3. *The State*, July 20, 1898.
4. Secretary of the Exterior to Tómas Estrada Palma, May 12, 1898, Emeterio S. Santovenia and Joaquín Llaverías, editors, *Actas de la Assembleas de Representantes y del Consejo de Gobierno Durante la Guerra de Independencia*, La Habana, 1932, vol. IV, pp. 61-63; Andrés Moreno de la Torre to Estrada Palma, Santiago de Cuba, Aug. 14, 1898, AN.
5. Varona Guerrero, *La Guerra de Independencia*, vol. III, p. 1676.
6. Escalante, *op. cit.*, pp. 539-40.
7. *The State*, Aug. 16, 1898.
8. Richmond *Planet*, July 30, 1898.
9. General Lawton to Adjutant General of the Army, Aug. 16, 1888, *Correspondence Relating to the War with Spain*, vol. I, p. 230.
10. Quoted in Millis, *op. cit.*, p. 364.
11. General Shafter to Adjutant General of the Army, Aug. 16, 1898, *Correspondence Relating to the War with Spain*, vol. I, p. 230.
12. Adjutant General of the Army to Lawton, Aug. 16, 1898, *ibid.*, p. 231.
13. *The State*, July 31, 1898.
14. Copy of leaflet in Clara Barton Papers, Box 53, Library of Congress.
15. Quoted in Millis, *op. cit.*, p. 317.
16. New York *World*, July 12, 1898.
17. *The State*, July 30, 1898.
18. New York *World*, July 20, 1898; New York *Tribune*, Aug. 7, 1898.
19. *The State*, July 28, 1898.
20. *Literary Digest*, vol. XVII, July 30, 1898, p. 123.
21. *The State*, Sept. 11, 1898.
22. Kennedy, *op. cit.*, pp. 281-82.
23. *The State*, Sept. 11, 1898.
24. Day to McKinley, Sept. 30, 1898, William McKinley Papers, Library of Congress.
25. *The State*, Sept. 21, 1898.
26. *Ibid.*, Oct. 24, 1898.
27. *Ibid.*, Dec. 22, 1898.
28. *Ibid.*, July 25, Oct. 24, 1898.
29. Reprinted in *ibid.*, Nov. 20, 1898.
30. *Ibid.*, Sept. 28, Oct. 17, 1898.
31. *Ibid.*, Nov. 20, 1898.

32. *Exposición al Presidente de los Estados Unidos del Consejo de Gobierno Revolucionario*, Santa Cruz del Sur, Sept. 1, 1898, AN.
33. Bartolomé Masó, *Mensaje que dirige a la Asamblea de Representantes el Presidente de la República de Cuba*, 24 de Octubre de 1898, Publicado en la revista Maceo, Año I, de noviembre, 1898, p. 21; *Documentos Históricos*, La Habana, 1912, pp. 63-64; *The State*, Nov. 1, 1898.
34. *Actas de las Asambleas de Representantes*, vol. V, pp. 62-63.
35. Albert G. Robinson, "Cuban Self-Government," *The Independent*, vol. LII, Dec. 13, 1900, p. 2970: Healy, *op. cit.*, p. 45.
36. *The State*, Nov. 3, 1898.
37. Healy, *op. cit.*, p. 46.
38. *The State*, Sept. 24, 1898.
39. *New York Herald*, Sept. 26, 1898; *The State*, Sept. 28, 1898.
40. *Washington Post*, Nov. 9, 1898; *The State*, Nov. 22, 1898.
41. *New York Sun*, Oct. 17, 1898.
42. *The State*, Sept. 28, 1898.
43. *Ibid.*, Dec. 3, 1898. Rubens, *op. cit.*, pp. 392-93.
44. Sergio Aguirre, "La desaparición del Ejército Libertador," *Cuba Socialista*, Diciembre, 1963, pp. 54-55.
45. Rubens, *op. cit.*, p. 389; "Report of the Commission Sent to Washington," February 25, 1899, *Actas de las Asambleas de Representantes*, vol. V, pp. 152-54; Porter, *Industrial Cuba*, pp. 204-10; Healy, *op. cit.*, pp. 47-48.
46. *Congressional Record*, 56th Cong., 2nd Sess., vol. XXXIV, pp. 3041-42; *Actas de las Asambleas de Representantes*, vol. V, pp. 158-59; Sterling, *op. cit.*, pp. 39-44.
47. García to Morgan, undated, *Actas de las Asambleas de Representantes*, vol. V, pp. 160-65; Healy, *op. cit.*, p. 49.
48. *Actas de las Asambleas de Representantes*, vol. V, p. 157; Healy, *op. cit.*, p. 50.
49. *Foreign Relations*, 1898, pp. LXVI-LXVII; *The State*, Dec. 5, 1898.
50. *New York Tribune*, Dec. 6, 1898; *New York World*, Dec. 6, 1898; *London Standard*, Dec. 7, 1898, reprinted in Healy, *op. cit.*, p. 51.
51. *Patria*, Dec. 23, 1898.
52. Julio Le Riverend, *La Republica: Dependencia y Revolución*, La Habana, 1966, pp. 8-10.

## CHAPTER XVIII

### The Treaty of Paris

1. "Treaty of Peace between the United States and Spain," *Senate Document 62*, 55th Cong., 3rd Sess., p. 3; Portell Vilá, *op. cit.*, p. 269.
2. Day to McKinley, Sept. 30, 1898, William McKinley Papers, Library of Congress.
3. *Senate Document 62*, *op. cit.*, pp. 22, 27, 41, 46, 190-200.
4. Day to McKinley, Oct. 12, 1898; McKinley to Hay, Oct. 13, 1898, both in William McKinley Papers, Library of Congress.
5. Day to McKinley, Oct. 14, 1898, *ibid.*
6. *Foreign Relations*, 1898, pp. 932-33; *Senate Document 62*, *op. cit.*, p. 97;

Day to Hay, Oct. 27, 1898, B. F. Montgomery Papers, Hayes Memorial Library.
7. Leech, *op. cit.*, p. 342.
8. New York *Journal of Commerce* reprinted in *The People*, Sept. 25, 1898; *United States Investor*, vol. X, Sept. 24, 1898, pp. 817-18.
9. *Foreign Relations*, 1898, p. 930; *Senate Document* 62, *op. cit.*, pp. 108, 119, 223; Bernabe Africa, "Did the United States Acquire the Philippines from Spain by Purchase?" *Philippine Social Science Review*, vol. I, Nov.-Dec. 1929, pp. 147-53; Frye to McKinley, Oct. 30, 1898, B. F. Montgomery Papers, Hayes Memorial Library; *The State*, Nov. 25, 1898.
10. *Foreign Relations*, 1898, pp. 831-40.
11. Undated memorandum, William McKinley Papers, Library of Congress; Day to McKinley, Dec. 12, 1898, *ibid.*
12. "Speech of Albert J. Beveridge at Marquette Club, Chicago, September 25, 1900," *ibid.*
13. Charles E. Chapman, *A History of the Cuban Republic: A Study in Hispanic American Politics*, New York, 1927, pp. 93, 644; Harry F. Guggenheim, *The United States and Cuba: A Study in International Relations*, New York, 1934, p. 52.
14. *The State*, Oct. 19, 1898.
15. Day to McKinley, Nov. 19, 1898, William McKinley Papers, Library of Congress.
16. Sidney Margolies, "The Influence of Cuba in American Politics with Special Reference to the Spanish-American War and the Platt Amendment," unpublished M.A. thesis, Columbia University, 1939, p. 41.
17. Maria C. Lanzar, "The Anti-Imperialist League," unpublished Ph.D. thesis, University of Michigan, 1928, pp. 19-25.
18. Richmond *Planet*, Aug. 27, 1898.
19. Millis, *op. cit.*, p. 392.
20. New York *Evening Post*, Aug. 19, 1898; Carl Schurz, "Our Future Foreign Policy, Aug. 1898," Carl Schurz Papers, Library of Congress; Schurz to Hoar, Dec. 1, 1898, *ibid.*; Edward Atkinson to William McKinley, Aug. 25, 1898; Edward Atkinson to R. S. Ashton, Aug. 26, 1898, Edward Atkinson Papers, Massachusetts Historical Society; Andrew Carnegie, "Distant Possessions—The Parting of the Ways," *North American Review*, vol. CLXVII, August, 1898, p. 242; Robert L. Beisner, *Twelve Against Empire: The Anti-Imperialists, 1898-1900*, New York, 1968, pp. 95, 172-73; John W. Rollins, "The Anti-Imperialists and Twentieth Century American Foreign Policy," *Studies on the Left*, vol. III, 1962, p. 18; Indianapolis *News*, April 15, 1899, in "Cuba Annexation, Newspaper Clippings compiled by Robert P. Porter," scrapbook in New York Public Library. Hereinafter cited as "Cuba Annexation."
21. Richmond *Planet*, July 30, 1898.
22. *The State*, Nov. 6, 11, 13, 18, 1898.
23. Samuel Gompers, "Imperialism, Its Dangers and Wrongs," *American Federationist*, vol. V, 1898, pp. 179-80.
24. *The People*, June 26, 1898.
25. *Ibid.*, Aug. 21, 1898.
26. New York *Evening Post*, Jan. 23, 1899.

## NOTES

27. Fred H. Harrington, "The Anti-Imperialist Movement in the United States," *Mississippi Valley Historical Review*, vol. XXII, Sept. 1935, p. 215.
28. Elmer Ellis, *Henry Moore Teller, Defender of the West*, Caldwell, Idaho, 1941, p. 314.
29. *Congressional Record*, 55th Cong., 3rd Sess., p. 20.
30. *Ibid.*, pp. 325-27.
31. *The State*, Dec. 20, 1898.
32. Indianapolis *News*, April 15, 1899, in "Cuba Annexation."
33. J. A. Foraker to General James H. Wilson, July 24, 1899, James H. Wilson Papers, Library of Congress. Emphasis mine. P.S.F.

## CHAPTER XIX

## MILITARY OCCUPATION: THE BROOKE ADMINISTRATION

1. McKinley to Brooke, Dec. 22, 1898, copy in William McKinley Papers, Library of Congress.
2. *Annual Reports of the Secretary of War*, 1899-1903, Washington, 1904, pp. 131-22.
3. *Civil Report of Major General John R. Brooke, U.S. Army, Military Governor, Island of Cuba*, Washington, 1900, p. 6.
4. *The State*, Dec. 30, 1898; New York *Evening Post*, Dec. 29, 1898.
5. Teller to McKinley, Dec. 30, 1898, William McKinley Papers, Library of Congress.
6. *Civil Report of General John R. Brooke*, pp. 6-7; New York *Tribune*, Dec. 30, 1898; Healy, *op. cit.*, pp. 53-54; Ortiz, *op. cit.*, vol. I, p. 23.
7. *Civil Report of General John R. Brooke*, p. 7; Ortiz, *op. cit.*, vol. I, pp. 24-26.
8. *Civil Report of General John R. Brooke*, p. 8.
9. Ortiz, *op. cit.*, vol. I, pp. 26-28.
10. Albert G. Robinson, *Cuba and the Intervention*, New York, 1905, p. 107.
11. *Civil Report of General John R. Brooke*, p. 330.
12. *Ibid.*, p. 8.
13. Martínez Ortiz, *op. cit.*, vol. I, p. 31.
14. José Rivero Múniz, *El Movimiento Obrero durante de la primera Intervención: Apuntes para la historia de proletariado en Cuba*, Universidad de Las Vilas, 1961, p. 35.
15. *Civil Report of General John R. Brooke*, p. 9.
16. José María Cespedes, *La Intervención*, La Habana, 1901, p. 12.
17. *La Lucha* reprinted in *The State*, Feb. 5, 1899.
18. Johnson, *op. cit.*, vol. IV, p. 133; *Civil Report of General John R. Brooke*, p. 414.
19. Charles T. Andrews, "Sketches of Cuba and Porto Rico, 1899," *op. cit.*
20. *Annual Reports of the Secretary of War*, 1899-1903, pp. 18-19.
21. *Ibid.*; Healy, *op. cit.*, p. 63.
22. Charles T. Andrews, "Sketches of Cuba and Porto Rico," *op. cit.*
23. Matthews, *New-Born Cuba*, pp. 95-96, 118-34.
24. Charles T. Andrews, Sketches of Cuba and Porto Rico," *op. cit.*
25. *House Document* 2, 55th Cong., 1st Sess., vol. IV, pp. 223-32.

26. *Civil Report of General John R. Brooke*, p. 343.
27. Porter, *Report on Condition of Cuba*, p. 10.
28. Johnson, op. cit., vol. IV, pp. 155-62.
29. Foraker to Wilson, May 22, 1899, James H. Wilson Papers, Library of Congress.
30. *The State*, Nov. 22, 1898.
31. Reprinted in *ibid.*, Dec. 31, 1898.
32. Marion Wilcox, editor, *Harper's History of the War in the Philippines*, New York, 1900, p. 123.
33. *The State*, Feb. 6, 1899.
34. Adams to Elizabeth Cameron, Feb. 26, 1899, in Worthington C. Ford, *Letters of Henry Adams, 1892-1918*, Boston and New York, 1938, vol. II, p. 220.
35. Martínez Ortiz, op. cit., vol. I, p. 133.
36. Nichols, "Domestic History," op. cit., p. 167.
37. *The State*, Aug. 13, 1898.
38. Gómez de la Maza, *Máximo Gómez y la Asamblea*, Habana, 1899, p. 9.
39. Orestes Ferrara, *Mis relaciones con Máximo Gómez*, Habana, 1915, p. 220.
40. Martínez Ortiz, op. cit., vol. I, pp. 33-34; Leuchsenring, *Gómez*, p. 46.
41. Gómez, *Diario de Campaña*, p. 420.
42. *La Discusión*, Jan. 17, 1899; Martínez Ortiz, op. cit., vol. I, pp. 40-41.
43. Sterling, op. cit., p. 72.
44. Indianapolis *News*, April 15, 1899, in "Cuba Annexation."
45. New York *Evening Post*, Feb. 28, 1899.
46. Robert P. Porter, *Special Report on the Visit to General Gomez and in Relation to the Payment and Disbandonment of the Insurgent Army*, Washington, 1899.
47. *Ibid.*; Souza, *Gómez*, p. 73.
48. Porter, op. cit.
49. Aguirre, op. cit., p. 60; New York *Tribune*, Feb. 25, 1899.
50. *Civil Report of General John R. Brooke*, p. 16
51. *Actas de las Asambleas de Representantes*, vol. V, pp. 87-97.
52. *Ibid.*, pp. 68, 101-02; *The State*, March 24, 1899.
53. Salvador Cisneros Betancourt, *Appeal to the American People on Behalf of Cuba*, New York, Aug. 14, 1900, pp. 10-11.
54. *The State*, March 13, 15, 1899.
55. Aguirre, op. cit., p. 66.
56. *Civil Report of General John R. Brooke*, p. 16; *The State*, March 16, 30, 1899; Adjutant-General of the Army to Brooke, March 17, 1899, copy in William McKinley Papers, Library of Congress.
57. *Actas de las Asambleas de Representantes*, vol. V, pp. 138-45.
58. New York *Tribune*, April 4, 1899; *Congressional Record*, 55 Cong., 3rd Sess., vol. XXXII, p. 2809.
59. *The State*, April 5, 1899.
60. *Ibid.*
61. New York *Tribune*, April 17, 18, 1899; *The State*, April 18, 1899.
62. *The State*, May 27, 1899.
63. Russell A. Alger to McKinley, May 17, 1899, William McKinley Papers; *Civil Report of General John R. Brooke*, pp. 16-17.
64. *Civil Report of General John R. Brooke*, pp. 16-17.

NOTES 683

65. *New York Times*, June 7, 1899.
66. *The State*, March 13, April 14, May 19, 1899.
67. Aguirre, *op. cit.*, pp. 63-64; letter of Sergio Aguirre, Mariano, marzo 6, de 1966, in possession of author; interview with Sergio Aguirre, University of Havana, Department of History, July 27, 1966; letter of Julio Le Riverend, undated, La Habana, in possession of author; Euclides Vázquez Candela, "El 'Baragua' Que No Tuvimos," *Bohemia*, April 21, 1965, pp. 106-07.
68. Varona Guerrero, op. cit., vol. III, pp. 1704-08; Leuchsenring, *Gomez*, pp. 176-80.
69. Sterling, *op. cit.*, p. 63.
70. Brooke to H. C. Corbin, May 24, 1899, William McKinley Papers, Library of Congress.
71. *Havana Herald*, June 4, 1899; *The State*, June 5, 1899. My emphasis. P.S.F.
72. Marriott in *Review of Reviews*, Jan. 1899, p. 131; reprinted in *The State*, Jan. 11, 1899.
73. Martínez Ortiz, *op. cit.*, vol. I, p. 107; Carlos M. Trelles, *El Progreso (1902 a 1905) y el retroceso (1906 a 1922) de la republica de Cuba*, La Habana, 1923, p. 5; Portell Vilá, *op. cit.*, p. 267; Chapman, *op. cit.*, p. 105; Robinson, *op. cit.*, pp. 133-34; Johnson, *op. cit.*, vol. IV, pp. 145-55.
74. Brooke to H. C. Corbin, May 24, 1899, William McKinley Papers, Library of Congress.
75. Charles T. Andrews, "Sketches of Cuba and Porto Rico," *op. cit.*
76. *Ibid.*
77. Reprinted in *The State*, Nov. 18, 1899.
78. Rivero, *op. cit.*, pp. 42-45.
79. New York *Tribune* reprinted in *The State*, April 21, 1899.
80. The text of Ludlow's order is reprinted in Rivero, *op. cit.*, pp. 200-01.
81. Chicago *Times-Herald*, June 6, 1899.
82. Leech, *op. cit.*, p. 391.
83. Bonifacio Byrne, *Mi bandera*, La Habana, 1904, p. 35.

## CHAPTER XX

## Military Occupation: The Wood Administration

1. *The State*, March 9, 1899.
2. Foraker to Wilson, July 24, 1899, James H. Wilson Papers, Library of Congress.
3. *Civil Report of General John R. Brooke*, p. 8.
4. Charles T. Andrews, "Sketches of Cuba and Porto Rico," *op. cit.*
5. William Edwin Diez, "Opposition in the United States to American Diplomacy in the Caribbean, 1898-1902," unpublished Ph.D. thesis, University of Chicago, 1945, p. 31.
6. *Studies on the Left*, Summer, 1963, p. 4.
7. Chicago *Times-Herald*, June 9, 1899.
8. Roosevelt to Wood, July 10, 1899, Theodore Roosevelt Papers, Library of Congress.

9. Cf. Robert Bacon and James B. Scott, eds., *The Military and Colonial Policy of the United States: Addresses and Reports of Elihu Root*, Cambridge, Mass., 1916.
10. Wood to Roosevelt, July 12, 1899, Theodore Roosevelt Papers, Library of Congress.
11. Brooke to McKinley, Sept. 26, 1899, William McKinley Papers, Library of Congress.
12. Indianapolis *News*, April 15, 1899, in "Cuban Annexation."
13. Wilson to Foraker, May 12, 1899, James H. Wilson Papers, Library of Congress.
14. Wilson to Roosevelt, July 5, 1899, Theodore Roosevelt Papers, Library of Congress.
15. Wood to McKinley, April 27, 1899, William McKinley Papers, Library of Congress.
16. *New York Times*, June 24, 1899.
17. Wood to McKinley, Sept. 26, 1899, William McKinley Papers, Library of Congress.
18. Wood to McKinley, April 27, 1899, ibid.; *New York Times*, June 24, 1899.
19. Charles T. Andrews, "Sketches of Cuba and Porto Rico," *op. cit.*
20. *General Wood's Policy in Cuba is a Downright Failure*, pamphlet in Spanish signed "La Opinion Pública," Santiago de Cuba, April, 1901. Copy in Harvard College Library.
21. Roosevelt to Lodge, July 21, 1899, Theodore Roosevelt Papers, Library of Congress; Foraker to Wilson, May 20, 1899, James H. Wilson Papers, ibid.
22. Root to Roosevelt, Dec. 18, 1899, Elihu Root Papers, Library of Congress.
23. *Civil Report of General Leonard Wood for the Period from January 1 to December 31, 1901*, Washington, 1902, vol. I.
24. Wood to Root, Dec. 22, 1899, Leonard Wood Papers, Library of Congress.
25. Charles T. Andrews, "Sketches of Cuba and Porto Rico," *op. cit.*
26. Valentine, *op. cit.*, p. 32.
27. Wood to Root, Dec. 30, 1899, Leonard Wood Papers, Library of Congress. Emphasis Mine. P.S.F.
28. Gómez to Wood, Dec. 30, 1899, ibid.,
29. Wood to Root, Dec. 30, 1899, ibid.; Hagedorn, *Leonard Wood*, vol. I, p. 266.
30. Wood to Root, Dec. 30, 1899, Leonard Wood Papers, Library of Congress.
31. *The State*, July 25, 1901.
32. Chapman, *op. cit.*, p. 104; Johnson, *op. cit.*, vol. IV, pp. 155-56.
33. *The State*, July 17, 1900.
34. Antonio Iraizoz, *Outline of Educational Systems and School Conditions in the Republic of Cuba*, Habana, 1924, p. 15; *Civil Report of Wood*, 1901, vol. VII, p. 7; Fitzgibbon, *op. cit.*, pp. 45-51.
35. *The State*, Aug. 14, Dec. 5, 1898.
36. Report of Major C. W. Gorgas in *Civil Report of General Leonard Wood for the Period from January 1 to December 31, 1901*, vol. I, pp. 6-8; *The State*, April 17, 1901.
37. *The State*, March 23, 1902.
38. Fitzgibbon, *op. cit.*, p. 31; Johnson, *op. cit.*, vol. IV, pp. 162-63; Martínez Ortiz, *op. cit.*, vol. I, pp. 427-38; Trelles, *op. cit.*, p. 5; Juan M. Leiscea,

     *Historia de Cuba,* Habana, 1925, pp. 448-49; Pánfilo D. Camacho, *Estrada Palma, El Gobernante Honrado,* La Habana, n.d., pp. 181-82.
39. Hagedorn, *op. cit.,* vol. I, p. 329.
40. William Herbert Hobbs, *Leonard Wood Administrator, Soldier, and Citizen,* New York, 1920, p. 67. See also Hon. James Bryce, "Some Reflections on the State of Cuba," *North American Review,* vol. CLXXIV, 1902, p. 456.
41. Albert G. Robinson, "Cuban Self-Government," *The Independent,* Dec. 13, 1900, p. 2968; "Our Legacy to the Cuban Republic," *Forum,* June, 1902, p. 456.
42. Jenks, *op. cit.,* p. 65.
43. Carleton Beals, *The Crime of Cuba,* Philadelphia, 1933, p. 160.
44. *New York Times,* June 24, 1899,
45. Herminio Portell Vilá, *Historia de Cuba en sus relaciones con les Estados Unidos y España,* Habana, 1941, vol.IV, p. 9.
46. Healy, *op. cit.,* p. 186.
47. *The State,* Jan. 30, 1901; Wood to Root, June 18, 1900, Jan. 8, 1901, Elihu Root Papers, Library of Congress.
48. New York *Evening Post* reprinted in *The State,* Jan. 30, 1901.
49. Bacon and Scott, *op. cit.,* pp. 190-91.
50. R. H. Jesse to G. K. Harroun, Dec. 1, 1898, Cuban Educational Association Papers, Library of Congress.
51. *The State,* April 23, 1900.
52. *The State,* Feb. 4, 1899.
53. Pamphlet dated August 24, 1900. Copy in Harvard College Library.
54. Wood to Root, Jan. 13, 1900, Elihu Root Papers, Library of Congress.

# CHAPTER XXI

# U.S. Economic Penetration of Cuba During the Occupation

1. Gonzalez, *op. cit.,* p. 52.
2. New York *World,* July 20, 1898. "Capital will be the next invasion of Cuba," read a headline in the Springfield *Republican* of Aug. 12, 1898.
3. Charles Morris, *Our Island Empire,* Philadelphia, 1899, pp. 162-64.
4. Matthews, *op. cit.,* pp. 204-06; Jenks, *op. cit.,* p. 67; Springfield *Republican,* Aug. 10, 1898. See also the later statement of Herbert G. Squires to John Hay, Sept. 17, 1904, Dispatches from U.S. Ministers to Cuba, NA.
5. *National Business League, Opinions of United States Consuls, Prominent Business Men and Educators on the Establishment of Permanent International Expositions and Trade Courts in the Great Commercial Centers of the World in Reply to Letters Suggested by Volney W. Foster,* Chicago, 1902, p. 12.
6. Charles T. Andrews, "Sketches of Cuba and Porto Rico," *op. cit.*
7. *Lumbermen's Review,* reprinted in *The State,* July 4, 1898.
8. Marriott in *The State,* Jan. 11, 1899.
9. Washington *Evening Star,* Feb. 10, 1898, and reprinted in *Congressional Record,* 55th Cong., 3rd Sess., vol. XXXIII, p. 2807.

10. Foraker to James H. Wilson, July 24, 1899, James H. Wilson Papers, Library of Congress.
11. *Congressional Record*, 55th Cong., 3rd Sess., vol. XXXII, p. 2572.
12. *Ibid.*, pp. 2807-11; Healy, *op. cit.*, pp. 82-84.
13. *Congressional Record*, 55th Cong., 3rd Sess., vol. XXXII, p. 2812.
14. Foraker to Wilson, July 24, 1899, James H. Wilson Papers, Library of Congress.
15. *The People*, Dec. 19, 1900.
16. Jenks, *op. cit.*, pp. 69-70; *The State*, Feb. 12, 1901; Cisneros, *Appeal to the American People*, . . . pp. 1-7.
17. Wood to Foraker, Dec. 21, 1900; Wood to Root, Dec. 22, 1900, both in Elihu Root Papers, Library of Congress.
18. Jenks, *op. cit.*, p. 162.
19. Wichita (Kansas) *Eagle*, July 9, 1899, in "Cuba Annexation."
20. Enrique H. Moreno Pla, *Gonzalo de Quesada, Estadista*, La Habana, 1962, p. 17.
21. Hopkins to Spooner, March 14, 1900, John C. Spooner Papers, Library of Congress. Emphasis in original. P.S.F.
22. New York *Sun*, July 12, 1900. See also *The State*, Nov. 9, 1900.
23. New York *Sun*, Dec. 8, 1900.
24. Philip C. Jessup, *Elihu Root*, New York, 1938, vol. I, pp. 296-98.
25. Foraker to Wood, Jan. 7, 1901, Leonard Wood Papers, Library of Congress.
26. *New York Times*, Dec. 17, 1900.
27. Jenks, *op. cit.*, p. 153.
28. *The State*, Sept. 12, 1898.
29. *Commission on Cuban Affairs*, pp. 1-2.
30. Porter, *Industrial Cuba*, pp. 198-99.
31. J. K. Elwell to Clara Barton, Nov. 18, 1898, Clara Barton Papers, Box 51, Library of Congress.
32. Albert G. Robinson in *The State*, June 5, 1902.
33. Wilson to Adjutant-General, Division of Cuba, May 9, 1899, Records of the U.S. Military Government of Cuba, NA; Brooke's comment on Wilson's letter in *ibid.*; Brooke to General H. C. Corbin, May 24, 1899, copy in William McKinley Papers, Library of Congress; *Civil Report of Major General John R. Brooke*, pp. 12-13; Healy, *op. cit.*, pp. 93-94.
34. Report of the Department of Agriculture, Commerce, and Industry, March 5, 1901, in *Annual Reports of the War Department for the Fiscal Year Ended June 30, 1901*, Part 4, pp. 4-9; Healy, *op. cit.*, p. 190.
35. *Report of General Wood for the Period from January 1 to May 20, 1902*, Part i, p. 13.
36. *Civil Report of General Leonard Wood*, 1902, Vol. I, p. 196.
37. Porter, *Report on Cuba*. p. 11.
38. New York *Daily People*, June 18, 1901.
39. Jenks, *op. cit.*, p. 154.
40. *Ibid.*, p. 153.
41. Charles T. Andrews, "Sketches of Cuba and Porto Rico," *op. cit.*
42. Jenks, *op. cit.*, pp. 130-31.
43. *Ibid.*
44. *Ibid.*, p. 130.

45. *The State*, Sept. 10, 1901; May 2, 1902; *Congressional Record*, 57th Cong., 1st Sess., p. 4423.
46. Jenks, *op. cit.*, pp. 131-32; Weigle, *op. cit.*, p. 260.
47. Weigle, *op. cit.*, p. 260.
48. Ramiro Guerra y Sánchez, *Sugar and Society in the Caribbean; An Economic History of Cuban Agriculture*, New Haven, 1964, pp. 73-74.
49. Jenks, *op. cit.*, p. 141.
50. *Ibid.*
51. *The State*, Sept. 28, 1898.
52. Concord (New Hampshire) *Patriot*, Nov. 9, 1899, in "Cuba Annexation."
53. Rochester *Democrat-Chronicle*, Nov. 9, 1899, in *ibid.*
54. Quoted by Nicolas Guillen at First National Writers and Artists Congress, Havana, *Cultural Bulletin*, Republic of Cuba, vol. I, No. 4, 1961.
55. Jenks, *op. cit.*, pp. 141-48.
56. *Ibid.*
57. Bernard Fernandez, in Marquette (Michigan) *Journal*, Oct. 8, 1900, in "Cuba Annexation."
58. Jenks, *op. cit.*, pp. 156-58; *Daily People*, Jan. 29, 1902.
59. New York *Evening Post*, May 23, 1901.
60. Jenks, *op. cit.*, pp. 160; *Daily People*, June 1, 1901.
61. Gonzalo de Quesada, *Cuba*, Washington, 1905, pp. 231-33; Victor H. Olmsted and Henry Gannett, *Cuba: Population, History, and Resources*, Washington, 1909, p. 78.
62. "The Cuban Revolution: Fall of Machado," *Foreign Policy Reports*, Nov. 18, 1935, p. 250.

## CHAPTER XXII

## The Cuban Labor Movement During the Occupation

1. José Rivero Muñiz, *El Movimiento Obrero durante la primera Intervención: Apuntes par la historia de proletariado en Cuba*, Universidad de Las Villa, 1961, p. 41.
2. *Civil Report of Major General Leonard Wood, December 20, 1899 to December 31, 1900*, n.d., vol. I, p.. 8-13, 79-80.
3. These figures are based on the estimate of the census made by Victor S. Clark in his study, "Labor Conditions in Cuba," *Bulletin of the Department of Labor*, No. 41, Washington, July, 1902, p. 689.
4. Charles Albert Page, "The Development of Organized Labor in Cuba," unpublished Ph.D. thesis, University of California, 1952, p. 38.
5. Rivero, *op. cit.*, pp. 11-12.
6. *Ibid.*, p. 21.
7. Clark, *op. cit.*, p. 677.
8. *Ibid.*, p. 678.
9. Clark, *op. cit.*, p. 748.
10. Rivero, *op. cit.*, p. 11.
11. Clark, *op. cit.*, p. 665.
12. *The State*, Feb. 4, 1899; Charles T. Andrews, *op. cit.*

13. Rivero, op. cit., p. 31.
14. Ibid., pp. 37-39.
15. Quoted in ibid., p. 55.
16. Charles T. Andrews, op. cit.
17. Rivero, op. cit., p. 82; The State, April 10, 1899.
18. Rivero, op. cit., pp. 80-85.
19. Ibid., p. 84.
20. Ibid., p. 114.
21. José Rivero Muñiz, El Primer Partido Socialista Cubano, Universidad Central de Las Villas, 1962, pp. 38-79, 99-104; Joaquin Ordoqui, Elementos Para la Historia del Movimiento Obrero en Cuba, La Habana, 1961, p. 15.
22. Rivero, El Movimiento Obrero, . . . op. cit., pp. 92-108. See also Patria, Sept. 24, 26, 1899. All references to Rivero hereinafter are to El Movimiento Obrero. . . .
23. Bliss to Chafee, Aug. 26, 1899, "Strikes in Cuba," Records of the United States Military Government of Cuba, Selected Documents Concerning Strikes in Cuba, 1899-1908, NA. Hereinafter cited as "Strikes in Cuba," NA.
24. Rivero, op. cit., pp. 109-16; Annual Report of Brigadier-General William S. Ludlow, United States Army, Military Governor Havana, "Strikes," October 4, 1899, pp. 184-85.
25. Rivero, op. cit., pp. 116-20.
26. Ibid., pp. 123-24.
27. Ibid., p. 125.
28. Ibid., pp. 124-25.
29. Ibid., pp. 126, 133.
30. Ibid., pp. 127-28.
31. Rivero, op. cit., pp. 129-32; The People, Oct. 8, 1899.
32. El Diario de la Marina, Havana, Sept. 28, 1899; Rivero, op. cit., pp. 147.
33. Patria, Sept. 28, 1899; Rivero, op. cit., pp. 147-48.
34. Rivero, op. cit., pp. 132-33.
35. Ibid., pp. 134-35.
36. Ibid., p. 135.
37. Ibid., pp. 141-42.
38. Ibid., pp. 142-50.
39. Ibid., pp. 152, 149-50.
40. Ibid., p. 149.
41. Ibid., p. 160; Page, op. cit., p. 39.
42. Annual Report of Brigadier-General William S. Ludlow, op. cit., pp. 186-87.
43. The Carpenter, Oct. 1899, p. 4; Coast Seamen's Journal, Dec. 27, 1899, p. 4; Labor Advocate, Sept. 30, 1899.
44. The People, Oct. 1, 1899.
45. Proceedings, General Assembly of the Knights of Labor, "Committee on Legislation," Boston, November 14-23, 1899, p. 79.
46. Proceedings, A.F. of L. Convention, 1899, p. 16.
47. Philip S. Foner, History of the Labor Movement in the United States, vol. II, New York, 1955, pp. 379-80.
48. Samuel Gompers, "A Trip to Cuba," American Federationist, vol. II, March, 1900, p. 61.

49. *Proceedings*, A.F. of L. Convention, 1900, p. 30.
50. Hermann Hagedorn, *Leonard Wood*, New York, 1931, vol. I,p. 275.
51. Gompers, "A Trip to Cuba," *op. cit.*, pp. 59-60.
52. Rito Estaban, *Sobre el movimiento Obrero de America y Europa*, La Habana, 1946, p. 87.
53. Gompers, "A Trip to Cuba," *op. cit.*, p. 62.
54. *Ibid.*, p. 62.
55. Rivero, *op. cit.*, pp. 175-77.
56. Mayor Frias to Richards, Adjutant General, Havana, Feb. 23, 24, 1900; Frias to Wood, Feb. 23, 27, 1900, "Strikes in Cuba," NA.
57. Edwin F. Atkins to Wood, Feb. 21, 26, 1900; Frias to Wood, Feb. 27, 1900, *ibid.*
58. Lt. Stokes to Adj. General, Havana, Jan. 1, 2, 3, 4, 1901; Wood to Lt. Stokes, Jan. 2, 1901; Capt. Foltz to Adjutant General, Jan. 4, 1901, *ibid.*; *The People*, Jan. 13, 1901.
59. *The People*, Jan. 13, 1901.
60. *National Labor Standard*, Jan. 10, 1901.
61. For a detailed discussion of the National Civic Federation, see Philip S. Foner, *History of the Labor Movement in the United States*, vol. III, New York, 1964, pp. 61-110.
62. Lt. W. W. Wallace to Adjutant General, Matanzas, Feb. 14, 1901; Hickey, by command of Major General Wood, to Col. Noyes, Feb. 8, 1901; Noyes to Adjutant General Department, Matanzas, Feb. 9, 11, 12, 1901, "Strikes in Cuba," NA.
63. *New Yorker Volkszeitung*, 29 Mai, 1901; *The Worker* (New York), June 2, 1901.
64. Unsigned letter to Chief of the Detective Bureau, Havana, Feb. 19, 1901, "Strikes in Cuba," NA.
65. *Daily People*, Feb. 19, 1901; Commanding Acting Chief Rasco, Rural Guard, to General Wood, March 14, 1901; Capt. Walter B. Barker, to Lt. Frank McCoy, March 20, 1901, "Strikes in Cuba," NA.
66. R. G. Ward to Col. H. L. Scott, Aug. 11, 1901; Scott to Adjutant General, Sept. 5, 1901, "Strikes in Cuba," NA.
67. Ricardo Puertas in *El Combate*, Aug. 6, 1901, original newspaper clipping in Spanish, in "Strikes in Cuba," NA.
68. Louis V. Cavaiarc to General Wood, Departamento de Policía de la Cuidad de la Habana, Sección Secreta, Feb. 15, 19, 1901; Juan Rios to Wood, May 14, 1901; Unsigned letter to the Chief of the Detective Bureau, Havana, Feb. 19, 1901, "Strikes in Cuba," NA.
69. Rivero, *op. cit.*, p. 165.
70. Clark, *op. cit.*, p. 678.
71. La Habana, 1936, pp. 24-25.
72. Rivero, *op. cit.*, p. 168.
73. *Daily People*, Feb. 19, 1901.

## CHAPTER XXIII

## Failure of the Annexationist Drive

1. Janet Smith, editor, *Mark Twain on the Damned Human Race*, New York, 1962, pp. 14, 20. For a study of Mark Twain's evolution into the leading anti-imperialist writer of this period, see Philip S. Foner, *Mark Twain: Social Critic*, New York, 1958, pp. 239-308.
2. Robert P. Porter, *Industrial Cuba*, New York, 1899, pp. 32-46. See also Robert P. Porter, "The Future of Cuba," *North American Review*, vol. CLXIII, April, 1899, pp. 418-23.
3. Tom's River (New Jersey) *Courier*, June 29, 1899, "Cuban Annexation."
4. Boston *Globe*, June 20, 1899, "Cuba Annexation."
5. Astoria (Oregon) *Oregonian*, June 28, 1899, *ibid*.
6. Chicago *Tribune*, Aug. 7, 1899 and other papers of that date in *ibid*.
7. Savannah *Press* quoted in *The State*, Oct. 3, 1898.
8. New York *Evening Post*, Oct. 11, 1898; *The State*, Oct. 3, 1898.
9. Worcester (Mass.) *Gazette*, Aug. 14, 1899, "Cuba Annexation."
10. Bellert (Illinois) *Democrat*, Aug. 15, 1899; Lansing (Michigan) *Journal*, Aug. 7, 1899, "Cuban Annexation";
11. Binghamton (N. Y.) *Leader*, April 15, 1899 and other newspapers of that date, "Cuban Annexation."
12. *The State*, April 22, 1899.
13. Chicago *Chronicle*, Sept. 12, 1899, "Cuban Annexation."
14. Binghamton (N. Y.) *Leader*, April 15, 1899, "Cuba Annexation."
15. Chicago *Tribune*, Nov. 26, 1899 and other papers under that date, "Cuba Annexation"; *Workers' Call*, Nov. 25, 1899.
16. Cf. Chicago *Times-Herald*, Nov. 22, 1899; Chicago *Inter-Ocean*, Nov. 20, 1899; St. Paul *Pioneer Press*, Dec. 3, 1899; Kansas City *Star*, Nov. 11, 1899; Boston *Herald*, Nov. 12, 1899; St. Louis *Star*, Oct. 12, 1899; New Haven *Leader*, Sept. 25, 1899; Cleveland *Leader*, Nov. 15, 1899; Dallas *News*, Dec. 12, 1899; Boise *Statesman*, Dec. 1, 1899; Portland *Oregonian*, Oct. 12, 1899, all in "Cuba Annexation."
17. New York *Evening Post*, Nov. 9, 1899; New York *Tribune*, Nov. 25, 1899; Richmond *Times*, Nov. 9, 1899; St. Louis *Globe-Democrat*, Nov. 11, 1899, last two in "Cuba Annexation."
18. Foraker to Wilson, Nov. 20, 1899, James H. Wilson Papers, Library of Congress.
19. Healy, *op. cit.*, p. 116.
20. *La Discusión*, Nov. 14, 1899; *Patria*, Nov. 18, 1899; *La Tarde*, Havana, clippings from original papers and English translations in Records of the United States Military Government in Cuba, 6462, National Archives.
21. Messages and telegrams in Civil Governor of Santa Clara Province to Secretary of State and Government, Nov. 30, 1899 and Dec. 1, 1899; Civil Governor of Havana Province to Secretary of State and Government, Nov. 29, 1899; Civil Governor of Matanzas Province to Secretary of State and Government, Dec. 1, 1899; Secretary of State and Government to General Brooke, Dec. 1, 2, 5, 1899, all in Records of the United States Military Government, National Archives. See also Washington *Post*, Nov. 27, 1899.

## NOTES

22. *La Discusión*, Nov. 29, 1899, clipping from original paper and English translation in *ibid*.
23. *Washington Post*, Nov. 29, 1899.
24. Rathbone to Root, Dec. 4, 1899, Elihu Root Papers, Library of Congress.
25. *New York Tribune*, Dec. 4, 1899.
26. *Annual Report of the Secretary of War, 1899-1903*, pp. 41-44. Emphasis mine, P.S.F.
27. *The State*, Dec. 3, 1899.
28. See reprints of Cuban newspapers in *New York Tribune*, Dec. 4, 1899.
29. *New York Tribune*, Dec. 6, 1899. Emphasis mine. P.S.F.
30. *The State*, Dec. 6, 1899.
31. Wilson to Goldwyn Smith, Dec. 27, 1899, James H. Wilson Papers, Library of Congress.
32. *Philadelphia Times*, May 2, 1900; *Detroit Free Press*, June 15, 1900, and and other papers in "Cuba Annexation."
33. *New York Times*, April 2, 1900; *New York Sun*, April 13, 1900.
34. Richard B. Olney, "The Growth of Our Foreign Policy," *Atlantic Monthly*, vol. LXXXV, March, 1900, pp. 289-301.
35. Cf. newspapers of March-April, 1900 in "Cuba Annexation."
36. *The State*, May 5, 18, 1900.
37. Wilson to Whitelaw Reid, Aug. 3, 1900, James H. Wilson Papers, Library of Congress.
38. *The State*, March 29, 1900.
39. See newspapers of April, 1900 in "Cuba Annexation."
40. Theodore P. Wright, Jr., "United States Electoral Intervention in Cuba," *Inter-American Economic Affairs*, vol. XXII, Winter, 1959, p. 54.
41. *St. Louis Globe-Democrat*, March 31, 1900, in "Cuba Annexation."
42. *The State*, April 20, 21, 1900.
43. *New York Tribune*, April 22, 1900.
44. Root to Paul Dana, Jan. 16, 1900, in Jessup, *op. cit.*, vol. I, p. 305.
45. Wood to Root, Jan. 13, Feb. 6, 23, 1900, Elihu Root Papers, Library of Congress.
46. *Civil Report of General Leonard Wood for 1900*, vol. I, part 1, pp. 36-38.
47. Healy, *op. cit.*, pp. 131-32.
48. *New York Tribune*, June 16, 1900; Wright, Jr., *op. cit.*, pp. 55.
49. *The State*, June 17, 1900.
50. *Ibid*.
51. *Civil Report of General Leonard Wood for 1900*, vol. I, part 1, p. 52; Root to Wood, June 20, 1900, Elihu Root Papers, Library of Congress.
52. Reprinted in *The State*, June 24, 1900.
53. *The State*, June 23, 1900.
54. Hopkins to Spooner, John C. Spooner Papers, Library of Congress.
55. Platt to Atkins, June 11, 1900, marked "Personal and Confidential," Orville H. Platt Papers, Connecticut State Library.
56. *The State*, March 29, 1900.
57. *New York Evening Post*, Dec. 5, 1899.

## CHAPTER XXIV

### THE CUBAN CONSTITUTIONAL CONVENTION

1. Wood to Root, Feb. 16, 1900, Elihu Root Papers, Library of Congress.
2. Rodríguez to McKinley, June 21, 1900, William McKinley Papers, Library of Congress.
3. George S. Boutwell, "The President's Policy of War and Conquest Abroad, Degradation of Labor at Home," *Liberty Tract* #7, Chicago, 1900, pp. 8, 13.
4. Moorfield Story, "Is It Right?" *Liberty Tract* #8, Chicago, 1900; Edwin B. Smith, "Republic or Empire with Glimpses of 'Criminal Aggression,'" *Liberty Tract* #9, Chicago, 1900; Carl Schurz, "For the Republic of Washington and Lincoln," *Liberty Tract* #10, Chicago, 1900. These addresses had been delivered at the League's Philadelphia conference, Feb. 22-23, 1900.
5. David Starr Jordan to Bryan, Feb. 7, March 7, 1900; Ewing Winslow to Bryan, July 24, 1900, William Jennings Bryan Papers, Library of Congress.
6. James E. Runcie, "American Misgovernment in Cuba," *North American Review*, vol. CLXXX, Feb. 1900, pp. 284-94.
7. Joseph L. Bristow, *Fraud and Politics at the Turn of the Century*, New York, 1952, pp. 98-130.
8. *Social Democrat Herald*, May 26, 1900.
9. Reprinted in *The State*, May 26, 1900.
10. *Congressional Record*, 56th Cong., 1st Sess., vol. XXXIII, pp. 5591-96.
11. Platt to Wood, June 1, 1900, Leonard Wood Papers, Library of Congress.
12. Wood to Root, June 3, 1900, Elihu Root Papers, Library of Congress. See also Wood to Root, June 21, 1900; Wood to McKinley, June 22, 1900; Wood to Teller, June 21, 1900; Wood to Aldrich, June 21, 1900, copies in Leonard Wood Papers, Library of Congress.
13. Wood to Root, June 18, 1900, Elihu Root Papers, Library of Congress.
14. Philip S. Foner, *Mark Twain: Social Critic*, p. 259.
15. Wood to Lodge, Aug. 8, 1900; Wood to Root, July 6, 1900, copies in Leonard Wood Papers, Library of Congress.
16. Wood to Roosevelt, April 20, 1900, Theodore Roosevelt Papers, Library of Congress; Healy, *op. cit.*, p. 146.
17. *Chicago Record*, July 7, 1900.
18. Kirk H. Porter, *National Party Platforms*, New York, 1924, pp. 211-34.
19. Wood to Henry Cabot Lodge, Aug. 8, 1900, copy in Leonard Wood Papers, Library of Congress.
20. *House Document No. 1*, 55th Cong., 2nd Sess., p. 358; Ortiz, *op. cit.*, vol. I, pp. 161-62.
21. *The State*, May 28, 1900.
22. Rubens, *Liberty*, pp. 400.
23. *House Document No. 1*, 55th Cong., 2nd Sess., p. 358.
24. *New York Times*, Aug. 6, 1900.
25. *The Nation*, Aug. 2, 1900, p. 85.
26. *New York Evening Post*, Aug. 1, 1900.
27. *The State*, Aug. 3, 1900.
28. *Ibid.*, Aug. 8, 1900.

29. *Daily People*, Aug. 29, 1900.
30. Cisneros, *op. cit.*, pp. 15-16.
31. Wood to McKinley, Aug. 31, 1900, copy in Leonard Wood Papers, Library of Congress; Wood to Root, Sept. 8, 16, 1900, Elihu Root Papers, Library of Congress.
32. Wood to Root, Aug. 13, 1900, Elihu Root Papers, Libarry of Congress; Wright, Jr., *op. cit.*, p. 55; *The State*, Aug. 27, 1900; *New York Times*, Aug. 27, 1900; *Daily People*, Sept. 4, 1900; Cisneros, *op. cit.*, pp. 15-16.
33. Martínez Ortiz, *op. cit.*, vol. I, pp. 178-79.
34. *New York Times*, Sept. 19, 1900; *Daily People*, Oct. 26, 1900.
35. Wood to Root, Sept. 26, 1900, Elihu Root Papers, Library of Congress.
36. *The Nation*, Oct. 25, 1900, p. 324.
37. Leonard Wood, "The Cuban Convention," *Independent*, Nov. 1, 1900, p. 2605.
38. *New York Times*, Nov. 6, 1900.
39. *House Document No. 1*, 55th Cong., 2nd Sess., p. 359; Sterling, *op. cit.*, pp. 76-77.
40. *Daily People*, Nov. 6, 1900.
41. *New York Times*, Nov. 6, 1900; Feb. 8, 1901.
42. *The State*, Nov. 6, 1900.
43. *Daily People*, Nov. 7, 1900.
44. *New York Times*, Nov. 7, 1900.
45. Chicago *Inter-Ocean*, Nov. 7, 1900.
46. *The State*, Nov. 9, 1900.
47. Philadelphia *Ledger*, Nov. 8, 1900.
48. *Daily People*, Nov. 7, 10, 1900.
49. Leopoldo Herrego Estuch, *Juan Gualberto Gómez: Un Gran Inconforme*, La Habana, 1954, pp. 155-57.
50. María Virtudes Morán, "Church and State in Cuba," unpublished M.A. thesis, Columbia University, 1950, pp. 44-45.
51. *A Treaty of Peace between the United States and Spain*, Protocol No. 20, Conference of December 6, 1898.
52. C. M. Pepper, *To-Morrow in Cuba*, p. 268; *Civil Report of Major General John R. Brooke*, p. 15.
53. *Civil Report of Major General John R. Brooke*, pp. 13-18.
54. *Civil Report of Brigadier-General Leonard Wood . . . for the period December 20, 1899, to December 31, 1900*, vol. I, pp. 80-86; Moran, *op. cit.*, pp. 55-56.
55. *Diario de Sesiones de la Convención Constituyente*, Número 16, p. 164. 25 de enero de 1900.
56. Herrego, *op. cit.*, pp. 158-60.
57. Chapman, *op. cit.*, p. 134. For a discussion of the problem in Latin America, see Lloyd Mecham, *Church and State in Latin America*, Chapel Hill, North Carolina, 1934.
58. *The State*, Dec. 30, 1900.
59. See, for example, Herrego, *op. cit.*, pp. 160-61.
60. *Constitution of the Republic of Cuba*, Havana, February 21, 1901.
61. New York *Journal*, Jan. 28, 1901.
62. *Daily People*, Feb. 5, 1901.
63. *New York Times*, Dec. 4, 1900.

64. "Report of the Secretary of War, 1901," 57th Cong., 1st Sess., *House Document*, vol. 2, p. 49; *The State*, Nov. 28, 1901.
65. *The State*, Dec. 28, 1900.
66. *Review of Reviews*, vol. XXII, Dec. 1900, p. 708.

## CHAPTER XXV

### Origin of the Platt Amendment

1. Wood to Root, Jan. 4, 1901, Elihu Root Papers, Library of Congress; copies of letters to Aldrich, Foraker, and Platt in Leonard Wood Papers, *ibid*.
2. Root to Wood, Jan. 9, 1901, Leonard Wood Papers, Library of Congress.
3. Root to John Hay, Jan. 11, 1901, Elihu Root Papers, Library of Congress. Emphasis mine. P.S.F.
4. *The State*, Jan. 15, 1901.
5. *Ibid*.
6. Philadelphia *North American*, Feb. 2, 1901.
7. *The State*, Feb. 4, 1901.
8. *Ibid*.
9. Orville H. Platt to Wood, Jan. 18, 1901, Leonard Wood Papers, Library of Congress.
10. Henry Cabot Lodge to Wood, Jan. 15, 1901, *ibid*.
11. *Daily People*, Feb. 1, 1901.
12. Louis Arthur Coolidge, *Orville H. Platt, An Old Fashioned Senator*, New York, 1910, p. 338.
13. Leon Burr Richardson, *William E. Chandler, Republican*, New York, 1940, pp. 604-05.
14. Platt to Root, Feb. 5, 1901. Elihu Root Papers, Library of Congress.
15. Washington *Post*, Feb. 8, 1901.
16. Root to Wood, Feb. 9, 1901, Leonard Wood Papers, Library of Congress.
17. *Ibid*.
18. Hagedorn, *op. cit.*, p. 350.
19. Robinson, *Cuba and the Intervention*, p. 236.
20. Wood to Root, Feb. 25, 1901, Elihu Root Papers, Library of Congress.
21. Wood to Diego Tamayo, Feb. 21, 1901, copy in Leonard Wood Papers, Library of Congress.
22. Wood to Root, Feb. 24, 1901, Elihu Root Papers, Library of Congress.
23. *The State*, Feb. 22, 1901.
24. New York *Sun*, Feb. 25, 1901.
25. *The State*, Feb. 17, 1901; *Daily People*, Feb. 18, 1901.
26. *Daily People*, Feb. 27, 1901.
27. Wood to Root, Feb. 27, 1901, Elihu Root Papers, Library of Congress.
28. Pánfilo D. Camacho, *Estrada Palma, el Gobernante Honrado*, La Habana, pp. 175-76.
29. *The State*, Feb. 27, 1901; *Daily People*, Feb. 27, 1901.
30. Healy, *op. cit.*, p. 174.
31. Benigno Souza, *Máximo Gómez, el generalísimo*, La Habana, n.d., p. 286.
32. Horrego, *op. cit.*, p. 161.

## NOTES

33. "Report on the Relations which ought to Exist between Cuba and the United States, presented by the respective Committee, February 26-27, 1901," copy in Elihu Root Papers, Library of Congress. See also, Robinson, Cuba and the Intervention, p. 238; Ortiz, op. cit., vol. I, pp. 272-77.
34. Daily People, Feb. 28, 1901.
35. Wood to Root, Feb. 27, 1901, Elihu Root Papers, Library of Congress.
36. Daily People, March 2, 1901.
37. Harry F. Guggenheim, The United States and Cuba, New York, 1934, p. 74.
38. The State, June 3, 1901.
39. Congressional Record, 56th Cong., 2nd Sess., p. 2954.
40. Both the first draft marked "Preliminary," and the second marked in Platt's handwriting "Propositions Submitted to the President by me," are in the Orville H. Platt Papers, Connecticut State Library, Hartford.
41. Orville H. Platt, "The Pacification of Cuba," Independent, vol. LIII, June 27, 1901, p. 1467.
42. Platt to John H. Flagg, Jan. 18, 1904, Orville H. Platt Papers, Connecticut State Library, Hartford.
43. See also Coolidge, op. cit., p. 353.
44. Platt to Wood, April 21, 1901, Leonard Wood Papers, Library of Congress.
45. Walter Wellman, "Elihu Root: A Character Sketch," Review of Reviews, vol. XXIV, Jan. 1904, p. 38.
46. Jessup, op. cit., p. 311.
47. Quoted in Hagedorn, Leonard Wood, Vol. I, p. 421.
48. Joseph B. Foraker, Notes of a Busy Life, Cincinnati, 1917, vol. II, p. 352.
49. Coolidge, op. cit., p. 352.

## CHAPTER XXVI

## Congress Adopts but Public Opinion Rejects the Amendment

1. Congressional Record, 56th Cong., 2nd Sess., vol. XXXIV, p. 3025.
2. Ibid.
3. Ibid., pp. 3036-42.
4. Ibid., pp. 3145-51.
5. Ibid., pp. 3147-52.
6. Coolidge, op. cit., p. 344.
7. Congressional Record, 56th Cong., 2nd Sess., vol. XXXIV, pp. 3132-34.
8. Ibid., pp. 3145-46.
9. The State, Feb. 4, 1901.
10. Congressional Record, 56th Cong., 2nd Sess., vol. XXXIV, p. 3132-35.
11. Ibid., pp. 3151-52, and World Almanac 1901 which lists the party affiliations of the Senators, and Eric Foner, "The Platt Amendment," unpublished paper, 1962, Columbia University Seminar, p. 29.
12. Congressional Record, 56th Cong., 2nd Sess., vol. XXXIV, p. 3335.
13. Ibid., p. 3340.
14. Ibid., pp. 3340, 3341, 3347, 3380.

15. Ibid., pp. 3332, 3334, 3341, 3348, 3349, 3356.
16. Ibid., pp. 3331-36; *New York Times*, March 2, 1901.
17. *Congressional Record*, 57th Cong., 1st Sess., p. 3.
18. Root to Wood, March 2, 1901, Leonard Wood Papers, Library of Congress.
19. *New York Tribune*, March 6, 1901.
20. Ibid., March 1, 2, 1901; *New York Evening Post*, March 4, 1901; *The State*, March 6, 8, 1901.
21. *The State*, March 10, 18, 1901.
22. "Democratic Responsibility," *Journal of the Knights of Labor*, March, 1901.
23. Root to Wood, March 2, 1901, Leonard Wood Papers, Library of Congress.
24. *Literary Digest*, vol. XXII, No. 10, March 9, 1901, pp. 273-74; *Philadelphia Press*, March 3, 1901.
25. Coolidge, *op. cit.*, pp. 348-49.
26. Orville H. Platt, "The Pacification of Cuba," *Independent*, June 27, 1901, p. 1467.
27. Albert J. Beveridge, "Cuba and Congress," *North American Review*, April, 1901, pp. 545, 550.
28. Robinson, *Cuba and the Intervention*, pp. 247-48.
29. *Public Opinion*, March 7, 1901, p. 293.
30. Ibid.
31. Reprinted in *New York World*, March 1, 1901.
32. Reprinted in *ibid*.
33. *New York Evening Post*, Feb. 26, May 2, 1901; *Public Opinion*, March 7, 1901, p. 293.
34. *New York World*, March 10, 1901.
35. *Public Opinion*, March 7, 1901, p. 293.
36. *The State*, Feb. 26, March 1, 5, 1901. See also, *Public Opinion*, March 7, 1901, p. 293.
37. *The State*, March 5, 1901.
38. *Public Opinion*, March 7, 1901, p. 292.
39. Reprinted in *New York World*, March 11, 1901.
40. *Chicago Times-Herald*, March 3, 1901; *Public Oponion*, March 7, 1901, p. 292.
41. Reprinted in *Journal of Knights of Labor*, March, 1901.
42. *The People*, March 3, 1901.
43. *Journal of the Knights of Labor*, Feb., March, 1901.
44. *The Railway Conductor*, May, 1901.
45. *Social Democratic Herald*, May 9, 1901.
46. *The Challenge*, March 27, 1901.
47. *Journal of the Knights of Labor*, March, 1901.
48. "A Startling Program. Vast Scheme of World Dominion Outlined by a Republican Leader," *National Labor Standard*, May 23, 1901.
49. "The New Imperialism," *Railroad Trainmen's Journal*, April, 1901.
50. H. Wayne Morgan, *William McKinley and His America*, p. 449.
51. Edwin Lehman Johnson, Columbia, in *The State*, March 7, 1901.
52. *The Worker*, April 28, 1901.
53. *Springfield Republican*, March 29, 1901.
54. *The State*, March 10, 1901.

## CHAPTER XXVII
## Cuba Resists

1. *New York Times*, March 2, 1901; Albert G. Robinson, "Some Cuban Opinions," *Independent*, May 9, 1901, p. 1056.
2. Emilio Roig de Leuchsenring, *Historia de la Enmienda Platt*, La Habana, 1961, vol. I, p. 163.
3. Wood to Root, March 2, 1901, Elihu Root Papers, Library of Congress.
4. Root to Wood, March 2, 1901, Leonard Wood Papers, Library of Congress.
5. *La Discusión*, March 4, 1901 reprinted in Leuchsenring, *Historia de la Enmienda Platt*, vol. I, pp. 151-57; *New York Tribune*, March 3, 1901.
6. *New York Evening Post*, March 8, 1901; J. B. White to McKinley, March 6, 1901, William McKinley Papers, Library of Congress.
7. *Daily People*, March 7, 1901.
8. Robinson, "Some Cuban Opinions," *op. cit.*, p. 1059.
9. Leuchsenring, *Historia de la Enmienda Platt*, vol. I, p. 160.
10. *Alma Cubana o La Enmienda Platt*, Biblioteca Cubana, 1901 Copy in Harvard College Library.
11. Robinson, *Cuba and the Intervention*, p. 250.
12. *New York Evening Post*, April 16, 1901.
13. Reprinted in *The State*, April 10, 1901.
14. *Ibid.*, April 6, 1901.
15. Wood to Root, March 4, 6, 8, 20, 23, 1901, Elihu Root Papers, Library of Congress.
16. *New York Times*, March 28, 1901.
17. *The People*, April 5, 1901.
18. *New York Times*, May 20, 1901.
19. Wood to Root, May 8, 1901, Elihu Root Papers, Library of Congress.
20. Atkins to Platt, June 3, 1901, Orville H. Platt Papers, Connecticut State Library, Hartford.
21. *New York Times*, May 9, 1901; *New York Herald*, May 9, 1901; *Daily People*, May 9, 1901.
22. Leuchsenring, *Historia de la Enmienda Platt*, vol. I, pp. 220-22.
23. Orville H. Platt, "The Pacification of Cuba," *op. cit.*, p. 1496.
24. *The People*, March 24, 1901.
25. Wood to Root, March 6, 30, 1901, Elihu Root Papers, Library of Congress.
26. Root to Wood, March 20, 1901, Leonard Wood Papers, *ibid.*
27. A. G. Robinson in *New York Evening Post*, March 12, 1901.
28. Root to Wood, March 29, 1901, copy in Elihu Root Papers, Library of Congress.
29. Wood to Root, April 2, 1901; Root to Wood, April 2, 1901, *ibid.*
30. Robinson, *Cuba and the Intervention*, pp. 260-61; Wood to Root, April 4, 1901, Elihu Root Papers, Library of Congress.
31. "La opinion de Manuel Sanguily. Importante entrevista. Declaraciones transcendentales," *La Discusión*, marzo 21, 1901, and summarized in Leuchsenring, *Historia de la Enmienda Platt*, pp. 217-19.
32. *Vota Particular Contra la Enmienda Platt por Salvador Cisneros y Betancourt, Marqués de Santa Lucia, Presentada en la Convención de 1901*, 15 de Marzo de 1901, Habana, 1901, pp. 16-23. Reprinted, La Habana, 1963.

33. "Ponencia del Sr. Juan Gualberto Gómez a la Convención," *Revista de la Biblioteca Nacional*, Segunda Serie, Año V., No. 2, Habana, pp. 23-41. For a brief summary of Gómez's views in English, see *Literary Digest*, May 4, 1901, pp. 531-32.
34. Robinson, *Cuba and the Intervention*, p. 261.
35. Enrique H. Morena Pla, *Gonzalo de Quesada, Estadista*, La Habana, 1962, pp. 14-17, 30-32.
36. Robinson, "Some Cuban Opinions," *op. cit.*, p. 1058.
37. *New York Times*, April 13, 1901.
38. *Ibid.*, April 13, 1901.
39. *New York World*, April 7, 1901.
40. *The State*, April 9, 1901.

## CHAPTER XXVIII
## Cuba Yields to Force

1. Wood to Root, April 15, 1901, Elihu Root Papers, Library of Congress.
2. *Daily People*, April 20, 1901.
3. *Ibid.*, April 24, 1901.
4. *The State*, April 26, 28, 1901.
5. The discussion on the commission's visits with McKinley and Root are based on the following sources: "Reports of the Committee Appointed to confer with the Government of the United States, Giving an Account of the Results of its Labors," Copy in Elihu Root Papers; Platt to Root, April 26, 1901, *ibid*; Sterling, *op. cit.*, pp. 187-213; Leuchsenring, *Historia de la Enmienda Platt*, vol. I, pp. 185-214; Document M, no. 72, in *Memoria de los trabajos realizados durante las quatro legislaturas y sesíen extraordinaria del primer periodo congresional 1902-1904, predida de una mención documentada sobre los hechos históricos que dieron, como resultado defiinitivo, la independencia de Cuba y su establecimento en República*; *La Patria*, May 25, 1901; *Congressional Record*, 5th Cong., 1st Sess., p. 4011; Jessup, *op. cit.*, p. 319.
6. Jessup, *op. cit.*, pp. 320-21.
7. *New York World*, April 29, 1901; *The State*, May 2, 1901.
8. *The State*, May 2, 1901.
9. *New York Press* reprinted in *The State*, May 7, 1901.
10. Providence (R. I.) *Journal*, undated typed editorial but marked May, 1901 in Orville H. Platt Papers, Connecticut State Library.
11. Springfield *Republican* reprinted in *The State*, April 13, 1901.
12. Orville H. Platt, "Solution of the Cuban Problem," *World's Work*, vol. II, May, 1901, pp. 728-29.
13. Published in English and Spanish in Ortiz, *op. cit.*, vol. I, pp. 301-03.
14. Camacho, *op. cit.*, pp. 176-77.
15. Wood to Root, May 17, 1901, Elihu Root Papers, Library of Congress.
16. Root to Wood, May 17, 1901, Leonard Wood Papers, Library of Congress.
17. *The State*, May 20, 1901; Robinson, *Cuba and the Intervention*, pp. 270-71.
18. *New York Times*, May 29, 1901.

## NOTES

19. Reprinted in *ibid.*, May 30, 1901.
20. *New York Times*, May 30, 1901.
21. *The State*, May 21, 1901.
22. New York *Evening Post*, May 20, 1901.
23. *Daily People*, June 3, 1901.
24. Wood to Root, May 28, 29, 1901, Elihu Root Papers, Library of Congress; Root to Wood, May 28, 1901, Leonard Wood Papers, *ibid.*
25. *New York Times*, June 1, 1901.
26. Root to Wood, May 28, 1901, Leonard Wood Papers, Library of Congress; Jessup, *op. cit.*, p. 322.
27. New York *Tribune*, June 5, 1901; *New York Times*, June 3, 1901.
28. Dr. M. F. Coomes to Bryan, William Jennings Bryan Papers, Library of Congress.
29. Wood to Root, June 1, 1901, Elihu Root Papers, Library of Congress.
30. Martínez Ortiz, *op. cit.*, vol. I, pp. 315-16; Leuchsenring, *Historia de la Enmienda Platt*, pp. 234-35.
31. Springfield *Republican*, June 25, 1901.
32. Jessup, *op. cit.*, p. 315.
33. See for example, Jack Davis, "The Latin American Policy of Elihu Root," unpublished Ph.D. thesis, University of Illinois, 1956, p. 129.
34. Philip C. Wright, *The Cuban Situation and our Treaty Relations*, Washington, 1931, p. 20.
35. Wood to Roosevelt, Oct. 28, 1901, copy in Leonard Wood Papers, Library of Congress.
36. J. R. White to McKinley, March 6, 1901, William McKinley Papers, Library of Congress.
37. *Daily People*, March 23, 1901.
38. Jessup, *op. cit.*, p. 314.
39. *Ibid.*, p. 315.
40. *Ibid.*, p. 317.
41. Edwin M. Borchard, "Commercial and Financial Interests of the United States in the Caribbean," *Proceedings of the American Academy of Political Science*, vol. VII, pp. 386-87.
42. *The Nation*, Aug. 1, 1901, p. 81.
43. *Weekly People*, July 27, 1901.
44. New York *Evening Post*, May 23, 1901.
45. Sterling, *op. cit.*, pp. 217-18.
46. Orville H. Platt, "Solution of the Cuban Problem," *World's Work*, vol. II, May, 1901, p. 729.
47. Quoted by Representative Crowley, Illinois, in *Congressional Record*, 56th Cong., 2nd Sess., vol. XXXIV, p. 3372.
48. Ralph Halstead Parker, "Imperialism and the Liberation of Cuba, 1868-1898," unpublished Ph.D. thesis, University of Texas, June, 1935, pp. 338, 347-48.
49. Robert Bacon and James Brown Scott, *The Military and Colonial Policy of the United States; Addresses and Reports by Elihu Root*, Cambridge, 1916, p. 188.
50. Philip S. Foner, *History of Cuba and its Relations with the United States*, vol. II, p. 359.
51. See, for example, Fitzgibbon, *op. cit.*, p. 93.

52. Jenks, *op. cit.*, p. 85.
53. Wood to Roosevelt, Oct. 28, 1901, copy in Leonard Wood Papers, Library of Congress.

## CHAPTER XXIX

## THE BATTLE OVER RECIPROCITY

1. Wilson to Foraker, May 12, 1899; Wilson to Root, Nov. 3, 1899, James H. Wilson Papers, Library of Congress; U.S. Tariff Commission, *The Effects of the Cuban Reciprocity Treaty of 1902*, Washington, 1929, pp. 376-78.
2. *The Effects of the Cuban Reciprocity Treaty of 1902*, p. 377.
3. *Ibid.*, p. 387.
4. Olcott, *Life of William McKinley*, vol. II, pp. 381-83.
5. Wood to Roosevelt, May 9, 1901; Roosevelt to Wood, May 14, 1901, Theodore Roosevelt Papers, Library of Congress. Emphasis mine. *P.S.F.*
6. Wood to Root, Oct. 25, 1901, Elihu Root Papers, Library of Congress.
7. Wood to Roosevelt, Oct. 28, 1901, Theodore Roosevelt Papers, Library of Congress. Emphasis mine. *P.S.F.*
8. Roosevelt to Wood, Nov. 11, 1901, *ibid.*
9. *U.S. Foreign Relations*, 1901, pp. xxi-xxxii.
10. Roosevelt to Wood, Oct. 12, 1901; Roosevelt to Nelson P. Aldrich, Nov. 18, 1901, Theodore Roosevelt Papers, Library of Congress.
11. *The State*, Dec. 21, 1901.
12. *Cuban Sugar Sales*, Testimony taken by the Committee on Relations with Cuba, 57th Cong., 1st Sess., Washington, 1902, pp. 24, 194-205. Hereinafter cited as *Cuban Sugar Sales*.
13. Wood to Root, Jan. 4, 1902, Elihu Root Papers, Library of Congress.
14. Wood to Colonel Scott, Sept. 27, 1901, with sample letter enclosed, in Records of the United States Military Government of Cuba, Box 201, 1901, 3759, National Archives.
15. *Cf.* letters and petitions in *ibid.*
16. Wood to Root, Sept. 12, Oct. 6, 22, 1901, Elihu Root Papers, Library of Congress.
17. *House Document No. 679*, 57th Cong., 1st Sess., p. 6; *New York Times*, Oct. 6, 1901; *The State*, Oct. 8, 1901.
18. *Outlook*, vol. LXX, Jan. 18, 1902, pp. 169-71.
19. *The Effects of the Cuban Reciprocity Treaty of 1902*, p. 386.
20. *Civil Report of General Wood for the Period from January 1 to December 31, 1901*, vol. I, Part I, pp. 33-34.
21. The full story of Wood's activities together with an itemized statement of funds expended is in *House Document No. 679*, 57th Cong., 1st Sess. See also testimony of Francis B. Thurber in *Cuban Sugar Sales*, pp. 422-25.
22. *North American Review*, vol. CLXXXIII, Dec. 1901, pp. 768-73.
23. *Cf. Journal of Commerce and Commercial Bulletin*, Jan. 29, 1902.
24. *Cuban Sugar Sales*, pp. 24, 194-202, 220-35.
25. Richard D. Weigle, "The Sugar Interests and American Diplomacy in Hawaii and Cuba, 1893-1903," unpublished Ph.D. thesis, Yale University, 1939, pp. 262-64.

## NOTES

26. *Cuban Sugar Sales*, pp. 121-38.
27. *House Document No.* 335, 57th Cong., 1st Sess., p. 173.
28. *Literary Digest*, vol. XXIII, Dec. 21, 1901, p. 791.
29. *New York Tribune*, Dec. 8, 1901; *Journal of Commerce*, Dec. 7, 1901.
30. Root to Wood, Jan. 10, 1902, Elihu Root Papers, Library of Congress.
31. *House Document No.* 535, 37th Cong., 1st Sess., pp. 1-30.
32. *Ibid.*, p. 90; *The Public*, Feb. 1, 1902.
33. *Ibid.*, p. 49.
34. *Ibid.*, pp. 62-66, 69-70, 549-51.
35. Wood to Root, Jan. 16, 1902; Wood to Roosevelt, Jan. 16, 1902, Elihu Root Papers and Theodore Roosevelt Papers, both in Library of Congress.
36. *House Document No.* 535, pp. 44-67.
37. Wood to Root, Jan. 27, 1902, Elihu Root Papers, Library of Congress.
38. Root to Wood, Feb. 7, 1902; Wood to Root, Feb. 8, 1902, *ibid.*
39. *House Document No.* 535, pp. 166-218.
40. Roosevelt to Nicholas Murray Butler, Feb. 4, 1902, Theodore Roosevelt Papers, Library of Congress.
41. Orville H. Platt to Roosevelt, Feb. 3, 1902, *ibid.*
42. Root to Wood, March 7, 1902, Leonard Wood Papers, *ibid.*
43. *Congressional Record*, 57th Cong., 1st Sess., p. 3491; *House Report* 1276, 57th Cong., 1st Sess.; *Literary Digest*, March 8, 1902, pp. 315-16; March 29, 1902, pp. 419-20.
44. *Congressional Record*, 57th Cong., 1st Sess., p. 3606; *The State*, March 3, 6, 1902.
45. *Congressional Record*, 57th Cong., 1st Sess., p. 3606.
46. *Ibid.*, pp. 4455-56.
47. *Ibid.*, p. 4523.
48. Weigle, *op. cit.*, pp. 296-97.
49. *New York Times*, June 12, 1902.
50. *Ibid.*, June 13, 1902.
51. *Ibid.*, June 13, 15, 1902.
52. *Outlook*, vol. LXXI, June 21, 1902, p. 477.
53. Boston *Evening Transcript*, June 12, 1902.
54. Roosevelt to Spooner, June 10, 1902, Theodore Roosevelt Papers, Library of Congress.
55. *Congressional Record*, 57th Cong., 1st Sess., p. 6720.
56. *The Effects of the Cuban Reciprocity Treaty of 1902*, pp. 417-19.
57. *New York Times*, Jan. 18, 1902.
58. *Ibid.*, June 19-20, 1902.
59. *Congressional Record*, 57th Cong., 1st Sess., p. 7305.
60. *The State*, Feb. 6, 13, 1902.
61. *Ibid.*, April 9, 1902.
62. *Congressional Record*, 57th Cong., 1st Sess., pp. 7638-43.
63. Ernest Untermann, "Sugar as an Educator," *Appeal to Reason*, July 19, 1902. See also editorial in *ibid.*, Jan. 18, 1902.

## CHAPTER XXX

## The Republic of Cuba

1. *The State,* Nov. 28, 1901.
2. *Daily People,* April 20, 1901.
3. Wood to Root, Feb. 27, 1901, Elihu Root Papers, Library of Congress.
4. Martínez Ortiz, *op. cit.,* vol. I, p. 352.
5. *The State,* July 8, 1901.
6. *Ibid.,* July 3, 1901.
7. Martínez Ortiz, *op. cit.,* vol. I, p. 353.
8. *Ibid.,* pp. 353-54.
9. *Ibid.,* pp. 350-51.
10. *Ibid.,* pp. 351-52.
11. *Ibid.,* p. 355.
12. *Ibid.,* pp. 359-65.
13. Horrego, *op. cit.,* p. 171.
14. Martínez Ortiz, *op. cit.,* vol. I, pp. 366-69.
15. Reprinted in *The State,* Sept. 28, 1901.
16. Horrego, *op. cit.,* pp. 172-75.
17. Wood to Roosevelt, Oct. 28, 1901, Theodore Roosevelt Papers, Library of Congress.
18. Martínez Ortiz, *op. cit.,* vol. I, pp. 372-73.
19. Horrego, *op. cit.,* pp. 175-76.
20. Martínez Ortiz, *op. cit.,* vol. I, pp. 373-74.
21. *The State,* Jan. 4, 1902.
22. *New York Tribune,* Jan. 2, 1902.
23. *New York Evening Post,* Jan. 2, 1902.
24. Unnamed and undated London newspaper clipping, probably the London *Times,* in Estrada Palma Papers, Archivo Nacional.
25. Martínez Ortiz, *op. cit.,* vol. I, pp. 375-76; *The State,* March 28, 1902.
26. *The State,* April 17, 1902; *New York Tribune,* April 21, 1902; *Daily People,* April 18, 1902.
27. Leon Wolff, *Little Brown Brother: How the United States Purchased and Pacified the Philippine Islands at the Century's Turn,* New York, 1961, pp. 356-57.
28. Reprinted in *The State,* May 5, 1902.
29. *Ibid.,* May 8, 1902.
30. *Ibid.,* May 18, 1902.
31. *Ibid.,* May 23, 1902.
32. *Ibid.,* May 21, 23, 1902; *New York Times,* May 21, 22, 23, 1902.
33. René E. Reyna Cossio, *Estudios Histórico-Militares Sobre la Guerra de Independencia de Cuba,* Habana, 1954, p. 67.
34. *Harper's Weekly,* May, 18, 1902.
35. *New York Tribune,* May 21, 1902; *New York Times,* May 22, 1902.
36. *The State,* May 20, 1902; *Springfield Republican,* May 20, 1902.
37. *The State,* May 20, 1902.
38. *New York Evening Post,* May 20, 1902.
39. *Daily People,* May 21, 1902.

40. *Journal des Debats, Independence Belge,* and *Saturday Review,* reprinted in *Literary Digest,* June 14, 1902, pp. 814-15.
41. Havana *Post,* reprinted in *The State,* May 21, 1902. *See also* reprint of editorials from the Havana *Post* in ibid., Feb. 25, 1902 and in New York *Evening Post,* Feb. 7, 1900.
42. Unidentified, undated London paper, probably the London *Times,* in Papers of Estrada Palma, Archivo Nacional.
43. Reprinted in *Literary Digest,* June 14, 1902.
44. Philadelphia *Press* reprinted in *ibid.,* June 29, 1901.
45. *The Public,* May 24, 1902.
46. Jacob Schurman to "My dear Mrs. Lowell," Dec. 10, 1903, Jacob Schurman Papers, Cornell University Library.
47. Jacob Schurman to the Editor of the New York *Tribune,* Jan. 19, 1904, *ibid.*
48. The program of the Filipino Progress League is in the Jacob Schurman Papers. *See also* Pomeroy, *op. cit.,* pp. 204-05.
49. Howard Beale, *Theodore Roosevelt and the Rise of American World Power,* Baltimore, 1956, p. 75.

# Index

Abad, Luis, 599, 625-26
Abarzuza, Buenaventura de, 406
Abbott, Lyman, 453
Abrei de Estévez, Marta, 107-08
Acosta, Baldomero, 89, 91
Adams, Brooks, 289
Adams, Henry, 289
Adams, John Quincy, xvi, 204, 657
Adams, Robert, Jr., 188
Addams, Jane, 453
Agramonte, Ignacio, 463
Agüero, Aristides, 151, 159-60
Aguinaldo, Emilio, 124-25, 374, 391, 409, 432, 515, 626
Aguirre, Francisco, 79
Aguirre, Sergio, 141, 437, 445, 626-27
Akers, Charles E., 83
Albertinini, Ricardo Díaz, 164
Aldave, García, 53
Aldrich, Nelson P., 527, 559
Alemán, José B., 554, 626
Alfaro, Eloy, 155
Allen, William V., 187, 583
Aller, Juan, 494, 496
Alger, Russell A., 248, 265, 340, 341, 352, 372, 443, 454, 467
Altgeld, John P., 453
Amari, Caniazza, 650
American Anti-Imperialist League, 453, 507, 534, 591
American Asiatic Association, 304
American Beet Sugar Company, 637, 641
American Cigar Company, 481
American economic domination of Cuba, 647-58
American Federation of Labor, 174-75, 415, 418, 453, 504-05, 509, 587
American imperialism, x-xi, xxviii-xxxiii, 153-55, 159, 290-310, 381, 405-06, 410-13, 417-18, 421, 431-33, 453-54, 465, 466-83, 538-40, 546-47, 549-50, 557-58, 563-64, 566, 587-89, 599, 618, 623-24, 626-31, 633-35, 669-72
American labor, and Cuban Revolution, 172-76
American National Red Cross, 130
American Sugar Refining Company, 478-79, 629, 640-42, 643, 647. See also Sugar Trust
Anarchists, 127
Anarcho-syndicalism, 491
Andrews, Charles T., 449, 453, 476
Angell, James B., 415
Angoncillo, Felipe, 409-10
Angoncillo, Tedoro, 126
Annexation of Cuba, movement for in United States, xvii, xxviii-xxxiv, 216-19, 223, 239, 271-72 279, 392-94, 396, 397, 408, 413, 416, 446, 452, 456, 467, 472, 473, 481, 492, 515-33, 537, 546-47, 564, 573, 595, 628-29, 634-35, 651, 656, 657
Anti-imperialism, 413-21, 432, 453, 503, 518-19, 525, 534-37, 541, 549, 562, 574, 580, 584, 587-90, 592, 597, 619, 623, 627, 648, 651, 662, 668
Anti-Imperialist League, 413-16
Antiplattistas, 655, 657-58, 660-61, 670
Anti-Trust, 648
Appeal to the American People on Behalf of Cuba, 464-65, 543-45
Appeal to Reason, 285-86
Appel, John C., 175
Argentina, 157
Armas López, Francisco de, 494, 496
Arnauto, Ricardo, 450-51
Arocha, González, 98

Associated American Interests in Cuba, 640
Associated Press, 356-57, 364, 371, 394
Association of Landowners and Agriculturists of Cuba, 475
Astor, John Jacob, 306-07
Atkins, Edwin F., 105, 182-84, 190, 196-97, 206, 207, 223, 246, 478, 479, 508, 517, 531, 578-79, 628-29, 634, 640, 642-43
Atkinson, Edward, 417, 420-21
Atrocities, 60
Autonomist Party, 45, 47, 100-01, 134, 214
Autonomy, for Cuba, 128-29, 132-35, 147, 181-82, 192, 196-98, 207, 209, 218, 222-27, 229, 236, 259-60
Auxier, George W., Jr., 288-89

Bacon, Augustus O., 536-37
Bailey, Thomas A., 292
Bald, Ralph Dewar, Jr., 295
Banco de la Isla de Cuba, 482
Banco Español de la Habana, 482
Banco Nacional de Cuba, 483
Banderas, Quintín, 19, 37, 53
Banking, in Cuba, 482-83
Barcan, Arthur, 293-94
Barnes, Harry Elmer, 288
Barton, Clara, 131-32, 382, 383, 384, 386, 387
Basadre, Jorge, 157
Bates, John C., 426
Batista, Fulgencio, 282
Battle, of Ayachuco, 87; of Artemisa, 75-76; of Caliseo, 58; of Candelaria, 75; of Ceja del Negro, 85; of Consolación del Sur, 82; of El Caney, 359-60; of Gabriel de Lombello, 83; of Guáimaro, 121; of Guantánamo, 348-49, 356; of Iguará, 53-54; of La Palma, 81; of La Reforma, 120; of Las Guásimas, 357-58; of Mal Tiempo, 56-57; of Mentezuelo, 85; of Paralejo, 37-39, 376; of Paso Real, 75; of San Juan Hill, 359-61; of Santiago de Cuba, 360-65; of Sao de Indio, 39; of Tumbas de Estorino, 85; of Victoria de Las Tunas, 121-22
Baylor, Charles G., 391, 417
Beale, Howard K., 292
Beard, Charles A., 288, 291
Beet sugar interests, 636-38, 640-41, 642, 645-47, 651
Beisner, Robert L., xi

Belligerency, U.S. policy toward, 181-91
Bemis, Samuel Flagg, 292
"Benevolent Assimilation," 587
Berlin Conference, xxx
Bermejo, Segismundo, 230, 231
Bernabé, Polo de, 250, 259-60
Betances, R. E., 107
Betancourt, Ana, 15
Betancourt, Pedro, xxiv, 38, 613, 658
Bethlehem Steel Company, 482
Beveridge, Albert J., 546-47, 584, 589
Blaine, James G., xxviii
Blanco, Ramón, 125, 129-30, 134-36, 218, 230, 246, 259
Bliss, Tasker H., 426, 493
Blue, Victor, 348
Bolivia, 152, 160
Bolívar, Simón, 277
Bonifacio, Andreis, 124
Bonsal, Stephen, 115, 664
Borchard, Edwin M., 629
Borrero, Francisco, 8
Bosc, Juan, 232
"Boxers," 538-39
Boza, Bernabé, 19-20
Brazil, 154, 160
Breckenridge, J. C., 233
Bristow, Joseph L., 535
"Bronze Titan," xxx, 46. See also Maceo, Antonio
Brooke, John R., 422-30, 433, 436, 437, 439, 440, 442, 446, 447, 448, 449, 450, 452, 454, 455, 456, 457, 458, 459, 467, 474, 475, 483, 487, 488, 551
Brooks, Paul, 179, 180
Browne, Herbert J., 647
Bryan, William Jennings, 202, 292, 415-16, 539, 542, 549, 583, 666
Burgess, John W., 607
Busto, Sarafí del, 494
Byrne, Bonifacio, 451

Cabrera, Raimundo, 108
Calhoun, William J., 113-14, 117-18, 213-14
Call, Wilkinson, 166
Callejas, Emilio, 110
Camacho, Simón, 494, 496
Cambon, Jules, 374
Cameron, Don, 185-86
Canada, 133
Canadian Pacific Railroad, 471, 472
Canalejas, Don José, 232-33
Cannon, Joseph, 241
Cannon Emergency Bill, 241-42

## INDEX

Capote, José Manuel, 152
*Captain Jinks, Hero,* 590
Cárdenas, Nicolás de, 151
Cárdenas, Rafael de, 493, 502
Carillo, Francisco, xxiv
Carlington, J. C., 531, 533
Carlist Wars, 76
Carnegie, Andrew, 171, 415, 416, 417, 671
Caro, Miguel, 156
Carpenter, Luis, 426
Carpetbaggers, 541
Casiero, C. V., 497
Castellanos, Gerardo, 31
Castro, Fidel, 72, 281
Cespedes, José Maria, 427
Central Cuban Relief Committee, 115, 130-32
Cerero, Rafael, 406
Cervera, Pascual, 230, 231, 245, 343, 353, 361, 362
Chadwick, French Ensor, 349, 360
Chaffe, Adna R., 359, 475, 493
Chamberlain, Daniel H., 627
Chamberlain, Joseph, 395
Chandler, William E., 565
Chapman, Charles E., 553
Chicago *Interocean,* 392
Chicago *Tribune,* 392
Chile, 108, 152, 153-54, 156, 157
China, 255, 294-95, 302-03, 309, 538-39
Chinese, role of in Second War for Independence, 102
Choate, Joseph H., 393
Church and state, 550-53
Churchill, Winston, 53-53, 194
Cienfuegos, Camilo, 72
Cigar makers, 173
Cigar Makers' International Union, 173
*Círculo de Hacendados y Agricultureros de la Isla de Cuba,* 600
*Círculo de Trabajadores,* 103, 493
Cisneros, Salvador Betancourt, 15, 41-42, 43, 46, 47, 49, 54, 86, 211, 439, 441, 464-65, 503, 543-44, 545, 546, 569, 603-04, 626
Civera, José, 121
Civil Order No. 445, 547-48
Clark, Victor S., 486, 512
Clavell, González, 358, 359
Clergy, role of in War for Independence, 98-99
Cleveland, Grover, xxix, 146, 154, 177-207, 285, 299, 415
Clews, Henry, 374, 389, 455, 474

Cockerell, Francis M., 583
Coen, C. M., 438
Collazo, Enrique, 3, 341, 427, 448-49
Colombia, 156
Colonial Reform Commission, xvii-xviii
Committee on Relations with Cuba, 77, 537, 571-73, 578, 621, 647, 649
Conde, Rosalía, 114
Congress of Cuban Historians, 177, 199, 204
Constitution, of Guáimero, 550-51; of Jumagüajú, 551; of La Yaya, 551; of Republic of Cuba, 555-57
Constitutional Convention, in Cuba, 538-58, 569, 593, 594, 600, 612, 613-14, 621, 624, 625-26, 627, 628
Coomes, M. F., 624-25
Corbin, Henry C., 353, 432
Cosio y Cisneros, Evangelina, 169
Costa Rica, xxiii, 57, 152, 157
Coudert, Frederick R., xxxii
Council of Government of the Republic of Cuba, 273, 397-98
Council of the Veterans of Independence, 520-21
Crea, Enrique, 103, 502
Credit, for Cuban farmers, 474-75
Creoles, xv-xvii
Crombet, Flor, 2, 7
Crosby, Ernest H., 590-91
Crowinshield, Arent S., 225
Cuba, abolition of slavery in, 15; American economic domination of, 628, 647-54; American occupation of, 466-83; annexation of favored in United States, xvii, xxviii-xxxiv, 271, 279, 392-97, 408, 412-13, 414, 446, 467, 472, 473, 481, 492, 515-33, 536-37, 564, 573, 629, 634-35, 651-52, 656, 657; as model for American imperialism, 670-72; as model for neo-colonialism, 672; attitude of people toward Second War for Independence, 98-103; banking in, 482-83; bonds of, 166, 220-22, 217-72, 438-39, 470; conservatives in fear masses more than American imperialism, 599; Constitution of, 12-13, 550-51, 555-67; Constitutional Convention in, 538-58; debt of, 407-09, 413; devastation in during Second War for Independence, 379-87, 428-29; disbanding of army of, 398-402, 431-48; economic crisis in during 1894-95, xxxiii; education in, 23, 450-51, 459-60, 461-62; effect on of U.S. tariffs, xxxiii; inde-

pendence movement in before 1895, xvi-xviii; labor movement in, 127, 484-513; Liberating Army of, xix, 19-25; looted by Spain, 428; and *Maine* explosion, 237-48, 251, 255; monetary system of, 487; municipal elections in, 528-31, 534; Negro in, 360, 485-86; opposition to annexation in, 530-32; opposition to Platt Amendment in, 603-11, 655, 657-59, 660-61, 670; plan of U.S. to purchase, 241, 249-50; population of, xvi; postal scandals in, 535-36; presidential election in, 655-62; protests in over American occupation, 396-97; racism of Americans in, 450; railroad built in, 471, 472, 476, 531; and reciprocity, 559-60, 564-73, 635-54, 600, 615-19; recognition of independence of refused by U.S., 261-76; *reconcentrados* in, 110-18, 130, 131, 132, 226, 248-49, 283, 381; relief for *reconcentrados*, 115, 130-32, 384, 386, 387; Reform Commission in, xvii-xviii; resources seized by Americans, 465-83; resists Platt Amendment, 593-626, 657-59, 660; role of Martí in, xix-xxxiii; role of Negroes during struggle for independence in, xviii; Rural Guard in, 436, 456, 500, 511, 523; slavery in, xvii; Socialists in, 490-91, 653-54; strikes in, 491-512; Ten Years War in, xviii-xix; wages in, 512-13; working class in, 485-86
Cuba Central Railroad, 476
Cuba Company, 472-73, 511
Cuban-American relations during Spanish-American War, 339-79
Cuban-American Sugar Company, 477
Cuban Army, disbanding of, 398-402, 431-48
Cuban Assembly, 398, 399-400, 427, 432-42, 445, 548, 553, 571
Cuban belligerency, recognition of by U.S. Congress, 227-28
Cuban belligerent rights, 224-25
Cuban bonds, 166, 220-22, 247-48, 271-72, 438-39, 470
Cuban Cabinet, 422-30, 454, 457, 551
Cuban Census, 528
Cuban Central Railroad, 473, 531
Cuban Central Relief Committee, 382, 383, 384-86, 387
Cuban Commercial League, 519
Cuban Commission, in Washington, 399-403, 620-24

Cuban Council of Government, 221-22, 389
Cuban debt, 411, 413
Cuban Educational Association, 464
Cuban independence, resolution in Congress favors, 205-06
Cuban *Junta*, 41, 163-68, 176, 218, 222, 226, 233, 234, 236, 248, 273, 277, 290, 344, 346, 371, 372-73, 375
Cuban League of the United States, 164
Cuban Liberty League, 171
Cuban loans, 445. *See also* Cuban bonds
Cuban National Party, 530, 534, 543, 545
Cuban reciprocity delegation, 639-44
Cuban Relief Committee, 474
Cuban Revolutionary Party, xx-xxvi, 15, 18, 19-29, 107, 108, 109, 151, 155-56, 405
Cuban Socialist Party, 490-91
*Cubano Libre, El,* 32, 60-62
Cubans, excluded from surrender by Spain, 366-69; not invited to Treaty of Paris, 406-07; oppose annexation, 518-23, 652; slandered, 356-61, 362, 388-89

*Daily People,* 550, 623, 662-63
Dalzell, John, 598
Dana, Charles A., 11
Daniel, John W., 268
Davis, Cushman K., 406
Davis, George W., 426, 486
Davis, Richard Harding, 102, 591
Day, William R., 213, 222, 223, 224, 229, 234, 248, 250, 256, 374, 385, 406, 407, 408, 409, 412, 413
Debs, Eugene V., 453, 536
Declaration of Independence, 664
de la Concepción Valdés, Gabriel, 11
del Busto, Serafín, 496
del Castillo, Cánovas, 126
del Castillo, Enrique Loynez, 12, 51
De Leon, Daniel, 172, 283
Democratic Union Party, 530
Depew, Chauncey M., 539, 672, 673
Desvernine, Pablo, 425
de Truffin, Nicolas, 16, 20, 26, 29, 62, 70, 82, 85, 93, 103, 118, 119, 120
Dewey, George, 240, 276, 295, 374
Díaz, Alberto J., 145
Díaz, Pedro, 92, 119
Díaz, Porfirio, 157-58
Dickens, Charles, 650

INDEX 709

Dingley Tariff, 396, 637
Dinsmore, Hugh A., 266-67
*Discusión, La,* 520, 522-23, 594-95, 597, 602
Disfranchisement of Negroes, 549
Dobson, Charles M., 482
Dodge Commission, 361
Domínguez Cowan, Nicolás, 158
Dozer, Donald Marquand, x
Duany, Castillo, 358
Du Bois, W. E. B., 99, 415
Ducase, Juan E., 82
Duke of Tetuán, 217
Dulles, Foster R., 291
Dunne, Finley Peter, 339
Dupuy de Lome, Enrique, 178, 194-96, 204, 210, 220, 223, 232-36
De Lome letter, 232-36

Ecuador, 155
Egan, Patrick, 153, 154
Egypt, 395, 461, 561
Eight-hour day, 493-505, 512
Election, of 1896, 202-03; of 1900, 504, 534, 535, 539-42, 544, 549, 586
Elkins, Stephen B., 652
Emery, Frederick, 286
Endicott, Williams, 415
England, 282, 254-55, 395
Escalante Beatón, Aníbal, 121, 351
Escoto, Gustavo, 233
Estenoz, Evaristo, 494, 500, 501
Esthninius Mamby, Juan, 31
Estrada Palma, Tómas, 15, 18, 25, 40, 43, 44, 48, 49, 55, 82, 84, 88, 107, 122-23, 128, 145, 147-49, 151, 152, 157, 158, 159-60, 163, 164-66, 170, 182, 184, 197, 208, 218, 220, 222, 228, 234, 259, 272-73, 274, 340, 346, 355, 363, 371, 373, 375, 389, 401, 405, 434, 435, 570, 620-21, 642, 655-67, 670
European intervention, 254-58

*Facts About Sugar,* 641
Farquhar, Percy, 467
Faulkner, Harold U., 288, 291
Federal Steel Company, 482
Ferer, José N., 625
Fernández de Castro, José, 626
Fernández de Castro, Rafael, 660
Fernández Barrot, Eugenio Lepoldo, 341
Fernandina plan, 2-3
Figueroa, Sotero, xxi, 167, 571

Filibustering, 17-18, 164, 178-81, 211, 582-87
Filipino Progress League, 671
Finlay, Carlos, 460-61, 479
Fish, Hamilton, xvii
Fish, Stuyvesant, 306-07, 418
Flagler, Henry M., 303
Flint, Grover, 31, 99, 344
Florida, Cuban tobacco workers in, 108-10
Foraker, Joseph B., 220, 267-69, 421, 431, 452, 456, 457, 468-69, 519, 537, 559, 577, 579, 636
Foraker Amendment, 469-71, 472-73, 520, 537, 573, 582
Foreign Policy Association, 483
Fortún, Louis, 626
Fowler, George R., 644
Fraga, José, 494
France, 255, 282-83
Francisco Sugar Company, 478
Free Federation of Workmen of Puerto Rico, 508-09
"Fruta madura" policy, 204-05
Friedel, Frank, 28, 672
Frye, Alexis Everett, 450, 462-63
Frye, William P., 406, 411
Funston, Frederick, 28, 123, 626

García, Calixto, 18, 20, 32, 50, 89, 120-21, 123, 128, 340-44, 346-48, 349, 350-56, 359, 362, 365, 367, 369-71, 372, 373, 390-91, 399, 400-03, 405, 437
García, Carlos, 501-02, 510-11, 518-19
García, César, 496
García, Ezequel, 659
García, Gualterio, 405
García, Ramón, 249
García Menocal, Mario, 122, 343, 450, 476, 477, 488, 521
García Pinto, Domingo, 501
García Ponce, Manuel, xxiv
García Vieta, Gonzalo, 341
Garnica, José de, 406
Garrich, Leopoldo, 52-53
Gates, John, 306-07
General League of Cuban Workers, 490, 491-94, 499-500, 502
General strike, 494-95
Germany, 217, 255, 256, 627-28
Giberga, Eliseo, 545, 554, 568
Gómez, José Miguel, 453, 546
Gómez, Máximo, xix-xxiii, 1-4, 7-10, 14, 19, 20, 21, 22-26, 32, 35, 39-41, 43-45, 49-50, 52, 53-54, 70-71, 77-80, 85-86, 93, 94, 97, 99, 105, 110,

116, 120, 127, 128, 139, 146, 151, 156, 157, 207, 261, 269, 277-78, 284, 342, 343-46, 352, 369, 370, 375-76, 399, 423, 424, 433-47, 458, 521, 553, 600-01, 620, 655-57, 659, 661, 663, 666
Gómez Toro, Francisco, 84, 92-93
Gompers, Samuel, 173, 415, 418, 453, 504-07, 587
Gonzáles, N. G., 149-50, 208, 343-46, 397. See also State, The
Gonzáles Llorento, Pedro, 613
González Lanuza, José Antonio, 425, 426
González Pérez, Antonio, 417
González Pintado, José, 496
Gorgas, Silliam, 460-61
Grajales de Maceo, Mariana, xxiii, 36, 70
Grant, Ulysses S., 223
Gray, George, 406, 410
Griggs, John, 257
Griswold, A. Whitney, 292
Grito de Baire, 4, 9, 14, 103, 124, 158
Grito de Balintawak, 124
Grito de Yara, 18, 46, 546
Grosvenor, Charles H., 272
Gualberto Gómez, Juan, xxiv, 3-4, 401-02, 544, 546, 550, 552, 553, 554, 571, 593, 600, 603-11, 626, 628, 659, 660, 661
Guam, 411, 413
Guerra, Angel, 8
Guerra, Benjamin J., xxi, 137, 164, 184, 371
Guerra, y Sánchez, Ramiro, 278, 479-80
Guerrero, Rafael, 124
Guerrilla warfare, 28-32

Hacker, Louis, 288
Hagedorn, Hermann, 461
Haiti, xv, 99, 159-60, 279, 280, 516, 528, 545, 554, 628
Hale, Edward, 527, 533
Hale, Eugene, 186
Hamedoes, S. E. F. C. C., 97
Hanial, J. A., 600
Hanna, Marcus A., 307, 438, 469, 509
Hanna, Matthew E., 463
Hardie, Keir, 282, 283
Harrison, Benjamin, xxix
Harroun, Gilbert K., 464
Harvard University, 459, 463
Hastings, Elbert G., 31
Hastings, J. Syme, 166
Havana Commercial Company, 481

Havemeyer, Harry, 650, 651
Havemeyer, Henry O., 478-79, 517, 636
Havemeyer, Theodore, 477
Hawaii, annexation of, xxviii-xxix, 263, 285, 294-95, 302, 308-09, 414-15, 630, 644, 651-52
Hawley, R. B., 476, 477
Hay, John, 274, 403, 406, 408, 409, 560, 591, 652
Haymarket Affair, 246, 494-95
Healy, David F., 143, 270, 462
Hearst, William Randolph, 163, 168, 169, 233, 238, 288, 346
Henna, Julio, 373
Hernández, Carlos, 341, 347
Hernández, Eusebio, 88
Hernández Ríos, Salvador, 341, 348, 546
Henry, Guy V., 353
Herrick, Myron T., 308
Heuraux, Ulises, 156
Hevia, A., 441
Hill, James J., 472
Himley, Henry A., 144, 181
Hinds, Asher S., 275
Hitchman, James Harold, 631
Hitt, Robert R., 188
Hoar, George F., 186, 416, 580, 582
Hobson, J. A., 286-87
Hofstadter, Richard, 293
Home Rule Bill, 100
Homestead strike, 171
Hopkins, George B., 471-72, 531
Hostos, Eugenio Maria, 108
House of Morgan, 509
Howells, William Dean, 415
Huau, J. A., 108-09
Hubbard, Elbert, 340
Hymn of Bayamo, 666
Hymn of the Invasion, 121, 151, 666

Ibero-American Union, 153
Iglesias, Santiago, 103-04, 509
Imperialism. See American imperialism, Anti-imperialism
Inclán, Suárez, 82
In Darkest Cuba, 344-46
Independencia, La, 396
Industrial Cuba, 514, 640
International Sugar Conference, 645-46
Invading Hymn, 12, 551, 666
Invasion of the West, 40-59, 99, 157
Ireland, John, 256
Isle of Pines, 481, 607, 622

## INDEX

Island of Cuba Real Estate Company, 480
Isthmian Canal, 628, 649

Jai-Alai Company, 470
Jamaica, 340, 341
Janney, Samuel, 220-21, 222, 236-37
Janney-McCook Syndicate, 271-74
Jenks, Leland H., 290, 462, 480, 603, 631
Jessup, Philip C., 628-29
Jiménez Castellanos, Adolfo, 424
Jiménez Pastrana, Juan, 102
Joint Resolution of Congress, 274-75, 372, 388, 398-99, 421, 447, 596, 604, 610, 621
Jones, James K., 579
Jordan, Thomas, xxxii
Johnson, Edward Lehman, 590
Johnson, Willis Fletcher, 556
Josephson, Matthew, 291
Juragui Iron Company, 482

Kaiser Wilhelm, 627
Kasson, John Adam, 305-06
*Katipunan*, 124
Kelly, Hugh, 643
Kendrick, John F., 339
Kennedy, Robert P., 468
Kennedy Board, 469
King, Clarence, 71, 90
Knights of Labor, 95, 172-74, 504, 587
Kohlsatt, Herman H., 300, 470

Labor movement, in Cuba, 484-513
Labor movement, in U.S. and strikes in Cuba, 503-06
Lacoste, Perfecto, 128, 148, 149, 424, 502
Lacret Marlot, José, 554, 626
Lainé, François, 245-46
Lamont, Daniel S., 304, 466
"Large Policy," 290-310
Lawson, Victor F., 367
Latin America, and Cuban Revolution, 151-60
Lawrence, Frederick W., 199-201
Lawton, H. W., 358, 359, 362, 380, 391, 392, 400
Lee, Algernon, 285
Lee, Fitzhugh, 131, 135, 137, 169, 198, 207, 225, 227, 228, 229, 230, 236-37, 239-40, 259, 304-05, 391, 426, 466-67
La Feber, Walter, 153, 299-301
Lenin, V. I., 288, 292, 293
Leo XIII, 256

Leuchtenberg, W. E., 292
Lloyd, Henry Demarest, 453
Liberal Party, 126
*Liga Filipina*, 124
*Liga General de Trabajadores Cubanos*, 490, 491-94, 499-500, 522
Linares, Arsenio, 355
Liliuokalani, Queen, xxix
Lincoln, Abraham, 596
Lindsay, William, 269-70
Lodge, Henry Cabot, 166, 190, 208, 276-77, 289, 292, 293, 295, 304, 415-16, 454, 469, 539, 564
Logan, Rayford W., 202
London *Times*, 101, 107
Long, John D., 225, 228, 229, 230, 235, 239, 240, 374
Loomis, Francis B., 301
Lora Héctor, 38
Lord Cromer, 461
Louis, Paul, 283
L'Ouverture, Toussaint, 96, 97
Lowell, Josephine Shaw, 671
Luciano Díaz, Manuel, 274
Ludlow, William, 423, 426, 446, 450, 489, 496-504, 506
Lundberg, Ferdinand, 246
Luque, Enrique, 52
Lynchings, 417, 450, 597

McCook, John J., 220-24, 247, 271-74, 303
McCormick, Thomas, 299-300, 302
McDonald, Timothy G., 309-10, 410
McDowell, William O., 164
McKenna, Joseph, 228
McKibben, Chambers, 366-67
McKinley, William, x, 139, 144, 202-03, 209-80, 293, 298, 299, 303, 307-10, 365, 375, 384, 387, 392, 409-13, 415, 417, 421, 423-24, 434, 436, 438, 440-41, 454, 455, 456, 457, 504, 514-15, 521, 525, 534, 535, 541, 542, 543, 544, 548, 557, 563, 566, 574, 576, 582, 586, 591, 594, 595, 597, 614-15, 617, 618, 623, 628, 634, 672
McKinley Tariff, xxxii
McLaurin, John L., 416
Maceo, Antonio, xviii-xix, 2-10, 14, 18-19, 24-25, 32, 36-72, 73-86, 104, 106, 108, 119, 128, 142, 144-46, 152-53, 157, 165-66, 171, 194, 279, 376, 437, 443, 458, 463, 663, 665
Maceo, José, 7, 44, 46, 84, 86, 345
Mackey, John W., 472
Magoon, Charles E., 375

Mahan, Alfred T., xxxi, 289, 295, 301-02
Maine, 225-31, 237-48, 251-52
Maine explosion, 237-48, 251, 252
Mambises, xviii, 31-32, 102, 120, 341, 344, 345-46, 363
Manduley, Rafael, 626
Manifesto of Montecristi, 4
Mariano Torres expedition, 18
Marín, Sabas, 73, 110
Marina Cubana, La, 657-58
Marinello, Juan, 70
Marion, Francis, 30, 346
Márquez Sterling, M., 383, 446, 616, 630
Martí, José, xix-xxxiii, 1-6, 8-10, 11, 15, 40, 58, 93, 94, 124, 142-44, 156, 162, 165, 167, 274, 279, 405, 435, 437, 463, 484, 490, 494, 547, 554, 569, 591, 631, 665, 666
Martínez Campos, Arsenio, 14, 15, 16, 33, 36-39, 49, 50-51, 52, 53, 57, 58, 60, 61-62, 73-74, 75, 129, 138
Martínez Ortiz, Rafael, 384, 567, 658, 661
Masó, Bartolomé, xxiv, 43, 44-45, 46-48, 123, 248, 375, 398, 439, 458, 657-58, 660, 661
May, Ernest R., 175, 207, 251, 258, 280, 307
Méndez Capote, Domingo, 371, 389-90, 425, 426, 427, 546, 559, 613, 614, 621, 623, 658, 659
Mercado, Manuel, 11
"Message to García," 340-41, 356
Messonier, Enrique, 491, 500, 502
Mestro, A. E., 383
Mexican War, x
Mexico, 157-60, 421
Miles, Nelson A., 228, 340, 341, 342, 352-53, 364-66
Miller, Warren, 298
Millis, Walter P., 96-97, 116, 119, 128, 200, 245, 393
Miró, José, 67-68, 69, 71, 76, 91, 152, 458
Moncado, Guillermo, xxiv
Monetary system, 487
Money, Hernando de Soto, 574
Monroe Doctrine, 154-55, 611, 615, 616, 618, 622, 630
Montero Ríos, Eugenio, 406
Moore, John Basset, xxx
Moreno Plá, Enrique H., 148
Moret, Sigismund, 127

Morgan, H. Wayne, 143, 235-36, 248, 251, 339
Morgan, John T., 166, 185-86, 402-03, 419, 441, 518, 579
Morgan, J. Pierpont, 307
Morris, Charles, 465
Morton, Levi P., 472
Müller y Tejeiro, José, 363
Mullin, Jack, 479
Muñiz Rivera, José, 513

National Association of Manufacturers, 296-98, 305, 309
National Business League, 467
National Civic Federation, 59, 587
National Party, 545
National Sugar Refining Company, 647-48
Navarro, Pedro A., 491
Neely, Charles F., 535-36, 561
Negroes, 5-6, 98-99, 170-71, 361, 417, 464, 485-86, 526, 529, 600
Negro Republic, fear of, 42, 159-60, 194-95
Negro suffrage, 530, 549, 554, 643
Nevins, Allan, 191
Neo-colonialism, 672
Newlander, Francis G., 651
New York Evening Post, 435
New York Journal, 233
New York Merchants' Association, 643
New York Produce Exchange, 643
North American Sugar Company, 644
North American Trust Company, 48, 426
Núñez, Emilio, 344, 546, 601, 624-25, 658, 666

O'Connor, Nancy Lenore, 295
Offner, John L., 251, 308-09
Oliver, Fernando, 52, 54
Olney, Richard B., 144, 154, 170, 177, 179-80, 191, 193-201, 203, 205, 207, 210, 526-27, 562
Order No. 445, 609-10
Oriente, war in, 37-51
Orr, A. E., 303
Ortega y Rubio, Juan, 71
Our Island Empire, 465
Oxnard, Henry T., 637, 641, 644

Pact of Biac-na-bato, 125
Pact of Zanjón, 46, 81, 207
Palmer, Truman G., 647
Pan-American Company, 470
Pan American Conference, xxviii

## INDEX

Pan-Hispanic movement, 153
Panic of 1893, 293
Paris, Treaty of, 406-21, 530, 551, 561, 567, 573, 604, 606, 621
Partido Comunista de Cuba, 142
Partido Republicano Independiente, 660
Partido Revolucionario Cubano, El, xx-xxvi
Partido Socialista Cubano, 490-91
*Patria*, xxi, xxv, 4, 15, 109, 167, 499, 520, 525, 602, 611
Pauncefote, Julian, 257-58
Payne, Sereno E., 645, 646
Payne bill, 649, 651-52
Pechet, Antonio, 506
Peninsulares, xv, xvii
*People, The*, 392, 418
Pepper, Charles M., 526
Pérez Carbó, Francisco, 65, 145
Pérez, Pedro A., 348, 363
Peru, 87, 151, 152, 156-57
Philippines, 76, 123-26, 156-57, 240, 294-95, 302, 309-10, 368, 374, 391, 406, 407, 409-13, 418, 419, 431-33, 443, 445, 467, 515, 520, 524, 535, 539, 549, 574, 582, 587, 596, 599, 626-27, 630, 656, 663-64, 671-72
Picasso, 70
Placé, Louis V., 196, 642, 643
Plácido," 11
Planters' Association of Cuba, 476
Platt, Orville H., 171, 278, 469, 527, 531-32, 537-38, 559, 563-64, 565, 566, 574-76, 577, 578, 584, 585, 597, 599, 614, 616-17, 619-20, 623, 628-29, 630, 645
Platt, Thomas, 597
Platt Amendment, 149, 560-633, 635, 638, 642, 652, 668-69
Polavieza, Camilio de, 125
Polo de Bernabé, Luís, 235
Pomeroy, William J., 599
*Ponencia a la Convención*, 603-11, 628
Ponopol Mining and Transportation Company, 482
Populists, 291, 453
Portell Vilá, Herminio, 134, 217, 237, 240-41
Porter, John Addison, 394
Porter, Robert P., 387, 402, 434, 435-36, 439, 447, 450, 476, 514-15, 518
Portuondo, Juan Miguel, 123
Portuondo, Rafael María, 18, 44, 161, 442, 613, 614, 615, 616, 626
Postal scandals, 535-36
Pratt, Julius W., 289-90
Pratt thesis, 290-301, 307

Preston, Andrew W., 478
Proctor, Redfield, 132, 248, 306, 600
Protectorate, 452, 455-56, 589, 631, 669
Protest of Baraguá, 94
*Provenir, El*, 167, 392
Puertas, Ramón, 511
Puerto Rico, xxi, 285, 302, 342, 343, 368, 374, 392, 406, 407, 412, 413, 418, 419, 445, 468, 508-09, 520, 535, 625, 630, 644, 672
Pulitzer, Joseph, 168, 238

Queralta, López de, 2
Quesada, Gonzalo de, xxx, 12, 15, 18, 44, 148, 163, 164, 166, 184, 248, 258, 273-74, 380, 399-400, 405, 434-35, 436, 439, 447, 471, 546, 554, 569, 620, 659
Quilez, Joaquín, 611-12, 619, 620

Rabí, Jesús, 8, 37, 152, 348, 350, 354
Racism, 5-6, 450
Ramírez, José, 47
Rand, Charles J., 183
Rathbone, Estes G., 428, 523
Rea, George Bronson, 247
Recio, López, 347
Reciprocity, 559-60, 564, 572-73, 576, 600, 615-19, 633-55
*Reconcentrado, El*, 442, 450-51
*Reconcentración*, 77-78, 110-18, 130, 146
*Reconcentrados*, 110-18, 130, 131, 132, 226, 248-49, 283, 381, 384-85, 663-65
Red Cross, 384, 386, 387
Redpath, John Clark, 471
Reed, Thomas B., 275
Reformist Party, 100-01
Reid, Whitelaw, 208-09, 242, 262, 279, 411
Remington, Frederick, 163
*Report on the Commercial and Industrial Conditions of the Island of Cuba*, 514-15
*República Cubana, La*, 660
Republic of Cuba, 42, 371, 374, 654-72
Revolutionary Governing Council, 261
Reyna Cassio, René E., 667
Richmond *Planet*, 391
Riverend, Julio Le, 142-43, 445
Rivero Muñiz, Manuel, 502, 506
Ríos, Hernández, 341
Rizal, José P., 124, 125
Robinson, Albert G., 135, 461-62, 474-75, 544, 585, 597, 611-12, 636, 640

Roca, Blas, 142
Roca, Pedro, 500-01
Rockefeller, John D., 303
Rockefeller, William, 306-07
Rodríguez, Alejandro, 534
Rodríguez Martinez, Juan, 511
Rodríguez López, José, 511
Rodríguez, José Maria, 119
Rodríguez, Mayía, 3, 49, 63, 80, 109, 435, 439, 458
Roig de Leuchsenring, Emilio, 139-41, 204
Roloff, Carlos, 2, 18
Roloff-Sanchez expedition, 18
Romero, Matias, 166
Romero-Abaruza bill, 101
Roosevelt, Theodore, x, 225, 227, 228-29, 240-41, 289, 292, 293, 294, 295, 299, 354, 358, 415, 456, 457, 549, 628, 635, 636, 637, 643, 645, 649-50, 662, 666, 672
Root, Elihu, 454, 455, 457, 458, 463, 473, 522, 523, 524-25, 529-30, 531, 534, 538, 540, 542, 545, 546, 557-58, 559-61, 563, 564, 565, 566-67, 571, 573, 576-77, 582, 584, 591, 593-94, 598, 601, 614, 615-18, 621, 622, 623, 627-29, 631, 633, 634, 635, 639, 642, 643, 644, 645, 650, 655, 664
Rosado, Antonio, 108
Rosario, Marios de, 8
Rough Riders, 339, 358
Rowan, Andrew S., 340-42, 356
Rubens, Horatio S., xxvii, 3, 108, 163, 164, 233, 234, 236, 248, 251-52, 258-59, 270-71, 371, 399, 530, 541
Ruiz, Joaquín, 134
Ruiz Rivera, Juan, 457-58, 493, 658
Ruiz, Richard, 213
Runcie, James E., 530, 535
Rural Guard, 436, 456, 500, 511, 523
Russia, 255, 411

Saenz Yanez, Adolfo, 425
Sagasta, Práxedes M., 16, 126, 128, 129-30, 249
Salas, César, 8
Samar, 663-64
Samoa, xxix-xxx
Sampson, William T., 238, 348, 349, 353, 354, 382
Sánchez, Juan Augustín, 19
Sánchez, Juan Manuel, 92
Sánchez Figueras, Silverio, 91
Sánchez, Serafín, xxiii, 2, 63
Sánchez Hechavarría expedition, 18
San Carlos Club, 456
Sanguily, Julio, xxiv, 14, 151, 344, 546

Sanguily, Manuel, 48, 439, 441, 442, 481, 546, 552-53, 554, 593, 602, 620, 625, 659
Santo Domingo, 4-5, 21, 31, 76, 156
Sartorius, Manuel, xxvi
Saveth, Edward N., 293-94
Savio, Gervasio, 340-41
Schomburg, Arthur A., 97
Schlesinger, Arthur M., 291-92
Schuman, Jacob, 671
Schurz, Carl, 416
Second War for Independence (in Cuba), atrocities during, 60; attitude of Cuban people toward, 98-103; autonomy issue during, 128-29, 132, 135; battles during, 37-39, 53-54, 56-57; 58, 75-76, 82, 83, 85, 121-22; beginning of, 1-3; rejection of autonomy by Cubans during, 128-29, 132-35; Cuban strategy during, 21-25; description of independence fighters, 344-46; destruction of sugar crop during, 104-06; devastation of Cuba during, 379-87, 428-29; dissidence in Cuban government during, 85-87; economic conditions during, 104-08; failure of Weyler's policies during, 128-29; financing of, 104, 107-09; invasion of West during, 40-99, 376-80; Latin America and, 151-60; military situation in spring of 1898, 135-50; most Cuban leaders oppose U.S. intervention in, 135-50; Negro domination issue during, 159-60; number of soldiers in Cuba during, 135; origins of, xix-xxxiii; racism during, 86-87; reconcentrados during, 110-18, 130, 131, 132, 226, 248-49, 283, 381; relation of insurrection in Philippines to, 123-26; role of Chinese during, 102; role of Negroes in, 5-6, 98-99; role of tobacco workers in, 3, 108-10; Spain in financial difficulty as a result of, 125-26; Spanish and Cuban armies contrasted, 16-21; Spanish strategy in, 33-34; suppression of trade unions during, 103-04; war in Oriente, 35-51

Seward, William H., x
Shafter, William R., 349, 350-51, 353, 354, 355, 356-57, 359-60, 362-63, 364-65, 366-69, 370, 371, 372, 392, 395, 400, 432
Sherman, John, 113, 209, 212, 213, 215, 217, 218, 229
Siboney Indians, 37
Sickles, Daniel E., 170

## INDEX

Sigsbee, Charles D., 225, 230, 237, 239
Silva, Manuel R., 593, 626
Simpson, Jerry, 453
Sklar, Martin R., 296-97
Slavery, in Cuba, xv-xvii, 15
Slayden, James L., 612
Smith, A. C., 220
Smith, Charles Emory, 265, 298
Smith, Goldwyn, 525
Smith, William Alden, 228, 259
Social Darwinism, 291
Socialism, for Cuba, 653-54
Socialist Labor Party, 172, 283, 297-98, 393, 418, 504, 623
Socialists, xxi
Socialists in U.S., and Cuban revolution, 171-72
Socialist Party of the United States, 653
Soto, Carlos, 90
South America, 159-60
Spain, armies of contrasted with those of Cuba, 16-21; colonies of achieve independence, xv; corruption of in Cuba, xvi; favors annexation of Cuba by U.S. rather than independence, 408; forced to fight two-front war, 125-28; hopes to achieve alliance of European powers, 244-58; in financial difficulties during war in Cuba, 125-26; and Latin America, 153; loots Cuba, 428; offers armistice, 259-61; offers Cuba autonomy, 133-34, 135; opposition in to war in Cuba, 125-26; strategy of in war in Cuba, 33-34; reconcentration policy of, 77-78, 110-18, 130, 146; rejects reforms for Cuba, 101
Spanish-American War, causes of, 281-310; Cuban-American relations during, 339-78; Cubans excluded from surrender by Spain during, 366-69; destruction of Spanish fleet during, 361-62; end of, 374-78; official end of, 415-16; outbreak of, 276-77; role of Cubans is slandered in, 356-61, 362; role of Negro soldiers in, 344, 361; U.S. changes military plans during, 342-43; U.S. unprepared for, 351-55. See also García, Calixto; Shafter, William R.
Spanish bonds, 254-55
Spanish Treaty Claims Commission, 647
Spanish Volunteers, 442
Spaulding, Thomas M., 233
Spooner, John C., 531, 574, 576
Spooner Amendment, 574, 582, 583
Spotoron, Juan B., 207

Springfield *Republican*, 364, 619, 670-72
Squiers, Herbert C., 274, 652
Standard Beet Sugar Company, 637, 641
Standard Manganese Company, 482
Standard Oil Company, 303
*State, The*, 258, 343-44, 397, 401, 403, 411, 413, 418, 459, 540-41, 562, 586, 589-90, 592, 597-98, 618
Steinhart, Frank, 483
Stevens, John L., xxix
Stillman, Oscar B., 207
Strikebreaking, 488-89, 493, 494-505, 507-09, 510-11
Strikes, 487-89, 493-505, 507-08, 509-11
Sugar crops, destruction of, 104-06
Sugar industry, 473-75
Sugar Trust, 478-79, 517-18, 519, 628-29, 633, 634-42, 643, 644-45, 647-48, 649, 652
Supreme Court, 561-64, 625
Swanberg, W. A., 200, 246-47
Syme-Hastings, J., 95
Syndicates, 467

Tamayo, Diego, 568, 593, 600-01, 613, 626, 658
Tariff, 559-60, 564, 573, 575-76, 615-17, 617-20, 632-55
Taylor, George Edwin, 97
Tejera, Diego Vicente, 490, 491, 501, 512
Teller, Henry M., 270-80, 419-20, 423-24, 469, 527, 563, 580, 646-47
Teller Amendment, 270-75, 278-80, 392-93, 402-03, 413, 419-20, 514, 516-17, 531-32, 537, 540, 546, 579, 630
Ten Years' War (1868-1878), xvii-xix, 10, 16, 18, 21, 31, 34, 41, 46, 74, 76, 81, 87, 94, 99, 120, 121, 155, 207, 223, 267, 567
Thomas, Hugh, 307
Thomas, Samuel, 472
Thurber, Francis B., 639, 642, 648
Tillman, Benjamin R., 415, 579, 583-84
Titherington, R. H., 349
"To the People Sitting in Darkness," 514
Tobacco Trust, 481
Tobacco workers, xxv-xxviii, 3
Toral, José, 365-67
Toral, Secundino, 510-11
Trade unions, 103-04, 486-513
Treaty of Guadaloupe Hidalgo, 421
Treaty of Paris, 406-21, 530, 551, 561, 567, 573, 604, 606, 621

Treaty of Zanjón, xix
Trelles y Govín, Carlos M., 115
Trocha, 33-34, 50, 65, 78, 81, 89, 90
Trujillo, Enrique, 167, 392
Trusts, 304, 481. See also Sugar Trust
Turpie Amendment, 267-70
Twain, Mark, 415, 514, 539

Union Democratic Party, 545
Union League Club, 657
United Fruit Company, 477-78
United States, and annexation of Cuba, 271, 279, 392-97, 408, 412-13, 414, 446, 467, 472, 473, 481, 492, 515-33, 536-37, 564, 573, 629, 634-35, 651-52, 656, 657; and Cuban belligerent rights, 49, 189-91, 224-25; economic penetration of Cuba by, 466-83; favors autonomy for Cuba, 181-82, 192, 196-98, 203, 207, 224-25; fears Negro domination in Cuba, 196-97, 214; "fruita madura" policy toward Cuba, 204-05; and independence of Cuba, 205-06; investments of citizens of in Cuba, 188-89; loss of American investors in Cuba, 231-32; people of support Cuban independence, 168-76; plan in to purchase Cuba, 241, 249-50; policy of Cleveland Administration toward Cuban Revolution, 177-207; policy of McKinley Administration toward Cuban Revolution, 209-80; racism in, 124; refuses to recognize Cuban independence, 261-76; scheme in to purchase Cuba, 220-33; rise of imperialism in, 290-310; role of in Second War for Independence, 89-90; supports Spain in Ten Years' War, xviii; unprepared for Spanish-American War, 351-55; was its intervention necessary to defeat Spain, 139-50. See also American imperialism
United States Export Association, 639
University of Havana, 459
Untermann, Ernest, 652-53
Uruguay, 157

Valdés, Ramón, 157
Valdés, Suáres, 52
Valdés y Molina, Suárez, 83
Van Horne, Sir William, 471-74, 476
Varg, Paul A., 302
Varona, Enrique José, 15, 151-52, 450, 499
Varona Guerrero, Miguel Angel, 17
Vázquez Candela, Euclides, 445
Venezuela, 154-56
Venezuela boundary dispute, 154-55
Vest, George, 419

Vest Resolution, 419
Victoria, Guadalupe, 157
Vidal, Leyte, 84
Villa-Urrutía, W. R. de, 406
Villalón, José R., 441, 457
Villuendas, Enrique, 593
Voto Particular Contra La Enmienda Platt, 602-03

Wages, 512-13
Wall Street, xxxii
Ward, R. G., 511
Warner, W. S., 384
Washington, Booker T., 415, 453
Wellman, Walter, 558, 576-77
Western Federation of Miners, 505
Weyler, y Nicolau, Valeriano, 73-96, 103, 104, 105, 106, 109-12, 118, 120, 126, 127, 128, 129, 134, 136, 146, 213, 218, 226, 227, 232, 245-46, 379, 518, 522, 571, 597, 663, 664, 665
Wheeler, Joseph, 356-57, 358
White, Andrew D., 217
White, J. R., 595
White, Stephen M., 186
White, William A., 239
Whitehead, James Louis, 283
Whitney, William C., 304
Wilhelm II, 256
Williams, James R., 581
Williams, William Appleman, 191, 298-99
Wilson, James H., 269, 426-27, 452-53, 455, 456, 457, 519, 525-26, 576, 577, 633, 636
Wilson-Gorman tariff, xxxii, 300
Wisan, Joseph E., 288
Wolff, Drummond, 219-20
Wood, Leonard, 184, 367, 382-83, 384, 392, 426, 436, 454-65, 467-68, 475, 476, 482, 483, 484, 506, 507, 508, 509, 510, 511, 512, 515-16, 519, 523, 530, 531, 534, 535, 538, 539, 540, 545-46, 547-48, 592, 593-95, 597, 598, 600, 601, 612, 613, 614, 621, 623, 624, 628, 631, 633, 634, 636, 637-40, 642, 643, 644, 647, 648, 650, 656, 660-61, 666
Woodford, Stewart L., 136, 139, 215-17, 218-19, 226, 255, 257
Workers' Circle, 493
Wright, Philip C., 628
Wright, Theodore P., 528

Yellow fever, 450, 460-61
Yellow Fever Commission, 459
"Yellow Press," 168, 169, 213, 238, 260, 288, 290, 293
Young, S. B. M., 394-95

Zayas, Alfredo, 546, 626, 659